Living Through the Soviet System

Living Through the Soviet System

Edited by Daniel Bertaux, Paul Thompson & Anna Rotkirch

Memory and Narrative Series

Transaction Publishers
New Brunswick (U.S.A.) and London (U.K.)

First paperback edition published in 2005 by Transaction Publishers, New Brunswick, New Jersey, by arrangement with Routledge.

© 2004 Editorial matter and selection, Daniel Bertaux, Paul Thompson, and Anna Rotkirch; individual chapters, the contributors.

All rights reserved under International and Pan-American Copyright Conventions. No part of this book may be reproduced or transmitted in any form or by any means, electronic or mechanical, including photocopy, recording, or any information storage and retrieval system, without prior permission in writing from the publisher. All inquiries should be addressed to Transaction Publishers, Rutgers—The State University, 35 Berrue Circle, Piscataway, New Jersey 08854-8042. www.transactionpub.com

This book is printed on acid-free paper that meets the American National Standard for Permanence of Paper for Printed Library Materials.

Library of Congress Catalog Number: 2005053815
ISBN: 1-4128-0487-6
Printed in the United States of America

Library of Congress Cataloging-in-Publication Data

On living through Soviet Russia.
   Living through the Soviet system / Daniel Bertaux, Paul Thompson, and Anna Rotkirch, editors.—1st pbk. ed.
      p. cm.—(Memory and narrative series)
   Originally published: On living through Soviet Russia. New York : Routledge, c2004.
   Includes bibliographical references and index.
   ISBN 1-4128-0487-6 (pbk. : alk. paper)
   1. Soviet Union—Social conditions—Case studies. 2. Communism and family—Soviet Union—Case studies. 3. Soviet Union—Social life and customs—Case studies. 4. Soviet Union—Moral conditions—Case studies. 5. Oral history. I. Bertaux, Daniel. II. Thompson, Paul Richard, 1935- III. Rotkirch, Anna, 1966- IV. Title. V. Memory and narrative.

HN523.O6 2005
306'.0947—dc22   2005053815

CONTENTS

Notes on contributors   ix

1 Introduction   1
DANIEL BERTAUX, ANNA ROTKIRCH AND PAUL THOMPSON

PART I
Creating Soviet Society

2 The cultural model of the Russian popular classes and the transition to a market economy   25
DANIEL BERTAUX, IN COLLABORATION WITH MARINA MALYSHEVA

3 Equality in poverty: the symbolic meaning of *kommunalki* in the 1930s-50s   54
VICTORIA SEMENOVA

4 Coping with revolution: the experiences of well-to-do Russian families   68
EKATERINA FOTEEVA

PART II
Personal and Family Life

5 'What kind of sex can you talk about?': acquiring sexual knowledge in three Soviet generations   93
ANNA ROTKIRCH

CONTENTS

6 Family models and transgenerational influences: grandparents, parents and children in Moscow and Leningrad from the Soviet to the market era   120
VICTORIA SEMENOVA AND PAUL THOMPSON

7 'Coming to stand on firm ground': the making of a Soviet working mother   146
ANNA ROTKIRCH

8 The strength of small freedoms: a response to Ionin, by way of stories told at the *dacha*   176
NAOMI ROSLYN GALTZ

PART III
The Marginal and the Successful

9 Memory and survival in Stalin's Russia: old believers in the Urals during the 1930s-50s   195
IRINA KOROVUSHKINA PAERT

10 The returned of the repressed: survival after the Gulag   214
NANCI ADLER

11 Success stories from the margins: Soviet women's autobiographical sketches from the late Soviet period   235
MARIANNE LILJESTRÖM

12 Epilogue: researching with interview sources on Soviet Russia   252
DANIEL BERTAUX, PAUL THOMPSON AND ANNA ROTKIRCH

Bibliography   258
Index   271

CONTRIBUTORS

Nanci Adler is Associate Professor at the Center for Holocaust and Genocide Studies of the Royal Netherlands Academy of Arts and Sciences. She is author of two books, *The Gulag Survivor* and *Victims of Soviet Terror*, and of many articles on the consequences of Stalinism.

Daniel Bertaux is Directeur de Recherches at the Centre d'Etudes des Mouvements Sociaux, Ecole des Hautes Etudes en Sciences Sociales, Paris. He has been a researcher for the CNRS since 1968, and his originally quantitative research on social mobility led him to discover the value of qualitative life stories. His researches have included studies of bakers, of families and social mobility in France and in Russia, and of absent fathers. He is founder of the Biography and Society Research Committee of the International Sociological Association, and first President of the Sociological Association of France. His books include *Destins personnels et structure de classe*, *Biography and Society*, *La mobilité sociale*, *Les récits de vie*, and (with Paul Thompson) *Pathways to Social Class*.

Ekaterina Foteeva was a researcher at the Institute of Sociology, Russian Academy of Sciences, Moscow, from the mid-1980s to the mid-1990s. She participated in various projects on family sociology and social policy, and oral-history studies of family social mobility. In 1996 she moved to Canada to work on a project on migration, and she now lives in Toronto.

Naomi Roslyn Galtz is an Assistant Professor in the School of Interdisciplinary Studies at Miami University. Her work focuses on everyday life, play/space, material culture and sustainable consumption. Presently she is pursuing a new US-based project on discourses of simplicity in consumption.

Marianne Liljeström is Professor of Women's Studies at the University of Turku, Finland. She has published articles on Nordic and Soviet women's history, and a book (in Swedish) on the Soviet gender system, and she is currently writing a book on Soviet women's autobiographies.

Marina Malysheva was an interviewer with the Bertaux Russian families project, and is a researcher at the Institute for Socio-Economic Studies on Population, Moscow.

Irina Korovushkina Paert is a Lecturer in History at the University of Wales, Bangor. She began researching on the Old Believers as a student at the Urals State University, Yekaterinburg. Her book on this, *Old Believers, Religious Dissent and Gender in Russia*, is forthcoming with Manchester University Press.

Anna Rotkirch researches in Sociology at the University of Helsinki, Finland. She has specialised in comparative research on families and sexuality, autobiographical research and Russian studies. She is author of *The Man Question: Loves and Lives in Late Twentieth Century Russia* and co-editor of *Women's Voices in Russia Today*.

Victoria Semenova is a Lead Researcher at the Institute of Sociology, Russian Academy of Sciences in Moscow, and she teaches sociological methods at the Russian State Humanities University in Moscow. She is author of a book on qualitative methods in Russian and of articles in *Family and History* and *BIOS*. She is especially interested in narrative analysis and in intergenerational issues.

Paul Thompson is Research Professor in Sociology at the University of Essex, and a Fellow at the Institute of Community Studies in London. He is Founder-Editor of *Oral History* and Founder of the National Life Story Collection at the British Library National Sound Archive, London. His books include *The Voice of the Past*, *The Edwardians*, and *The Work of William Morris*. He is co-author of *Growing up in Stepfamilies*, of *The Myths We Live by* (with Raphael Samuel), and (with Daniel Bertaux) of *Pathways to Social Class*.

1

INTRODUCTION

Daniel Bertaux, Anna Rotkirch and Paul Thompson

For a period of over seventy years after the October 1917 Revolution in Russia, talking about the past, either political or personal, became extremely dangerous for many. In a society dominated by a giant system of internal espionage, talking about yourself could always leave perilous clues, hostages to fortune. Who could know which neighbours or friends were informers to the authorities? And to reveal that any relative or close connection had ever been in political trouble, or fought on the wrong side in the Civil War, or was descended from aristocrats or well-to-do peasants (*kulaki*) or even shopkeepers, could put anyone at risk of unemployment or banishment to the political prison camps in Siberia and elsewhere. In such a context, there was no chance of successful interview-based research, either by Russians or by outsiders, and understanding of what was really going on in Russia was thus generally left, in terms of politics, to 'Kremlinologists' whose prime skill was reading between the lines of *Pravda* and other official newspapers or, for economy and society, to a painstaking wringing-out of perspectives from published statistics, policy documents and literature.[1]

The situation changed dramatically with the new policy of *glasnost* at the end of the 1980s. In parallel, Soviet society began to re-examine its own pasts, while Russian family members began opening up their own family secrets. The result was a flood of reminiscence, almost nightly on television, and more formally collected by new Russian oral history groups and also by Western researchers. Daniel Bertaux and Paul Thompson both began collecting in-depth life-story and family-history interview material in the early 1990s, working with two overlapping Russian groups of interviewers. The two projects – which we detail in the Epilogue – shared an intergenerational perspective, and gathered altogether fifty family case-history interviews (from the Bertaux project) and forty-seven life-history interviews from a further twenty-five families (from the Thompson project). The most important immediate outcome was a book in Russian published by the Bertaux team, which has proved widely read and influential.[2] This new book builds on those initial findings, and at the same time brings the two earlier projects together with other more recent work based on different kinds of autobiographical material.

Thus the first four chapters of *On Living through Soviet Russia*, written by Daniel Bertaux, Victoria Semenova and Ekaterina Foteeva, are based directly on the Bertaux project, while a further chapter, by Semenova and Thompson, draws on both the Bertaux and the Thompson interviews. To these we have added two more chapters by other current researchers who have been using life-story interviews (Naomi Roslyn Galtz and Irina Korovushkina Paert), and four others (one each by Nanci Adler, Marianne Liljeström and two by Anna Rotkirch) by authors who have been analysing Russian written autobiographies. This is by definition a unique book, not only because no similar material was collected earlier, but also because, newly released from earlier suppression, memory of the Soviet era was exceptionally full and vivid in the *glasnost* era. Indeed Russia, then in a moment of free flux, has since moved to another kind of fearful society, with its own new barriers to free talking.

The coherence of the book is based on the use throughout of autobiographical material, and this has necessitated some discussion of issues of memory in a formerly totalitarian society. However, while this book does raise important questions of method for future researchers, our aim here is not primarily methodological. It is rather to analyse, through personal accounts, how Russian society operated at a day-to-day level, and also how people coped with these operating mechanisms – topics on which there was scarcely any serious work up to the end of the 1980s.[3] This volume contrasts the different social integration of different social groups, from the descendants of the pre-revolutionary upper class to the new industrial working class. It examines in turn the implications of family relationships, working mothers, absent fathers and caretaking grandmothers; patterns of eating together, communal living, and of housing; the secrecy of sex; the suppression of religion; and the small – but, in the context, so relevant – freedoms of growing vegetables at weekends on a *dacha* plot. Because of its basis in direct testimonies, *On Living through Soviet Russia* reveals in a highly readable and direct style the meaning for ordinary men and women of living through those seven turbulent decades of a great European nation.

UNDERSTANDING SOVIET SOCIAL STRUCTURES

Of all the deliberate social experiments which have taken place in human history, Soviet society was one of the largest ever undertaken, and it was sustained over a vast part of the world's surface for as long as seventy years.[4] It claimed to offer an alternative to capitalism, providing full employment for its citizens, cheap housing for all, free health care and free education. Although we now know that it was a never-achieved utopia which cost millions of lives, for most of the twentieth society it provided a crucial worldwide symbol that there was a viable alternative to capitalism, that the logic of industrial capitalism need not invariably prevail, and that resistance to class oppression could be progressive, on the side of the future. Indeed, without Soviet society, it seems unlikely that Western Europe would have achieved, between Communism and the pure capitalist market society, compromises in the form of welfare capitalism and the social market – compromises which have more recently become much more difficult to defend. Once represented as pragmatic reforms, they are now criticised as if impossible utopias. Soviet Russia's claims for economic and social success were taken very seriously for decades, both by Russians and by Westerners, and even in the 1960s, it looked briefly as if Russian scientists would succeed in leading the Americans in the race to conquer outer space. The cracks in the Soviet system only began to be widely recognised in the 1970s under the extreme pressure of the armaments race, and its final demise took place with a rapidity which scarcely anybody – either in Russia or in the West – had dared to imagine.

Many older Russian men and women in the early 1990s had memories encompassing the entire Soviet era. They had experienced the drama of its twisting evolution. There was, first of all, the collapse of the old social hierarchies of the Tsar's Empire through its defeat in the First World War and the twin 1917 Revolutions; then a period of chaos, followed until 1920 by Civil War, which cost two million lives. For a while the New Economic Policy of the early 1920s allowed some slow reconstruction, but soon, with Stalin's takeover, much more radical changes set the whole society rocking again.

From the late 1920s Stalin began a series of drastic initiatives for the creation of the new socialist state. The class of medium peasants – branded as *kulaki*, a derogatory word – was eliminated from the countryside and the land turned over almost entirely to collective farming. Small entrepreneurs were also eliminated from the towns, and a massive programme of industrialisation and urbanisation launched. Under the first two five-year plans, from 1928 until 1938, the urban population of Russia doubled. Still more dramatically, Stalin used forced labour from his growing network of prison camps in an attempt to colonise the bleak Russian north, constructing canals and railways through the frozen wilderness and forcing colonists to create new outposts of Soviet society there. (From many such regions, with the collapse of Soviet industry, over half the population has fled back to western Russia since 1990.) Stalin also even set up an autonomous Jewish state in 1928 in Siberia's far east, Yiddish-speaking Birobidzhan, although this eccentric colonisation project proved an early victim, struck by Stalin's own Great Terror in 1936–7.[5]

At the same time, family relationships were thoroughly transformed and the power structures between generations and sexes dramatically altered through the abolition of larger private property, the partial spread of communal forms of housing for the urban working class, and also – at a time when, in Western societies, married women were largely excluded from professional work – a requirement for both men and women to undertake paid work. The numbers of women rose from 24 per cent to 39 per cent of the whole Soviet workforce between 1928 and 1940. In total contrast to the gender conventions of Western culture, Stalin even set up three regiments composed entirely of women fighter pilots, who fought at Stalingrad and in every battle involving the Red Army up to the defeat of the Nazis in 1945.[6] More typically, Russian women could be found in a whole range of occupations, from manual jobs in agriculture and industry to skilled and professional work from engineering to medicine.

The third phase was the return of chaos and slaughter with the Great Patriotic War, in which much of western Russia was occupied by Germany, and some 27 million more Russian soldiers and citizens died at the battlefront, in prison camps, or as the result of starvation, massacre and illness. Finally, after 1945 there was a much more ordered phase in the history of Soviet society, beginning with post-war reconstruction, and then from the late 1950s more serious attempts by the Communist elite to raise the ordinary standard of living, produce enough food, get goods into the shops, build family housing, and create a renewed society which really worked. By the 1980s that, too, had failed, and the whole Soviet infrastructure was running down, with food and industrial production in decline and the credibility of the Soviet leadership evaporating. With Gorbachev's arrival in 1985, the final gamble was made: *perestroika* (restructuring), and *glasnost* (the end of secrecy). But the tensions, now released into the open, destroyed the system.

While from the late 1920s, millions of Russians suffered from Stalin's radical strategies to create a new Soviet society, many losing their homes and their jobs, many of them 'repressed' by being kept permanently workless, or made to migrate or serve for years as prison labour (around 11 million exiled or executed), it is equally important to remember how many Russians believed they were indeed helping to create a new world. 'People had real spirit here', one Siberian pioneer remembers.[7] Even where the changes brought mortal famine to the countryside, which we now know was deliberately imposed by Stalin on groups such as the Cossacks whom he regarded as potential opposition, the victims were simply bewildered, unable to imagine the source of their destructive fate. Ordinary Russians were more likely to pray to Stalin than to imagine him as a source of their sufferings. The relentless propaganda made its impact: the heroic celebratory booklets like *Building the White Sea Canal*, which never mentioned that most of the workforce was convict labour, or the mid-1930s film *Seekers of Happiness*, depicting the journey of an American Jewish family who moved to Siberia to escape the unemployment of the Great Depression. Everywhere, Soviet children were taught through their membership of socialist youth movements the ideals of communism – solidarity, equality, justice, peace, brotherhood, the supremacy of the collective. Equally they learned to disapprove of their opposites – individualism and divisive or 'anti-social' behaviour. We can assume that almost all Soviet citizens to some extent internalised these anti-capitalist and pro-socialist values. Among the strongest believers were the teachers. The Bertaux team collected stories of idealistic young teachers who, even in the 1960s, wanted to bring their educational practices closer to Communism, and moved then to Siberia in order to have the freedom to set up new, more ideal schools. They found other young teachers there with similar attitudes. But, paradoxically, even such efforts to realise the ideals of Soviet society regularly ended in suppression, and sometimes the repression of their initiators, for changing local institutions without the approval of the relevant Communist Party authorities.

Soviet society was thus not only utopian, but also perplexingly contradictory, and hence difficult for most contemporaries to interpret. Because it fell far short of what it claimed to be, the actual rules of Soviet society had to remain hidden from view – hidden not only to foreigners, but to Soviet citizens too. It was a 'secret' society, whose official public pronouncements had to be minutely checked before their release. These pronouncements and the controlled official press and radio became the staple material of Western Sovietologists, who thereby created whole libraries of critical studies of Soviet society without ever being able to gain much understanding of the real lives of Soviet citizens. The only Russians they could freely interview during the whole Soviet period were those who had escaped to the West, and it was never possible to know how far their experiences had been typical.[8]

It is unlikely, in any case, that ordinary Russian citizens could have explained the fundamental workings of Soviet society, precisely because these were deliberately hidden from them. Even in the democratic West, only a minority of specialised professionals fully understand the workings of the capitalist market and its full power – not only because of its complexity but also because its workings also are partly deliberately hidden – although the market is fundamental to the social exchanges and inequalities of Western societies. In Soviet Russia it could be argued that, from the 1950s, the workings of the system and the rules of the game did become increasingly well understood by Russians themselves, and that was one of the reasons for the system's downfall.

Soviet society was structured around power rather than possessions. Money – despite popular pride in the possession of a stable and reliable national currency – was much less relevant in everyday Soviet life than in the West, because there were severe restrictions on what it could buy: there was no market in housing, few goods for sale in the shops. Many of the key things came free, like health care and education, or very cheap, like bread, housing and electricity. But since supply seldom never enough, access to them was either through the black market – flourishing from the late 1930s, where dealings could be either in cash or in barter – or through accessing a mixture of formal rights and informal network connections. Hence, getting what you wanted depended to a high degree on your networks, your social capital. You could not simply reserve a table for a meal in a restaurant: you had to use your connections to get the table, because otherwise you would be told it was booked, when in fact the food intended for the restaurant might have been bartered by the work team for something more useful to them, say a group holiday in Yalta. It seems that it was connections as means to favours, the informal deals expressed in the rhetoric of friendship which Russians called *blat*, which were the basic currency of Soviet life, the equivalent to money in the West.[9] But how such connections were built, social capital accumulated, is much less clear. We explore in the chapters which follow how social capital took different forms in different contexts: information networks for migrants, getting jobs or housing through work contacts, the pull of old family connections, or the transmission across generations of intellectual skills or approaches to dealing with crisis. Family relationships gained a new importance in this economy of exchange, paradoxically precisely at the same moment as the influence of family was being deliberately undermined by government policies in housing and schooling, and at the old elite level family connections had to be hidden for fear of persecution. Connections were therefore perhaps as often made through neighbours and workmates, through specially close friendships (*druzhba*), through politics, and also through religious or political dissidence.

From this followed the Soviet class structure. Again, secrecy made this hard to study, because social classes had officially been abolished. Perhaps this is one reason why there has been considerable contention on the issue, with the views of historians and socialists ranging from those who see the Soviet system as being in reality not significantly different from that of the West, to those who interpret it either as a survival from the past – for example, with 'Estates' rather than classes – or as a new and wholly different system.[10] But, for the research projects on which this book is based, we have assumed that there was in practice a hierarchy along the following broad lines. First, at the top there was an upper class of those with access to political power, headed by the *nomenklatura*, with the middle- and lower-level party cadres in their wake. Next there were the two major blocks of the working population at all occupational levels: the urban population, from professionals to unskilled, and well below them the peasantry. However, within these blocks some professions, such as the intelligentsia, or at a lower level, hairdressers or shop assistants, evidently could gain more access to useful connections, yet there has not been enough information to make any systematic distinctions among them. Lastly and much more obviously, there was the large group of marginalised or repressed citizens, the more fortunate of the latter released and 'assigned' to the least popular parts of the country such as Siberian outposts, the worst off still prisoners working their sentences in the network of Stalin's *lager* system. This social structure seems clear enough in retrospect, but it is important to understand that not only is its nature still a matter of debate, but also, more importantly for our purposes, not at all of it was obvious to most of those who were living through Soviet Russia.

The oral and written autobiographies on which this book is based are not only vivid, but also often painful. In one form or another, they all reflect the loss or disappearance of close family members, the sufferings from the crushing of the *kulaki*, from Stalin's purges, and from two major wars. But it is equally striking that they do not portray an anomic, destabilised population, reeling from incessant and incomprehensible change. On the contrary, many interviews convey a stoic acceptance of difficult life paths, and also moments of stillness. Often they reflect a yearning for order, and a calm associated with the presence of grandmothers, or simple common domestic activities such as gathering berries in the forest, or even an icon left nailed to the wall. They also bring out the strategies which ordinary people used to better their lives, to find spaces for self-expression, or by word or deed to protest. Both oral interviews and written interviews, in short, reflect not only the great structural clashes of Soviet society, but also, as with ordinary people's autobiographies in the West, how Russians experienced both the stresses and also the small freedoms and pleasures of ordinary life, and how they acted in the face of the structures which framed their life choices.

INTERPRETING AUTOBIOGRAPHICAL MEMORIES

Working with autobiographic memories always raises key issues of validity and representativity, which we have fully discussed elsewhere.[11] There are, however, some special problems in interpreting Russian autobiographical material.

The first question is how far, in a society in which both secrecy and deception have been so pervasive, can memories have any validity at all? In Soviet Russia for seventy years, remembering was dangerous, not only to yourself, but to your family and friends. The less that people knew about you and your family story the better, because most information was potentially dangerous, could be twisted into material for a denunciation. In politically comfortable Western democracies, telling stories about yourself is commonplace, the currency of everyday conversation as well as the essence of relationships between intimates. This was not so in Russia. Soviet citizens learned to wear masks in both public and private life, even with close friends and intimates. Irina Sherbakova, for example, found in her interviews with survivors of the *gulag* that many of them not only concealed their prison years from their own children, who could too easily talk, but even, if they married after their return from prison, from their own spouses.[12] And such habits die slowly. Some of us were struck on early visits to Russia not only by the continuation of personal mistrust (often well-based) between colleagues, but also by how little they are likely to know about each other's personal lives.

One of the first points which strikes a Western life-story sociologist or oral historian is the number of interviewees who mention with regret the gaps in their knowledge of the family's story. This was as true of active Communists as of those outside the establishment. Thus, among our own interviewees, Igor Smirnov (b. 1923), a party political worker with the military like his father, remarked: 'We prefer not to talk about our relatives, who they are.' He knew that his grandmother, with whom he lived as a child, 'was brought up in a noble family, she was a well-bred person ... Unfortunately she never told me sincerely about her life.' Valentin Aleksandrovich (b. 1933), whose mother was a pioneer Communist heroine in Murmansk, was mystified by the joint photographs of his grandparents, in which his grandfather's image had been deliberately cut out: 'I can say nothing about it, because this issue was never discussed in our family. The Civil War mixed people up and people were not ashamed of their relatives, they were simply afraid that ... memories about them would cause troubles for the rest of the family.' It was still worse for those who knew for certain that their family history was a heavy handicap. For example, the father of Petr Andrienko (b. 1923) had been a village shopkeeper and small trader in machinery, but after collectivisation he was arrested as an 'Enemy of the People' and never reappeared. Afterwards, whenever Petr needed to fill in one of the many forms which regulated Soviet life, for example to get a factory job, he lied about his origins: 'There were questions about your relatives: were they repressed or not? ... That made me very downcast ... No doubt it *is* better to keep silent about it.'

Hence a significant part of Russian family history was undoubtedly obscured through the need for secrecy over such a sustained period. But a great deal was nevertheless handed down. As these very examples indicate, quite often such family 'secrets' were withheld by one member of a family, but known and transmitted by others. In particular, as Semenova and Thompson show in their chapter here, in many Russian families there were stronger lines of communication between grandparents and grandchildren than between parents and children.

The early 1990s, moreover, may seem in retrospect as years exceptionally favourable to autobiographical candour in Russia. Perhaps the very uncertainty about the future made the appraisal of the Soviet past all the more intense. The era of *glasnost* had initiated a huge questioning of the public past, and there was a vast public outpouring of autobiographical reinterpretation. For the first time since the 1917 Revolutions, many people felt free to speak uninhibitedly, not only about their own lives, but about their parents and grandparents too. The organisation Memorial – whose documentation is used by Nanci Adler in her chapter here – was originally a semi-clandestine dissident network for recording the fates of repressed men and women, but now became transformed into a national exercise for documenting the deaths, deportations and imprisonments suffered by Russians under the Soviet regime of terror. One of its first exhibitions about the concentration camps, held in the Moscow Palace of Culture in 1988, was a particularly extraordinary turning point, seen by thousands of people, where lone old men and women could be seen holding up the names of lost parents, or with notices round their collars – 'Does anyone else remember X Camp?' – just wanting others to remember with; a need which Memorial responded to by setting up monthly memory circles.

Yet at this time the direction of the future was still unclear, so that there was not yet a new self-censorship against the past. Thus, in 1993, Victoria Semenova recorded an elderly woman who had belonged to the top Soviet *nome–klatura*: she described in full her pioneering role as a woman geologist, and her later high responsibility as head of a Ministry. But she began the same interview with a proud declaration: 'I have a long story to tell you about my life. In fact I came from noble origin and my family lost everything during the Revolution. Even my grandson has learned the truth about my origin only recently ... '[13]

Some experienced Russian oral historians argue that, now once again in the post-*glasnost* era, Russians, and particularly older Russians socialised into reticence, are reluctant to give candid interviews. 'Every Soviet citizen had *two totally different biographies* at hand, each of which could be presented in several versions. They differed from each other in terms of the facts selected, interpretation, the character of presentation, as well as the sphere of public the person ought to speak in.' In the post-Soviet period these habits have often continued, so that people often do not speak in an interview in the way that they would in private conversation. Partly because of the rise of violence and racketeering, and also because some Russians have taken to making money from being interviewed, quite often their 'narratives rather resemble textbook phrases that reproduce officially accepted opinions'. To get 'real' information, authentic personal narratives, these researchers suggest, 'one has either to have high credibility by belonging to the periphery of the respondent's social network, or to get access to his/her "private" realm through a third person enjoying the respondent's trust.' In a recent project at the Centre for Independent Social Research in St Petersburg on ex-Soviet immigrants to Berlin, Viktor Voronkov found that the early interviews resembled newspaper articles rather than personal experience. These first interviews had been conducted by German co-researchers. But when Russian interviewers took over, there was an immediate change in the type of interview. When Voronkov asked his first interviewee what he had told the German sociologist who had interviewed him previously, he was answered emphatically: 'Never mind, I told them as it ought to be!' (*'Tak, kak nado!'*)[14]

It may well indeed be true that the years in which candour came most easily have passed. Yet it would be a mistake to suggest that, ten years later, Russians are back to a new phase of secrecy as acute as under the Soviet regime. Effective research using life stories, oral history or written autobiographies continues, even if it demands a higher level of skill in gaining the confidence of interviewees. In an interesting new development, Memorial sponsored a national essay contest in 2000 and in 2001 for teenage schoolchildren on 'Man and history, the twentieth century', for which the children were strongly encouraged to do their own interviews. These competitions attracted 1,700 and 2,000 entries respectively. The majority of the entries came from the smaller towns rather than the biggest cities, and a typical entry was a family story based on interviews with various kin, including a grandfather who was a dispossessed peasant.[15] It looks to be far too soon to announce that the new culture of remembering has passed.

We should note that, in any case, telling what 'it ought to be' in an interview can give revealing insights into the social values of a period. Indeed, in her chapter here, Marianne Liljeström uses precisely the formalised character of the published success stories of Soviet women to reveal the qualities which were believed to be crucial for success. In their collection of oral histories with women, *A Revolution of Their Own* (1998), Barbara Engel and Anastasia Posadskaya-Vanderbeck include a number of life stories of Communist activists which – although recorded after the collapse of Soviet power – are equally striking, both in terms of their continuing political faith and in their denial of discrimination against women in Soviet Russia. Interviews such as these are valuable precisely because they confirm the deep hold which Communist ideology had upon key sections of the population, including some of the most intelligent. Similarly, at a more typical everyday level, the way in which Russians almost always describe *blat* as a practice of others, while maintaining that they themselves only gave favours for friendship, should be interpreted not so much as denial, but as a sign that the practice, while almost universal, was always viewed with ambivalence. In fact the ideal interview contains a mixture of broader social attitudes with the direct and often contradictory experience of the interviewee, for it is that very tension which provides one of the springs for individual and collective social action.

This is linked to another problem which was encountered by some of the first Russian oral historians. They found that, when people lacked a firm overall historical picture within which to place their own experience, memories of individual experience also seemed to lack certainty. Thus a fieldwork trip interviewing survivors of the deliberately induced Kuban famine of 1933 found that many informants still could not give coherent accounts of their own personal experiences and suffering, or come to terms with the possibility that the famine might have been imposed on them by their own government. Similarly, two excursions to conduct interviews in the city of Vladimir brought strikingly different outcomes. On the first, before *glasnost* in 1984, it was not yet publicly acknowledged that the ancient monastery above the city's railway station housed one of Russia's chief political prisons. Most interviewees said they did not know about the prison, and few said they had any direct contact with it. But four years later, when the extent of the prison system had become public knowledge, the same people, re-interviewed, not only claimed to have known about the prison all along, but in some cases to have worked or been prisoners in it. While some of these new accounts seemed credible, others seemed to be adapted from television or newspaper reports, even if the informants had come to believe in their own stories.[16]

In terms of shifts in public consciousness and memory, this evidence is interesting in itself, a striking demonstration of how different the Soviet past was. Certainly it does emphasise the need for caution and skill in the interpretation of interviews. On the other hand, it is equally important to recognise that the very instability of official history – to the extent that the school textbooks were withdrawn while our own fieldwork was in progress – combined with the unreliability of most official statistics, which were more likely to represent what had been called for in the plans rather than what had actually happened, made direct personal accounts a particularly precious form of evidence. Indeed, given the systematic deception imposed by the Soviet elite, what would we know of the *gulag* without the autobiographical testimonies of survivors such as those collected by Aleksandr Solzhenitsyn or by Memorial? Could we have successfully reconstructed its history with just the voluminous mendacity of the judicial archives? Would we understand ordinary Soviet families better, if our only sources were official propaganda and the methodical documentation by the secret services of deliberate falsehoods about neighbours provided by informers?

Solzhenitsyn summed up the choice which he himself had faced in gathering material for *The Gulag Archipelago* (1974):

> I have never had the chance to read the documents. In fact, will anyone ever have the chance to read them? Those who do not wish to *recall* have already had enough time – and will have more – to destroy all the documents, down to the very last one.
>
> This book could never have been created by one person alone. In addition to what I myself was able to take away from the Archipelago – on the skin of my back, and with my eyes and ears – material for this book was given me in reports, memoirs, and letters by 227 witnesses, whose names were to have been listed here ... But the time has not yet come when I dare name them.[17]

If we want to understand living through Soviet Russia, we simply cannot do without the direct testimony of the Russians who lived through it.

A further important difference between life-story work in Western countries and in Russia is that Western researchers typically assume that their informants are 'actors', who themselves make 'choices' which shape their subsequent life paths. Indeed, one key contribution of life-story research to the understanding of social change has been precisely to highlight the hidden dynamic which comes from the private decisions of individuals whether or not to marry, have children, take a job, move house, or migrate between districts of countries, when these are aggregated into millions of choices.[18] But the overwhelming view of our Russian colleagues was that older Russians see themselves not so much as 'actors' but as 'victims'. And indeed, in the Soviet Union it was much more difficult than in the West, even for dedicated Communist party workers, to feel they were in control of their own destinies. Travel was restricted and internal migration narrowly controlled by bureaucratic procedures, as also were the housing and job markets. Among ordinary workers the cocoon of community and workplace could be hard to escape, except in periods of severe dislocation such as war or famine. Many families lost key members – particularly men – in each generation, as victims of international or civil war and political imprisonment.

There was certainly much in our interviews to confirm this perspective on Soviet citizens as essentially being trapped in their suffering. But, as we shall see, what is equally remarkable is the extent to which people found their own ways of manipulating the system. This was especially true of precisely those families who suffered most because of their social origins or their politics, who became marginal to the protective social system, and who were therefore only able to survive by breaking the rules or following them in decisive individual life choices.

Lastly, as in any life-story research, there is the question of representiveness. We have already noted how the nature of the Soviet class structure was itself a major unsolved issue. But, more than that, the very secrecy of the Soviet system also made some of the standard solutions for random or quota sampling impossible. In the early 1990's there were not even published phone directories for Moscow and St Petersburg. We were therefore fortunate that, through Victoria Semenova, some of our work could be linked to one reliable cross-Soviet longitudinal survey, with a sample of school-leavers born in 1965–7 and interviewed when entering work in 1984, and again in 1990 and 1993.[19] But while that is invaluable in relating evidence to the present, it would certainly be impossible to take the families of schoolchildren in the 1990s as being representative of the whole Russian population in earlier decades. Such families are by definition survivors, and we know that in the older generations huge swathes of people, and especially of men, had been eliminated earlier through industrial accidents and disease, death and imprisonment in war (especially in western Russia), famine (such as in the Kuban) and repression (above all among the former elites, *kulak* families and religious minorities). In principle, the past would therefore be better represented through a quota sample, designed to compensate for these imbalances brought through history – and indeed, this was the approach tried by Ray Pahl and Paul Thompson,[20] and in a more specialised way, by Irina Korovushkina Paert in her account here of the Old Believers. The drawback however is that, while it is certainly possible to rectify the imbalance between men and women, and to achieve a broad cross-representation of the occupational structure, the lack of earlier reliable statistical information means that to go much further would depend to a large extent on guesswork.

Two other approaches to representativeness are also used in this volume. The first possibility – which has only been used here with written autobiographies – is to treat a set of autobiographical testimonies simply as a documentary cache of clues to the past in need of evaluation. This is the standard approach of historians, and the spirit in which Nanci Adler uses the evidence collected by Memorial on the *gulag* in her chapter. It is also used by some sociologists, the difference being that they initiate the creation of the documentary cache rather than simply finding it. Thus Anna Rotkirch has based her chapter on Soviet sexuality here on an autobiography competition, in a tradition of sociological research which goes back to Florian Znaciecki in Poland in the 1920s, and which is a well-established approach in Nordic countries.[21] Neither of these types of source, of course, is socially unbiased; their contents depend on what kind of person was sought out to provide testimonies, and who chose to cooperate. Recognising what kinds of testimonies are missing or over-present is therefore crucial to successful interpretation.

Finally there is the use of single cases. This is the approach used here in chapters by Naomi Roslyn Galtz and Anna Rotkirch, and in Daniel Bertaux's account of a single working-class family. Ekaterina Foteeva uses a sub-group of elite families from the Bertaux project, but chosen with a similar rationale. Bertaux points out that, by collecting information on whole transgenerational families, a set of some fifty family accounts will provide over 2,000 individual trajectories. It is then possible to pick out a family, or even a single witness, whose life experience fits closely with what we know from history – experiences of collectivisation, war, urbanisation and industrialisation – so that the testimony becomes an epic, revealing how an ordinary Soviet man or woman felt about these transitions and their generating mechanisms, and the devices which they used to survive them. A notable example is his account with Marina Malysheva of the life of a Russian countrywoman, Maria Zolotarfeva. In their commentary they point out both how her story opens up new dimensions, especially in terms of gender, but also how it can be seen to fit with known history, for it 'embraces almost all the main events and processes of the sovietisation of the villages and its consequences: collectivisation and extortion, forced migration and machinations over passports, social isolation and homelessness, deprival of benefits and hunger, unpaid labour on the kolkhoz, and the constant struggle for survival'.[22] In this book, four of the chapters use a similar approach: Rotkirch explores gender through the case of one woman's autobiography; Galtz looks at leisure through the story of one woman and her *dachi*; Foteeva selects a group of well-to-do families to examine how they dealt with the advent of Soviet power; and Bertaux himself uses a single but very complex family of rural and industrial workers to interpret the creation – both through the accidents of industrialisation and through deliberate policies – of a remodelled Soviet working class.

* * *

So what insights into Russian Soviet society can we learn from the chapters which follow? The book's first section presents three perspectives on the creation of a distinctive Soviet society. It opens with Daniel Bertaux's interpretation of the experiences of a single proletarian family. His question is, what was their own cultural model of Soviet society? Was it possible that a mass of illiterate and deeply religious peasants could have made their own an official discourse that was supposedly inspired by one of the most radical and sophisticated thinkers that Europe ever produced, Karl Marx? And when their grandchildren finally turned their back on the Communist Party, was this because, as some American observers claimed, Russians had rejected egalitarian values and were dreaming of a market society and political democracy, or because they had come to believe that the Party itself had betrayed the very values it had preached? In the Soviet case, the Communist Party claimed to speak for the Soviet people with a single voice, so there were no public opinion polls until the 1960s, and even elections had only one candidate. There were thus few contemporary clues offered for answering such questions, so that retrospective interviews become invaluable.

Bertaux's chapter grew from a set of remarkable interviews carried out by Marina Malysheva, a co-worker in his Russian research team in the early 1990s. Malysheva had interviewed several men and women belonging to the same kinship network, called here the Zamochins, and it was thus possible to construct a case history of that extended family. Its oldest members had come in the

1930s, when they were in their late teens, from the hunger-haunted countryside to take up manual jobs in Moscow. Their children grew up crowded in semi-collective *baraki* and became adults during Krushchev's thaw. The third generation came of age during Brezhnev's 'stagnation', when the huge gap between Communist rhetoric and everyday social reality was becoming clear to most people. Thus the members of each historical generation developed their own set of shared values and taken-for-granted beliefs and representations, which crystallised during their youth and thereafter stayed little changed for the rest of their lives. These successive 'sediments' of ideology, shaped partly by official discourse but also by the direct experience of material conditions of work and everyday living, can be observed within this one family, which in Bertaux's view can be seen as representative of millions of other families who went through similar processes of migration to the city and socialisation into controlled Soviet patterns of urban living, and then eventually found themselves facing the slow re-emergence of individualism and privacy.

Beginning with a matter-of-fact narrative of the vivid accounts from Zamochin family members of working and living together, and of the ways in which extended family members could help each other or alternatively lose contact and disappear, Bertaux picks up from these narratives a number of indications of a transgenerational 'moral economy' which all seem to point towards belief in egalitarian values. In the second half of the chapter, his analysis moves to a different level, and he suggests how the sources of these egalitarian values may lie in earlier Russian social history: in particular, in the rural commune, and in the spirit and semantics of the Orthodox religion.

In Victoria Semenova's chapter, the focus deepens to examine the consequences of Soviet urban housing policies. The extraordinarily rapid urbanisation of Russia from the 1920s resulted in a drastic shortage of housing, above all in the great cities of Moscow and Leningrad. In the unregulated housing markets of the West, such shortages had resulted in heavy overcrowding in ageing buildings, and stark differentiation between urban neighbourhoods which ranged from affluent elegance to insanitary slums. In the Soviet Union the housing problem was tacked through central planning and bureaucratic allocation (mediated through the influence of connections and networks). Residence in Moscow quickly became limited by the issue of residence permits *(propiski)*. On the periphery, clusters of wooden huts *(baraki)* were built near the new industrial factories to house the new labour force which was coming – often illegally, as with the Zamochins – from the villages. And in the city itself, families were piled up in larger apartments and houses which had belonged to the former upper classes, now divided by flimsy partitions with no more than a room for each family: the famous *kommunalka* form.

Semenova's chapter deals with the sociological consequences of this last type of accommodation. The chapter is based on the testimonies of two generations: those, now quite old, who spent much of their adult years living in *kommunalki*; and the younger generation, who lived in them only as children. In a manner very rare in world history, families of extremely different origin, from the rural and urban poor to the former pre-revolutionary elites, were forced to live closely together and share the same common domestic spaces. Because families typically had only a single room, meant for living and sleeping, the women cooked in a communal kitchen and the children played in a communal yard, thus fostering the development of new values through peer-group influence. Semenova explores the long-term consequences on such a constrained way of life, in which privacy was reduced to very little and intimacy – the most private aspect of privacy – to almost nothing (a point which links to Anna Rotkirch's paper on sexuality later in this volume). She suggests that in this type of housing it became particularly difficult for the educated or one-time upper-class families to pass on their cultural capital and everyday domestic patterns to their children. As a consequence, the earlier highly differentiated Russian social cultures were gradually immersed in a new common culture of equality in poverty, the culture of the ordinary Soviet person: a culture which stressed adherence to the collective rather than individualism, nonconformity or personal achievement.

In the last chapter of this section, Ekaterina Foteeva turns to the top of the social structure to examine the experiences of a group of well-to-do Russian families of the pre-revolutionary era. One of the most fascinating topics of Soviet studies is, indeed, the fate of families which belonged to the upper classes before the Bolshevik takeover. Many fled to the West, but what happened to those who remained in the new situation in which their background had become a formal disadvantage? What about their children, whose social origin was meant under Stalin's rule to deny them entry to higher education or to many of the better jobs? What about their grandchildren? Since successful social revolutions are so rare in history, they can be examined almost like social experiments: and in this case, again using family interviews as our source, we can ask how far members of the new ruling class were able in reality to eliminate the better-educated old elites, and through what strategies?

Foteeva draws her interpretation from a set of family interviews, chosen to represent a range of formerly wealthy families: from aristocrats and rich merchants to industrialists and well-educated priests. She is able to show that, while whole families of wealthy peasants were repressed, the urban elites were much more selectively targeted. Most often it was only the established older professional men who were repressed. Their sons and daughters could take up manual jobs and survive. Since women were considered by the regime to be less dangerous than men, many of the daughters were able to find refuge in non-manual work which required cultural knowledge or foreign languages. As for the sons, quite often, hiding their social origins, they succeeded in getting an education by joining evening training courses for workers, the *rabfak*, which the new regime set up in the hope of forming a new intelligentsia from the ranks of the industrial proletariat. Some went on to become professionals and academics, and a few even Communist political activists. In terms of transmission, according to Foteeva, the key challenge which these families faced was to hide their origins while at the same time passing on their cultural capital to their children; and the stratagems and tactics which they used make fascinating reading.

The second section of the book concerns personal and family life. Here the first chapter takes us to the opposite end of the early Soviet society – that of poor and illiterate peasants. Anna Rotkirch uses the rare published autobiography of Aleksandra Chistiakova, who worked for the state railways from the 1940s to the 1970s, in order to trace how the officially imposed Soviet gender contract was lived out in everyday life. It has been suggested by some critics that Soviet women accepted gender inequalities because of their passive traditional attitudes, but Chistiakova's story strikingly illustrates how women were prepared to struggle for survival independently, only choosing to use traditions which they found supportive.

According to the gender ideology which was established under Stalin and remained basically unchanged until the demise of the Soviet Union, women's paid work was coupled with their responsibilities for unpaid care work, often carried out by female kin of the working mother. Chistiakova's life is, however, very far, not only from the official success stories of Soviet women, but also from middle-class women's complaints about their double burden. She depicts both extreme material and physical hardship, and also the challenge of coping with her husband's drinking and violence. Her story suggests why many Russian women, in the hope of winning more practical and emotional support, were willing to subscribe to 'traditional' views on male dominance and decision-making in a selective, pragmatic way. Her story also illustrates the positive achievements of Soviet power in providing both girls and boys with basic education and in granting women personal and professional independence. For finally it was, above all, Chistiakova's own working life which enhanced her personal freedom and self-esteem and provided a basis for the well-being of her whole family.

Chistiakova's life story also provides an example of the patterns of extended motherhood responsible for childrearing and cultural transmission in Soviet family life. This is again a key issue in the chapter by Victoria Semenova and Paul Thompson. They ask how far the typical patterns of childrearing of the Soviet period can be related to the attitudes of Russian men and women to work, and in particular to their responses to crises when work became much more difficult to find. For this they draw on the evidence of both the Thompson and the Bertaux interviews.

They show, first, the contrasts in attitudes to formal school education between working-class families, who preferred to leave their children's education to the teachers and not interfere, and the much more specific encouragement of professional parents. Equally important, middle-class families were far more likely to have collections of books, including Russian novels, poetry and history, or to teach their children to draw or to play music, thus not only transmitting some of their intergenerational cultural capital, but providing education at home as well as at school. There is striking evidence from the interviews that working-class children could be well aware that, although their peers were 'all the same grey mice' in identical uniforms, and with little difference in material well-being, these home-educated children from professional families, much more often the teachers' pets, had immense advantages over them.

There was a parallel contrast in the transmission of family models. In proletarian families, with the parents away at work for most of the day, housing so crowded that there were rarely family mealtimes for talking together, there was very limited opportunity for transmitting a specific family model: children were much more likely to pick up ideas in a more generalised way from their peers, playing in the communal yards. Working-class fathers were typically severe authority figures, and so were many in the middle class: indeed, overall, the predominant model of Russian parenting, not only in the Soviet period but also today, has above all sought to encourage social conformity and obedience, and backed it with the ultimate sanction of physical discipline. Nevertheless, there were some middle-class families which had their own distinctive order, with the father deliberately taking his son to the workplace and trying to enthuse him with its values, and above all, the encouragement of discussion rather than the mere imposition of orders by use of the belt. Probably more important than this broad social class distinction, however, was that two in every five families with children were also living with grandmothers or other extended kin, and in many of these homes the grandmother was the principal carer for the child. The interviews suggest that the atmosphere in these households was typically much gentler and less punishing, and there was very often a confiding intimacy between grandmother and grandchild. This did not necessarily lead to the transmission of earlier family values – both because the stories were of women who were mostly illiterate and from peasant backgrounds, and because so many family stories were too dangerous to pass on – but there were exceptions, particularly in educated middle-class families.

Semenova and Thompson conclude by looking in special detail at the backgrounds of a small group of young men and women who – in sharp contrast to the great majority of Russians – took advantage of economic change to set themselves up as independent entrepreneurs in the early 1990s. They are thus exemplars of adaptability in the face of change, and indeed many hold values which emphasise personal freedom, independence and self-direction. It is, therefore, striking to find that in their families most often either the father was absent or his authority was not accepted by the mother or grandmother; or, alternatively, the sons had to win their independence against strong parental opposition. Paradoxically, then, the strength of the younger Russian generation in facing the dramatic changes of the 1990s would seem to have come less from conventional intact nuclear families, and much more from extended and split families headed by mothers and grandmothers.

Sexual knowledge and morality is also affected by both intergenerational transmission and change between one generation and the next. Since practically all types of public reference to sexuality and nudity were prohibited in the Soviet Union from the 1930s until the late 1980s, sexual knowledge could only be transmitted through informal social networks, and it is therefore only possible to trace the patterns of this transmission through autobiography or oral memory. In her chapter on the transmission of sexual knowledge, Anna Rotkirch uses a large collection of autobiographies, dividing its authors into three generations. The older generation, the generation of silence, came of age in the 1940s and 1950s and, because they no longer lived in the countryside and did not usually have access to information from books and brochures, they probably had even less sexual information than their own parents and grandparents. They typically learnt what they knew from their peer groups, including childhood friends in the *kommunalka* or the *dachi*. The second generation, which came of age in the 1960s and 1970s, was the generation of learned ignorance. They did have access to a variety of sources of sexual knowledge, from Western pornographic films to Hungarian contraceptives, and the word *seks* was introduced into the Russian language in the 1970s. However, they had no common forum in which to discuss changes in sexual behaviour and attitudes, and lacked any shared morality or expectations. By contrast, for the youngest generation, the generation of articulation, who began to come of age in the 1980s, the situation did change fundamentally, for sexuality became an accepted topic for the public sphere: in media commercials, in school education and in pop culture.

In the last chapter of this section, Naomi Roslyn Galtz addresses the question of the meaning of personal freedom in a highly authoritarian society by looking at family and personal leisure activities in the form of work-based garden activities and the *dachi*, the small summer cottages on garden plots which were so common on the peripheries of Russian cities. Galtz tells the story of one cooperative *dacha* settlement organised in the early 1980s by a Moscow technical institute, and in particular of one of its members, a retired 63-year-old woman. *Dachi* were very popular among urban Soviet families, not only because they offered proximity with nature (also an attraction in Western European countries with a still-meaningful peasant legacy), but also because they gave an opportunity to hold and manage a form of private property. They were spaces for personal initiative and for seclusion: one could be on one's own on the *dachi*, till the soil, and – within the limits of the regulations – arrange the environment, spending weekends away from the omnipresent control of 'Them'. Hence Galtz's attempt to move from the experience of the *dacha* to an understanding of freedom, the 'small freedoms' in an otherwise highly controlled society. In the cities themselves, kitchens and cafés could also provide similar parallel spaces, where young intellectuals could talk freely with close friends.

As Galtz shows, the issue of freedom is very complex. The received wisdom of Westerners is to think that Soviet people were totally without freedom. By contrast, some Russian intellectuals – such as Leonid Ionin, writing in the post-Soviet period – have argued that Soviet people did develop a sense of freedom which was unique, and which their Western counterparts could not understand because they had no experience of it. Indeed, there is nothing like repression to generate an acute appreciation of the smallest chance to exercise choice. Galtz argues that both points of view are oversimplifications, for it is not just the overall degree of control, but norms relating to class, to gender, and perhaps to age which shaped such experiences. We cannot assume, for example, that a male intellectual and a working-class female shared the same experiences of 'small freedoms'.

The final section of the book concerns minorities: first the marginal, and second the successful. Irina Korovushkina Paert's study of the Old Believers in the Urals during and after Stalin's time describes a uniquely non-Soviet group that somehow managed to survive at the margins of Soviet society. Relying on oral sources which often provide the fullest evidence of such persecuted minorities, she paints a picture of utter repression. Not only were the leaders and many members killed or deported, and their churches converted to barns or youth centres, but some of the Old Believers' cemeteries were even turned into football pitches. But these accounts also hint at resilience. The regime had aimed to erase them completely, not only materially but also in terms of meaning: and there were perhaps other religious groups which were altogether eliminated. But with the Old Believers the very survival, transmitted through families and communities, of memories and meanings is itself a witness of resilience; even though the price of survival was often the passing down to grandchildren of a muted identity, protecting them from repression by never revealing to them their whole faith and full religious identity.

For such children and grandchildren there would often come a moment when they understood the political situation into which their heritage had projected them, and they faced the same dilemma as all those others whose families stood for values condemned by the Communist authorities. The dilemma was between remaining faithful to the commitments of one's parents, and as a consequence being ostracised for life, or joining the winners' side, the world of Communist youth groups, Pioneers and *komsomols*. The choice was, as Max Weber would have put it, between a value-rational choice and an instrumentally rational choice. Many of the most active and energetic young people would opt for this latter 'rational choice', opening up much fuller life chances for themselves, but at the moral cost of betraying the values of their parents and kin. They faced, in short, the kind of choice which in all societies faces the young of disapproved, marginalised minorities, religious, ethnic or cultural: your freedom or your heritage.

Nanci Adler writes of those who formed the lowest group in the Soviet social structure, the millions of men and women who were sentenced under Stalin to serve years of imprisonment in the *gulag*. Many of them would be shot there, or die from ill health or work accidents. Some did survive the terrible conditions, eventually to be released. But they were unable to return to normal life. Their documents identified them as ex-convicts, and a *zek* was not a free citizen, but was instead assigned to residence somewhere on the outskirts of the Soviet Empire. To the authorities they remained suspects, so that ordinary citizens feared to deal with them, and it was very hard for them to find either work or lodging. Ex-prisoners also lived in constant fear of being re-sentenced, so that their inner psychological wounds remained bleeding. For the same reason, little is known about how they lived after the *gulag*. Most preferred to remain silent.

Adler has used a combination of written testimonies collected with Memorial and her own interviews with survivors. They are the only possible source for such experiences. Her chapter recalls the testimonies collected for Solzhenitsyn's classic eye-opening book, *The Gulag Archipelago* (1974), although his concern was with the *gulag* itself rather than with survival after it. It is difficult not to be moved by these fragile voices, which stood against arbitrary bureaucratic and apparently unlimited power just as a courageous and unarmed individual will sometimes decide to stand alone against the forces of organised destruction. Adler compares the oblivion of this group in public consciousness to a Freudian repression in the psyche, and their experiences in later speaking out to the 'return of the repressed' in the collective mind of Soviet and post-Soviet society: a society still reluctant to fully acknowledge their existence, or take responsibility for what was done to them.

In the final chapter, Marianne Liljeström considers another minority, but this time at the opposite end of the spectrum: that of successful Soviet women. She uses in a novel way three published life histories, a genre which has usually been dismissed as stereotyped and uninformative because of the need to conform to official expectations. In the case of women's autobiographies, however, there was an inherent underlying tension, because on the one hand, women were expected to be portrayed with appropriate femininity, while on the other, the image of a revolutionary hero, although intended in principle to be gender-neutral, was *de facto* masculine. Liljeström shows how women quietly challenged the male bias of the male revolutionary story and created a 'female signature', and points out that, rather than being uniform, her three authors take very different positions in relation to the popular masses, male soldiers and women in their published autobiographies.

There were so many minorities in Soviet society that it is important to have a glimpse of them here. But above all the concern of this book is with living through the Soviet era as experienced by the vast masses of Russian citizens – hence our starting point, the journey of the Zamochin family from their peasant origins to the industrialised Soviet city – to which we must next turn.

Notes

1 Notable examples include Vera Dunham, *In Stalin's Time: Middleclass Values in Soviet Fiction* (Cambridge University Press, Cambridge, 1976) and (from policy documentation) Mary Buckley, *Women and Ideology in the Soviet Union* (Harvester Wheatsheaf, New York and London, 1989).
2 Victoria Semenova, Ekaterina Foteeva and Daniel Bertaux (eds), *Sud'by liudei: Rossiia XX vek. Biografii semei kak ob'ekt sotsiologicheskogo issledovaniia* [The Fates of People: Russia in the 20th Century. Biography as an Object of Sociological Research], (Institut Sociologii RAN, Moscow, 1996).
3 Almost the only work to deal with such issues was Viktor Shlapentokh, *Public and Private Life of the Soviet People. Changing Values in the Post-Stalin Russia* (Oxford University Press, Oxford 1989), chapter 9. It is illuminating to make comparison with the arid statistical approach, which conveyed little sense of the real changes taking place since

INTRODUCTION

the mid-1980s, of David Lane, *Soviet Society under Perestroika* (Unwin Hyman, Boston, 1990), chapter 7, 'Reproducing society: gender, family and generations'.
4 The most obvious comparison is with Chinese Communism, which involved a larger population but for a shorter time.
5 'Russia's lost tribe', *Guardian*, 15 December 2001.
6 Six of 'Stalin's falcons' were interviewed for 'The very few', *Guardian Weekend*, 15 December 2001.
7 *Guardian Weekly*, 20–26 June 2002.
8 Michael Glenny and Norman Stone, *The Other Russia: The Experience of Exile* (Faber and Faber, London, 1990). The earliest project of this kind was the United States State Department Soviet Interview Project, the interviews of which are held both in the Library of Congress and at the Russian Research Center, Harvard.
9 Alena Ledenova, *The Russian Economy of Favours Blat, Networking and Informal Exchange* (Cambridge University Press, New York, 1998).
10 There is a substantial Russian literature on this issue. Our own concern here is simply to situate the interviews used in this book, both in terms of the sample strategy used, and of how class impinged on individual experience and identity. On identity, a good starting point would be Sheila Fitzpatrick, 'Ascribing class: the construction of social identity in Soviet Russia', *Journal of Modern History*, 50, 4 (1993): 745–70.
11 Paul Thompson, *The Voice of the Past* (Oxford University Press, Oxford, 1978, revised editions 1988 and 2000); Daniel Bertaux (ed.), *Biography and Society: The Life History Approach in the Social Sciences* (Sage, London, 1981); Daniel Bertaux, 'Social genealogies, commented and compared: an instrument for studying social mobility in the "longue durée"', *Current Sociology/La Sociologie contemporaine*, special issue, 'The Biographical Method', 43 (1995): 69–89; Daniel Bertaux, *Les récits de vie* (Nathan, Paris, 1997).
12 Irina Sherbakova, 'The Gulag in memory', translated by Paul Thompson, in Luisa Passerini (ed.), *Memory and Totalitarianism*, International Yearbook of Oral History and Life Stories, Vol. 1 (Oxford University Press, Oxford, 1992): 103–16.
13 Victoria Semenova and Sergei Rozhdestvesky, 'The experience of suffering passed down through generations', paper to the IXth International Oral History Conference, Göteborg, 13–16 June 1996.
14 Ingrid Oswald and Viktor Voronkov, 'On the interview situation in post-Soviet society', foreword to 'The "Public" in Soviet Society', forthcoming in *European Societies*.
15 We are grateful to Alastair McAuley and Rose Glickman for information on the Memorial competitions.
16 Daria Khubova, Andrei Ivankiev and Tonia Sharova, 'After *glasnost*: oral history in the Soviet Union', in Luisa Passerini (ed.), *Memory and Totalitarianism*, 89–102; and transcript at meeting at British Library National Sound Archive, 21 March 1990. An important discussion in French of the public contestation of memory in Eastern Europe as a whole can be found in Alain Brossat *et al.* (eds), *À l'Est la mémoire retrouvée* (La Découverte, Paris, 1990): 'La mémoire disputée', 321–565.
17 Aleksandr Solzhenitsyn, *The Gulag Archipelago 1918–1956: An Experiment in Literary Investigation* (Collins and Harvill Press, London, 1974): xi.
18 Paul Thompson, 'Life histories and the analysis of social change', in Daniel Bertaux (ed.), *Biography and Society: The Life History Approach in the Social Sciences*, (Sage, London, 1981): 289–306.
19 Ludmilla Koklyagina and Victoria Semenova (eds), *Doklad o tret'em etape longit'udnogo issledovaniia puti odnogo pokoleniya* [Report on third wave of longitudinal survey: paths of one russian generation] (ISAN, Moscow, 1993).
20 Ray Pahl and Paul Thompson, 'Meanings, myths and mystifications: the social construction of life stories in Russia', in C. M. Hann (ed.), *When History Accelerates: Essays on Rapid Social Change, Complexity and Creativity* (Athlone Press, London, 1994): 130–60.

21 Daniel Bertaux (ed.), *Biography and Society: The Life History Approach in the Social Sciences* (Sage, London, 1981).
22 Marina Malysheva and Daniel Bertaux, 'The social experiences of a countrywoman in Soviet Russia', in Selma Leydesdorff, Luisa Passerini and Paul Thompson (eds), *Gender and Memory*, International Yearbook of Oral History and Life Stories, IV (Oxford University Press, Oxford, 1996): 31–44.

Part I

CREATING SOVIET SOCIETY

2

THE CULTURAL MODEL OF THE RUSSIAN POPULAR CLASSES AND THE TRANSITION TO A MARKET ECONOMY

Daniel Bertaux, in collaboration with Marina Malysheva

INTRODUCTION

Of all the state secrets concealed by the Communist regime, one of the best kept was surely that of everyday life, its practical contexts, its rules and long-term effects: of the daily efforts of families to survive, to improve their living conditions and to pass on some of their resources to their children in order to help them to live better. It was not just a question of maintaining the credibility of an official representation of social reality that would have been shattered by the public revelation of the manifold difficulties of daily life, nor even of preventing awareness of the growing distance between the official model of meritocratic selection of the elites and how they were really composed. It was, also more fundamentally, a matter of protecting the monopoly that the Party seized for steering the historical direction of social change. This monopoly assumed that the only legitimate force for change, the historical Subject, was the Party. It involved a two-fold moral *diktat*: that all individual and collective energies were supposed to be directed along the lines marked out by the Party, and that any effort to divert a part of this to further individual, family or clan strategies for the improvement of living conditions was inadmissible. Recognising the existence of this kind of effort would have meant recognising the existence and legitimacy of Subjects for action other than the Party itself.

To what extent did Soviet people really internalise this viewpoint? Was it possible to live in this way, generation after generation? Or can we suggest that a semi-conscious strategic mode of thought led individuals or small groups of mutual support (above all, families) to try to make the most of the collective frameworks imposed on them, so as to improve their own living conditions?

By putting this question, we are already highlighting an initial contradiction: the central resource of 'Communist societies' was not money, as in the West, but power. However, those who exercised it were not supposed to use it for their own advantage – on the contrary, it was they who were responsible for combating individualism. Had they not been recruited on the basis of their ardour in publicly defending the ideals of collectivism and values of altruism?[1] Here we are confronting the paradox that would eventually erode the credibility of the entire system.

The question has been put, but how can we study it? We are proposing an empirical approach that responds to the nature of the phenomenon being studied. Based on the collection of lived experience by means of life stories and family histories, it focuses on the behaviours of individuals and families in as far as they were oriented *over the long term*. It is in this sense that we can speak about strategic forms of behaviour in the minimal sense of the term. Minimal because, for Soviet citizens, both the horizon of possibilities and the resources available were extraordinarily limited, for these limits were imposed not only by the command economy, but also from the very low level of general development and hence of resources, which was closer to that of the nineteenth-century industrial West than that of the twentieth century. Minimal also because of the stigmatisation by official ideology of anything resembling individual Subjects behaving according to their own rather than the collective interest.[2] Minimal but not non-existent: for this is not only our own central hypothesis, but was also the spectre that haunted Communist leaders. It preoccupied them particularly when they thought, for example, of the families of the former ruling classes, whose strategic capacity they precisely feared and whose opportunities for action they systematically endeavoured to obliterate.

Fortunately, our testimonies give a privileged glimpse of how far official Soviet values were really internalised by Soviet people; and it is this point that this chapter deals with. For a long time, their values did not appear to be of much importance. Through its very structure, the command economy was supposed to allow scarcely any initiative on the part of individual agents, and to strictly control their behaviour. Yet the very emphasis placed on the continual repetition of the same ideological slogans, and the tight control imposed on the public expression of non-conformist values or opinions, hint at the continuing doubts of the Soviet elites as to the lasting success of their programmes for inculcating collective values (Colton 1980).[3]

In order to give a better idea of the issues at stake, we have therefore chosen to tell the story of a working-class family of peasant origin. Their trajectory is one experienced by innumerable other Soviet families from the 1930s to the present day. The contexts within which its successive generations grew up, worked, loved and lived are contexts that have been experienced by millions of other Soviet families. It is, in this sense if not statistically, representative: a single story paralleled by countless others.

THE BRIEF HISTORY OF ONE WORKING-CLASS SOVIET FAMILY

The Zamochins

Ivan Zamochin and his wife *Alexandra* were born in Siberia, of peasant families of European Russian origin. They were married in 1911, and by 1917, when the revolutions in St Petersburg took place, they had four children. 'The land to the peasants', said the new government. Ivan and Alexandra fixed on a plan to sell their poor farm, leave Siberia and return to the village of Alexandra's parents, Osnovo, in the region of Tambov (Lower Volga). As soon as the Civil War calmed down, they put their plan into action. They took over a farm in Osnovo; Ivan cleared and cultivated the land while Alexandra looked after the animals and gave birth to four more children.

Things took a turn for the worse in 1929 when Stalin decreed the collectivisation of the land. Ivan submitted grumbling to the directives and joined the *kolkhoz*, hoping that he would do reasonably well out of it. A vain hope: it very quickly became apparent that the real purpose of collectivisation was to take the maximum amount of food from the peasants to feed the cities. Soon people in the countryside were very hungry. As for the compulsory work on the land of the *kolkhoz*, it was not paid in money but in bits of paper, the *trudoden'* (days of work), that had practically no value.

People said that in Moscow you could find things to eat. A brother of Alexandra's had already emigrated there; he was working at the railway station in Kazan, the very place where peasants from the Volga Basin were arriving in their thousands. As Ivan and Alexandra were now confined to the village by Stalin's new directive depriving peasants of the right to leave 'their' *kolkhoz* (1932), the uncle said 'no more than three'. They decided to send their three eldest children to Moscow.

Egor, 23, already married to a girl from the village, was put in charge of the expedition; he was accompanied by Nikolaï, 22, the 'intellectual' of the family (he had completed his seven years at primary school) and Masha, 20, who knew how to sew. So Egor arrived at Kazan station with his brother and sister one morning in the winter of 1935. Thanks to their uncle, the two others found a job straight away at the depot of this huge railway complex. A bed was found for them in extremely basic dormitories that the station had built for its employees. But Egor wanted a room he could bring his wife to. He heard that on the edge of the city, in the Medvedkovo district, a huge industrial area was being developed and that on waste ground shacks (*baraki*) were being built for the workers. Egor went there, found the building site and the shacks – long log houses, each of which was intended to house several dozen families. It so happened that they were looking for someone to be in charge of one of them. Egor made it clear that he was married, made a good impression (the man in charge was perhaps from the same region); in short, he got the job (which was very poorly paid) and above all a place in the shack. His wife soon joined him. Subsequently they would have two sons, Anatoly in 1936, Viktor in 1938.

Egor died in 1977, but his son *Viktor* was able to describe to us the *baraki* in Medvedkovo among which he grew up.

> The people were used to village life, so they felt at home here in Polegorodok – 'the little town in the fields', that's what we called it. They were among their own kind. If you like, Polegorodok wasn't any bigger than a Russian village. It consisted of several single-storey long wooden *baraki*, with vegetable gardens all around. At one end of the *barak*, there were a communal kitchen and toilets. It had a central corridor with doors. Each family had its own door and window, but inside you could separate out the space as you wished. There were no dividing walls. People put up partitions, but they were, in a way – symbolic. Everyone knew everyone, everyone knew everything about everyone. You never locked the doors, of course, and nobody would have taken a carrot or even a radish from your vegetable garden, even if you hadn't put a fence around it. We children ran all over the place. Our mothers were at work all day, but they weren't worried: they knew that there was no danger, it was like in the village, there was always someone left to look after us.
>
> Of course, as soon as the snow melted, people spent all their evenings working on their vegetable gardens. They talked to one another from one patch to another. There were some who had built a wooden shed to keep a pig, or one or two sheep and some chickens. Some even had a cow. People grew vegetables and then sold them at the markets in Moscow; it paid well. My uncle Ivanchik, my father's younger brother, had noticed that there was a steam-pipe that passed underground near to his shed; he was crafty, he sowed vegetables there before the winter. People said to him, 'You're mad', but the vegetables grew. In the middle of winter, he harvested onions, cabbages, lettuces, parsley and fennel, and he made some dosh out of it.
>
> People had no money at all. It was very difficult in the years after the war, even in the 1950s. But the atmosphere was friendly. In the middle of Polegorodok, we built a big hall, constructed of stone. During the holidays, we cooked giant crocks full of stew and shared the food amongst us. Everyone brought a plate, someone played the accordion, and we sang and danced.

Viktor's childhood memories can be dated with precision. Viktor was born in 1938 in the *barak* which his father Egor supervised. He was seven years old when the Great Patriotic War ended. His description therefore concerns the 1940s and the beginning of the 1950s, the years in which the legitimacy of the 'Soviet' cultural model, as redefined by Stalin, was at its height.

We are going to introduce other characters into this story, and move gradually from their living conditions to their working conditions, and then to their attitudes and values and their truly internalised cultural model: this is what we need to grasp from the inside, to understand whether and how long it retained its power over people's minds.

In the late 1930s, shortly after securing his job as supervisor of the *barak*, Egor brought to Moscow – or rather to Polegorodok, to his own *barak* – three other brothers (including Ivanchik, who was to excel in growing vegetables in the middle of winter). All three found jobs as workers in the factories of Medvedkovo. Only the two youngest sisters remained at the *kolkhoz* with their ageing parents: they were to remain peasants all their lives, with very bad living conditions which only marginally improved over a long time.

At this time, tens of thousands of peasants were arriving in Moscow despite the rules for the administrative authorisation of residence, *propiska*. There was a great need for labour in the factories and on the building sites of the Soviet metropolis. This was how the Chernovs came from the Smolensk region, and also the Sabakovs, who came from a village in the Orlov region and settled in Polegorodok. Later on, their children or grandchildren would mix their blood with that of the Zamochins.

THE CHERNOVS

Let us take the Chernovs next. *Tikhon* and *Tatiana* got married in 1918 in the village of Filipovo in the Smolensk region. They were prosperous peasants. They had only three children: Maria, the eldest, born in 1919 (she is one of our main witnesses; much later her daughter Rimma would marry Viktor Zamochin); Konstantin, born in 1926; and Valia, born in 1930.

Following the collectivisation of the land, the situation of wealthy peasants became catastrophic. Tikhon and Tatiana escaped the repression of the *kulaki* by very quickly joining the *kolkhoz*; but with the work vouchers they were given, they did not even have enough to buy shoes for their children. Tikhon then decided (in 1934) to leave for Moscow. He succeeded in getting work in a metalworking factory which lodged him in a hostel for single workers. He tried to save to send money to his family, but his salary was too small.

Even before their eldest daughter *Maria* had finished her seven years of compulsory schooling in the village, her mother Tatiana sent her to Moscow to join her father and find a job. This was in 1935, when Maria was only sixteen. In Moscow she was accepted on an accelerated training course as a vodka sales assistant (for which her seven years at school were not required). As her father could not keep her indefinitely with him in an entirely male hostel, he ended up by suggesting that she should share the room of a female friend of his. It did not take Maria long to realise that this woman was her father's mistress; she wrote to her mother describing the situation to her and adding that she wanted to return home to the village.

But Tatiana decided otherwise. She had scarcely received the letter before she packed her case, took her two young children (Nikolaï was nine and Valia six) and arrived without any warning at her husband's place in Moscow. This provoked a crisis: it was out of the question that Tatiana and her children should live in a hostel for unmarried workers. Tikhon made amends, broke off with his mistress, looked for accommodation for his family, but found only an extremely expensive hotel room. Tatiana was desperate. She did not even have enough money for a ticket home. In the end she decided that the only solution was to sell her house in the village of Filipovo. With the money from the sale, she managed to find a room in Medvekovo. The whole family was then crammed into it. (This was the common housing standard of the time.)

The two youngest children, therefore, went to school in Moscow. The boy, *Konstantin*, was conscripted into the army at the age of sixteen in 1941, survived the war and joined the police in 1945 (thanks to which he quite quickly – and very unusually – got his own room in another communal apartment). *Valia*, who had completed her secondary education, found a job as an assistant in a laboratory conducting secret research for the army. As for Maria, the eldest, she fell in love at the age of twenty with a young man of her own age, Iosif, a metalworker of peasant origin who was living in Polegorodok. He married her in 1941 and took her with him to the *barak* where his family lived. Everyone crammed in a bit more tightly to give the young couple a corner of the room.

Iosif, Maria's young spouse, born in 1922, was the youngest of a family of seven children. His parents, peasants from the Orlov region, came to Moscow – or rather to Polegorodok – with all of their children in the 1930s. He was nineteen in 1941, which was the year of his marriage; it is also the year the USSR entered the war. As he was a skilled professional (he knew how to work metal by hand), he was mobilised as an aspiring officer and began the war near to Moscow in a military academy. He was even allowed to visit his young wife. It was during one of these visits that their first child was conceived, Rimma, born in 1943. Then Iosif left for the front.

In spite of his age, Maria's father Tikhon was also called up. His wife Tatiana then found herself without resources (she didn't have a job) and moved in with her eldest daughter, Maria, in Iosif's *barak*. Maria gave birth to Rimma, only leaving her job as a sales assistant for two weeks; then she entrusted the baby to her mother and returned to her job. She was working in a large food shop, which gave her a certain facility of access to basic foodstuffs (bread, margarine), thanks to which there was always something to eat at home.

During the war years, the discipline imposed on workers was extremely harsh: all of our testimonies agree on this point. Arriving five minutes late meant losing your salary for the whole day. Unjustified absence could bring arrest and deportation. This discipline created particular problems for young women and mothers, problems that were virtually insoluble. No account was taken of the fact that they might be pregnant, or their child ill (the creches were full to bursting point), or that they could be suffering the consequences of a self-induced abortion. It was for this reason that Tatiana, Maria's mother, soon found herself in great demand in the *barak*: she was looking after not only her granddaughter, Rimma, but other children too. Childcaring quickly became virtually her profession, for which she was paid in foodstuffs and clothing, sometimes money – which was very timely, as her husband had sent no word and no money. This illiterate but calm, gentle and responsible peasant woman became a kind of mother figure for the *barak* community.

The war finally ended. Tikhon never came home. He had disappeared in the confusion. (In spite of the repeated requests made after the war by his second daughter, Valia, the laboratory assistant, who through her work was in contact with the military authorities, the latter would never supply any details about his fate.) Iosif, Maria's husband, was badly injured in the knee; he was to limp for the rest of his life. He returned with the Red Star medal, but he refused to speak about his years at the front. The memory was too painful.

Nine months after the return of the husbands to Polegorodok, a veritable flowering of babies re-peopled the *barak*. Among them was Natalia, Iosif and Maria's second daughter. A third child would be born ten years later in 1955; a boy called Iuri who was to be his mother's little darling (we shall meet him again).

In 1948, Maria's sister, Valia the laboratory assistant, married a secondary school teacher ten years her senior. He was *Evgenii*. He had been in the war, had been taken prisoner by the Germans (he didn't brag about it) and survived. He was passionate about history and pedagogy, an excellent teacher. However, one day an envoy from the local Party committee came to see the headmaster of his school: because of his captivity during the war, Evgenii had been deemed unreliable, and Soviet children were not to be entrusted to his care. Stalin had demanded that his soldiers should never surrender, so by allowing himself to be captured alive Evgenii had betrayed his fatherland, and by surviving the terrible conditions of captivity he had betrayed it a second time. 'You can count yourself lucky to have escaped the camps!' the civil servant in charge of purging the cadres told him. Totally prohibited from teaching, Evgenii now had to make do with a job repairing typewriters, spending his days with workmates who had no interest whatever in history or literature, but who were mainly concerned with their wages and their 'collective drinking binges'. Evgenii would have just one daughter, Natasha (born in 1950), who would later study economics at university.

As for Maria's brother, Konstantin the policeman, in 1951 he married a young woman who was also from the country, an unskilled worker. They would have two children: Sergei, born in 1954, who was later to study law (note the relationship between the father's profession and the son's choice of studies) and Tania, born in 1956, who like her mother left education very early and took up a modest job as a caretaker.

THE OLDER SOVIET-BORN GENERATION

Before pursuing the life paths of the suceeding generations, let us spend a moment looking at the generation of Maria and Iosif, Valia and Evgenii, Konstantin and his wife. They are all of peasant origin (apart from Evgenii), were born between 1917 and 1928, and came to Moscow with their parents in the 1930s to flee the *kolkhoz* (this was also the case of Egor's five brothers and sisters, born between 1912 and 1921, who emigrated to Moscow where their uncle had already settled, and that of Iosif's seven brothers and sisters). Almost all of them spent their teenage years, and later made a home, in Polegorodok, in an atmosphere of communal living. It was in overpopulated *baraki* that their children were born and brought up in the 1940s and 1950s. We have already briefly described Polegorodok's community spirit and the harshness of the working conditions. One last point remains to be added: the stability of employment.

This was strikingly illustrated by Maria's story. She had always worked as a simple sales assistant in the same chain of food shops. In 58 years of uninterrupted work, she only changed shop three times and was never promoted. She was 75 years old at the time of the interview. Maria told her life story without displaying any emotion. Her phrases were lack lustre. She described her life, now nearing its end, as long and grey without any highlights. There was nothing endearing or attractive about her. The weight of an entirely predetermined daily life made her what she is today. She doubtless had to get used to regarding her body like a machine, a machine made to suit the needs of her family and her work. Now the machine is broken (one leg paralysed) and she is no good for anything ...

Maria remained faithful all her life to her work and family. This loyalty, which she is unable to comment on because to her it is so self-evident, was only expressed when she was asked about the career paths of the members of her extended family. Without passion, but with a certain pride, she mentioned that most of them worked for the same 'administration' for most of their lives. This was the case with her brother Konstantin, who remained an ordinary policeman until he retired; and her sister Valia, laboratory assistant all her life in the same military research centre. And also her husband Iosif, who was a worker all his life in the same factory until his death in 1968, run over by a car. About him, she could manage to say nothing more than that when he died – when she herself was 49 – she was therefore obliged to resume very long working hours, from eight in the morning until eight at night for six days every week.

THE SECOND SOVIET-BORN GENERATION

There was the same stability of work for most of the next generation, those born in the 1930s and 1940s. Thus Maria's eldest daughter Rimma has been a kindergarten assistant for 27 years, her second daughter Natalia, a warehouse worker for 29 years, and her husband a turner in the same factory for 31 years. Victor, Rimma's husband, she says has been a bus driver for 37 years (she's still counting); and her own son, Iurii, a lorry driver for the same *combinat* (metal factory) for 20 years.

Maria's tone is that of observation, but of an observation that values stability in work and which seems to say: we did not look to improve our position, we did not look for easier jobs, we accepted tough working conditions and low salaries with courage. We showed ourselves to be dependable and loyal – good workers. We did our best in the jobs that were assigned to us.

> *Maria, you were a sales assistant all your life, how come you did not take advantage of your position? During the period of the zastojnyj (stagnation), all shop girls made substantial amounts of money, it is a well-known fact. Why didn't you?*

I was never able to steal. It's true that in the shop everyone did 'deals'. Apart from me and a few other old women. That's why I was never promoted: because the others that stole, and the bosses that stole even more, didn't trust me. They kept me out of things, and the bosses warned me: 'If you speak, you're out'. I never said anything.

Let us now move on to the life paths of the two generations that came after that of Maria. We shall see how they experienced the thaw under Khrushchev and the *zastojnyj*, the renewed freeze under Brezhnev, before being plunged into the turbulence of *perestroika* and the end of the USSR.

Let us consider first the two sons of Egor, the head of one of the *baraki* in Polegorodok. The eldest, *Anatolii*, was born there in 1936. He liked above all freedom of movement, doing what he wanted. He therefore preferred the company of comrades outside Polegorodok. This was how he discovered the advantages provided by anonymity within a giant metropolis. But his initiation into urban ways of life did not bring him luck.

According to his brother Viktor, he started associating with youths who hung about in the streets and ran on *spirt* (highly concentrated alcohol). He abandoned school, left home to do his military service, and returned already an alcoholic. He moved from one unskilled job to the next, could not find a woman that wanted him, and died (in 1971) aged only 35.

Viktor, Anatoly's younger brother (the one who described life at Polegorodok so well), had a very different character. Born in 1938, he studied persistently, and passed the entrance exam for the school of trolley-bus drivers in Moscow, a worker's profession that was respected and very well paid. Under the Soviet regime, the salaries of highly skilled workers were much higher than those of doctors, lawyers and other intellectuals. Even in 1993 a trolley-bus driver's salary was six times that of a researcher in the social sciences.

In 1963, Viktor was 25; he met Rimma, Maria's eldest daughter, and married her (so bringing the threads of our parallel stories together). On account of the acute shortage of housing, Rimma came to live with him in the *barak*. Their two daughters, Marina (1964) and Tania (1967), were born there.

But the era of Polegorodok was coming to an end. Khrushchev had finally succeeded Stalin and, in 1956, he twisted the knife in the wound by denouncing the crimes of his predecessor. For a while the rhetoric of Cold War gave way to proclamations of peaceful coexistence and competition over the people's well-being, asserting that soon the superiority of the socialist model would be demonstrated by better living conditions. Khrushchev had been to the USA and was captivated by the apartments of his American Communist friends. All the *baraki* must be razed to the ground, he declared on his return, and a huge programme must be launched to build small modern four-storey blocks, each family having its own apartment.[4]

Polegorodok, along with other *barak* neighbourhoods, was demolished at the end of the 1960s. The families were rehoused in different Moscow suburbs. Overcrowding remained the rule: three generations lived together in tiny apartments (the upper limit was twenty square metres per person; the lower limit, below which you could begin the procedure for requesting a larger apartment, was ten square metres per person). Mostly, moreover, they were still communal apartments, with several families sharing the same kitchen, bathroom and toilet, and the same telephone (when there was one). The uprooted peasants, who at Polegorodok had managed to recreate a village community in the middle of Moscow, were scattered in all directions and thus became aware of their alienation in the city. They felt marginalised there and were regarded as such by native Moscovites, despite the prevalent workerist rhetoric.[5] The communal spirit of the living conditions had thus disappeared. But it lived on at the same time in the workplace. Vikor and Rimma attest to this.

Rimma, Viktor's wife and Maria's eldest child, was born in 1943 in a *barak* in Polegorodok. Very sociable, interested in the welfare of others, and steeped in communal values (she was brought up by her peasant grandmother, Tatiana), she believed in socialism and passionately wished to serve it. Just as she was finishing her secondary education in 1960, the League of the Komsomols (Communist Youth) was launching a big campaign which consisted in sending the youth 'to rebuild the kolkhoz'. Four of her comrades wished to join it with her, but their parents were against it and threatened to cut off their support. The five friends then got jobs at the warehouse of the Medvekovo food shops in order to make some pocket money before setting off. Rimma herself was kept back at Medvekovo hospital by a nasty cut on her hand, while her friends, having discovered the reality of *kolkhoz* life, escaped and returned to Moscow at the first opportunity.

Recovered from her injury, Rimma resumed her job at the warehouse and was soon promoted. The local Party cadres spotted her dynamism and socialist convictions and gave her special responsibilities. In 1966 she was invited to join the Party, a mark of trust of which she is very proud. She enrolled at the Institute of National Economy, preparing for a career as a manager in large-scale distribution. But meanwhile she fell in love with a bus driver, who took her every evening to Polegorodok: it's our Viktor. They got married, she was expecting a baby and Viktor – who was on a good wage – told her to break off her studies in order to look after their baby. Rimma resigned herself to leaving the Institute, and instead began working as a kindergarten assistant. This became the profession that she still exercises. This cessation of her professional career as a result of marriage also ended her political activities. The kindergarten assistants were all women and – Rimma says – not interested in political activism.

On the other hand, her work environment was very integrated. Rimma (who was 50 at the time we interviewed her) remembers her first years as a kindergarten assistant with nostalgia: 'We all knew one another, we all got together on Sundays, fifteen of us in our two-room flat; we told one another everything, we shared everything, joys and misfortunes.' Without realising it perhaps, Rimma had recreated around her the communal atmosphere she had so loved during her childhood in Polegorodok, and of course as a young *komsomol*.

The nostalgia which Rimma expressed in 1992, after the fall of the regime, was not confined to nostalgia for her youth. It expressed a much deeper malaise, that of the irretrievable loss of the cultural model which created a social fabric integrating Soviet society through values that were shared, if not by everyone, at least by the vast majority. Her husband Viktor says the same thing, though more laconically: 'I still do the same job, I go to the bus depot every morning, but the atmosphere isn't the same. These days, no one needs anyone anymore.' Yet Viktor drives his trolley-bus as before. His objective working conditions have not changed. But a symbolic order has fallen apart, and so far nothing has replaced it.

Rimma's sister, Natalia, married a wood-turner and remained a skilled worker in the same factory. Her brother *Iurii* is a lorry driver. It was on him that his mother Maria had pinned all her hopes:

> When my Iurii was born I was already 36. He was very different from his sisters: always moving, noisy, stubborn, but very lovable. He did exactly what he liked. He had a lot of trouble finishing his compulsory education. But he was good at maths, so I put his name down for the entrance exam to a technical college. It was a very good college that trained radio technicians. I hoped so much that he would take the exam. He passed it. For one month, he left early in the morning, as if he were going to college, and he came home at the end of the afternoon.
>
> Then, one day, he came home in the middle of the day. Perhaps he was ashamed. I asked him, 'Why are you back so early today, Iurii?'
>
> 'Mum, I haven't stepped foot in college for two or three weeks. I don't want to study anymore.'
>
> I had such a shock, I stood there in the middle of the room speechless, rooted to the spot, unable to move or to utter a word ...

Iurii left to do his military service for two years, where he learned to drive. On his return, he became a lorry driver. He got married, fathered a little girl, but started drinking and his wife left him, taking the child. He returned to live with his mother. That was ten years ago. He is still there. He spends all his free time listening to his cassettes of rock music. He is drinking more and more.

So in this generation, that of Viktor and his brother Anatoly, of Rimma, Natalia and Iurii, you were born in the *baraki* – villages in the heart of the city – within an emerging working class, and in general you stayed a worker. Rimma might have pursued a career that would have led her to the status of a cadre, but that would have jeopardised her marriage. Her cousin Natasha, the only daughter of Valia the laboratory assistant, became an economist; she is an exception. Another cousin, Sergei, the policeman's son, was a lawyer; but now he has gone back to being a worker and earns a better living that way.

For this generation, who were in their fifties in the 1990s, remaining a worker was not demeaning. As they relate, apartments may have been tiny and foodstuffs scarce, but everybody was in the same boat. The standard of living was slowly improving, and life was predictable. Things were getting better, at least as far as daily life was concerned, and making plans had some meaning. But Gorbachev's *perestroika* destroyed all of that. The nostalgia of this adult generation is based therefore on an objective reality, as well as on a vague sense of a loss of meaning. Not just the loss of Empire but loss of everyday normality, security and togetherness.

THE POST-THAW SOVIET GENERATION

If Viktor and Rimma, who both work in the public sector, can see the transformation in work relations clearly, the end of the *Gemeinschaft* in the workplace, what can be said about their two daughters, Marina and Tania, three years between their ages, who are confronted with the new conditions of production? How are they, who belong to the rising generation, adapting to the changes?

On completing her secondary education in 1982, *Marina* found work at the state-run Central Market in Moscow, in a shop selling second-hand items. Very quickly she realised that all of the staff were dealing in the goods that were entrusted to them, and involved in illegal but all-pervasive racketeering. Her colleagues tried to initiate her into their schemes, but she could not settle in. The values of scrupulous honesty taught her by her grandmother Maria, and by her mother (a sincere Communist), made her too uneasy. So it got to the point where she was rejected by the staff team and she left her job – a job that is today highly sought after, and offered at a premium of hundreds of thousands of roubles because it is so very lucrative.

In fact, Marina's goal was to have her own apartment so as to start a family; in other words, to live normally, if need be as a housewife – an attitude shared by many of today's young women and encouraged by the 'democratic' politicians as a way of reducing unemployment. So the search for housing became her obsession. Marina had understood how much her mother Rimma had suffered from not having her own apartment.

Rimma had indeed waited until the age of 49 before getting her own apartment. She recalls regretfully:

> When Marina got married – of course she was living with us – she brought her husband to live in our two-room flat. They took one room and our other daughter, Tania, moved into our room [she was already 17]. Then Marina became pregnant, and her child was born. That made a lot of people. Then it was Tania's turn to marry. She went to live with her husband at her mother-in-law's, but it didn't last. She quarrelled with her and came back to us with her husband. For a year [1987], we were three couples in two rooms plus the baby, until Marina got an apartment.

This testimony does not describe an unusual situation, but rather the statistical norm. Although there has not been a national survey of the Soviets' housing since the end of the 1920s, for questions relating to housing were removed from censuses at that time and only reintroduced in 1989,[6] we can estimate that in over 80 per cent of cases a young married couple had no choice but to live with the parents of one of them for several years – at least in Moscow.

So Marina had long dreamed of having her own place. We should bear in mind that under the socialist regime there was nothing like a free housing market. You could neither buy nor rent, but simply put your name on a waiting list and waited ten or fifteen years, or longer, for the administration to see fit to grant you a new apartment in exchange for the old one. But Marina really wanted an apartment for herself. So she started working on a voluntary basis for an organisation in charge of apartment exchanges, as under their rules every employee could receive one after three years of voluntary service. She did not seek to take advantage of the privileged access to information that her position gave her; she waited confidently. After two years, the organisation was dissolved. It so happened that, fortunately, having got married (to a radio technician) in the meantime and finding herself pregnant, she had been put on a priority list at the last minute. Thus, despite her fundamental honesty, she finally gained possession of an apartment in Moscow. She now works as a check-out assistant, is bringing up her child, and does not complain about her lot. Her mother and maternal grandmother taught her 'to be content with what you have', to appreciate the 'simple things of life' to which honest work gives you access.

Marina's younger sister, *Tania*, has very different ambitions. Influenced by the wheeler-dealer atmosphere that now prevails, she wants 'to earn money'. She is resolutely 'modern'. Tania got a job in an independent 'cooperative', originally set up by a large state-run computing company which was seeking to house its managers; a cooperative which quickly became autonomous under the impetus of its director at a time when a Western-style housing market was developing in Moscow, fed by the very high demand for housing. Tania works well and long hours, and gets a good salary, which she negotiated herself: 'I went to see the boss and said to him, "I don't earn enough; I need a rise, otherwise I'll quit". He asked, "How much?" I said, "10,000 roubles" (ten times my mother's salary). He replied, "OK, you'll get it".'

But Tania is shocked by what she has discovered about market-economy work relations:

> Our managers are young men who are in constant competition with one another, do everything to push aside their colleagues and who at the same time use all the means they can to derive personal advantage from the company. Us women are not supposed to get involved in their deals; besides, the boss doesn't allow it. I would really like to help sell the apartments and take my cut from the sales. We women just prepare the files and keep the accounts.
>
> The boss is doing well, I have to say. The sale of apartments simply provides him with cash flow. In June [1992] we were scarcely out of the red. But he's set up a housing construction company in parallel; that's what he wanted from the beginning. Now all of our debts go to the company that set us up [the big computing company], while we keep the profits that come from the construction business. That's several million roubles.
>
> By rights we should share it out. Why? Because we're all members of the cooperative, we're paid out of the profits. When the company wasn't making any profit, we worked for no salary and even harder. Now the money's coming in but we don't have any clear criteria for sharing it out. The boss tells us: 'We're going to expand and take on more members of the cooperative, I have to keep a share for them.' Let them come, show us what they can do and make money for the company; then they'll be paid.
>
> The real problem is that the boss is pushing his sons. He always says that he's not working for himself but for his sons. The eldest has only just finished secondary school; his father has enrolled him on a special (private) accountancy course. It's very expensive and it's our company that's paying. Then he'll send him to the Institute for Higher Business Studies. That will cost even more. And immediately afterwards – he's told us – his son will take over the company. He comes to visit; he thinks he owns the place, he even makes passes at us, it's totally disgusting. When the younger one is old enough, his father will set up another company for him. So what about us? Who are we working for in the end?

In spite of her 'modern' values, Tania finds it hard to get used to the idea that the company she is working for is a *private* company. The initial ambiguity

(Gorbachev had authorised the creation of private companies, but used the term 'cooperatives' for them) has not yet lost all its meaning for Tania. How can it be right for profits generated by the work of dozens of people to be appropriated by one single person?

At one of the interviews, both Tania and her mother Rimma were together. The daughter asked her mother: 'Frankly, Mum, it's a question of principle. How can you call what you do [a kindergarten assistant] a *job* when it's so badly paid?' 'Yes, but there's the *responsibility*,' her mother replied straight away. Is that the moral feeling that held a whole social system together for half a century?

But Tania is not satisfied with an answer based on morality, a concept that in any case she doesn't understand: 'Mum, that's got nothing to do with my question. How much do you earn? [A rhetorical question, as she knows the answer: 1,000 roubles, about £3.50 a month.] I get 10,000 roubles, with prospects of earning 16,000 soon. What about you?' In answer to this rhetorical question, the mother replies in the same terms: 'Do you really think there's any point in talking about us?'

'Us': instead of talking about herself as an individual, Rimma uses the collective pronoun. 'Us' is the previous generation, the one that precisely still regarded itself as an 'us' and not as an accumulation of 'me's, or even 'I's. This fraternal 'we' into which the individual blends is thus the ultimate reference point, the source of meaning and identity for this generation of Soviet people, in the same way as the individual 'me' is for, let's say, an American. But today this 'us' is rapidly dissolving in the harsh climate of market-oriented relations.

Tania thinks differently. She makes a *direct* link between the quality and quantity of her professional activity and her income, which she regards in no way as a salary: she *makes money* for her company and collects her share. There is certainly an 'us' here, but it is economically judged, shot through with competitive rivalries, and has very little symbolic value – more a matter of compatibility. It is an opportunistic 'us'. If Tania finds a better job tomorrow (she is already thinking about it), she will leave this fairweather 'us' for another one without any regrets. Rational action presupposes an actor and a goal: under the new conditions, the actor is the individual and the goal is his or her bank account.

But even for Tania, who has grasped the new rules of the game very well, there are limits to individualistic forms of behaviour; a certain morality should govern people's behaviour. She has not yet succeeded in adopting the full mentality of the modern-day Raskolnikovs: now that Lenin is dead, anything that succeeds goes.

ANALYSIS

As schematic as this outline case study may be, it provides some useful elements for an anthropological understanding of the Soviet urban popular classes. The social history of the Zamochkin family is not unique. On the contrary, by virtue of the social trajectories of its successive generations, it constitutes a typical story in the creation of the urban proletariat in Russia. There are other family stories which are more tragic, and, conversely, other peasant or working-class families succeeded in placing their children on 'higher' career paths. This is therefore an average family. We do not claim that it is an ideal type, only that the *life experiences* of its members, and above all the sequence of contexts lived through – the migration from the village to the city, the long period living in *baraki*, and then in overcrowded apartments, their working contexts, their stability of employment – all of this was experienced and lived through by millions of other families. To the extent that we can see life experiences as internalised as a cultural model or *habitus*, and personal values and identity not as independent of life contexts and experiences but rather as their symbolised expression, it will be agreed that this particular story contains elements of general significance. It remains to separate them from the narrative and to reconstruct their coherence.

We are seeking to identify the constituent elements of the value system of the Soviet popular classes. We propose to do this in a historical perspective, tracing its genesis back to the pre-revolutionary period. But this genesis is not autonomous. The forms which this value system took in each era depended not only on the evolution of preceding forms, but also on the relationship established between the rulers and the ruled. A common thread will guide us on this journey: the concept of moral economy.[7] At each successive stage of the development of the Soviet system, the unspoken pact between those that govern and those that are governed (our 'popular classes') changes; the moment the moral economy of any society is destabilised, it seeks a new equilibrium.[8] We shall examine four stages: the traditional Russian peasantry at the end of the Tsarist regime, a peasantry from which the vast majority of the Soviet popular classes emerged, including, of course, the industrial working class; the creation of the 'Soviet model' under Stalin; the gradual moral disintegration of this model under Khrushchev, Brezhnev and even Gorbachev; and finally, the current period.

THE COMMUNAL/CULTURAL MODEL OF THE RUSSIAN PEASANTRY

What this short journey through a Soviet 'family' history has allowed us to glimpse is the potency of a cultural model – that might be described as *communal*. It clearly has its roots in the peasantry; but it has survived for a long time within the metropolis, supported both by the communal style of living and by the 'Soviet' form of work relations: stability of employment, the central importance of the 'collective' (the work team), and the absence of markets in the Western sense (job markets, housing markets). The type of social action (in Weberian terms) implied by this cultural model differs from the four types proposed by Max Weber, even if it contains elements that are borrowed from them. Indeed, it is only secondarily that it can be described as rational in goals, or rational in values, emotional or traditional (in the Weberian sense, a quasi-automatic action that is based on habit). None the less, it is certainly a type of behaviour that is entirely coherent. Its primary aim is the integration of the actor into the group, which also means an individual contribution to the integration *of the group*. This type of 'group-oriented' behaviour certainly contains an element of what Habermas called communicational action. However, what is aimed at is not so much communicational rationality as emotional and symbolic integration.

This communal cultural model has deep historical roots. These are particular to Russia, whose peasant cultural model had been shaped over the centuries by the Orthodox Church and by serfdom, and was based on the peasant commune, the *obshchina*, better known in the West by the name of *mir*.[9] To put it briefly, in most of Russia the peasants regarded the lands of the village, or rather the 'commune' (*obshchina*), as belonging *de jure* to the feudal lord, but also *de facto* to the commune itself. They were periodically redistributed by the council of the commune made up of the family heads, the larger families – counted by sons only, not daughters – being given the larger holdings. The feudal lords relied on this ancient custom to levy their taxes (unless it was the levying of taxes that kept the custom going – there is still uncertainty about this): they did not demand payment of these taxes from the head of each family individually, but from the commune as a whole. It was up to the commune to sort out how to divide up the cost between the households and to collect the dues.[10] The communes were thus obliged to meet frequently and to deliberate until a consensus emerged. This is one of the deepest roots of the communal idea in Russia.

But we must also take account of the considerable influence of the Orthodox Church. Its conception of the world was focused around several central ideas. First of all, that the Orthodox Church is the direct heir of Christ the Martyr, via Byzantium, and that the Church of Rome is merely a fraud. Second, the community of believers must unite around their religious leader and smooth out any differences of opinion among them; he is their guide, and any discussion of ideas, any theological debate, any division, is to be avoided. What is essential is union and true faith, that which comes from the heart. The heretical West, with its ideas of free discussion, democracy and modernisation, its intellectualism, stirs up division and confusion, from which the faithful need to be protected. To believe, to obey, submit and live in harmony with the community of believers: that is what the Orthodox Church expects of them.[11]

It is moreover striking to note the extent to which the Communist Party of the Soviet Union, or rather that of Stalin, put the 'programme' of the Orthodox Church into practice: isolation from the West and protection from its noxious influences by closed frontiers, both physical and symbolic; the requirement of faith, obedience, trust, respect for authority; the rejection of a critical spirit that was dubbed 'deviationism' (the Church spoke of 'heresy') and community spirit.

This communal model might have disintegrated if the migration to the cities had been accompanied by entry into a market-based society in which individualism would have developed. But the opposite occurred: the *barak* style of housing reproduced the life of the village. The administrative allocation of jobs, job security, and above all the lack of a direct relationship between the work carried out (both in terms of quantity and quality) within the 'collective' and the redistributed salary – all of these features of the Soviet system tended to discourage a spirit of initiative (in comparison with the market-economy regime that has structured the development of Western countries). What is more, the 'totalitarian' ideology developed under Stalin reinforced the power of the communal model, in that it was founded on familiar schemas, re-appropriating their contents while giving them an ostensibly new form, through collectivist language.

This was, of course, not without its contradictions. The peasants freshly arrived in the city, who had owned their *izba* (wooden house) in the village, perhaps did not appreciate being piled on top of each other in the collective *baraki*. But on the other hand, having just arrived in an unfamiliar world, they needed to stick together, to feel that they were surrounded by villagers like themselves. The popular Russian expression 'to feel someone's elbow' has a positive connotation.[12] Immigrants from the countryside keep one another warm, or help one another out.

One can, therefore, hypothesise that the communal model of the Russian peasantry was not destroyed but preserved by the particular manner in which they were received in the Soviet cities. It is even likely that a significant part of the Stalinist ideology drew its inspiration not from the texts of Marx and Lenin (who both despised the peasantry), but from the experience of the Russian peasants ... [13]

What is the relationship between this communal cultural model, which appears to be so potent among the Zamochkins, and among many other Russian families, with Soviet ideology? Is it primarily a matter of continuity, or of reinterpretation?

UNDER STALIN: THE CREATION OF THE SOVIET CULTURAL MODEL

Stalin's elimination of his rivals in the race for power, first by means of political struggle and then by policing and repression, constituted a radical break with the 1920s. We can speak of a 'revolution within the revolution', or, more accurately perhaps, of a counter-revolution within the revolution.[14] The dream of the emancipation of the workers proclaimed by Marx ended with Stalin's capture of power and the establishment of a totalitarian regime that abolished civil rights, freedom of expression and criticism, freedom of association and political rights, which had already greatly suffered after the October 1917 Revolution. The generation of old Bolsheviks was decimated by police repression. It was replaced in the positions of power by a generation of opportunistic apparatchiks.[15]

'Marxism–Leninism', an expression coined by Stalin which Lenin probably and Marx certainly would have vehemently rejected, became the official ideology, repeated *ad infinitum*. Millions of prosperous peasants, specialists trained at the time of the Tsar and ordinary peasants and workers, not to mention many sincere Communist activists, were thrown into prison, into camps or executed by a bullet in the neck.[16] Even today we do not know the exact number of victims of those leaden years; we only know that they run into the millions. Yet when Marina Malysheva asks Maria (born in 1919), for example, if her family suffered under the purges, the answer comes curt and to the point: 'That didn't concern us.'

Indeed, seen and experienced from the inside, totalitarianism presented a different face. The crimes of the state remained secret. The arrests were accompanied by justifications that were plausible in the eyes of people at the time: even those that carried out the arrests could believe in these motives. They were cogs in a gigantic machine which, subjectively, believed it was working to develop the country in the right direction, that of scientific socialism. As it was, the development was slow in coming: there was a very severe crisis in agriculture and a seizing-up of the machinery of the planned economy. On paper, the command economy was a perfectly rational model: 'it should have worked'. Since it hardly worked and there was no question of doubting the theory, it was the system's opponents who were doing their best to sabotage its implementation. A 'plausible' explanation for the time, which 'justified' the elimination of these opponents.[17]

The building blocks of Stalin's edifice were, of course, the power relationships set in place. Money had lost most of its social power. Education was secondary to the loyalty owed to the leaders. The dimension of political–administrative power structured the whole of society from top to bottom. There were no longer rich and poor, but merely different levels of power. Officially, Soviet society was made up of two productive social classes: the *kolkhozniki* and workers, and a layer of 'services' intended to organise, manage and aid production. More plausibly, Soviet society was made up of six strata defined by their position on the axis of power: first the ruling class (which in the USSR was known as the *nomenklatura*), then the layer of civil servants in positions of power, and third, the mass of free workers, manual workers in the cities. In fourth place were the mass of *kolkhozniki*, confined to their villages by the internal passport. Fifth, there were those under house arrest, former prisoners and suspects living in fear, and, finally, the inmates, the populations of the prisons and camps, who were invisible on the central stage.

It was necessary to give a positive meaning, a 'soul', to this iron cage: this came in the form of the Soviet ideology developed by Stalin and his associates (such as Makarenko for education). Presented as an original synthesis of the ideas of Marx, Engels and Lenin, this ideology in fact borrowed many elements from the communal model of the Russian peasantry, which in turn made it immediately comprehensible and assimilable by 'the people'. Hence the emphasis placed on the collective, the paternalism of the Party, the state and the supreme leader, on respect for the authorities and the submission to their will; the stigmatisation of non-conformity; the value placed on integration into the collectives to which you belonged and which fitted one into the other like Russian dolls – the team of *kolkhozniki* or in the workshop, factory, the region, the republic, the USSR. In other words, a holistic model in which the activity and life of each person could only have meaning in relationship to the 'wholes' of which each was a part.[18]

The power with which this holistic cultural model penetrated into people's consciousnesses surely derives, apart from its daily repetition, from its secret similarity with the communal model of the Russian peasants. Wladimir Berelowitch has provided a convincing demonstration of this with regard to the family.[19] The features that characterise the Russian peasant family – such as joint ownership, polynuclearity (cohabitation under the same roof of the parents and the young couples formed by their sons), patriarchal power, equal status among sons, the absence of responsibilities and rights of individuals as such – can be found one by one, albeit in an altered form, in the Soviet model of the urban family. Each of these features is assigned a new significance by the ideology, but the essential point is that values familiar to everyone were thus relegitimised by the same all-powerful Party that, a short time before, had advocated greater ease of divorce, free love and the rejection of patriarchal authority. In this way, clothed in new language, traditional intrafamilial relations were perpetuated; and the content of a very old anthropological structure could be preserved.

As Berelowitch points out, the principal change was perhaps in the symbolic domain: the figure of the father-patriarch being replaced by that of Stalin himself, of which the real father could only be a 'pale icon'.[20] This symbolic substitution did not come from out of the blue. The father of the family has indeed been dispossessed of all of his property, his legal authority over his children, his autonomy of decision-making. He was now nothing more than an ordinary employee, subject to the authority of his 'collective', the State and the Party. And who precisely now had control over all the property, legal authority and autonomy of decision-making if not the Party, embodied institutionally and symbolically by Stalin?

It thus fell to the all-powerful Party to replace the father of the family for everything relating to the education of his children, their health, growth and well-being. It gave them work, shaped them, gave them direction and mobilised them for a glorious task: the concentration of all the country's energies for the construction of socialism.

There are many among our older interviewees who believed in this model in their youth to the point of investing all of their youthful energy in it. The most ardent among them were those responsible for passing on the message in the 'public' arena – schoolmasters, teachers, philosophers and other intellectuals – and those on the receiving end of this educational message – primary and secondary schoolchildren and students. They had nothing to compare it to. Their parents, if they had been subjected to collectivisation or repression, may have had some doubts, but kept quiet to protect themselves, and above all to protect their children. It was only after months or years of working in a factory or a *kolkhoz* that the harsh realities of existence started to open their eyes.

In order to attempt to understand how this all-pervasive ideology could be so deeply internalised, it is interesting to note what kind of action it encouraged. It could not be action for individual ends: individualism was stigmatised as synonymous with selfishness. That luxury was reserved for those who took part at their own risk in the game of politics. For others, it was a mode of action that was guided by a sense of *duty*. Each person in their post had their task to perform, which was only meaningful when integrated into the task assigned to the work team by the plan. 'The others work for you and you would refuse to work for them?' It was impossible to escape this injunction, which was at the heart of the Soviet moral economy.

Moreover, this injunction was also passed on and reiterated by the people (the term 'individual' here would be anachronistic) themselves to their peers, thus laterally and not only vertically. If someone did not do his or her work, it was not only him but the whole team that was punished: the principle of collective responsibility, from which came a very strong and constant moral pressure on one another.

When the system started to lose its moral credibility, this collective responsibility flipped over into individual irresponsibility. But to the extent that the system was credible – and it remained so as long as it was impossible to criticise it openly – the mode of action guided by the norm was internalised not only as a sense of duty, but as what one might call, after Mauss, a sense of having received a gift and as a consequence of carrying both a collective and a personal debt, a debt that could never be fully repaid.

> We're all on board the same ship facing a terrible storm (the external enemy) and we're all in it together. Everyone has to do their bit. It doesn't matter if there's hardly any relation between my efforts and what I receive in return. Nobody is getting rich on my back because man's exploitation of man has been abolished. Others in our vast homeland are doing what they have to: the *kolkhozniki* give me food to eat, the textile and clothing workers clothe me, building workers are building my future apartment. Our soldiers are ready to give their lives to protect my family. They're all working for me, I must work for them. I need them, they need me.

'Me' – like Viktor the trolley-bus driver, who says, 'I'm just a cog in the machine, but an essential cog: without our trolley-buses, how would the factories and shops run?'

Is it not just such a feeling of social utility that Viktor regrets when he asks, 'These days, no one needs anyone anymore'? This is because money abolishes debts: 'I've paid you so I no longer owe you anything at all. If you're not happy, find yourself another job.' Money, the universal means of exchange, for Parsons a form of social mediation, is also what pushes everyone back into their individual autonomy. Relations based on the market reduce social relations to relations of commercial exchange and drown the other forms of social connection 'in the icy water of egotistical calculation'.[21]

This explains the feeling of strong nostalgia for an era when the collective had a meaning. The apogee of the communal model was certainly the post-war period (when Viktor was at primary school). All wars strengthen community feeling, especially if it is a defensive war where one's country is in danger. The 'Socialist' communal model became a key image of Russian values in the Great Patriotic War of 1941–5. Stalin was never as popular as during these years. It was scarcely whispered that the very heavy death toll in the first few weeks of the war, when the German tanks were stopped at the gates of Moscow by virtually unarmed men, could have been avoided if Stalin had not thrown the military high command into complete confusion and had placed a little less trust in his ally Hitler. The message was that the Soviet Union had truly triumphed over absolute evil at Stalingrad; it was they who defeated the hydra and chased it back to its lair in Berlin.[22] In Europe, the English, even the Americans, only had walk-on parts. Such was the discourse that considerably reinforced the credibility of the Communist regime ... and made it possible to allocate most of the country's resources to the military–industrial complex.

The extraordinary potency of the Stalinist cultural model would persist after the war, assisted by the Cold War. It was only after 1956, with Khrushchev's criticisms, that the first doubts appeared. But the experience of the war and the anchoring of the Stalinist model in the communal cultural model would prolong its existence for those generations who had internalised it when young.

It was during the 1960s, thanks to the relative Khrushchevian thaw, that a certain distancing of the popular classes from the Stalinist model started to appear.[23] But this distancing was slow and resistible. By accusing one man, Stalin, and one political orientation, the 'cult of personality', Khrushchev saved the essential: the leading role of the Party. 'This time', he said imperiously, 'we are on the right track. Keep on working hard, and soon we shall catch up with the United States and then leave them far behind.'

THE GRADUAL DISTANCING FROM THE SOVIET MODEL

If after the victory in 1945 the mass of the Soviet population adhered to the Communist ideology, it seems to be accepted that, by the beginning of the 1980s, they hardly believed in it any more – although, given the impossibility of publicly expressing such scepticism, this did not appear to threaten the stability of a regime which was then regarded as unshakeable. This long phase of transition is the one that is the hardest to describe and analyse. The study of the particular family history cited here provides little material, because it does not include detailed observation of those born in the 1950s. What it shows us, however, is the persistence in Viktor and Rimma's daughters of communal values, *in spite of* their rejection of the Communist model. This is the essential phenomenon that we need to consider apart here.

The structure of Soviet society, as modelled and consolidated by Stalin, was a class structure that divided the rulers from the ruled. But a *pact* bound these two groups together, a pact that could be formulated from the point of view of the ruling class as: 'We will govern, you work; we will command, you obey; but we will share out equitably the wealth jointly created. We will not take advantage of our power to line our own pockets.' Now this pact held good as long as those in power abided by it.

'A fish rots from the head down': this Eastern European saying sums up the evolution of the Communist regime from the 1960s to the 1980s. After Stalin's death, a tacit rule seems to have bound the members of the *nomenklatura* together: 'Let us banish violence amongst us; in our internal political struggles, let us agree that the victors will never again resort to the physical elimination of the defeated – they will merely be sidelined.'

From then on, the temptation to take advantage of positions of power to accumulate privileges was too great. Corruption started from the top and soon spread pervasively. And eventually it became apparent to those governed, as a kind of tacit public knowledge.

It was not just a question of the rapid development of special shops and luxury *dachi* (which were not very visible), but also, for example, of the takeover by families from the *nomenklatura* of the places in the best educational institutes of the Union, which became more or less reserved in advance for their children. Such examples abound in our case studies. From Brezhnev onwards, this practice spread and led to a veritable intergenerational reproduction of the ruling class.[24] The phenomenon had doubtless existed before, but within a very limited circle and in a covert manner. From the 1970s onwards, it became extremely widespread and, above all, visible.

In a pact founded on duty and debt, if one of the partners starts to cheat systematically, the pact as a whole falls apart. The cynicism of the leaders was soon echoed by that of the working masses, who reacted by displaying less and less ardour in their work: 'They pretend to pay us, so we'll pretend to work.' The rate of growth started to slow down. But that still did not threaten the stability of the system. Zinoviev, one of the most incisive analysts of the period, while laying bare the discrepancy between the rhetoric and the behaviour of the leaders, concluded that the situation suited the masses. They did not work too much, and were guaranteed job security and an essential minimum wage, which was gradually increasing.

From the 1960s onwards, however, a new phenomenon emerged in the USSR: that of *private life*. At the time it was a new idea, just as it had been in Western Europe in the eighteenth century.[25] But the desire to widen the small sphere belonging to oneself and one's family alone, protected from the intrusion of neighbours, the Party and social pressure, grew as the revolutionary romanticism waned.

The generation of peasants who arrived in the city needed closeness, were glad to 'feel the elbows' of those who shared their own historical experience. But the next generation found it intolerable not to have a place of their own. Is it a normal way of life in peacetime to share your bedroom with other adults and your kitchen with other families? Is it normal to have to scour the whole city, if not the country, to find meat, shoes or toilet paper to buy? Pretending to work is perhaps all right, but pretending to consume is completely pointless. The concept of *private life*, hitherto foreign to the culture of the Russian popular classes, developed all the more quickly in that it constituted a reaction against the continual intrusiveness of the central power and its local representatives. It was not so much a democratised, more public sphere that Russians wanted from the 1960s onwards, but an expansion of the more private sphere.[26] Hence, among other forms of behaviour, the search for solitude in the forests, in the immensity of untamed nature, as far away as possible from the centres of power and propaganda.

There was, therefore, growing disaffection with the Soviet model, now represented by doddering old men who were known to be vain and corrupt. In the West, and particularly in the United States, the idea then spread that, like the Hungarians and Poles, who were in a cultural sense 'going Western',[27] the Russians too, belatedly, were abandoning 'collectivist' ideas in favour of a cultural model based on individualism. Zinoviev does not share this view. According to him, *homo sovieticus* had settled comfortably into the double language: he only wanted security and to find a bit of meat. The hypothesis that we are attempting to develop here is different: that the Russian scepticism towards the Soviet model does not necessarily signify the abandonment of communal values and adherence to a Hobbesian or Darwinian vision of human societies.

Stalin-style 'Communism' had been set up as a religion. Like all religions, it included a moral code, a system of values and norms of behaviour, which in turn implied an ethical code. The country's leaders started by abandoning the ethical code while maintaining the appearance of moral behaviour and continuing to believe in their religion. Then the moral code broke down, followed, finally, by the breakdown of belief itself.

For the working masses, the order was reversed. What mattered to them was the currency which counted in daily life and in one's interaction with others: that is, ethics. They stopped believing official propaganda quite early, given the gap between the sermons and reality. The rules governing behaviour lasted for longer, because they were essential for the effective functioning of the living/housing collectives and of the work teams, although the mismanagement and corruption ended up by corroding this 'moral economy' too. But the ethical code remained – equality, justice, solidarity and mutual support, faith – as it formed the core of the cultural model of the Russian popular classes. The hypothesis that I am proposing is that this communal ethical code had been profoundly internalised under Stalin, particularly because it corresponded to the previous peasant ethical code and was suited to the living conditions of the uprooted peasants – that is, the vast majority of the urban population of the time. It became for them a second nature, their *habitus*.

Even if this *habitus* proved to be increasingly inappropriate from the 1960s onwards, the values on which it was founded persisted to the present day, not only in the hearts of the generations socialised under Stalin, but also in subsequent generations. Living conditions had a lot to do with this: for example, the form of salary (unrelated to performance) and the mode of housing (several generations cohabiting in a limited space). But also, because of the salaried work of the mothers and their long working hours, it was the grandmothers who brought up the children, thus teaching them their own values, those of the communal *habitus*, which so straddled a generation.

We may even wonder if the gradual rejection of Communist ideology, far from representing a move away from communal values, did not result more from disappointment at the increasingly obvious betrayal of these same values by a ruling class that was manifestly and mainly concerned with stacking up its own privileges.

When the *nomenklatura* realised that it must do something, Gorbachev was brought to power. A man of conviction, adhering as much to the Socialist code of ethics and morality (as far as a politician is able to, in any case) as to the Leninist secular religion, he believed that it was possible to rebuild the moral economy of the country on the basis of Socialist ideals. He saw these ideals as the best possible expression of 'universal human values', by which he probably meant the values of the Enlightenment philosophers: reason, liberty, equality, solidarity and social welfare. It is uncertain that the Russian people ever identified with those values, but in any case it was already too late: the pact had been betrayed from above. Too many repeated lies and too much incompetence had discredited the rhetoric of the leaders. And above all, no perceptible improvement in the standard of living came to confirm the rightness of the new direction; in fact the opposite occurred. When the sociologists of the opinion poll institute financed by the trade unions finally succeeded in including in a national survey the question: 'Which institution do you trust most to govern the country?', the response was irremediable: the Communist Party of the Soviet Union won a mere 14 per cent. It was the beginning of the end. The rest is history.

MARKET RELATIONS AND COMMUNAL ETHICS

Russian society in the mid-1990s was in a state of chaos. The old rules of the game had become largely obsolete, and the new rules brought in by a fully deregulated market economy have, as a result of their enforced introduction, suffered considerable distortion. Russian capitalism is, for example, a capitalism without competition, a capitalism of monopolist oligarchs who have taken control of this or that market and dictate their prices, a lawless capitalism fearing neither God nor man, and even less the state. It seems a little naive to think that, because this system of organising economic relations has made the USA's fortune, the Russians will accept it blindly. They are able to make up their own minds about this form of modernity.

We believe, on the contrary, that they have not lost their powers of appraisal, nor their cultural points of reference. They judge the new market relations by the yardstick of their own cultural code, which certainly is no longer the Communist code, but which is neither the American code nor a moral vacuum. This code is that of the communal cultural model, which does not exclude individual performance and its fair reward, but accommodates them *within* a larger whole which serves as an ultimate point of reference. This larger whole, this 'collective' point of reference, in the past was Soviet society. Today its size has shrunk considerably: it is no longer even Russia, it is the region in which one lives, even one's company. But the need to be linked to a whole remains strong. Individualism cannot be a source of meaning and morality; on the contrary, if it emerges as a principle of strategic rational action, it does so on the basis of a rejection of the moral dimension.

The American variety of capitalism, that which has been exported to Russia but without its accompanying regulations and rule-enforcing institutions, now recognises only one measure (short-term profit) and one moral principle (the equitable reward of individual performance), irrespective of all other considerations. But this is hardly a 'moral' principle: indeed, the relations of competition between actors ('the market', i.e. the markets) are supposed to regulate the supply and demand of performance and reward performances of variable quality at their market price. 'Market' stands here as shorthand for a complex set of bargaining relations between actors who can each draw on markedly different power resources. If one actor has nothing to offer, the market will leave him to starve, turning a deaf ear to ethical arguments. A good businessman is one who earns a lot of money, and it doesn't matter how: bending the rules to his advantage is merely evidence of his superior competence. And, as in post-Communist Russia, there are no longer any rules ...

In our empirical example, young Marina approves of the swindling carried out by her boss to the detriment of the institution that helped him to set up his company, but she questions the monopoly the male managers have arrogated to themselves regarding the sale of apartments and the lucrative bonuses that accompany this activity. And she does not see as fair – that is, as moral – the fundamental principle of capitalism, the private ownership of the means of production and the private appropriation of the ensuing profits.

CONCLUSION

This brief historical sketch of a moral economy has been divided into periods which correspond to those of power in Russia. This approach seems particularly appropriate for a society which, from the Tsar to the Bolsheviks and from Stalin to Brezhnev, has been constantly structured by the dimension of power. At each successive stage, those in power proposed a pact to the working population; this pact was supposedly binding upon the powerful as much as it bound those who were subject to it. This pact was imposed from above, leaving no room for the autonomy of the actors concerned. Hence ordinary citizens acted not according to some instrumental or strategic rationality (that game was reserved for the political class and governed their internecine struggles), but according to a sense of duty, of moral and social pressure. And the pact relied on administrative violence, not to say terror, to ensure that everyone accomplished their duty. This was a particular moral economy, certainly diametrically opposed to the American cultural model, yet one which those European peoples who still retain the memory of absolutism can understand.

While these elements remained constant, however, the transitions (which, in the event, were rather brutal) from one form of power to another changed the pacts proposed to the working classes. Proposing a pact is one thing; for it to be accepted and internalised is quite another. Coercion and propaganda are the tools of those in power; as for the common people, they have only their own values. My hypothesis is that a new pact only has a chance of being accepted and of establishing a moral economy in so far as it re-uses elements from the previous moral economy. You cannot change values like you change your socks. And when a generation has only its values to pass on to its children, these will fill the whole moral space.

Hence Stalin's work on meaning. He was faced with the difficult question: how should one translate Marx's rational, urban, critical and libertarian vision into terms acceptable to the Russian peasant? The solution was the 'Marxist–Leninist' ideology developed by Stalin in the context of 'Socialism in a single country', which borrowed more elements from the Orthodox Church's vision of the world than from Marx's, or even Lenin's.

Gorbachev attempted to restore a moral economy based on ethics. There was perhaps still a majority of Russians then who believed in such public ethics; but they also knew that most of their local Communist leaders had ceased to believe in them. How could they trust such leaders, how could they be mobilised by them? Gorbachev eventually failed. But what his 'liberal' successors propose to Russians is nothing else than the old 'winner takes all' game. The radical reversal of values they dogmatically propose is doomed to failure. Despising the moral economy inherited from the past, they seek to force their ideas through while counting on the legendary passivity of the Russian people. But even this has its limits.

The case study of the Zamochkin family, the scope of which we have tried to widen through broad generalisations, allows us to better understand the dilemma of post-Communist Russian society: how to reconcile the transition to a market economy with a pluralist democracy. We need first of all to specify the terms of this dilemma. For the Western powers, which historically have never been attracted to philanthropy, the project of transition to a market economy and political pluralism possesses a special significance. To put it brutally, for them 'democracy' means the stabilising and 'civilising' of the political regime of a nuclear superpower, and thus a substantial decrease in the risk of nuclear adventurism which, rightly or wrongly, the West associates with dictatorial power.[28]

As for the transition to a market economy, for the West it means quite simply the opening-up of the vast Russian market to their products and access to the enormous natural resources of the country – which, it will be agreed, is not exactly the same thing as the self-generated development of Russian capitalism, which would involve, on the contrary, an initial phase of political protectionism in most sectors (particularly the agricultural and industrial sectors). In the absence of this, whole sections of agriculture and industry will collapse in the face of competition from imported products (be they from the United States, Japan or China). This was well understood by the factory managers immediately after the deregulation introduced by Gaidar in January 1992: instead of setting themselves up overnight as entrepreneurs motivated solely by profit, they continued to supply one another with those products necessary for the functioning of their companies, at prices 'personalised' according to the financial capacity of the customer factory, or even on credit; and they exerted considerable moral and material pressure on those among them who wanted go it alone, so that they did not break the chains of solidarity that had been renewed in this manner.[29]

The grafting of a market economy oriented entirely towards import–export onto a command economy functioning on (the basis of) power and personal relations has inevitably given rise to a distorted form of capitalism, in which monopolies and mafias proliferate on the one hand, and inflation and redundancies on the other. While a new import-merchant bourgeoisie flaunts its unashamed success, the mass of employees have seen their purchasing power collapse, along with their access to public services (medical treatment, quality teaching) and the security in their living conditions (employment, housing) to which they were very attached. Given these conditions, how can we hope that these populations, if they are given the opportunity, will vote for an economic system that has their interests so little at heart? This is the question, it seems to us, that emerges from the case study of the Zamochins.

Notes

An earlier version of this chapter was published in French in the *Revue d'études comparatives Est–Ouest*, 4 (1994). It was translated by Simon Strachan and Paul Thompson.

1 Moshe Lewin, 'The social background of Stalinism', in Robert C. Tucker (ed.), *Stalinism: Essays in Historical Interpretation* (Norton, New York, 1977): 111–36.
2 Peter Kenez, *The Birth of the Propaganda State* (Cambridge University Press, Cambridge, 1985).
3 Timothy J. Colton, 'What ails the Soviet system?', in Erik P. Hofmann (ed.), *The Soviet Union since Stalin* (Academy of Political Science, New York, 1980): 179–99.
4 Gregory D. Andrusz, *Housing and Urban Development in the USSR* (Macmillan, London, 1984).

5 Moshe Lewin, *The Gorbachev Phenomenon: A Historical Interpretation* (University of California Press, Berkeley, 1988).
6 Andrei Volkov, *The 1937 Census of the Population of the USSR* (State Statistical Office, Moscow, 1990).
7 James Scott, *The Moral Economy of the Peasant* (Yale University Press, New Haven, 1976).
8 Viktor Zaslavsky, *The Neo Stalinist State* (M. E. Sharpe, Armonk, 1982).
9 Nicholas V. Riasanovsky, 'Khomiakov on *sobornost*', in Ernest J Simmons (ed.), *Continuity and Change in Russian and Soviet Thought* (Harvard University Press, Cambridge, Mass., 1955): 183–96; Martin M Malia, 'Herzen and the peasant commune', in Ernest J. Simmons (ed.), *Continuity and Change in Russian and Soviet Thought* (Harvard University Press, Cambridge, Mass., 1955): 197–217.
10 Dorothy Atkinson, *The End of the Russian Land Commune 1905–1930* (Stanford University Press, Stanford, 1983).
11 Pierre Pascal, *La réligion du peuple russe* (L'Age d'Homme, Lausanne, 1973).
12 A. I. Molotkov (ed.), *Dictionnaire phraséologique de la langue russe* (Soviet Encyclopedia, Moscow, 1967).
13 Lewin, 'The Social background of Stalinism'.
14 *Ibid*.
15 Zbigniew Brzezinski, *The Permanent Purge* (Harvard University Press, Cambridge, Mass., 1956).
16 Robert Conquest, *The Great Terror: A Reassessment* (Macmillan, London, 1992).
17 Robert Getty, *Origins of the Great Purges: the Soviet Communist Party Reconsidered 1933–1938* (Cambridge University Press, Cambridge, 1985).
18 Adam Ulam, 'Stalin and the theory of totalitarianism', in Ernest J. Simmons (ed.), *Continuity and Change in Russian and Soviet Thought* (Harvard University Press, Cambridge, Mass., 1955): 157–71.
19 Wladimir Berelowitch, 'De la famille patriarchale (à la difficile découverte de l'individu', in Anne Coldefy-Faucard (ed.), *Quelle Russie?* (Éditions Autremont, Paris, 1993); Basile Kerblay, *La société soviétique contemporaine* (Armand Colin, Paris, 1977); Basile Kerblay (ed.), *L'évolution des modèles familiaux dans les pays de l'Est européen et en URSS* (Institut d'Études Slaves, Paris, 1988); see Semenova, chapter 3, this volume, and Semenova and Thompson, chapter 6, this volume.
20 Berelowitch, 'De la famille patriarchale', 219.
21 Karl Marx and Frederick Engels, 'Manifesto of the Communist Party', *Selected Works* (Progress, Moscow, 1968): 38.
22 Alexander Werth, *Russia: the Post-War Years* (Macmillan, London, 1971).
23 John Bushnell, 'The "New Soviet Man" turns pessimist', in Stephen F. Cohen, Alexander Rabinowitch and Robert Sharlet (eds), *The Soviet Union since Stalin* (Indiana University Press, Bloomington, 1980): 179–99.
24 Mervin Matthews, *Privilege in the Soviet Union: a Study of Elite Life-Styles under Communism* (Allen & Unwin, London, 1978).
25 Richard Sennett, *The Fall of Public Man* (Knopf, New York, 1977).
26 See Galtz, chapter 8, this volume.
27 Joseph Held, 'Cultural development', in Stephen Fischer-Galati (ed.), *Eastern Europe in the 1980s* (Croom Helm, London, 1981): 257–78.
28 Richard Pipes, *US–Soviet Relations in the Era of Détente* (Westview Press, Boulder, 1981).
29 Irina Boeva, Tat'iana Dolgopiatova and Viacheslav Sironin, *Gosudarstvennye predpriiatiia v 1991–1992 gg.: Ekonomicheskie problemy i povedenie* (State enterprises in 1991–1992: economic and management problems) (Institute of Political Economy, Moscow, 1992); Oleg Kharkhordine, 'L'éthique corporatiste, l'éthique de *samostojatelnost* et l'esprit du capitalisme: réflections sur la création du marché en Russsie post-soviétique', *Revue d'études comparatives Est–Ouest*, 2 (1994): 27–56.

3

EQUALITY IN POVERTY

The Symbolic Meaning of *Kommunalki* in the 1930s–50s

Victoria Semenova

Sometimes the deep differences between the same social element, whether it be food, or sex, or – as here – housing, can be vividly revealed by the words and phrases which people use when talking about them. For example, if an Englishman or American or Frenchman is asked about his housing plans, he will usually reply using an active tense: 'I'll buy or rent a house', or 'an apartment in Beverly Hills' or 'in the *XVième arrondissement* of Paris'. A Russian citizen, by contrast, throughout the entire Soviet period, would answer the same question in the passive tense: 'I've been given an apartment/room', 'I was allocated an apartment/room at … ' Such phrases imply not only sharp differences in space for living – a house, an apartment, a room – but still more importantly, in the use of the active or passive tense, a hint at a totally different way of distributing housing space. For in Soviet Russia, housing was a common good, held as a monopoly by the State and distributed through State institutions. In this situation, the housing strategies of groups and individuals were not based on independent choices reflecting social position, and in parallel with other social choices, as such strategies are evolved in Western countries,[1] but instead on the total dependency of both individuals and groups on the State's chosen policy of housing distribution, shaped by the ideological preferences of the dominant power system.

There is clearly a wide range of cultural consequences for everyday experience and patterns of behaviour resulting from these differences, from the feeling of ownership – *khoziain* – and of a degree of self-control over one's own private space, through to the forming of patterns of social identity. Thus there have been fundamental differences between Western and Soviet attitudes to housing and its cultural meaning, whether to a permanent home in the city or a country second-home *dacha*. In this chapter we try to explore such sociocultural differences more deeply by focusing on a single period, the so-called 'Soviet classical period' from the 1930s to the 1950s, and on the single case of the most urbanised centre of that time, Moscow.[2]

SOVIET HOUSING POLICY

Let us begin by describing the Soviet approach to housing and urbanisation in that period. Rapid urbanisation started in Russia only in the late 1920s and early 1930s, much later than in the leading Western countries. When it came, urban expansion resulted from two causes: on the one hand, the Communist Party's belief in large-scale industrialisation, and on the other, the 'dispossession of the peasantry', the eviction of large numbers of *kulaki* or small farmers from the villages, precipitating a massive flow of rural population into the big cities. As a result, in the four years from 1930 to 1933 the urban population grew by 23 per cent, and by 1938 had increased by 32 per cent. Moscow doubled its population between 1926 and 1939, and grew by another 20 per cent up to 1959.[3] This rapid growth caused a housing crisis. While in 1927–8 each inhabitant had on average 5.9 square metres of housing space, by 1940 this had fallen to only 4 square metres, and it was to remain as low as this until the 1960s.[4] Moreover, this was not simply a housing shortage caused by rapid industrial growth, as had happened earlier in the West. In the Soviet case it was accentuated by deliberate political policies.

First, the housing policy, developed on the basis of the State ownership of land and buildings, was specifically aimed at achieving *uplotnenie* – higher lodging densities. There was no attempt to match the rapid urbanisation with the building of mass housing or the construction of a new urban infrastructure capable of meeting the new needs which had been generated. Instead, the settling of the newly arrived was achieved through a process of doubling up, of a denser level of lodging within the existing housing structures inherited from pre-revolutionary times. It was therefore achieved at the expense of a marked lowering of housing standards for those already in the city, most sharply in the case of those formerly privileged families whose homes were expropriated and packed with newcomers.

This policy of denser lodging typically meant that several families were placed in one apartment which had previously belonged to a single family, so that each newcomer family had only a single room of their own, and shared the communal kitchen and utilities with several other families. The result was a new type of housing, the *kommunalka* (communal apartment), which soon became the most widespread type of housing in the city. From the 1930s to the early 1940s, 80 per cent of Moscow's population were living in *kommunalki*.[5] This was a policy which attempted little more than to meet the bare physical, spatial needs of the ever-expanding population.

Second, the use of urban space including housing was controlled by State institutions. Housing was most often allocated through State-owned enterprises, so that it was also a form of control over the workforce: the disloyal and undesirable would become the victims of eviction, to be replaced by 'leaders of industry and people actively engaged in public life'. The priority given to the latter was officially part of the housing legislation of the period. Housing was also redistributed according to political allegiance, with political suspects such as former owners and others under repression being deprived of their living space in favour of the politically loyal – workers and ex-peasants, law-and-order staff, and the conforming intelligentsia. The determinative character of these housing strategies was also indicated by the local authorities. They made the decision about type of accommodation or place to live. A single room was invariably given to each family, and the only difference was its size, which depended on the number in the family. Thus, for most of the population, being housed was simply linked to being politically loyal.

Third, the State policy was of uniform urban aggregation rather than differentiation. In the early years, there was no distinction at all in housing by status: even newly arrived *nomenklatura* (leading industrial or political cadres) were allotted similar single rooms in joint flats. In the temporary housing barracks built on the outskirts of Moscow there was the same high housing density as in the crowded pre-revolutionary apartments of the city centre. Eventually it did become possible to observe some social distinction according to power relations, for a number of prestigious houses were built in central Moscow for the new *nomenklatura* elite; but these were very few, a mere twelve altogether being built between 1926 and 1937.[6] But for the majority of the population, right up until the 1964 Decree at last launched the first mass urban housebuilding programme, new housing was deemed unnecessary.[7] So there was only the one dimension of social distinction – those with the 'power' (only 2 per cent of Moscow's population) and 'the others'. Dense lodging was thought to be not merely sufficient, but meritorious.

The outcome of these housing policies was the emergence of a new communal type of urban housing, a barrack-like industrialised form, accommodating the rapidly growing semi-proletarian and semi-peasant industrial workforce.[8] In these *kommunalki*, constricted into very limited personal space and lacking any normal urban services, the new migrants to the city tended to stick as far as possible to their early modes of living. The result was a striking reversal of urbanised cultural progress, a lumpenisation of the population. On the one hand, the educated social groups, often evicted from their homes, were leached out of the city population; on the other, the proportion of the Moscow population made up of semi-literate, first-generation migrants rose rapidly.

How far, in this situation of enforced social mixing, could different social groups maintain their own cultures? How, swirling together in the cauldron of the *kommunalki*, did different social groups interact? Or alternatively, did a true mixing take place: did the restricted personal living space of the *kommunalka* generate a new form of everyday cultural experience and a new type of personality – the Soviet person, destined to be the leading type in the Russia of this period, the 'ordinary Soviet man'.[9]

BOURDIEU AND HOUSING AS *HABITUS*

In recent urban sociology the concept of physical urban space is seen theoretically as a 'metaphor', as Bourdieu puts it, for describing other social formations, such as social hierarchies or differentiations in social status. The relationship between physical and social space was thoroughly explored in the classic urban sociology of Georg Simmel, Max Weber, Louis Wirth and the Chicago school, and for decades was mainly seen as a general continuum between rural and urban culture. It is assumed that urban politics is guided by market forces, and 'the city (which is simply a society) is made up of the free initiatives of individuals and groups, which are limited, but not determined, by a problem of means'.[10] The control of power is basically restricted to economic control through a policy of housing and land prices in a city's different districts. This is how segregated districts evolve, each with a homogeneous stratum of inhabitants, ranging from prestigious neighbourhoods of the elite to the poor workers on the periphery. In such cities a family's housing implies its status in the social hierarchy, housing change may indicate upward or downward social mobility, and investment in housing is seen as a crucial family strategy.[11] Hence housing strategies are built around active choice and closely related to social status, mobility and identity.

By contrast, in Soviet Russia there was no system of economic control over space, but rather one of State political control, with disloyal or repressed groups being penalised. There have been some cases of direct political control of housing allocation in the West, but these have been rare aberrations, only affecting working-class housing in contexts of exceptional political pressure or housing shortage. In the Soviet case, by contrast, political control was the dominant urban system, and our concern is to understand the social and cultural consequences of such a monopoly of power over the allocation of space. For this purpose, Bourdieu's theoretical approach, seeing the connections between physical and social space and their cultural consequences in terms of power, seems particularly valuable.

Bourdieu sees three possible outcomes when a dominant power is held over space. The first is power over physical space. Exclusive ownership of space brings the power to manipulate its distribution, and this always implies the use of space to help the construction of homogeneous groups, the preservation of spatial distance, and the protection of space from unwelcome invasion from outside.

Second, spatial possession is usually a consequence of violence. The appropriated space is usually one of the places in which the new power claims legitimacy. Power in this form is carried out in its most cunning way as hidden or symbolic violence, but reaping both material and symbolic profit from it. At the same time, by creating a certain type of habitat or living space, power can also develop a certain kind of *habitus*.

Third, unifying people and material possessions within one and the same space makes it possible to unite them symbolically and to create an effect of common local influence, so that people associated with that space are to some extent labelled or branded by association with it. This branding may be positive; but similarly, the 'ghetto effect' manifests itself as a similar labelling when a group of people is deprived of all its social privileges; and association with others similarly deprived multiplies their deprivation, and makes them lose their own culture and practices.[12]

So, to return to the real situation in Moscow, how did the common habitat of the *kommunalki* change the cultural *habitus* of the two Russian city generations who came to live in them?

THE STATISTICS OF MOSCOW HOUSING

Let us first look at what the manipulation of Moscow's urban space and its housing system meant in statistical terms. In addition to the qualitative in-depth interviews we use later, we have the quantitative figures from our three-generational family interviews, which were computerised, providing information about housing moves by 2,000 people.[13] Out of the generation of 134 grandfathers born between 1900 and 1920, 80 had experienced living in joint apartments during the 1930s–50s – most of the rest, having not yet left the countryside, were still rural peasantry. We also have interview information from some of the children of these grandfathers, and the two sources together can help us to understand the housing strategies of these families. On the other hand, we have no information on the 'interrupted strategies' of families who were evicted from the *kommunalki* and repressed, although a fictional account of their different strategies can be found in Rybakov's novel, *Children of Arbat*.[14]

The grandfathers certainly indicated that moving into a *kommunalka* was a significant event in their housing history, although typically they were highly mobile, making previous and subsequent housing changes on average every two or three years. The experience of living in *kommunalki* was shared equally by former lower and upper strata. These multi-room apartments brought together in the social space of a collective dwelling families who had been socially extremely distant in pre-revolutionary times. For instance, one room might be occupied by a formerly well-to-do family who had been deprived of their own house; another by a peasant family who had migrated from their own plot of land and house in the village; a third room by a poor urban worker's family who had previously been living in a shared room (the *ugol*). Out of the diversity of the pre-revolutionary class-segregating system of settlement, which such contrasts illustrate, peasants, the urban poor and former well-to-do proprietors all now converged into communal apartments as the one common type of housing. That means that social space – as a metaphor reflected in the pattern of settlement – remained undifferentiated during the 1930s–50s. It reflected the new social model of 'equality in poverty'.

There were, however, some differences in the timing of housing moves. The urban poor and the expropriated upper classes typically moved into *kommunalki* in the 1920s; the new migrants came to the city in the 1930s. Moving out from *kommunalki* for most people came in the 1960s, when the new policy of *rasselenie* (separating) was launched. Usually the first to be given new separate apartments were the elite of the social hierarchy: the *nomenklatura* – party officials, highly educated professional specialists. The last to leave were the least privileged –

uneducated and unskilled workers, who were usually given low-grade housing on the city periphery. Consequently that was the end of the 'equality in poverty' model and the start of the new housing pattern which was socially differentiated and closer to the Western pattern.

Moving into a *kommunalka* also had a different meaning, depending where you came from. For poor workers, who had been sharing their room or even their bed with members of other families, to have a room of one's own in a communal flat was an upward move in living standards and so in status. For peasants, despite the loss of their private living space in their village homes, a move to the city was in itself seen as a rise in the hierarchy of the new society. For the former well-to-do, by contrast, the change in housing meant not only a material cut in living standards through 'denser living', but also a deprivation of their assumed civic rights: a loss of control over the private space in which previous generations had transmitted their cultural capital to them, but which they could not use in the same way for their own children – a point to which we shall return.[15]

In short, housing strategies from the 1930s to the 1950s were not governed by individual action or initiative, but were signs of change in a family's social status. Housing moves were imposed, initiated through State housing policies as a form of social control and a way of enforcing social equality, particularly on the pre-revolutionary privileged. By redistributing spatial rights, this State-backed policy aimed to establish an equality in social space which matched that in power. As a result, the former boundaries in everyday life between different social strata were breached, and the social basis for bourgeois individualism was eradicated. As Hannah Arendt observed, the equality of life conditions and absence of any autonomous zones within a society are among the characteristics associated with despotism.[16] The walls of reinforced concrete which had earlier separated social groups and enclosed them within their own spaces had now, through the radical social redistribution of living space, become porous, leaking partitions.

REMEMBERING THE LIFE OF THE *KOMMUNALKI*: THE OLDER GENERATION

In order to understand how spatial dominance can be a powerful but unconscious form of symbolic violence, let us try to look at the physical space of the *kommunalka*, its structure and its social use in everyday life, almost as a performance stage, as Erving Goffman had it, for *The Presentation of Self in Everyday Life*.[17] At this point we must call on the direct recollections which we have from our own informants.[18]

Most often a *kommunalka* was an older building, a former private house or mansion which had been crudely remodelled by dividing up the former spacious rooms with partitions into a series of cells, each usually occupied by a single family of three or four persons. In one of these cells the former owner might have been allowed to continue living. Thus Evgenii Mamlin (b. 1933) describes the flat which his parents moved into in the mid-1920s:

> Before the lodgers were moved in, it was the first floor of a private residence with a single family occupying six rooms, instead of the present fourteen rooms with fourteen families. Now the family of the former apartment owner had just one room, sixteen square metres [nine by nine feet]. The other families in the flat included a schoolteacher's and a doctor's family. The rest, as far as I can remember, were ordinary workers.
>
> It was an old stone-built mansion with a broad staircase. Before the Soviet time apparently the flat was a whole suite of rooms with ceilings four and a half metres high. Then the rooms were partitioned off into separate smaller ones, each entered either from the corridor or through the next-door room. We lived in a subdivided room only sixteen square metres, without any windows. The partition didn't go up as far as the ceiling so we could hear all the [neighbours'] conversations. There was a much more spacious kitchen, forty-five square metres, with gas stoves for all the families. Mother had to feed the Dutch stove in the neighbour's room so that some warm air could reach our room over the top of the partition. There was no bathroom or shower, just two sinks and two toilet cabins. Only cold water, no hot water. The stoves burnt wood. Gas stoves were only installed in 1949. Before that we cooked on oil and primus stoves.

Looking at the plans of these flats in Goffman's terms, each of these family rooms was a backstage area in which the particular family's relationships and culture were enclosed within a floorspace of no more than a few square metres. In this space family members ate, slept, did their schoolwork, received their own guests and relatives, and listened to the talks and quarrels of the neighbours on the other side of the partition walls. Some rooms were crammed with the remnants of old furniture hastily rescued from a former whole apartment; in some rooms the tenant had botched together some rough furniture himself; and in yet other rooms piles of books were used to prop up a damaged old sofa. In these rooms families did their best to maintain their earlier customs and social culture.

Nevertheless, the most important location for cultural struggle was 'the front stage' of the theatre – the kitchens and washing places shared by all the families, where private everyday life became a performance watched by the audience of the other families. On this stage you tried to act according to the rules of the new game, behaving yourself according to Soviet norms. You read the newspapers, sustained conversations, fought for your place in the kitchen, and observed the social rules of order and discipline. Here the sphere of private everyday life was brought onto the public stage.

Vladimir Birikov (b. 1954) remembers these relationships with neighbours in his childhood:

> I don't envy my parents, especially my mother. Sometimes there were big quarrels with our neighbours. I was not involved myself, but I remember the adults often quarrelling because of the crowdedness and something being amiss – one burner per family on the gas stove was not enough and people became embittered. The bill for the electricity supply was divided up *per capita*, to the last *kopeck*. The calculations were posted up and everyone knew how much to pay. My father was the man put in charge of the calculations. We didn't seem to quarrel so much ourselves with the neighbours, but we never celebrated holidays with them either. More often with our relatives.

The overcrowding meant that everyday life had to be strictly regulated, with the times for using communal facilities rigidly divided up between the families. Anna Belenkaya (b. 1910) told of the inconveniences she endured in such a cramped communal life. Each family took turns to use the bathroom, once a week at fixed hours. There was a notice on the bathroom door listing the washing day and hours for each family:

> Once my time came, and by the time I had done the laundry for the whole family and hung out the washing in the garret, it was already four in the morning – but at seven I had to take the kids to school. Cooking was also done by turn. And God forbid you use the wrong stove or saucepan – you'd soon be in trouble ...

Not only the stoves, but the gas burners on them, and the kitchen tables were all strictly allocated, and could only be used according to the timetable.

> Each family had its own cooker. First you cooked in the kitchen, then you ate in your room. Meals had to be taken into the rooms, of course – particularly when we had guests. The kitchen was too small.
>
> Well, the room was small too. So those who wanted to have a smoke, or whose kids were little, would go into the kitchen and sit there into the small hours. Some were doing crosswords, others were reading newspapers ...

Among the most important constituents of this 'communal boiler' introduced by the Soviet political system was the invasion of power relationships which it brought into every apartment. In its regulation of almost every aspect of daily life, the *kommunalka* system was, in fact, a form of State supervision over the private lives of its citizens. In every apartment 'a senior tenant' had to be elected or appointed. One of the life stories recalls how Praskov'ia Dobraikova (b. 1906), a Communist Party member, was appointed: 'Since', the tenants maintained, 'she is one of the Party, she is entitled to guide us.' Although Praskov'ia was not liked by her neighbours, they obeyed her peremptory shouts without fail. Her duties were as follows: to arrange the timetable and see to the maintenance of proper order in the use of the bathroom; to put up a schedule for the use of the kitchen stoves; and to calculate precisely from the meter readings how much everyone had to pay for the electricity supply. She was very aggressive, with a rough temper, but everyone tried to avoid a squabble with her. Praskov'ia thought herself entitled to reprimand anyone for any infringement of the rules for order in the life of the flat. So she demanded to be told about who was visiting whom; spotted those whose electricity consumption was above the norm; reprimanded those who missed their turn for washing the floors; and so on.

This local regulatory power relationship in everyday life, with its implicit acceptance of obedience to the authorities and deprivation of personal freedoms and privacy, was in the same mould as the political system of power and subordination in the wider society of that period. On the one hand, there was the tight hierarchy of vertical subordination; on the other, the weakness of communal or neighbourly links. Any person identified as a dissident 'object of guidance' would directly confront the accredited representative of authority in the person of the 'senior tenant', but could count on little support from 'the others'.

Not surprisingly, the loss of private living space was felt most acutely by formerly well-off families, who before the Revolution had lived by the norms of bourgeois individualism, and who regarded the family home as sacred and impregnable to any outside invasion. Elena Iakovleva (b. 1920) remembers:

> No matter how strange it may seem nowadays, I was born on this very leather sofa, and maybe it's here I'll die too. There's only a few people can boast of sticking to something with such constancy through our lifetime. The only difference is that we had the sofa in another room then. Previously our family used to own this house. It was bought by Mum, who brought us kids to Moscow from the far-off island of Sakhalin, where our family was in the fur trade. The house had been built by some famous architect ... After the Revolution the ground floor, which accommodated the trade premises, and later on rooms for the servants, was taken away from us almost immediately. The families of some workers settled there. Very nice people they were, by the way ...
>
> Our living space got narrower and narrower, until eventually we had only three rooms. Our last stronghold we thought. Then one day we were having dinner at the big table – and the family was a big one, with us three kids, Mum, and Mum's sister and brother. Well then, so we were sitting at the table when a man suddenly appeared – a military man, with a shoulder-belt. He said our rooms had taken the fancy of some commander, so he would like to move in here. 'After you finish your dinner,' the man said, 'please vacate two rooms and all of you

move into the third, the smallest one.' He looked about the walls and ordered the standard clock to be taken away – too noisy: 'as for the rest,' as he looked at the pictures on the walls, 'everything should stay here'. It was useless to make any complaints and there was nobody to complain to.

Of course, it was very hard for us to get used to our new life. Different families have different ways, you understand? But in the end we did get used to it, of course ... We had to gradually sell off our furniture, because there was no room for it in our tiny room, and it got in the way in the corridor.

Some families were more successful in resisting such violent seizure of their living space by using cunning strategies to make an alien invasion unlikely. Our interviews include examples of 'communal apartments' in which the formerly well-to-do owners had brought in other family members from throughout the city to fill up 'the surplus living space' with their own kin. The Voronov family, for example, succeeded in gathering together all their relatives in their apartment in Malaia Bronnaia Street, and they sustained this large but crowded familial apartment for over twenty years. Each family had only a single room of its own, but in this apartment all their neighbours were their own relatives. This meant that here, exceptionally, a social class homogeneity could be maintained among the flat occupants.

Only a very few well-to-do families were able to preserve their former living space because of exceptional circumstances. Before the Revolution the Zhurnalistov family had owned a small estate far to the south of Moscow. They managed to hold on to their family 'fortress' up to 1936 – despite giving up their apple orchard – due to the personal support they had from Kalinin, a member of the government. This rare delay gave sufficient time for the family to transmit its familial and class values unchanged to the younger generation. Such exceptional cases of struggles waged by pre-revolutionary well-to-do families to preserve their control over their family living space, however, only confirm the general rule. Such families resisted precisely because they feared losing the symbolic dominance conferred by their former homes and the living space within which their family's cultural class capital could be handed down to their children and grandchildren.

The world of the *kommunalki* implied not only the loss of families' symbolic space, but also of their actual role as property owners. The apartments were rented rather than owned, and everyday existence in them was under the control of the authorities, so that at any time the occupants could be evicted from their home by official order after, say, a hostile report from a neighbour. Thus families felt themselves merely temporary lodgers in their own homes. This is one reason why in later decades, when the mass acquisition of garden plots and *dachi* as country homes was launched, the response sprang especially from a popular wish to become an independent proprietor, here at least autonomous and no longer directly dependent on the authorities.[19]

The direct interaction between former class cultures within the confined local space of the communal apartment created a kind of cultural 'wash-boiler', in which the previously distinctive values of different groups were tumbled and spun together. It gravely hindered the intergenerational transmission of different social class and familial cultures.[20] It cut off ties with other members of the same cultural group, and even with other kin from the family, so striking at the social roots of family itself. The atomisation of families and the loss of physical space as a ground for class cultures tended to bleach out the old identities, and their destruction led to a search for changed identities within the new Soviet society.

Everyday neighbourly mixing did lead to a degree of solidarity along with a mutual rejection of the claims of separate cultures. The older generation clearly remembered the division of space in the apartments between 'one's own zone', the family's own room, and 'the other zone', the communal space divided for use among the tenants by time and space. The feeling of neighbourly solidarity is most often recalled in relation to moments of extreme stress and external threat, such as interventions by the authorities, war or natural disaster. On the other hand, not a single form of joint activity is remembered. And the memories do include many indications of mutual rejection or hostility: families who thought their meals considerably superior to those of their neighbours, perhaps because they always ate meat; a father who advised his wife not to mix too much with neighbours, and tried to get the children away to the country in the summer; families who simply could not get used to the habits of their neighbours.

Thus communal flats, by depriving the once privileged of their symbolic and material control over family living space, and by enabling the infiltration of public norms into private life, became one of the most cunning of the regime's strategies for seizing power in everyday life: a form of symbolic yet inconspicuous violence. The system of letting allowed, through the handling of communal space in the flats, the imposition of a new, common, everyday culture based on aggression and general obedience. Through it the State was able to mould a new type of ordinary city-dweller, embittered through overcrowding and poverty, a tenant with no security or rights, deprived not only of personal privacy, but also of class traditions and social roots.

THE EXPERIENCE OF THE *KOMMUNALKI* CHILDREN

While the older generation remember predominantly the feeling of mutual rejection of different cultures by the *kommunalka* tenants, their children, by contrast, typically recall how they imbibed their neighbours' habits and ways of life.

Unlike adults, children seem to have found it easy to understand and take in their everyday experience of communal mixing. Because of the lack of sufficient private living space, children were usually sent out into 'the common spaces' –

into the corridor or the open air. For most of them, recollections of childhood leisure times are about playing in the yard, for the whole family could rarely get together over dinner. Indeed in one family, when guests came to their flat, the children had to mix and play *under* the table, because there was no room for them at the table top. Children remembered the common space in the *kommunalka* not as regulated and divided up, but as a genuine environment for common living. For them, a corridor was a great place to speed along on a bike, while the yard was where their parents sent them to get out of their way. Doing their school homework provided an excuse for visiting one of the neighbours, a schoolteacher who had a lot of books and could help them. Children mixed with each other much more readily and had less difficulty in adapting to unfamiliar habits. They were less likely to get involved in disputes over the allocation of space, less aggressive towards neighbours and other adults, but faster in understanding those habits of neighbouring families which were different from their own. What they emphasise in their memories is the neighbourly solidarity of the *kommunalki*, mixing with neighbours' children, and playing together as teenagers, relatively free of the control of their parents.

It is clear that things in different *kommunalki* varied substantially, depending on their prevailing culture. Thus, if there were more formerly rural families among the tenants of a flat, then, as was normal in village communities, one of the women – a grandmother, perhaps, or a mother who did not go out to work – would mind all the families' children. For those who grew up like this, there are memories of baking tarts, treats and joint meals with other families. If the flat was made up of more urban working-class families, then memories of childhood more often emphasise how the mothers were eternally busy either out at work or about the house, while the fathers gathered together in the kitchen or the yard for purely male pleasures, such as reading the newspaper or playing dominoes; and after school the children were left totally free to play as they liked. If more of the families came from a cultured background, children from all the families – including the workers' families – might be lent books and helped with their school homework by an educated woman neighbour.

In any case, all the neighbourhood children went to the same school, which had a further influence on levelling class difference. As Alina Dobriaikova, the daughter of Praskov'ia the 'senior tenant', remembered the girls of her own age: 'all of us looked like just the same kind of grey mice in our identical school uniforms'. Thus the children of the *kommunalki* experienced 'an effect of branding', as Pierre Bourdieu puts it, by the milieu of their childhood. Living communally created a common *habitus*.

CONCLUSION

Thus, in examining the everyday life of the *kommunalki*, we uncover one of the sources which moulded the psychology of the ordinary Soviet city-dweller. The spatial fragmentation of previously separate cultures, and the remixing of these cultures within the communal spaces of the apartments, both numbed or destroyed earlier cultural traditions and resulted in the emergence from their wreckage of the new everyday culture of barrack socialism.

Yet recollections of life in the communal apartments present a less straightforward picture of how these changes were felt by those who lived through them. People did not think their experiences as beggarly, either at the time or even today. There were no others in better social situations with whom to compare their own. Nearly all the people they knew lived similarly, whether they were former owners, intellectuals, workers or former peasants. As they remember it, people paid little attention to the complexities of everyday life: they just got on with what they had to do. For older people especially, the message to us was: 'Our life was good. We had higher social ideals and aims to inspire us then.' There is in some of these interviews almost a nostalgia for poverty, which reflects a daily life experience deeply affected by political education. Here were people truly inclined to concern themselves, as Hannah Arendt was to put it, less with the cares of everyday living than with ideological dreams in terms of 'centuries' and 'continents'.[21]

The practice of doing everything by turn, and the indifference to living standards and everyday problems, helped to marginalise the idea of social comparison and reduce feelings of 'social envy'. The principal of communal living removed the space in which autonomous social groups could develop or be sustained. The consequence was a new urban working class, struggling for scarce everyday commodities, bitter with overcrowding and poverty, yet willing to accept the lowering of its living standards and reacting by emphasising that all should share on a level basis, 'so that everyone would live approximately in the way that I do'. This was fertile soul for moulding the mass psychology of the 'ordinary Soviet man': mixing aggressively, jostling, boorish and rude.

Hannah Arendt referred to this new politicised moulding of Communist personality as 'mass psychology'. It was a psychology propagated by the whole apparatus of public relations in Soviet totalitarianism, and above all by its initial laboratory, the system of camps for the politically repressed. But there were other laboratories in other contexts, including the case of the settling of city-dwellers in communal apartments which we have examined. The *kommunalki* fostered the psychology of 'equality in poverty': through the invasion of privacy by public power; through the overcrowding which brought aggression against those who stood out; through the generation of a feeling of being one of many, one of a mass with a low priority for living standards and individual needs but high common aspirations.

Thus the symbolic meaning of communal apartments as the prime means for housing city-dwellers from the 1930s to the 1950s, lying hidden behind the overcrowding and intensive aggregation in physical space, was the aggregation in social space. And the fundamental principle in the running of the *kommunalki* was the stark division between 'those in power' and the increasingly homogeneous mass of subordinates socialised through mass psychology. To understand this may also help us to understand how the psychology of the Soviet man was to prove so tenacious.

Notes

1 Peter L Berger and Thomas Luckmann, *The Social Construction of Reality* (Doubleday, New York, 1966).
2 Yuri Levada (ed.), *Prostoi sovetskyi chelovek* [The ordinary Soviet person] (Mirovoi Okean, Moscow, 1993).
3 Manuel Castells, *The Urban Question* (MIT Press, Cambridge, Mass., 1977).
4 Institute of Economic Problems of Moscow, 1987.
5 *Ibid.*: 15.
6 O. Trushchenko, 'Akkumuliatiia simvolicheskogo kapitala v prostranstve stolichnogo tsentra' [The accumulation of symbolic capital in city centre space], *Rossiiskii Monitor*, 1, (1993), 13–26.
7 Since 1964 a new form of residential differentiation has developed, based on the social and occupational segregation of different groups in the population, with different districts acquiring higher or lower prestige rankings. For more details on settlement policies from the Khrushchev era, see O. Trushchenko, *Prestizh Tsentra* [The Prestige of the Centre] (Socio-Logos, Moscow, 1995).
8 Rudolf Schlesinger, *The Family in the USSR: Changing Attitudes in Soviet Russia – Documents and Reading* (Policy Press, London, 1949).
9 Levada, *Prostoy sovetskyi chelovek*.
10 Castells, *The Urban Question*: 84.
11 Isabelle Bertaux-Wiame and Paul Thompson, 'The familial meaning of housing in social rootedness and mobility: Britain and France', in Daniel Bertaux and Paul Thompson (eds), *Pathways to Social Class: A Qualitative Approach to Social Mobility* (Clarendon Press, Oxford, 1997): 124–82.
12 Pierre Bourdieu, 'Social space and class genesis' (in Russian), in Bourdieu, *Sotsiologia politiki* (Socio-Logos, Moscow, 1993).
13 The set of eighty family histories, which included information on three generations of migration and settlement history, was part of the collective project, 'The Century of Social Mobility in Russia', headed by Daniel Bertaux, 1991–4. Altogether there were 2,000 respondents. The analysis was made by the SPSS programme (Victoria Semenova, Ekaterina Foteeva and Daniel Bertaux, *Sud'by Liudei. Rossiia XX vek* [The Fates of People: Russia in the 20th Century] (Institut Sociologii RAN, Moscow, 1996): 412–21.
14 A Rybakov, *Children of the Arbat* (Eesti Raamat, Tallinn, 1988).
15 Daniel Bertaux, 'Transmission in extreme situations: Russian families expropriated by the October Revolution', in Daniel Bertaux and Paul Thompson (eds), *Pathways to Social Class* : 230–58; cf. Foteeva, chapter 4, this volume.
16 Hannah Arendt, *Totalitarianism* (Harcourt Brace, New York, 1968): 20.
17 Erving Goffman, *The Presentation of Self in Everyday Life* (Doubleday, New York, 1959).
18 The interviews cited are from the Pahl–Thompson collection now at the School of East European Studies, University of London (Dobriakova, Mamlin, Belen'kaia, Gavrilova) and interviews for the Bertaux family histories project (Nikolai Z. and Zhurnalistov families, interviewed by V. Semenova; Voronov family, interviewed by V. Kuznetsova).
19 See Galtz, chapter 8, this volume.
20 Cf. Bertaux-Wiame and Thompson, 'The familial meaning of housing'.
21 Arendt, *Totalitarianism*.

4

COPING WITH REVOLUTION
The Experiences of Well-to-do Russian Families

Ekaterina Foteeva

> In Russia everybody lives peacefully and calmly protected by legality. No ... revolutionary attempts and aspirations of democratic, socialist or communist nature, born by delusions of our century, threaten the tranquillity and well-being of the peaceful Russian citizen: everybody sleeps placidly in his bed assured in the vigilant guarding of JUSTICE.

These words were written in the middle of the nineteenth century by Heinrich Schliemann, St Petersburg's first guild merchant of German origin, famous all over the world as an archaeologist for his sensational discovery of legendary Troy. The historical intuition which favoured Schliemann's excavations in Turkey deceived him in Russia. Less then sixty years after he had written, the country was to be turned upside down by the democratic revolutions of 1905 and 1917, the Bolshevik Revolution of 1917, and the ensuing seventy years of Communist experiments.

In a mere twenty years after the 1917 revolutions, the formerly prosperous social groups had disappeared from the new social structure of Soviet Russia, giving way to the proletariat, the *kolkhoz* peasantry and the so-called 'people's intelligentsia'. By the end of the 1920s the landowners had already been annihilated, and the social position of the bourgeoisie and the *kulaki* (the rural bourgeoisie) was much restricted. A couple of years later the Soviet authorities chose to put an end to the leftovers of the 'capitalist elements'. In 1934 Molotov, the Chairman of the Soviet of the People's Commissariat, declared that they existed 'just as a slight reminder' of the past.[1]

The revolutionary upheaval blew the former prosperous classes away from the social arena, but what exactly has happened to the individuals and families among them? Millions of people could not have simply vanished. Some found escape abroad, and many were killed in the Civil War or perished during the years of the Red Terror and Stalinist repressions. Nevertheless there were also many who survived somehow, adapted to the new social reality, and became a part of the new socialist society.

Until now there has been little information about how they survived and were incorporated into the post-revolutionary social structure. There was just one empirical research investigation on social mobility, conducted by Pitirim Sorokin very soon after 1917.[2] Soviet scholars used the scarce official statistics to describe the changes in the class structure in the course of socialist transformation. These studies were of a very general character and used broad macro concepts like class, estate and social group.[3] The voluminous works of Western scholars were free of the many ideological and theoretical constraints imposed on their Soviet colleagues. They are much more varied in their theoretical approaches and topics, more detailed and analytical, but focus especially on the issues of the Red Terror and Great Purges and relations inside the power pyramid.[4] Still, neither in Russia nor in the West, has there been any research focusing primarily on the social history of the former privileged groups of Bolshevik Russia.

The published recollections of members of the well-to-do social groups who witnessed the October Revolution and the first years of socialist transformation concentrated mostly on emotional descriptions of tragic family events and the painful experiences of life in Soviet Russia, the Bolshevik terror and forced emigration. In these narratives they often portray themselves as victims of historic circumstances. But the history of these well-to-do families has not yet been explored from the perspective of the positive (although hard and painful) experiences of the survival of those who stayed in Soviet Russia.

My intention has been to trace the life trajectories of individuals and families from the former prosperous classes, rather than the classes themselves, and to regard these people not just as victims of circumstances, but also as active agents who controlled their own lives and shaped their futures. I challenge the approach which conceives of these former well-to-do individuals as passive, intimidated people, deprived of everything they had and condemned by Soviet power to remain in the lower social groups of the socialist society with poor opportunities for upward mobility. On the contrary, I assume that they demonstrated impressive adaptive abilities and were able to employ the new 'rules of the game' in order to achieve their own objectives. My research aimed to analyse their patterns of survival and the social mobility of the family members through the early decades of Soviet rule.

The families studied come from the samples of two projects: 'The Century of Social Mobility in Russia', headed by Daniel Bertaux, and my own project, 'Strategies of Survival in Post-Revolutionary Russia: Entrepreneurs' Families' Experience'.[5] The samples include twenty-seven families prosperous before 1917: landowners, merchants, clergy, intelligentsia and wealthy peasantry. The life stories of those who were directly affected by revolution and post-revolutionary social changes were the focus of my interest.

Many – but not all – of these interviewees were initially contacted through merchants' organisations, and it may be that a tendency for the more successful to join such organisations could be one reason for the predominance of rising individual trajectories in the interviews. There are no reliable statistics for the group as a whole, but my own belief is that the data overall suggest that the tendency to social degradation is unlikely to have outweighed the group's upward dynamic.

After the socialist revolution, the former privileged families who stayed on in Soviet Russia found themselves in a totally different socio-political space. In the new society the dominating values, ideals, attitudes and behaviour patterns were mostly opposite to those they had held. While staying within the same territorial borders, they crossed 'symbolic boundaries', performing a 'symbolic migration' and becoming socio-cultural strangers in their native land.[6] Like immigrants entering a new country, they had to renounce their old style of life and learn the new rules. Once a dominant group in the 'old' society, they were now a socio-political minority. To survive they had to adjust to change and become incorporated into Soviet society.

There are many different models of migrants' adjustment to new environments. After the pioneering works of Chicago-school sociologists (Thomas's 'pluralism' and Park's 'cycle of assimilation'), scholars conceived of immigrants in terms of alienation and assimilation, resulting in the abandoning of the past. Modified versions of these concepts viewed assimilation not as a unilinear change but as a complex process composed of several interrelated subprocesses. Pluralistic models conceived of the host society as a melting pot in which immigrants were synthesised into a new, different entity, with distinct groups living side-by-side in relative harmony. By contrast the latest theory of transnational migration does not view immigrants as uprooted people, but instead explores how migrants sustain relations linking together their societies of origin and settlement.

Many ideas in these models are relevant to the objectives of my study. The term 'adaptation' is used here in a broad social sense to refer to the internal and external transformations of an individual challenged by a new socio-cultural environment. External (or functional) adaptation assumes modification of observable behaviour to conform with social norms, without necessarily involving modification of individual norms and values. Bringing the latter in line with the social norms implies the internal (normative and attitudinal) adaptation of an individual. As a complex phenomenon, adaptation may be measured by various sets of indicators, depending on the particular study: social and individual; objective and subjective; sociological and psychological, etc. The problem of quantification is not applicable to a qualitative biographical study. My objective was not to measure, but to describe, understand and explain the adaptation process. I gave priority to exploring social adaptation rather than psychological adaptation, on which the research data did not provide sufficient information. Hence I focus on traditional sociological indicators: education, occupation, professional attainments and social status. I take high educational and occupational status as an indicator of successful adaptation. Inability to get proper education and occupation, marginalisation or delinquent behaviour, point to low adaptation.

Societal and individual criteria of individual social adaptation often differ. The Soviet authorities deliberately impeded the upward mobility of the former well-to-do classes. They were more interested, above all, in their internal adaptation – in their absorption of Bolshevik ideology and their rejection of the 'old' culture, along with their assimilation into the new Soviet working masses. But despite persistent attempts to control individual consciousness alongside behaviour, the totalitarian regime was not very successful in achieving this. On the contrary, the life histories show that restoration of their lost social position was a very powerful impetus for individual upward social trajectories. But while some were able to transform their 'old' identity and internalise the new socialist values, others were unable to cope with such a shift in attitudes: and, overall, most of the pre-revolutionary well-to-do, alongside their functional adaptation and professional achievements, retained to some degree their earlier values and ethical norms, as well as some of their patterns of everyday behaviour.

For decades, Western studies of the post-revolutionary period were carried out on the basis of a totalitarian paradigm. The Soviet system under Stalin was seen as a monolithic, hierarchical dictatorship under an autocratic leader having almost unlimited control over all spheres of life. He passed his orders to the ruling elite, which transmitted them down to the bottom of the social pyramid. The country was ruled in a planned, systematic and functional way. Ordinary citizens remained outside the political process, were manipulated from above, and could never perform as independent historical actors. They had to adhere to prescribed rules of behaviour and share dogmatic ideological views. Social support for the regime was artificially induced by propaganda and enforced by terror. Those who were assumed to be unwilling to adjust to the new society, such as the bourgeoisie, opportunists, wreckers and so on, were labelled 'enemies of the people' and were prone to annihilation. The task of searching for and exterminating these enemies was laid on the secret police, but all citizens were encouraged to unmask hidden enemies.

Some more sophisticated researchers of totalitarianism assumed the presence of interest groups in the power pyramid which intervened in politics to promote and defend their own group interests. The growing evidence of non-monolithic manifestations, of confusion, chaos and disobedience, were incorporated in the totalitarian approach under the term 'inefficient totalitarianism'. In the 1970s a new generation of researchers began to enlarge the scope of research subjects and focus on society rather than the power pyramid. These scholars rejected previous assumptions of society's passive role and concentrated on State–society interrelationships.[7] Subsequently, rethinking the period has been supported by new access to the recently declassified Soviet archives, and, while much is still to be done, the most recent evidence accords with this more qualified view of Soviet totalitarianism.

* * *

Immediately after the Bolshevik Revolution, well-to-do families were deprived of their privileged social status. Unlike the bourgeois revolutions which had introduced formal legal equality for all citizens, the proletarian revolution announced legal inequality. The Russian language was enriched with the new word *lishentsy* – those deprived of civil rights. This category included a wide range of individuals who represented political, social or economic structures of the overthrown regime, lived on 'non-labour profits', or were employers of labour: noble landowners, clergy, Tsarist army officers, owners of factories and rural enterprises, merchants and traders, or policemen. Such social background brought a risk of political stigma and potentially a danger of becoming an 'enemy of the people'. Such enemies, real or potential, were to be exterminated.

In the interviewees' recollections, repression was one of the most common themes. Family members suffered from them throughout the period from October 1917 until Stalin's death in 1953, but three waves of repression were mentioned most often: the Red Terror of post-revolutionary years; the abolition of the New Economic Policy (NEP) bourgeoisie and the destruction of the rural bourgeoisie, from 1923 to the late 1920s; and the Stalinist purges of the 1930s.

None of those who were arrested between 1917 and the early 1920s had a court trial or received any proof of their guilt. Several interviewees had close kin who had fought against Soviet power as White Army officers, or had given financial support to the White forces. These overt enemies of the Bolshevik regime, if not killed in action, managed to emigrate and hence escaped. But the only guilt of their repressed relatives, who did not emigrate and had never fought against Soviet power, was their social origin and kinship ties with such 'enemies of the people'. Lenin in one speech regretted that the Bolsheviks had been too kind to the 'representatives of the bourgeois-imperialistic regime'. Obviously it was not Bolshevik kindness but other factors, most typically protection by members of the Soviet elite, which allowed some of those arrested to be quickly released. Thus Maxim Gorky helped Dmitrii Riabushinskii, a prominent scientist, founder of the Aerodynamic Research Institute and a member of a notorious tycoon family, to escape from prison and emigrate to France, where he worked as co-director of a laboratory at the Institute of Mechanics and lectured at the Sorbonne. In another family, the urgent economic need to manage a nationalised or State-controlled factory forced the authorities to cancel the execution of the factory's former owner. Other escapes may have been due to bribery, or simply to 'a lucky chance'. However, many families have not transmitted any detailed memories of arrests and escapes, so that a typical narration may just state: 'Grandad was arrested and released several times.' On the whole, the testimonies give an impression of chaotic decisions by local authorities, poor control by the central administration, and the 'arbitrariness of the street'.

The second wave of repressions was related to the period of the New Economic Policy and the annihiliation of the *kulaki*. From 1921 until the late 1920s the NEP had encouraged private enterprise in retail sales and customer services, food production, and light industry. The typical Nepmen bourgeois was a small- or medium-scale entrepreneur, usually from a pre-revolutionary private-sector background. Although initially the NEP bourgeoisie began to be pushed out by economic measures, by the later 1920s these were supplemented by direct repression.

There are three families in the sample who belonged to the NEP bourgeoisie (in each of them the family heads were arrested), and several families with close Nepmen kin. One narrator regretted that her relatives had trusted the Soviet power and become Nepmen, and hence were repressed:

> My grandfathers were too old to re-start the business, and my mother and her siblings were too young. Their age saved them. But mother's cousin unluckily trusted in the NEP, started his own small business and was arrested in 1926. He was imprisoned, then sent to exile, then he was rehabilitated and returned to Moscow and lived there illegally without the *propiska* [police registration of tenants]. My point is: the people who trusted in the NEP were haunted by it.

The policy of *dekulakisation* differed from the abolition of the NEP bourgeoisie. While Nepmen suffered individually, the *kulaki* were repressed on a family basis. The measure of their punishment depended on the level of their resistance to Soviet power, and ranged from imprisonment to partial property confiscation. Three out of four *kulak* families in my sample experienced all the forms of repressions applied to that social group: expropriation of the family property, imprisonment and exile. Only one family avoided repression, because it voluntarily gave its property to a collective farm and joined the farm with the other villagers. But this case was a rare exception.

The repressions of the 1930s were a theme cutting across all the narratives. This wave of repressions was the most harmful for the families, and people suffered irrespective of their age, sex, occupation or the support of their 'personal connections'. All the testimonies use the impersonal 'they' to refer both to the Soviet power and to its representatives, above all the secret police officers who made the arrests.

> 'They' arrested the young people:
> Who said 'they' didn't arrest children? Mitia was not 16 yet when 'they' took him. We were told that he was missing, but later we learned by chance that he perished in Siberia at a timber saw-yard. The prisoners were making rafts, Mitia got stuck under a raft and drowned.

Nor were the elderly spared: 'Nikolai was arrested as a German spy when he was already over 60. He died in prison in 1942.' Although being a woman was not a protection from arrest, it was mostly men who were arrested, particularly specialists whose professional knowledge could be used in prison. 'They' arrested the Red Army officers, teachers, doctors, scholars, engineers and also the priests.

The clergy, although reduced substantially in the repressions, were not completely eliminated like some other formerly privileged social groups, because the church as a social institution continued to function. One clergy family in my sample did not suffer from direct repression; nevertheless, they chose to quit their profession. Generations of the men of this family had been preaching in the same village for more then 130 years, but by the 1920s a priestly career had become dangerous. In 1926, after his father's death, one man, who could have 'inherited' his father's position, wrote in his diary: 'The younger generation could continue to preach in this village, but due to the 1917 Russian revolution I didn't dare to become a priest.'

There is still no reliable information on what categories of population suffered most from the repressions of the 1930s. This time the social range of victims was much broader than in the previous waves of repression. Some research based on limited statistical data has showed that top-level Party, State and military officials were the most probable victims, while the ordinary workers and the poorest peasants were the least probable.[8] Probably the next most vulnerable social group were the *kulaki*. In between were former merchants, intelligentsia, managers and clerical workers. Their families regarded their pasts as a constant jeopardy to their safety, even though in the mid-1930s the 'genealogical witch-hunt' was halted with an official declaration that sons were no longer responsible for the sins of their fathers. Nevertheless, for decades a person's past remained meaningful to the Soviet authorities, and having a 'history' provided a convenient and easy explanation for being repressed.

These family stories raise many questions about the logic of the repressions. Why, for example, was a harmless, elderly, small-scale merchant baker arrested, while the whole family of a former magnate was left in peace? Why arrest a family's teenagers while letting another family member enter the mid-level Soviet *nomenklatura*? It is known that sometimes the Soviet authorities protected prominent representatives of the former elites, but not other members of their families. Often questions regarding particular individuals remain unsolved: there is not enough information for any conclusions about the logic at an individual level. Researchers have suggested motives such as revenge or jealousy, local power struggles, ideological commitments and the specific economic conditions.[9]

Expropriation, in parallel with repression, was another common theme. Family memories have retained, in more or less detail, the history of their houses and the later deterioration of their living conditions. By contrast the story of their business expropriation was usually limited to mere phrases such as '"They" took away our factories' and 'Everything was seized', with no details given. One reason was that at the time of the event even the oldest interviewees had been no more than children and could not have witnessed the process of business expropriation. As time went on, their parents chose either to tell them nothing about the family's past or just to recollect the happier periods of the family's history. It was not thought safe to discuss with children why the factories were taken away. But the children saw how their houses were seized and their families thrown out of their homes.

The testimonies give much detail of the expropriation of houses and personal belongings, the evictions, the new way of life in crowded living conditions, and in many cases the violence and vandalism during expropriations. To take just one example: 'My grandmother told me so bitterly how the family was pushed away from their house in Petrovskii Park and how "they" made a fire and burned their luxurious library. "They" burned it all. Just two volumes of Pushkin survived. Our maids hid several small things under their aprons and saved them. All the rest was burned, ruined, robbed.' Comparisons of a 'before' and an 'after' also continue in the stories of Soviet fairly to maintain the expropriated property: 'You know about the "Black Swan" – the luxurious villa of Nikolasha?. [10] When "they" expropriated it in 1918 or 1919 "they" turned it into the soldiers barracks. And "they" ruined it completely'. Several families decided to give up some of their property voluntarily in the hope of avoiding repression and saving the rest of their belongings, but such attempts were not very effective. At the most, they only protected the remnants of personal possessions. Yet even such possessions might become crucial for physical survival in the years to come, when many families sold or exchanged these remnants for food at the flea markets.

The testimonies rarely convey the emotional sorrow which parents or grandparents must have experienced through the loss of their property. The one exception is from a former *kulak* family:

> Despite the organisation of a collective farm the people couldn't reconcile themselves to the loss of their property for a long time. Everybody still knew, that was his horse, and that was his cow. Each collective farmer tried to use his former horse when tilling the *kolkhoz* land, each woman tried to milk her former cow ... Their sense of property didn't vanish for ages.

More generally, members of once-prosperous families had lost their privileged position in exchange for a stigmatised *lishentsy* status. They had lost not only their property, but also their bank deposits, stocks and shares, gold, and their right to inherit: in short, their means of existence. Repressions continued to threaten their lives and freedom. For such families, survival had become the most acute problem.

The family histories show, except for one case of complete failure, that all met the challenge and started adapting to the new social reality. Although each history is unique, they shared many similar experiences and reactions to social challenges, and used similar strategies to restore their former status.

* * *

Survival under the Bolshevik regime implied first of all the creation of a defensive space. Arendt assumes that the greatest threat for the individual was represented not by the abolition of the private ownership of wealth, but by the abolition of private property in social space. The four walls of one's private home, or, as she called it, 'the living space of freedom', offer the only reliable hiding place from the public world, from being seen and being heard.[11] For the totalitarian state, space had become a political instrument of primary importance. By transforming private dwellings into communal (hence public) apartments, the Soviet authorities imposed permanent control over the private life of their inhabitants.

The efforts of the families to reorganise their social space were, in effect, attempts to retain control over their privacy. Since they could not resist the state policy of 'densification' habitation, some of them created 'an extended family communal flat' by accommodating several nuclear families related to them in an apartment formerly inhabited by a single nuclear family.

One interviewee relates:

> My grandad built that house ... for his mother. It was really good: two floors, basement, central heating ... After the revolution it was the only house which was not expropriated. And gradually all the family members who survived gathered to live there. I mean, the house was being 'densified' with our family members. There were three communal flats full of relatives. I was born in that house and spent 25 years there.

Another recalls:

> I asked the members of several merchant families: how did all of you survive? They said: we 'densified' ourselves. What was their first principle after the revolution? They selected an apartment where they all moved in. And they lived together and supported each other. Many people have very warm recollections about these communal flats, the relatives lived very peacefully there.

By gathering in one communal flat, such families tried to avoid the invasion of their reduced private space and still live with the safe and protective social surrounding of people from a similar background. But many other families had to share apartments with workers, former peasants, or Soviet employees.[12] The communal flats became a 'melting pot' of different socio-cultural groups, a domestic sphere for the formation of the 'ordinary Soviet citizen'. 'Ordinary' had a concrete meaning here: under the Soviet reality it implied becoming de-individualised, 'like everybody', as opposed to anything elite or original; easily controlled and manipulated by the authorities; and with only elementary needs.[13]

With the communal way of life came a constant feeling of fear of repression. 'People were never relaxed, always expecting ... the knock at the door which meant "they" had come to arrest us. Fear was a constant feeling.' This was amplified through the fear of the neighbours' surveillance and denunciation. Everybody was afraid of everybody, because the authorities 'showed mercy to nobody'. The fear of others spread to family relations and poisoned them. The resulting splitting of former extensive family networks into nuclear families was a by-product of this fear and a self-protective reaction:

> When all these repressions began, patriarchal extended Russian families tried not to have contacts with each other. It's understandable. They ... tried to lose as many relatives as possible, to forget them ... Our parents were so scared that they cut off all contact with their cousins. My mother didn't contact her cousin who lived just three steps outside. I have never even heard about him. They cut off all relations, can you imagine?

Such family atomisation and the abandonment of family support networks was a voluntary reaction: there was never any official policy forbidding or restricting contact with family members of repressed persons. But it was in line with the regime's overall strategy of 'divide and rule'. Separated and suspicious citizens are more easily surveyed and manipulated. This effect was strengthened by purges. They spread a shadow of suspicion over everybody who had any relations with a victim – from mere acquaintances to the closest relatives. 'The guilt of having relations with an enemy' appeared to be the most effective mechanism of atomisation.[14]

Although less prominent than fear, the theme of surveillance and denunciation is also common in the narratives. Quantitative research by Fitzpatrick suggests that denunciations in the Soviet period were not specifically directed against members of the stigmatised social minorities.[15] Nevertheless, 'class enemies' and their relatives were particularly at risk, and the limited space of a communal flat was a perfect setting for rooting out hidden class enemies. Other denunciations were motivated by personal objectives: desire to increase living space, or to obtain the personal belongings of the 'class enemies'. Neighbour-on-neighbour denunciations were supplemented by denunciations at work:

> When I was a post-graduate student a denunciation was sent to the Ministry of Health. There was a professor in my institute, his name was Kurdiumov. He was from my town, Astrakhan, and knew my history. And he sent a denunciation to the Ministry that I was a former Nepman. The Vice-Minister called for the director of our institute and they discussed what to do with me. I know all this because later the director showed me that letter. And still they decided to let me remain in the institute.

* * *

Some families used voluntary territorial mobility as a mechanism of escape from surveillance. Territorial mobility as a means of survival, in the sense of voluntarily becoming socially invisible, was used mainly by rural families (*kulaki* and priests) to escape the severe social control and lack of anonymity of village life. But some urban families also used this strategy:

I know that the order to arrest my grandmother was signed by Lenin personally. She was a widow in her 60s. And she left the house, escaped. Put a bunch of her things on her shoulders and went away. And she was wandering around Moscow, spent a night with some relatives, a night with another. She didn't have a permanent address and she escaped arrest.

While often effective, territorial mobility could not always provide safety and freedom. Nevertheless people saw it as one way out. Another was voluntary occupational mobility: 'My father frequently changed work places. He was anxious for my mother's safety – she was from a merchant family. So he moved from one job to another.'

An alternative escape strategy used by some families was to become 'invisible in a crowd', and thus remain unnoticed by the regime without territorial mobility. The tactic was to behave like everybody else: to find roundabout ways, never climb straight upward, avoid attracting attention, remain in the shadow. The implications were manifold. For example, in education it could mean preferring safety to quality: 'My uncle advised me not to enter Moscow University where "they" might check my social origin, but to choose an ordinary college.' Others would pretend they had less education than they really had: 'God forbid you wrote in your personal file that you knew foreign languages. In those years, if you wrote you knew the foreign languages, "they" would start to investigate your family origin. We preferred not to mention our knowledge.'

The attempt to behave like everybody else was a core feature of *homo sovieticus*, the social type which had reached its 'classical' form by the 1930s–40s. But for many of the sample families, this homogeneity with the ordinary masses, and loyalty and submissiveness to the regime, remained relatively superficial and did not influence their value systems. The principles of defensive behaviour were combined with pursuing personal and family agendas, even though these often contradicted the aims of the regime.

* * *

Another measure that helped to 'cut off the past' was the destruction or falsification of documents and concealment of the family history from the children. Several families kept photos with the images of some people cut out, leaving only the silhouette and the empty hole. Other people told me how their relatives had presented faked documents to the authorities. Telling half the truth or belittling their pre-revolutionary social positions was widely used in the autobiographies which every Soviet citizen had to submit when applying for a job or entry to an educational institution. One witness called this document a 'self-denunciation'. Another showed me his autobiography in which his father, a prosperous merchant and the owner of a fishery business, was referred to as an ordinary fish trader, while the narrator's own occupation during the NEP was described by the deliberately unclear phrase, 'helping my father'.

Although practices differed from one family to another, concealing the family history, or at least part of it, was more a common strategy than telling children the whole truth. No memory, no documents – hence, less evidence of the dangerous past to threaten current safety. However it was not invariable. At one extreme, interviewees said: 'I didn't know anything'; at another: 'My parents never concealed anything from me.' Most children managed to glean a few 'safe' parts of the family story and, unable to interpret these parts and reconstruct the whole picture, had ambivalent family identities: 'I felt that we differed from our neighbours, but I couldn't comprehend why.' A more complete uncovering of the family history often took place in the years of Khrushchev's 'political thaw', during the 1960s, but archival investigations were not possible until the collapse of the Soviet regime in the 1990s. Sometimes information about the family origin produced a shock effect:

> When I graduated from secondary school my father told me: 'It's time for you to know that your grandmother was Riabushinskaia ... And what?' It didn't mean much to me. I went to the library to check the encyclopaedia. When I found out about the Riabushinskiis, my hair stood on end. I started to read Lenin and found what he wrote about the Riabushinskiis, that they were number one enemy of the Soviet power. I felt I'd better keep silent about my family origin.

A more positive strategy, which some believed had helped their survival, was marriage. The testimonies illustrate both profitable marriages and misalliances. Before the revolutionary period the criteria of profit and misalliance had included religion, ethnicity and occupation, but above all wealth and social status. For both sexes, profitable marriage could bring both economic growth and upward social mobility. These notions survived the socialist revolution. Many people mentioned marital misalliances with someone of another social status, with 'lower' or 'higher' depending on who made the evaluation. For the regime, the social status of the former well-to-do classes was the lowest but, in making marital choices, they themselves thought in terms of their pre-revolutionary social status. Irrespective of their later occupations, they perceived themselves as above their working-class spouses. This feeling was supported by their unquestionably higher cultural level.

In the Soviet era the need to survive transformed the criteria of profitable marriage and added the notion of a politically profitable union, of marrying a person with a 'good' social origin or status. While many marriages were still socially heterogeneous, socially or politically profitable marriages were motivated by the hope of attaining social or political protection: 'Her parents hoped that her Red Army husband could protect the family,' or, 'He married a simple worker, took her family name and became free from his dangerous past.' Such marriages did not guarantee safety, but none the less they were seen as a means to family security.

The last survival mechanism, using personal connections, was very typical of Russia, and a deep-rooted pre-revolutionary tradition. After 1917, many support networks were broken up or became inadequate, but some did remain quite effective, and new ones also emerged to suit Soviet conditions. They served a wide range of objectives, including help to find work or to retain a room in a communal flat and thus stay in Moscow; or help in re-admission to university after expulsion. But the most important goal was escaping repression. Sometimes it was a form of thanks for help given earlier to the future Soviet officials by former Tsarist elites:

> The revolutionaries used to hide from the Tsarist police in my grandfather's house. I know about Bonch-Bruevich, Krasin, Nogin. Muralov Nikolai Ivanovich, [later] a Red Army commander, was working as a manager on grandfather's countryside estate ... My grandfather warned them of future searches, because the police informed him in advance. After the revolution, Muralov tried to protect our family members. They were only exiled, and no one was arrested or executed. But when Muralov was executed in 1937, all of them were sent to prison.

Protection could only last as long as the patron remained in power: the purges not only ruined the lives of Soviet officials, but threatened the well-being of all those within their social networks. Hence, protection through networks was temporary. Personal contacts brought two-fold consequences: they might help, though not necessarily, and at the same time they put people at risk of being repressed if their patron was purged.

* * *

These strategies of adaptation related mostly to post-revolutionary survival. For status restoration the families used other mechanisms. The most important among them was the education of the younger generations. Many descendants of formerly prosperous families managed to receive higher education and enter the Soviet intelligentsia.[16]

The interviews suggest there is a need to rethink the model of the 'people's intelligentsia' presented by Soviet scholars. They stressed social mobility from the working class and the peasantry as the dominant mechanism for forming the intelligentsia, and neglected the continuing pre-revolutionary component.[17] I hypothesise that, in spite of all the obstacles the Soviet authorities put in the way of pre-revolutionary intellectuals, the regime was ineffective in destroying their cultural capital. They transmitted educational and cultural values to the next generation, thus creating an intellectual bridge between the former Russian and new Soviet professional classes.

The Soviet authorities realised the importance of intellectuals for the socialist transformation of society. But while the former Russian intellectuals either rejected or were ambivalent to the Bolshevik Revolution, the groups who supported Soviet power were illiterate or poorly educated. The cultural and intellectual base of revolution was very limited, hence the campaign to create a new social base providing the intellectual background to reform, the 'people's intelligentsia'. But until this group, ideologically faithful and easily manipulated, had been created, the authorities tried to enlist the 'old' intellectuals, called 'bourgeois specialists', and use their intellectual potential. The forced use of bourgeois specialists and the negative attitude towards them were supplemented by the policy of discrimination in admission to higher education on grounds of social origin. Thus the 'old' intelligentsia was deprived of the social mechanism of self-reproduction.

For only a short period of time university admission was open to any person above sixteen years old, regardless of citizenship or sex. University fees, entrance examinations and minimum educational requirements for entrance were abolished. But in the early 1920s this freedom was abandoned and a system of nomination of politically and socially acceptable candidates by local Party, Soviet and trade-union organisations was introduced. A few remaining places were occupied by free competition between applicants who had to provide recommendations from the authorities. Because the educational level of workers and peasants was too low for university requirements, a network of preliminary training courses, or *rabfak* [worker's faculties] was opened to prepare future students. The pre-requisites for *rabfak* were as low as the ability to read and write fluently, the knowledge of the four basic arithmetical processes and an elementary knowledge of society and politics. The social composition of the students fluctuated from year to year, but the trend was a declining share of the former privileged in favour of people from workers' and peasants' backgrounds. Nevertheless, the interviews suggest that the share of students with 'social aliens' backgrounds in the 1920s was much higher than in the official figures, because the children of the formerly privileged had merged into different 'politically safe' social groups, concealing their social origin.

Esteem for education had deep roots in noble, intellectual, merchant and clergy families, and the preservation of their educational and cultural capital remained an important obligation for parents after 1917. But their children had serious obstacles in the way to secondary and higher education. Hence some preferred to get the knowledge without receiving a formal diploma. One woman who studied in the 1920s recollects:

> After the revolution my gymnasium was closed, because 'they' closed all private high schools. Only the state schools could function. I was 15 years old at that time and had to finish the high school course at home on a private basis. Then it was very difficult to enter any university. Where could I be admitted with my origin and my family name? So I just attended lectures at the Philological Department of Moscow University as an external student.

She had no diploma because she was not formally a student, although she took the whole university course. But a diploma was necessary for a future professional career, so others found alternative forms of education:

> I shall never forget how our principal once came to our class, pointed at me and said: 'Children, there is a daughter of the enemies of the people!' How do you think I could study or make a professional career, when so many members of my family had been arrested, repressed, sent to exile or even shot? ... After finishing school I was thinking over how to continue my education ... I knew that I would never be permitted to enter any day time or even night classes, so I had to study by correspondence. When I finished the second course of the Institute of Foreign Languages there was a campaign of checking our files – personal documents – and I decided to leave the Institute, otherwise they would purge me. So I quit and entered the University, also by correspondence courses, and I graduated from the University with the best marks.

The choice of an alternative form of education – by correspondence course in this story, for others by night courses and external education – was combined with a form of educational mobility and evasion to avoid being purged, for student purges are an issue in more than one family story.

* * *

Because social background was a prime obstacle to a successful education and professional career, the strategy of upward social mobility commonly demanded an intentional change of social background for the creation of a favourable class identity. Class identification was based on two criteria – actual occupation, and social origin. There are examples in the literature of young people with 'alien' social backgrounds who broke all visible ties with their parents to rid themselves of their pre-revolutionary class identity.[18] No such extreme cases occurred in my sample, but some of the interviewees were able to 'improve' their social origin by being adopted by people with a somewhat 'better past'.

A more common strategy in my sample was concealing one's social origin, deceiving the authorities by belittling the pre-1917 position of the family. Unless documents were requested, class origin was usually determined by the individual's statement. 'So,' one of my respondents remarked, 'why tell the truth?' Thus a factory owner turned into a simple employee, or a fishery business owner into an insignificant small trader. This trick was used by a wide range of people from the very top to the bottom of the social scale. The most common tactic was to declare oneself proletarian:

> My granddad perished in Ukraine in 1918 or 1919. Nobody knows how and where. He was a Tsarist officer before 1917, and I doubt that he

was in the Red Army after 1917. But we don't know how he died. So my father used to say that he was an orphan, just an orphan. When he graduated from school, he went as a voluntary unskilled worker to one of the 'great constructions of Communism'. It was in 1931. After having spent several years there, he had the right to call himself a worker and enter *rabfak* in Moscow. After *rabfak* he entered the Motor Transport Institute. In 1932, when the Military Motor Transport Academy was opened, the students were recommended to become officers. My father agreed ... and served in the Army for 43 years and became General-Colonel of the Engineering forces.

This pattern of basing an educational and professional career on the creation of a favourable class identity was widespread, and there are numerous similar examples. One woman from a noble background said there were many students with 'bad' social origins at the *rabfak* where she had studied. One earned his living as a builder and entered an institute after *rabfak*, but in two years was expelled from it having been identified as the son of a textile tycoon. So soon afterwards he married a woman of simple worker's origin and took her family name. Without the stigma of belonging to a famous bourgeois family, and with proletarian status, he once again entered the institute, this time choosing night courses, and successfully graduated with a diploma in civil engineering.

The persistence with which the descendants of nobles, merchants, clergy and intelligentsia tried to get higher education is impressive, but the motivation of formerly wealthy peasants who were not themselves educated is also striking. In one family the poorly educated parents, grieving at the degradation of their once-prosperous village after the creation of a collective farm, insisted their son continue his studies at a secondary school after completion of his primary schooling. He had to walk several kilometres every day to reach it. Then he went on to the nearest town to become an urban professional. For this family, education was not an intellectual transmission but a way to get out of a degrading setting.

* * *

In addition to formal education, the other component of becoming an intellectual was cultural capital: the cultural resources of a family transmitted through generations.[19] For family members this was associated with broad erudition, knowledge of art and foreign languages, good taste and the development of artistic abilities, good speech and behaviour, and some moral qualities. One older woman recalled:

We told our children that they must keep the values of our grandparents – honour and fairness. They respected their honour and never betrayed their values, neither my daughters, nor my grand-daughters. In a time when it was not permitted to talk about God, we thought about God and about our souls. And these thoughts saved our souls, our inner world.

Her daughter continues:

> Neither my grandmother and mother, nor I, ever concealed our family background, our history. My family never conformed, never pretended to be what it never was. Our parents and we children too carried through all our lives what we really were. We suffered the burden of our social origin, but never 'changed our colour', never conformed. We tried to be faithful to our inner truth. And this faithfulness helped us greatly ... If I hadn't had that inner support from my family, I wouldn't have succeeded in my life. Not to lose the family bond, the ties with your ancestors – that is a most important thing.

Such accounts stress the crucial role of transgenerational moral attitudes and models,[20] continuing personal identification with the family and respect for family memory as part of the family cultural tradition. But reconciliation of the past with the 'present' was a stressful and ambivalent process for individual identity formation:

> My grandfather and grandmother used to listen to the radio and discuss it in French. Once when they started to speak French I told them indignantly: 'I am sick and tired of your bourgeois prejudices! I will never ever stand for this radio-enemy and your speaking foreign languages!' They were shocked. Then my grandmother came to me, stroked my head and and said: 'Taniusha, you are wrong. You will understand everything later on.'

In other instances there was no such reconciliation between the generations:

> My grandfather knew five languages ... My father spoke three languages, just like my mother. They were not like us – we speak only one and know it poorly ... We are Soviets, they are people of another culture ...

> My mother never told me much about the family history ... Until the 1960s I didn't know my real family name. When I was 14 years old somebody, but not my mother, told me that I was from a family which was very famous before the revolution. What did I feel when I learned about my origin? To tell the truth – nothing, I didn't care much.

Such family histories show the role of the family memory and family traditions: when family members were able to keep them, cultural capital could be transmitted to the younger generations, while disruption of the family memory and lack of identification with the family could result in a drastic cultural gap between the generations.

* * *

How far did gender affect the fates of the men and women in my sample families?

These family histories show that both sexes suffered from repressions which were not targeted specifically against men or women. Thus, the *kulaki* – men, women, and children of both sexes – suffered equally because the policy of *dekulakisation* was oriented towards the family unit. By contrast, repressions against other former privileged classes were individually oriented. Because men were more economically and politically active than women, they were also more vulnerable to repression. They were regarded by the new regime as the primary enemies of Soviet power, while the females sometimes suffered as 'substitutes' for their missing husbands, sons or brothers: '"They" came to arrest him, but he managed to go into hiding, so "they" arrested his wife instead.' The consequences of repression seemed to be more serious for males than for females: men were more often imprisoned and executed than women, whose punishment was more often limited to exile. This assumption, made on the basis of the research sample, finds some statistical support: according to NKVD (secret police) data for October 1946 the number of women living in exile in special settlements exceeded the number of men.[21]

The influence of gender on occupational career is more complicated. Before the Revolution the division of male–female roles in prosperous families was traditional: the husbands as breadwinners, the wives as housekeepers and childrearers. The Revolution destroyed the positions of men as family providers, so they had to find alternatives. With their high levels of education and professional qualifications they might have had good chances but for the policies of the Soviet authorities. Some men were indeed used by the new regime as 'bourgeois specialists', and even made successful professional careers as factory directors or top-level managers, high-ranking officers or scientists. But for most, the policies of social discrimination pushed them away from professional well-paid work to the sectors of unskilled and semi-skilled labour. The aim of this policy was to re-socialise the former 'exploiters' by hard manual work.

The position of women was somewhat different. The Soviet power proclaimed the emancipation of women, their political, economic and sexual equality with men, as one of its most important political objectives. Hence official attitudes to women from formerly privileged classes were ambivalent. As women they could expect some state support in realisation of their educational and occupational efforts:

> My grandmother was a very talented person, but she couldn't realise her professional ambitions before the Revolution, and she didn't receive higher education. She graduated from high school with a gold medal but couldn't continue her education. My mother, the next generation, she – a woman! – studied at the university, she got the right to do scientific research work. Well, my point is: it was possible to live and make a career under socialism.

On the other hand, women were discriminated against in occupational spheres as members of the 'alien classes'. Since social characteristics were much more significant for the authorities than gender, the primary implication of Soviet policy towards women from 'alien classes' was a new right to suffer discrimination equally with men.

A lot of women from the privileged backgrounds entered the paid labour force soon after the Revolution, and many of them were motivated by economic necessity. In several families, where males were repressed, women remained the only breadwinners and had to provide for elderly parents and relatives, children, or even for the elderly maids and nannies who lived with them as family members. As a rule the females utilised their pre-revolutionary knowledge. The most typical kinds of jobs among them were as teachers of foreign languages, music or art, translator or interpreter, typist or secretary, bookkeeper or accountant, or in handicraft.

* * *

Analysis of the occupational histories of both sexes has revealed a high level of intra- and intergenerational mobility. The members of the oldest generation, born in the 1870s–80s, were socialised and educated long before the Revolution. By 1917 they were adults or elderly people with successful careers and a high social status. This generation suffered most of all. They experienced a sharp loss of status which many of them were unable to overcome, particularly those who survived repressions but spent many years or even most of their life in exile. Usually these people had to abandon their professional skills and acquire some other skills to help them to survive.

Those family members whose life was not ruined by repressions adapted occupationally in three different ways. First, there were many people who could not find any proper and stable work. They switched from one unskilled job to another because they were expelled from their previous ones as representatives of the 'alien classes'. This group were relatively poorly adapted. The second group utilised their pre-revolutionary knowledge, demonstrating a medium level of adaptation. Third, and occupationally the most successfully adapted, there were a number of individuals who simply continued their pre-revolutionary careers as doctors, actors, artists, writers and even factory directors. The next generation started to restore the lost social positions of their parents, and on the whole they succeeded in this. Though they were born before 1917, they encountered the Revolution as young people, and occupationally the active part of their lives still lay ahead. Their hopes for a better life, chances to make a career and anticipation of professional success inspired them to social advancement. The upward intragenerational mobility of this generation was most impressive compared to others. They got jobs demanding at least secondary education, while many became professionals with university diplomas. The social positions of this generation ranged from secretaries, accountants and nurses to university professors, doctors, Soviet Army generals and members of the mid-level State *nomenklatura*.

Building on the improved positions of the second generation, their children in turn attained even better results. Unlike their parents and grandparents, who had to adjust themselves to a totally different social system, this generation was born under socialist rule. They did not have a 'before' and an 'after' the Revolution with the consequent need to adjust to a new social system. The stigma of their social origin had lessened as the regime strengthened, and many of them did not even know their family origin. Most of them moved upwards within the middle classes with the help of university diplomas, obtained by much simpler paths than those of their parents or grandparents. Some of them also had Ph.D. degrees. As one woman concluded:

> We belong to a generation whose members were not killed in the revolution and were not repressed after it. We worked, we graduated from the universities, and became professionals. We have clever heads. Nobody and nothing stood in the way of our generation. It was a common thing in Russia for your own head, not your parents, to define the outcome of your life.

* * *

Although no job or social position was safe from the post-revolutionary repression, there were some which made life easier and others which made for still greater hardships. Those who had a profession necessary to the Soviet power, such as a doctor or an aircraft engineer, could expect some privileges even in prison:

> Grisha was arrested before the war. He worked in '*sharashka*' with Tupolev [the famous Soviet aircraft constructor]. Do you know what '*sharashka*' is? All the best specialists were arrested and they worked as professionals, as specialists in prison. They had good working and living conditions: they didn't enjoy freedom, but they were well supplied with everything. They were separated from their families and they had to obey the severe prison regime, but they had everything for their professional work.

In another way, in the hungry post-revolutionary years any job connected with food made life easier. One grandmother sent all her children 'closer to food', to spend summers in an agricultural cooperative where her ex-husband worked as an agricultural consultant. Another family bartered with a brother-in-law who had access to food through his work:

> My sister and her husband [Kolya] saved my sons from hunger. Kolya was mobilised to work as a medical orderly, accompanying wounded soldiers on a train. He always brought back some food from those trips which he exchanged for different things we gave him: old dresses, cotton kerchiefs, fake jewellery.

Food has a powerful symbolic meaning in Russia, a nation which has never had a proper choice of food, so much so that even today, when fear of famine is no longer on the agenda, many investment companies have tried to attract low-income clients through advertisements focusing on the 'food theme'. But in the post-revolutionary years with which these memories are concerned, access to food was above all a condition of survival.

Belonging to a non-Russian national minority could also bring added problems. Although the one Byelorussian family in my sample did not experience any added difficulties, the experience of the two merchant Jewish families was more distinctive. Before 1917 the civil rights of the Jews had already been legally restricted. Most could live only within the designated areas of the Jewish Pale; only limited quotas of Jewish children could be admitted to secondary schools and universities; and they were prohibited from owning land and practising some professions. The socialist revolution cancelled these limitations, and in this sense the Jews gained from it. Under Soviet rule there were no Jewish massacres, as had often previously occurred in some regions. But the negative attitude of Stalin and the authorities to the Jews, and the anti-Semitic spirit of the society, was not a secret. Such attitudes strengthened in the years of the NEP. Some researchers argue that many Jews whose pre-revolutionary occupation was in trade became Nepmen. This concentration of Jews among successful Nepmen intensified anti-Semitism in Soviet Russia to the point that being a Nepman became synonymous with being a Jew.

Although the Nepmen relatives were repressed in both Jewish families, the family histories did not suggest any other direct influence of nationality on their adaptation. One man told me that in the post-revolutionary decades he did not feel his nationality as an obstacle. The main problem was the social origin of the family: in the student purges of the mid-1920s he was expelled from the medical institute because he was a merchant's son. By the 1930s the negative criterion was less social origin than having been repressed. He was denounced several times, and in the 1930s the denouncers 'reminded the authorities' that he was a 'repressed Nepman', neglecting his social origin and nationality. However, the Jewish factor reappeared more directly on the agenda in the 1950s during one of the last waves of Stalinist repressions when, along with several other Jewish professors, he was expelled from his work.

* * *

In conclusion, my primary interest has been not in the politics and personalities in the ruling of Russia, but in the private lives of families and their strategies for adapting to official Soviet policy. Of course, not all the stories of these families were fortunate. Particularly in the older generation, there is also a minority of failed social trajectories. Typically these were of people who fell victim to repression and spent a large part of their lives exiled in the *lager*. Yet, even among these, there are examples of successful careers after release from prison. But I have chosen to concentrate here primarily on upward trajectories, because my purpose has been to analyse the mechanisms of social status restoration.

My interviews challenge the widespread portrayal of Soviet citizens as being the passive objects of manipulation from above. They show how, on the contrary, to a large extent people shaped their life careers and pursued their own agendas, mobilising both their inner individual and their family resources to achieve not only successful functional adaptation but also, despite deliberate Soviet official restrictions of their social opportunities, a significant degree of social mobility.

Notes

1 Viacheslav M. Molotov, *Stat'i i Rechi: 1935–1936* [Articles and Speeches: 1935–1936] (Gospolitizdat, Moscow, 1937): 45.
2 Pitirim A. Sorokin, *The Sociology of Revolution* (Howard Fertig, New York, 1967).
3 I Ya Trifonov, *Klassy i Klassovaia Bor'ba v SSSR v Nachale NEPa: 1921–1925* [Classes and Class Struggle in the USSR in the Beginning of NEP: 1921–1925] (Izdatelstvo Leningradskogo Universiteta, Leningrad, 1969); I. Ya Trifonov, *Likvidatsiia ekspluatatorskikh klassov v SSSR* [The Liquidation of the Exploitary Classes in the USSR] (Politizdat, Moscow, 1975); Grigorii Glezerman, *Likvidatsia ekspluatatorskikh klassov i preodolenie klassovykh razlichii v SSSR* [The Liquidation of the Exploitary Classes and the Overcoming of Class Differentiation in the USSR] (Gospolitizdat, Moscow, 1949); Valeriia Selunskaia et al. (eds), *Izmeneniye sotsial'noi struktury sovetskogo obshchestva: Oktiabr' 1917–1920* [Changes in the Structure of Soviet Society: October 1917–1920] (Mysl', Moscow, 1976); S. A. Fediukin, *Sovetskaya Vlast' i burzhuaznyie spetsialisty* [Soviet Power and Bourgeois Specialists] (Mysl', Moscow, 1965); S A Fediykin, *Velikii Oktiabr' i intelligentsia* [The October Revolution and the Intelligentsia] (Nauka, Moscow, 1972).
4 To mention just basics: Arch Getty, Jr and Roberta T. Manning (eds), *Stalinist Terror: New Perspectives* (Cambridge University Press, Cambridge, 1993); Alan M. Ball, *Russia's Last Capitalists: The Nepmen 1921–29* (University of California Press, Berkeley, 1987); Charles Bettleheim, *Class Struggles in the USSR: First Period, 1917–23* (Monthly Review Press, New York, 1976); Charles Bettleheim, *Class Struggles in the USSR: Second Period, 1923–30* (Monthly Review Press, New York, 1978); Edward H. Carr, *The Bolshevik Revolution: 1917–1923* (Macmillan, London, 1950–53); Edward H Carr, *Socialism in One Country*, 3 vols (Macmillan, London, 1958–1964); Robert Conquest, *The Great Terror: A Reassessment* (Pimlico, London, 1992); Moshe Lewin, *Russian Peasants and Soviet Power: A Study of Collectivisation* (Northwestern University Press, Evanston, 1968); Moshe Lewin, *The Making of the Soviet System: Essays in the Soviet History of the Interwar Russia* (Pantheon Books, New York, 1985).
5 This project was sponsored by the Research Support Scheme of the Central European University.
6 On 'symbolic boundaries', see Anthony P. Cohen, *The Symbolic Construction of Community* (Ellis Horwood, Chichester, 1985).
7 Getty and Manning, *Stalinist Terror*; Sheila Fitzpatrick, *Education and Social Mobility in the Soviet Union, 1921–1934* (Cambridge University Press, Cambridge, 1979); Sheila Fitzpatrick, Alexander Rabinowich and Richard Stites (eds), *Russia in the Era of NEP: Explorations in Soviet Society and Culture* (Indiana University Press, Bloomington, 1991); Sheila Fitzpatrick, *The Cultural Front: Power and Culture in Revolutionary Russia* (Cornell University Press, Ithaca and London, 1992).
8 Arch Getty Jr and William Chase, 'Patterns of repression among the Soviet elite in the late 1930s', in Getty and Manning, *Stalinist Terror*: 225–46.

9 Lynne Viola, 'The second coming: class enemies in the Soviet countryside, 1927–1935', in Getty and Manning, *Stalinist Terror*: 65–98.
10 Nikolai P. Riabushinskii, a playboy and philanthropist.
11 Hannah Arendt, *The Human Condition* (University of Chicago Press, Chicago, 1958): 70; Hannah Arendt, *The Origins of Totalitarianism* (Meridian Books, Cleveland, 1966): 466.
12 For a detailed analysis of the communal way of life, see Victoria Semenova, chapter 3, this volume.
13 Yuri A. Levada (ed.), *Prostoi Sovetskyi Chelovek* [The Ordinary Soviet Person] (Mirovoi Okean, Moscow, 1993): 8.
14 Arendt, *Origins*: 321.
15 Sheila Fitzpatrick, *Signals from Below: Soviet Letters of Denunciation of the 1930s*, unpublished paper, 1994.
16 I use the term 'intelligentsia' here in a rather narrow functional way in terms only of the educational and cultural levels of the individual.
17 Selunskaia *et al.*, *Izmeneniye sotsial'noi struktury*; M. P. Kim *et al.* (eds), *Sovetskaja intelligentsija: Istorija Formirovanija i rosta, 1917–1965 gg* [The Soviet Intelligentsia: A History of Its Formation and Growth, 1917–1965] (Mysl', Moscow, 1968).
18 *Ibid.*: 26–7.
19 For the first approach see Pierre Bourdieu, *Distinction: A Social Critique of the Judgement of Taste* (Harvard University Press, Cambridge, Mass., 1984); for the second, Daniel Bertaux, 'Les transmissions en situation extrême: familles expropriées par la Revolution d'octobre' (*Communications*, numero speciale 59, 1994: 'Génerations et filiation'), 77–97.
20 Paul Thompson, 'Women, men, and transgenerational influences in social mobility', in Daniel Bertaux and Paul Thompson, *Pathways to Social Class* (Clarendon Press, Oxford, 1997): 32–61.
21 *Moskovskie Novosti* [Moscow News], 1990: 41.

Part II

PERSONAL AND FAMILY LIFE

5

'WHAT KIND OF SEX CAN YOU TALK ABOUT?'

Acquiring Sexual Knowledge in Three Soviet Generations

Anna Rotkirch

INTRODUCTION

In a small Siberian town, the teachers went on strike for the first time in the spring of 1997. The reason was not, for instance, that their wages had not been paid during the last months – indeed, it had no direct connection to Russia's economic or social problems. The teachers participated in the nationwide protests against the first program of school sex education.[1]

As this controversy showed, Russia lacked a cultural consensus about how sexual knowledge should be transmitted. More than a decade after the end of Communist censorship of sexual and erotic topics, pornography is now sold in the metro stations of the cities, but 13-year-old girls living in the same cities may still be unprepared for their menstruation.[2] The availability and use of modern contraceptives (the pill and the IUD) is spreading, but abortion remains one of the main ways of birth regulation.[3] Russia lacks coherent legislation concerning family planning and reproductive rights.[4] In this transitional, paradoxical situation, it was possible for the Ministry of Education to develop and adopt the programme of sex education mentioned above – a programme that, whatever its good intentions, was bound to have problems being approved by the provincial cities.

This lack of consensus on sexual issues is a legacy from the post-war Soviet period and the almost total absence of public discourse – whether educational, entertaining, pornographic or philosophical – on sexuality.[5] Notably, the Soviet Union had no 'sexual revolution' in the 1960s similar to that in the West. There were only minor changes in the sexual policy of the Communist regime. At the same time, the actual sexual behaviour of Soviet people in some ways followed the developmental trends of other industrialised countries, including earlier onset of sexual life and a greater number of extramarital affairs and divorces.[6] This chapter will ask whether we detect traces of a smaller, later, or perhaps mixed and half-realised analogue to the Western sexual revolution in Soviet Russia. Can we talk about any distinct generations of Soviet sexual culture? I will focus on the ways of obtaining sexual knowledge in different periods of Soviet history. The term 'sexual knowledge' will here be approached on two levels. The first understands sexual knowledge as concrete information about intercourse and reproduction (pregnancy, contraceptives, personal hygiene, etc.). This form of sexual enlightenment can be greatly influenced by schools and other State institutions. It has been shown to have a significant positive impact, especially on women's health and sexual satisfaction.[7]

On the second level, sexual knowledge encompasses reflective assessment of questions of sexual mastery, identity and self-fulfillment, especially in reference to what one (now) thinks one should have known earlier in life. In biographical research, these two levels are of course not clearly separable, and they will alternate throughout the chapter. For example, I will discuss the channels for obtaining sexual information that are mentioned in autobiographies by members of three Soviet generations. But these biographies about past experience were written, a few years after the liberalisation of all kinds of discourse about sex in Russia, a fact which prompts the authors of all generations to reflect on their 'sexual knowledge' in the broader sense.

My main material is of two types, quantitative and qualitative: first, the statistical evidence of a representative survey of the population of St Petersburg, conducted in 1995;[8] and second, forty-seven in-depth written autobiographies. In addition, comparisons are made with the biographical and survey material on sexuality collected in Finland and Estonia presented by Osmo Kontula, Elina Haavio-Mannila and J. P. Roos.[9] The Russian autobiographies which I am using were collected in 1996 through a competition organised by Alexandr Klyotzin and Liza Lagunova from the Institute of Sociology in St Petersburg. Through an advertisement in the weekly newspaper *Chas Pik* and additionally distributed leaflets, people were invited to write about their love life and sexual life. The jury eventually selected six 'winning' autobiographies. In addition to the promised monetary awards for the winning autobiographies, an effective inducement to write seems to have been the title question of the competition announcement: *'Is there sex in Russia?'* The question alludes to the famous sentence uttered by a Russian woman in a *perestroika*-time TV-show: 'We have no sex in this country.' I will return to the answers given in the autobiographies throughout the chapter.

'IS THERE SEX IN RUSSIA?': THE TWO-SIDED ANSWER

Only a handful of academic works have appeared about sexuality in Russia and the Soviet Union, along with a little more in memoirs, travel accounts and journalism.[10] The recent, and by far the most authoritative and comprehensive monograph, *The Sexual Revolution in Russia*, is written by Russia's leading sexologist, Igor Kon. In this book, Kon distinguishes between four periods of sexual policy in the Soviet Union. The first was a short 'daring and progressive' period in the early 1920s with radical legislation, pluralistic discussion and social experimentation. This grew into the second period of 'brutal repression' under Stalin, where sexuality became unmentionable and love was ideologically confined to the married, monogamous, heterosexual couple. Kon describes the third period that followed, the late socialism of Khrushchev and Brezhnev, as the 'domestication' or 'awkward taming' of sexuality: research on sexuality was again partially allowed, and some kind of information and advice featured in medical journals. Fourth, the Gorbachev politics of *glasnost* led to the liberalisation of the printed word and a Russian 'sexual revolution' in the late 1980s.[11]

From being the world's most radical country on sexual and reproductive policy in the 1920s, the Soviet Union had perhaps the world's most hypocritical and prudish regime in the 1970s. Igor Kon vehemently criticises the Communist regime for creating unnecessary suffering. He talks about the lack of erotic culture, about the 'primitiveness' and 'ugliness' (even the 'nakedness') of Soviet sex.[12] In our material, biographical authors of all age cohorts also complain about a lack of adequate sexual knowledge.

> Soviet power talked about strengthening the family, but they prevented sexual enlightenment and only God knows how many families fell apart because of that. I am sure that if my wives and I had been sexually enlightened, I would have had half as many wives.
> (Man (28), higher education, born 1932, married four times)

> The first time I took a book about sex in my hands I was 40 years old. This was a good [informative] book, written by some German doctor and writer. I didn't read it all ... But I understood one thing – everything in our sexual life had been normal, inside the frame of normal sexual life.
> (Woman (8), journalist, born 1945)

> I had [when I was 21 years old] an *idée fixe* to get married as a virgin, I was afraid of pregnancy as of fire, of children born outside of marriage and such things. I had only vague ideas about the methods of birth control ...
> (Woman (19), librarian, born 1964)

This ignorance creates an understandable indignation among scholars and doctors, and is found in other accounts of Soviet sexuality. Soviet 'backwardness' is also accentuated by a comparison with contemporary Western sexual education and culture. Moreover, many of the key critical authors wrote their books in the USA, which provided political asylum for Popovsky and Stern and academic working peace for Kon. According to Igor Kon, the sexual revolution, or liberation, arrived in Russia in the late 1980s, and then in a raw, unsophisticated and commercialised form: in short, 'Russian sexual culture generally lags about 25 years behind that of the West.'[13]

Kon also stresses the violence present in Soviet sexual culture, for example in the high frequency of gang rapes conducted by boys or young men.[14] Mikhail Stern, who spent five years in a Soviet labour camp in the 1970s, goes as far as seeing the male camp culture of extreme hierarchical violence as the core of Soviet sexuality: 'The Soviet Eros is no more than the demon of Gulag society which has taken refuge in the lower depths of Soviet society and the Soviet psyche.' Life outside the camps is for him merely a milder version of institutionalised rape and humiliation.[15] On the one hand, then, we are presented a picture of 'totalitarian' sex: primitive, repressed, impoverished and violent. The Bolsheviks had 'no sex', because their ideology was against private life, individual choice and intimate, sensual pleasure. One of our biographies clearly expressed this ideological judgement:

> Alas, many of us had got the *sovkovyi* [Soviet] sexless version of dividing society into bosses and employees, the heroes of work and the retarded ... The conflicts between these opposed sides filled our phony literature, where love affairs were castrated and overshadowed by passions of production.
> (Man (35), archaeologist and artist, born 1945)

Much more common, however, was 'lack of sex' due to social problems and the hardships of everyday life. Take this laconic statement on the housing situation: 'Practically all our private life took place before the eyes of our relatives' (Woman (6), higher education, born 1937). Or the following description:

> We got married. Those were happy years. I loved him enormously. I tried to always be by his side. The whole day I was longing to see him again. And my heart was beating anxiously when, at last, he came home. But we did not have 'sex' during all those thirteen years that I lived together with him. Although we protected ourselves [condoms and interrupted intercourse], I was chronically pregnant. It looked like this: we were terrified [of a pregnancy], made it, then I was pregnant – again all those horrors: a suffocating headache, nausea, vomiting, irritation – then an abortion with all its pleasant attributes,

then we were not allowed to, and then the circle began again. What kind of sex can you talk about!!!

(Woman (9), nursery school assistant, born 1946)

This ironic outburst assumes that sometimes, somewhere, there does exist (better, relaxed, real) sex. And in fact, with one lover, this woman had already experienced it.

On the other hand, Igor Kon describes everyday Soviet sexual life as being in other ways similar to Western patterns. Thus in the 1960s it was already 'clear that both the value orientations and the sexual conduct of Soviet youth were moving in the same direction as those of their counterparts in the West'.[16] This direction includes general modernisation features such as smaller families, the earlier starting of sexual life, a greater tolerance of premarital sex and of homosexuality, and a tendency towards more equality between the sexes. Kon also points out that intolerance and opposition to sex education is found in the United States as well as in (post)-socialist Russia. Also, the American rape rates are much higher, and Russia in this respect is less violent (although he here omits the complicated question of reporting rates). In this second picture, Russians had sex just like everybody else – or even more of it. Due to disappointments in official working lives, private relations were given more time and energy during late socialism, and this included lovers.[17] This is the point made by the following autobiographer:

> Now you can hear people saying that there has been a sexual revolution in Russia. And that programme [the TV programme referred to earlier], with the sentence, 'We have no sex in Russia', I was looking at TV then. It was very funny. My whole life was saturated with sex. The working day began with talks about who had spent his night how. In the factory department there was no married woman without lovers, and the men hooked wherever they could ... Therefore I have made the conclusion that in fact there was sex precisely in the Soviet Union, but nowadays for people who are poor and don't have a normal apartment there is indeed no sex ... For me personally there is no more sex in Russia.
>
> (Man (37), born in 1954)

The Soviet experience of sexuality is thus presented as both shockingly different and just the same, if a little retarded. This paradoxical two-sided argument – Russia as both the 'same' and the 'other' – of course has a long tradition in the European history of ideas. Boris Groys, among others, has stressed that Russian philosophical identity is built on a view of Russia as Europe's 'other', which from the Renaissance onwards mirrors Western European developments in a retarded and grotesque form.[18] But in research on sexuality it might also partly stem from the methods used. Statistical material obtained through surveys shows that average behaviour followed Western developmental trends. But Kon's book also relates the experiences of his own generation and that of his students, and here, in the subjective memories, appear the anecdotes, the anger, the frustration, much of the violence, and other 'pecularities' of Soviet sex.[19] This is why biographical material seems a particularly promising ground for capturing the terrain between statistical averages and random personal memories, especially the importance of different class and social milieus with respect to sexual knowledge.[20]

SEXUAL POLICY AND SEXUAL GENERATIONS

The four main periods of Soviet sexual policy which we have identified may be dated approximately as follows: first, progressive sexual policy (1917–mid-1930s); second, repression (mid-1930s–early 1960s); third, domestication (early 1960s–1988); and finally, sexual revolution (from 1987).

This can be contrasted with developments in Finland which have only one great turning point – the 1960s, when the generation of 'baby boomers' was young. We can thus talk about three distinct sexual generations in Finland (and many other Western countries), with the generation of sexual revolution, encompassing those born between 1937 and 1956, as the main reference point. Before this was the generation of restraint, and after – people born between 1957 and 1974 – the generation of equality (in which the behaviour of men and women becomes still more similar).[21]

If we take the formative years as a potential generational criterion also in Russia, we could expect to find generational differences for people born, first in 1908–23, second in 1923–45, third in 1945–72 and finally after 1972. In the autobiographies we have life stories of people from the three most recent age cohorts. The impact of the early progressive policy of the 1920s is thus only indirectly present, and remains outside the scope of this discussion. Suffice it to say that debates about and experiments with 'free love' were limited to the intellectual elite and young people. The majority remained untouched by or suspicious of them.[22] The heritage of Bolshevik theorists on sexuality such as Alexandra Kollontai is still little known in Russia, and not once mentioned in any of our autobiographies. The 'progressive' period of Soviet sexual policy did influence the lives of ordinary people, especially women, mainly through the right to free abortion (which the Soviet Union was the first European country to stipulate, in 1920), and in acknowledging *de facto* marriages and the right to divorce.[23]

THE GENERATION OF SILENCE

> I am a product of my time, of the period in our country about which it is said and written: 'There is no sex in the Soviet Union.' For the biggest part of my life, talk about sex and erotica were

considered forbidden and shameful themes. Nevertheless love, sex and erotica are an integral part of the life of every person, and play an enormous role, wherever he lives. In my life they played a dominating role.

(Woman (5), higher education, born 1937)

The first generation I shall discuss here consists of people born between 1923 and 1944, who had their formative years during 1937–60. In the ways of acquiring sexual knowledge they are quite similar both to each other, giving the reader a taste of a specific generational experience, and to Finnish biographies from the same age group. I shall talk about a sexual generation of silence in Soviet Russia, for two reasons. First, this was the silenced generation. Liberal sexual policy had, since the early 1930s, turned to its opposite, in what Igor Kon calls the period of brutal repression. Abortions were a crime between 1936 and 1955; and the family laws in force from 1936 and 1944 to 1968 made divorce procedures difficult and expensive, and stigmatised those children born out of wedlock.[24] Psychoanalysis had been banned in the late 1920s and Sigmund Freud classified as a bourgeois scientist whose works were available only to professional experts with special permission. Along with Freud, other discussions such as that on childhood sexuality (the Marxist psychologist Pavel Blonskii published one as late as 1934) disappeared.[25] Soviet ideology from the 1930s onwards propagated only the monogamous, heterosexual nuclear family and increasingly soft and domesticated ideals of femininity.[26] Still, we should keep in mind that this kind of repressive sexual policy and gender ideology was still an unquestioned norm in other European countries of the time. France, for instance, legalised abortion only in the 1970s. The special trait of the Soviet regime in this respect was not so much repression as the gradual silencing of public discourse, with censorship in the arts, literature and science.

The second reason for talking about a generation of silence comes from the autobiographies themselves. They show no lack of sexual events – in fact, many of the richest sexual autobiographies come from this generation. The oldest woman (no. 1, born 1923, who we shall call Natalya V.) had several marriages and lovers in a life story that we will presently follow more thoroughly. The men of this generation who participated in the autobiography competition were exceptionally sexually active – they have a median of over ten sexual partners, which in fact was typical for only one-third of the whole age cohort. But for practically everybody in this generation, sexual matters were something to be silent about. For instance, every one of the respondents in the survey born between 1922 and 1941 said that sexual matters were kept secret in the family, 96 per cent that they had had no sex education in school, and less than 30 per cent that sex was something they discussed with same-sex friends.[27] Valerii Golofast has suggested a distinction between three levels of biographical narrative: routine, events, and hidden, secret things. For the generation of silence, sexuality belongs totally in the realm of secrets.[28] Therefore, acquiring knowledge is an event that stands out clearly in the memory: there is a distinct point at which you learned the basics. And telling about this personal secret – breaking the silence – is also an event for people of this generation writing their autobiographies, especially for the educated women. I have classified ten female and eleven male autobiographies as belonging to this generation (i.e., born before 1945/46). Of these, all of the professional women or those with higher education mention 'how they found out' as being an event. Two of the four women workers with lower educational qualifications, by contrast, do not pay special attention to sexual knowledge at all, except that one of them complains of being unprepared for her menstruation.[29] True, finding out is an 'event' for both well- and less well-educated men, but then it is often connected not to abstract knowledge, but to the first sexual experience and the pressure to succeed.

Natalya V.'s autobiography is an exemplary illustration of Soviet upward social mobility and, as a part of that mobility, of the desire to learn, professionally as well as privately. Her parents were born in the mid-1880s. Both had four years in school and became factory workers. Shortly before the Second World War, Natalya V. started her studies in a technical field, but they were interrupted by the war. She was evacuated to a small town where she met her first husband, who worked at the same military factory. She was pregnant with his child when her mother persuaded her to return to St Petersburg, where she gave birth to her daughter in 1944. Natalya V. then lived as a single mother for more than ten years and since then has been married several times. At the moment of writing, she was living with her fourth husband, who had a relatively prominent position. She had a successful career, taking a higher education degree and rising from factory worker to become a researcher in a project institute. In 1996, she was retired and working part-time as a cloakroom attendant.

Natalya V.'s story is richer in life events, but otherwise in several respects it is typical of the autobiographies of people born in the 1920s and 1930s. For Soviet citizens born in the 1920s, there was usually no mention of sexuality at home. In the case of Natalya V., the 'silence' is channelled through a religious upbringing. Notwithstanding the new atheist regime, Natalya V.'s mother continued to provide her children with a traditional Christian education. There was little physical contact in the family:

> Mother was the head of the family – a Petersburg family, kind but strict and demanding ... My father somehow went unnoticed in our family, he was a man of few words, who hardly took part in our education, but loved us. I was his favourite, he often patted me on the head and called me not by name, but *dochenka* [my little daughter] ... Mother was religious and tried to raise us in accordance with the Christian commandments. Mother was restrained in caresses, she patted and kissed us only on the head. We did not dare to lie, steal, be lazy, misbehave towards elderly people, go to strangers' apartments or go playing in the yard without permission. In the room there was a picture with

the face of Jesus, and mother said: 'He sees everything'. I looked at the little god from different corners of the room, and everywhere he looked directly at me.

(Natalya V. (1), higher education, born 1923)

Natalya V. and her sisters had to sleep with their hands on the blanket, and were not allowed to stay in bed while awake. She emphasises that she did not see naked men, except small boys in the *bania*. 'But in the *bania* they did not make any impression on me, although I probably remembered their well-proportioned bodies.' Her knowledge and experience of the other sex came from children's games. 'When I was five I saw a small boy without trousers, perhaps that was the reason [that I once asked my mother to transform me into a boy]. The sight made a strong impression on me, I felt shame and some inexplicable feeling.' The same feeling occurred at eight years, when she felt another child's hand between her legs during a game of hide-and-seek, or when she saw animals copulate.

CHANNELS OF SEXUAL KNOWLEDGE IN THE GENERATION OF SILENCE

Natalya V.'s biography describes several situations characterised by an inexplicable sense of 'shame, and something else'. In the relationship between adults and children, and later between spouses and lovers, sexuality was for this generation usually something unmentionable. Of this generation, about 40 per cent thought it was either very or rather difficult to talk about sex with their partner. And one-fifth thought it had become easier to talk about it during the last five years! In the following two generations the numbers of those finding it difficult to talk about sex are less than 30 per cent and less than 15 per cent, respectively.[30]

More typically for the generation of silence in Russia (as well as in Finland and several other European countries), children received their first knowledge about sex mainly from peer groups. The children who provided information were, in the Soviet context, neighbours in the shared *kommunalka* apartments, playmates in the yard, cousins in the countryside, and children at summer pioneer camps. The stories of childhood sex games are often set in the countryside, where the children spend the summer at their grandparents' place, or in small provincial towns where Leningrad children were evacuated for several years during the siege of the city. One woman (no. 6, born 1937) describes how, when the village girls at the *dacha* 'played "marriage" in the *banya*, the "husband" commanded: *lozhis, bliad!* [lie down, you whore!]'

The second main way of acquiring information was just by keeping one's eyes and ears open. Once, Natalya V. overheard two men talking. 'One of them says, "*Vse liudy kak liudy, a ia kak kh.. na bliude* [All people are like people but I'm like a dick on a dish]".' Taking the expression literally, she tried for a long time to picture herself like this.[31]

In this generation, the ways and forms of childhood sexual knowledge in Russia resemble those of other traditional societies – for instance, Finland at the same time period, but also Victorian England of the late nineteenth century. In his account of how sexual information was obtained in Victorian England, Peter Gay describes the very same principal sources of knowledge as those which characterise the Soviet period: peer groups, and following the doings of adults or animals.[32]

The biggest difference between the Soviet Union and Finland is that for Soviet people the period of no, or only very diffuse, knowledge continued, especially for women, later into the lifecycle. The women from St Petersburg were over 18 years old in some cases (nos 4, 5 and 9), whereas the Finns tell about being 14 or 15 when first finding out about child-making and birth.[33]

> In my time neither the parents nor school gave us any kind of information on questions of love, sex and even hygiene ... My naivety in these questions was ridiculous and actually stupid. Now it is probably hard to believe that before 20 I did not know where children are born from – I thought it was from the behind.
> (Woman (5), higher education, born 1937)

> I learned how children are born when I was 18, from a girlfriend. I was horrified. I did not believe her. I understood that they are not found in cabbageheads [the Russian equivalent of the stork or the gooseberry bush], I had seen pregnant women, but I had never thought about how she came to have the baby there. After that I could not look at my parents without disgust, especially at my father, when I imagined what they are doing. And you can imagine – they were doing it in a room of 16 square metres and with two adult daughters!
> (Woman (9), nursery school attendant, born 1946)

The biggest difference from the situation in Victorian England is that, in addition to the main ways of acquiring sexual knowledge – via peer groups and curiosity – Soviet reality provided almost nothing, except by practice alone. Victorian society had, by contrast, an urban culture of 'erotic education'. Peter Gay mentions prostitutes, fashion, artistic and bohemian milieus that provided (men, at least) with erotic and sexual information.[34] In Soviet Russia, the public arena was devoid of such features.

THE JOYS OF ART: MAUPASSANT AND MICHELANGELO

The generation of silence was also the first to grow up in the educational framework of *kulturnost* developed by Stalinism. Selected readings, manners and a certain general education were systematically taught to all Soviet citizens, and especially the first generation of urban dwellers. The result reflected in the autobiographies is that, for working class girls, and for both sexes from the educated classes, crucial impressions were obtained from fiction: 'The little I knew I either read in books – and I loved to read and read much – or from my observations of adults or animals' (Woman (5), higher education, born 1937).

It was especially French novels from the previous century which provided female Soviet culture with information and ideals about love:[35]

> Secretly, during the interval, we read Maupassant ... and Kuprin ... they haunted us and attracted with something unknown and enigmatic.
> (Woman (6), higher education, born 1937)

> My first acquaintance with love happened in childhood, when every day I could hear my parents calling each other by tender names, and I saw how they hugged and kissed cheek to cheek. [Such sensuality was, according to this author herself, exceptional for those times] ... In later years I learned about love mainly from books. An especially strong impression was left in my unconscious by the books of Guy de Maupassant.
> (Woman (3), higher education, born 1926)

> Real expressions of human feelings were to be searched for in the novels of Emile Zola, Stendhal, Jorge Amado and Gabriel Garcia Marquez, Françoise Sagan and other Western authors.
> (Man (35), archaeologist and artist, born 1945)

> When I was 18, I did not have the slightest idea of how children are born and what spouses do in bed. Somehow all that went by me, I was not at all interested in it ... I learned how children are born at the age of 19 from literature. In one novel by [Theodore] Dreiser it was depicted in detail. And I was very suprised, I thought it happened in a totally different way, that's how stupid I was!
> (Woman (4), unqualified worker, born 1935)

Again, a comparison with Victorian England is appropriate. Soviet youth in the 1950s actually read the very same French novels that English youth had read in the 1880s, containing, among other things, mentions of menstruation that came as a shock for readers of both historical epochs. For women, the onset of menstruation was often the first big confrontation with the problem of not knowing.

No women, and only two men of this generation, mention reading (popularised) scientific books about sexuality. One of them describes wartime, when he spent his years from 18 to 22 working up to twelve hours each day in a military factory in Leningrad:

No time for girls, although there were many of them working there ... My 'sexual development' was limited to listening to the stories of the experienced guys about their successes and failures in love, learning foul language (on which Master Vedov even gave production orders), and the book *Man and Woman* [by Shchukin] – which by the way was really vulgar – which I saw at a neighbour's house.

(Man (25), mathematician, born 1924)

In addition to information from fiction, the men (but again no women) also recalled looking at and distributing pictures. Again, these came from the legitimate high culture of the Stalin period.

My ideal of femininity was built on classical ideals. Looking through an album with works by Michelangelo, I was impressed by the sculpture 'Night' on his grave. I copied her several times during one school lesson or another, and even on demand; I had great success. I still remember the expression of voluptuous exhaustion on her face. Then came the time of romantic love, I wandered around in the halls of the Hermitage; once during the winter holidays I fell in love with a portrait of a lady with very strange eyes, they seemed to look at me persistently and tenderly, and as the portrait was quite small and hung in a hallway, this created an intimate atmosphere. I was for a long time infatuated with this look.

(Man (36), archeologist and artist, born 1949)

One man tells an exceptional story of how he got hold of erotic pictures. During the war, he lived with his grandparents in a small village that was eventually occupied by the Germans. They threw out heaps of books from libraries, pedagogical institutes and schools on the streets and yards:

That way I got free access (in 1941) to literature of all genres and directions. True, the Bolshevik regime had severed the scope of themes and writers a Soviet person could get hold of, but I still managed to read a lot that would have been out of reach if not for the war – from Maupassant and Boccaccio to a leaflet by Professor Shchukin called *Man and Woman in Sexual Life*.

(Man (28), higher education, born 1932)

Again, this level of printed information parallelled Victorian England for its content, but was much smaller in scale.

Thus the experiences of the generation of silence give some validation to the sensationalist part of the 'two-sided' argument: the claim that Soviet Russia during Stalin belonged to one of the cultures in world history that knew the least about sexuality.

I was sexually close to a woman [for the first time] only after the army. She was twelve or fifteen years older than me, somehow dogged by bad luck, unhappy and alone, and I felt sorry for her ... We undressed, I was even more ashamed than she ... How would I know what should be done and how to behave, since I had evaded even talks about amorous escapades during leave from the army. They were bragging and cynical. That hurt me.

When I had finished my first try unsuccessfully, I was ashamed to learn from my woman that I had gone for the wrong hole ... I simply needed serious knowledge about sex, but that was nowhere to be found. Once I got hold of a semi-underground photocopy of a translation of an English author. But he never allowed himself to leave the academic world for reality.

(Man (30), unqualified worker, born 1936)

We can take a last example of a traumatic first sexual experience by returning to Natalya V. As a teenager, she describes herself as an active, outgoing girl, who did well in school and was socially active. But at the same time, she had 'sharp experiences of the feeling of shame' concerning everything that had to do with romance, beginning with kissing. In 1940, Natalya V. attended a military training camp in Leningrad. Her trainer arranged to sleep in the same room as her, and had forced sex with her. Natalya V. was so ashamed and surprised that she 'froze'. 'It did not hurt, but I did not like him and even found his thick lips disgusting ... I could not look at him in the morning, I was so ashamed. I felt empty and dirty.'

THE SPLIT GENERATION OF LEARNED IGNORANCE

> They say there is no sex in Russia. There is. And I have passed all its hypostases: marriage without sex, sex in marriage without love, and sex in love, but without marriage.
> (Woman (12), head of warehouse department, born 1946)

On the basis of both the shifts in the Soviet regime and the biographical evidence, the generation of silence can be said to expand to include those born immediately after the war. A change arrives with the cohorts born in 1945, whose formative years were the 1960s. Soviet citizens of this period grew up in the liberalised climate after Stalin's death in 1953. A wave of migration into the cities and the increase in material standards also contributed to changes in sexual life and youth culture, as Kon shows that all Soviet surveys of the 1960s indicate. But, although abortions were allowed in 1955, a more liberal family law had to wait for over a decade. One of the reasons is supposed to be that

Nikita Khrushchev himself had participated in the making of the repressive 1944 law.[36] Post-Stalin sexual policy was, therefore, a gradual opening-up rather than a complete break. This led to one of the biggest contemporary cultural divisions between the West and Eastern Europe: their different 'sixties'. The Soviet *shestidesiatniki* were a distinct political generation, representing the (eventually failed) attempt at socialism with a human face. But they are not remembered for any wider public discussion of youth, sex and gender, like that taking place during and after the Western sixties.[37]

Instead, the Soviet 'sexual sixties' meant some limited debate in journals of the early 1960s, the renaissance of sex research (in the form of questionnaires) and the development of the field of so-called sexopathological research,[38] of some sexual therapy, and of pedagogical advice on the proper upbringing of boys and girls. The word 'sex' itself also first became widely used at this time. True, the newspaper articles of the period mostly continued to prefer *intimnye otnosheniia* (intimate relations).[39] But nevertheless the word *seks* came to be used alongside the traditional popular Russian expressions for intercourse, such as *trachanie* and *ebanie*. This is also pointed out in one autobiography:

> In a certain way I agree with the opinion that 'we had no sex', as there was no such word as 'sex'. The whole of Russia managed with other simple, everyday, life words. And I still do not quite understand why it is totally decent to say *zanimaius' seksom* [I have sex], *zanimius' polovym aktom* [I have intercourse] or *vstupal v polovuiu svjaz* [I engaged in sexual intercourse] ... while the same meaning [this action as a verb or a noun] expressed in Russian, beginning with *e* or *io*, is seen as indecent.
>
> (Man (31), worker with higher education)

Somewhat paradoxically, then, 'sex' was actually introduced, even if reluctantly, into Russian society in the Soviet prime time, the Brezhnevian 1960s.[40] The term carried with it a Western connotation, an implicit comparison with the development during and after the sexual revolution in the West. But the main emphasis of the Soviet 'expert advice' on sex was to warn against the dangers of masturbation, and the risk of getting venereal diseases. Still more significantly, the Soviet experts did not constitute the kind of broad expert systems that could 'pull' towards active reflection on sexual identities.[41] By contrast, in the West, psychotherapy, marriage counselling and various forms of self-help groups started to expand during the early 1970s.

Even the hesitant and moralising post-Stalin public discussion of sexuality regularly provoked counter-attacks and calls for censorship. I therefore propose to call the generation subject to the policy of 'domestication' the generation of learned ignorance. The term 'learned ignorance' is first used by the historian Peter Gay, who contrasts it with sheer lack of knowledge. Mere innocence, he stresses, is an easier condition to cure, for it 'may always be alleviated by pertinent new information'.[42] This was the case for many members of the generation of silence. Learned ignorance is in a way more resistant, giving rise to lifelong false convictions. Gay's main example for Victorian England is masturbation, which was seen as being seriously harmful. The same anxiety over, and disinformation about, teenage masturbation existed in the Soviet Union after the 1960s.

This is how one man found an old issue of the magazine *Sem'ia i shkola* (School and family), talking about masturbation:

> One article was about teenage masturbation; only then did I learn the name of the thing I was doing. I understood and became scared, because the article said that masturbation has negative effects on the body. It suggested teenagers should go in for sports more, or collect something, shortly, to distract oneself from the harmful deed.
> (Man (43), theatre director, born 1968)

Another example of 'learned ignorance' is the way in which Soviet doctors told young women that the risks of terminating a first pregnancy with abortion were greater than with later pregnancies. Otherwise, the (very real) health risks connected with induced abortions as they were performed in the USSR were understated, and some women even believed abortions were good for the body.

Once again, my attaching a label to a generation seems to be biased towards the experiences of educated women. The Soviet intelligentsia – and among the intelligentsia, the girls more than the boys – were subject to Soviet (dis)information propaganda, since they read professional medical and pedagogical journals. At the other extreme from this kind of 'learned ignorance' is the autobiography of a male from a poor working-class milieu (no. 40, born 1960), in which he describes a dramatically different sexual culture, beginning with sexual initiation through gang rapes in his early teens.[43]

CHANNELS OF SEXUAL KNOWLEDGE IN THE GENERATION OF LEARNED IGNORANCE

In our biographical material, I classified nine women and seven men as belonging to the second generation of learned ignorance. The main channels for acquiring sexual knowledge continue in this generation. A man born in 1968 (no. 43) recalls secretly watching slides from the Hermitage with the neighbourhood girls. Another man, born the same year (no. 44), tells us he learned about the world mainly through the library of his friend, where he found Balzac, Zola, Stendhal, Maupassant, and later Walter Scott and Dumas.[44]

Against this background of continuity, the autobiographies differ from those of the previous generation in three respects. First, for most autobiographies, obtaining sexual knowledge is no longer an event. On the one hand, family sex education had become slightly more common.[45] On the other hand, a few popularised books about sexuality had become available. The only mention of getting sexual knowledge by way of an 'event' is connected to this kind of publication. Three women, born in 1946 (no. 11), 1958 (no. 17) and 1964 (no. 19), all mention a handbook in gynaecology as being the main source of their knowledge of sex. Still, for the young women from St Petersburg in the first post-war generation, the problem is not learning about sex, which is gradually becoming more of a self-evident routine. Instead, the problem is whether to get married as a virgin. Interestingly, this is not mentioned by any of the older women. This is probably due both to shortage of men after the war and to the changing social norms with regard to premarital sex, which gave rise to misunderstandings and conflicts between dating men and women. Having intercourse only after marriage had been obvious behaviour for the older generation, but now became more a matter of negotiation. Whereas almost 50 per cent of the men and almost 60 per cent of the women from the generation of silence thought that sexual intercourse should not happen before the couple were planning to get married or were already married, the numbers fall in the next generation to almost 30 per cent for the men and less than 40 per cent for the women.[46]

The second theme articulated only in the second generation is homosexuality, described by one woman and one man. The latter especially complains about disinformation and lack of anything that could have helped him.

The third distinction is the lack of a common generational experience. The autobiographies of this second generation are more disparate, and could often belong in either the previous generation or the following one. Some autobiographies are written in the style and with the flavour of 'sexual emancipation', humorously relating different sexual adventures. In other accounts, different parts of Natalya V.'s experiences from the previous generation are repeated almost verbatim:

> The atmosphere in our family was always quite puritanical, no 'bodily tenderness' between my parents or with us, the children, no suggestive talks when the children were listening nor too-explicit books and reproductions. Neither did my mother have any 'enlightening' talks with me. The result was that when my period began at the age of 11 I did not know what it was, and where children come from I learned even later, and I am still almost ashamed to kiss my own brother or my father.
> (Woman (17), nurse, born 1958)

> My mother said she could not give any advice, because for her and my grandma it was all dirt and sin. They did not find any pleasure in sex. Even though grandma had seven children and a womanising man.
> (Woman (19), librarian, born 1964)

Similar stories are also found in the autobiographies of Finnish women from the second sexual generation, which Kontula and Haavio-Mannila call that of the 'sexual revolution'. Still, the level of ignorance does seem to me quite unimaginable in a Western European country in the 1980s, when this Russian woman was in her late teens:

> It is typical that I did not have any idea of the actual physical side of love, and neither had I anywhere to learn this from. As I had a sharp feeling of the 'sinfulness' of my hobby [drawing erotic pictures], I hid it carefully. I promised myself to stop all this, but ... I started again, and so it continued until I got married, and I got married when I was 26 years old. As for masturbation, I did not understand I could have gone into my panties, but caressed myself on the breasts ... Later I read in one of the many 'sexual encyclopedias' that there is nothing wrong about that. But I thought otherwise, and all my actions in that direction were accompanied by an enormous feeling of shame.
> (Woman (19), librarian, born 1964)

It is worth noting that this hobby of drawing erotic pictures for herself is not mentioned in any of the Finnish sexual autobiographies.

Thus the forms of acquiring sexual knowledge became more varied, but also more stratified and 'randomly' distributed. You might, or might not, find a handbook of gynaecology at your friend's house, and this created a significant difference in your understanding about sex. You might have access to Western or *samizdat* publications, or not. This adds a further meaning to the 'ignorance' defining these age cohorts. Due to the censoring of public discussion, Soviet people also had very little information about social milieus which were not within immediate reach. In the following example (although written by a man from the third generation), a teenage boy does not know the common word for 'gay':

> I did not know anything about homosexuality ... I read [about it] in the Big Soviet Encyclopedia: 'a sexual perversion' and so on. I did not understand the colloquial word *goluboi* [bugger/gay]. When they were teasing me for being *goluboi* in the army I did not get offended, because I thought that *goluboi* was just a synonym for the word *drugoi* [not like everyone else].
> (Man (43), born 1968)

The generation of 'learned ignorance' can therefore not be called a sexual generation in the strict sense, with shared crucial experiences.[47] It was a 'split' generation, where tradition disappeared, and with it a common understanding – albeit seldom articulated, and differing by class and gender.

THE GENERATION OF ARTICULATION

If we start from the periods of Soviet sexual policy, a third 'sexual generation' could only be expected in the age cohort born after 1972. Their formative years came after the mid-1980s, when both sexual policy and the debate about sexual issues began to be liberalised and Westernised.

However, a certain stylistic and experiential difference is felt already in the autobiographies written by people born after 1965, and growing up in the late Brezhnevian 1970s. With regard to sexuality, both men and women are direct and outspoken. The general tone is ironic, often rather detached. While previous generations described feelings of shame and curiosity, the youngest generation now speaks about 'my libido' (nos 44 and 45). In contrast to the previous disparate generation, the young St Petersburg people showed traces of shared generational experiences. Sexual behaviour continued to change. The average age of first steady dating, which had been eighteen, dropped to below seventeen years. The average age of first intercourse also dropped, becoming about seventeen for young men and about eighteen for women. In this generation, around three-quarters of each sex reported having used various sexual techniques, such as different positions and oral sex.[48] More significantly, sexual knowledge now became articulate, using the terms of popularised sexology and psychology. Sexual knowledge was no longer just 'learning about It', or – for women – whether or not to preserve one's virginity. Instead of 'finding out' traumatically, one woman (no. 21, born 1966) remembers how as a six-year-old she looked for the main four-letter word in the Great Soviet Encyclopaedia and was surprised not to find it. Later, her schoolteacher told the class about sex, which she became happily curious about.

In this generation, the focus is on reflecting one's own sexual tastes and personal aspirations. Thus, separate attention is given to masturbation, one-night-stands, contraceptives, prostitution and homosexuality. I have therefore called this the generation of articulation – this is the generation that consciously started talking about sex.[49] This generation grew up under the impact of Hollywood movies; of Western TV soap operas – notably *Santa Barbara* – which introduced Western discussions of sexual and gender problems such as rape, incest and harassment to the Russian audience; and of Western advertisements with their commercialised sexual images and ads for products such as Tampax.

If we contrast Russian and Finnish youth, their behaviours and attitudes converge. One crucial exception is the gender gap: in Finland, men and women born in the late 1960s report practically identical sexual behaviour, while in Leningrad/St Petersburg the gender gap remained, although it was diminishing. There are also big national differences in the experiences of sexual relations for money or other material reward, which were sharply increasing in Russia. Two of the four male Russian autobiographies mention meetings with prostitutes, while Finnish youth had less experience with prostitutes than did older generations in Finland. The generation of articulation was, of course, also the generation of commercialisation. Indeed, commercialisation and the project of sexual enlightenment were the two driving forces behind the articulation of sexuality.[50]

OPPOSING SHAME

In their autobiographies, men and women of this generation approached sexuality mostly in the context either of 'communication' or of 'pleasure'.[51] For both sexes, marriage or children are only exceptionally seen as a part of sexuality. Approaching sexuality as a field of separate, pleasure-serving issues, many of their stories are about transcending the shame traditionally attributed to the premarital loss of virginity, to masturbation and to homosexuality.

The women now suggest a different relationship to sex. Instead of wanting to get married as virgins, they now describe wanting to get rid of their virginity:

> After finishing school I applied to an institute [of higher education]. I remember that I was terribly weighed down by my viginity, which I had not yet had the opportunity to get rid of. Significantly, I gave the absolutely opposite impression (perhaps I tried to do so very hard) – that of a fallen woman who had tried everything ... Then one beautiful day, and more precisely on the 1st of May, I returned from the demonstration (oh, these obligatory demonstrations!), and when I left the escalator at the metro station I was stopped by a playboy with a moustache, aged 35. He was to become my first man ...
>
> I very much wanted to get rid of my viginity. Why? Well, first of all, as self-confirmation, and then, of course, to finally be able to sleep with V. [with whom she was in love]. I wanted so badly to appear experienced in his eyes!
>
> For that I needed somebody like that [the playboy's] type ... I do not have any special memories. It was practically painless, and there was only a little blood. He turned out to be quite tender and caressing, in one word – no ecstasy, of course, but quite nice.
>
> (Woman (21), higher education, born 1966)

Compared with the intense, shameful and/or devoted descriptions given by older women, this young woman was very matter-of-fact about the whole event. She did not mention the use of contraceptives in her first sexual intercourse, but one man and some of the women of her generation did, in strong contrast to the previous generation, who take up the issue only much later in their life course, after having children and abortions. Neither did this woman want any deeper relations with the man whom she had chosen as her first:

> Our relationship had no future. And I understood it perfectly. But he for some reason saw it differently. The difficulty in getting rid of a man you are fed up with – that's a whole different story, and I learnt that lesson at the very beginning of my way as a woman.
>
> (Woman (21), higher education, born 1966)

The same attitude was adopted by another young woman, who consciously chose a man with extensive sexual experience for her first intercourse. It is also clear she had acquired basic sexual and physiological knowledge well in advance:

> He was stubborn, with an incredibly big ego. His nose and his member were also both incredibly big ... His sexual experience was also very big, and I never regretted that I chose him to be my first man. Having almost finished his medical studies, eight years older than me, experienced, beautiful, clever, sharp – that was what my first should be like. And I never wanted my first to be my one and only.
> (Woman (23), born 1972)

This autobiography provided the only light-hearted sexual memoir written by a woman in my material, identifying her lovers by their astrological signs and praising equal, explorative sexual relationships without plans for further commitment. Another woman (no. 20) also had a selection of lovers, albeit justifying this with a complex idea of 'purification by sin'. There are thus less signs of women's ambivalence to sexuality in these autobiographies. But still, very few young women wrote at all, as compared with both the other generations and the entries to the Finnish autobiographical competition. And the liberated, individualised lifestyle quoted above is presented in a provocative tone, as if building on the assumption that a man-like, completely sexually emancipated woman is different from most traditional women who follow the usual codes of everyday morality and its accompanying shame.

This generation was also the first to write in detail about masturbation. For instance, one woman depicted it as a joyful experience without any need for shame:

> I do not remember the age when I started masturbating. Perhaps in the seventh or eighth grade. It gave me lots of pleasure. I took a volume from the *Thousand and One Nights* off the shelf, found an erotic scene and, reading it several times and pressing my legs together, had an orgasm ... I told the girls at school that I was masturbating without any shame whatsoever. Now I would without doubt not share such private secrets with my women friends. But I think that rich experience of masturbation helped me to have practically no problems in reaching orgasm in my relationship with my husband.
> (Woman (21), higher education, born 1966)

This approving attitude was not unopposed even in the 1990s. One of the leading sexologists, Sergei Golod, described masturbation as psychologically harmful for men (women's masturbation was not mentioned).[52] But Golod was from the older generations. The young men stress, by contrast, either that masturbation is 'nothing to be ashamed of', or that it is something they have now learned not be ashamed of:

> Once in the bathroom I got to know the helpful friend of all men – masturbation. There is nothing shameful in that, because only a sick

person or somebody without any genital functions does not masturbate ... It was an indescribable pleasure.

(Man (44), born 1968)

I would be lying if my story did not include such a phenomenon of teenage life as masturbation. When did it begin with me? It is hard for me to answer that, I only remember I was over ten. The sensation of something forbidden, those were the first feelings that overwhelmed me. But even if I cannot remember the day, where it was, or even the time of year, I clearly remember what happened. I was already familiar with having an erection, but what next? From my experience and the explanations of my [female] cousin, I approximately knew the algorhythm of action. That's why during the first attempt I did not experience anything except for a sweet pain. Enough for today, I decided. Next morning in school was like being tortured. By general opinion (*obshchestvennoe mnenie*). Could it really be written all over my face, are my suddenly sweating hands telling the story of what I did last night?

I had not discussed this [the masturbation] with father and mother. Therefore I started to think through and analyse street jokes and stories, and naturally I came to some kind of conclusions. Strange as it may seem, it was 'The Wall' by Pink Floyd which helped me realise the importance of my new knowledge; it was precisely because of that film that I suddenly stopped seeing what I was doing in such a degrading and disgusting light.

My parents guessed, but did not take any steps to expose me, just limited the quantity of porn magazines, a few of which were lying in the hallway.

(Man (45), born 1974)

Similarly, homosexuality is not only mentioned, but personally related to, in heterosexual autobiographies only from the youngest generation. One of the young men explicitly denied having had any homosexual relationships during his army service. 'My service passed driving trucks, but without any women. I did not notice any homosexual aspirations on my part. I still cannot understand: how could you do it with a man, in the arse? Of course everybody has his own peculiarities (*zamorochki*).'

Another man told a quite remarkable story of a Soviet school class protesting against a teacher who displayed homophobic attitudes:

> Although our class was divided into groups according to living area, we were all friends with each other and had sympathy for one another's sorrows. Thus, when the history teacher called one classmate something much worse than 'gay' (*goluboi*), notwithstanding the shattered relations, everybody stood up and left the room. Of course, from

today's perspectives provided by a university education, one could attribute any kind of motivation for the event, but at the time it was great.

(Man (45), born 1974)

This account is not very clear – does 'one another's sorrows' allude to the boy being gay? What is another 'kind of motivation' a university education could offer – a psychoanalytical explanation? But the main message is clearly permissive. The same man mentioned attending gay meeting places, *geiiovskie tusovki*, together with his girlfriend. This is of course not to say that male homosexuality had ceased to be socially taboo, or that it was easy to adopt a homosexual lifestyle.

But again, the notion of 'generation' deserves some question marks, because this process of articulation in many ways concerned everybody, not just the new Russian youth. Our autobiographies were written in 1996, ten years after the beginning of *perestroika* with its larger availability of contraceptives, pornography and more-or-less educative books on sex. The majority of our autobiographies mentioned reading explicit printed sexual information for the first time in the 1980s, or even later. Thus, for one young man born in 1968 (no. 43), it was during one dramatic day in 1995 that reading a novel by James Baldwin – whose writings had been unacceptable during the Soviet period – led him to a re-evaluation of his previous love life and his coming-out as a homosexual.

Let us return to Natalya V. to get another example of the change this introduced. Today, Natalya V., regrets her complete lack of knowledge and sex education. She even says, with respect to her first experience of forced sex, that:

> If I had known about virginity, I would have behaved otherwise ... I read my first information on sex between newly-weds in a gynecologist's waiting room at the age of 60. During my whole life I had read only one special leaflet, 'Women's hygiene'.
>
> (Woman (1), born 1923)

Natalya V. today is an exceptionally happy retired woman, financially well off and luckily married to her fourth husband. During the last years, she has been reading psychoanalytical literature – she mentions Freud and Jung – which probably influences her ways of remembering her childhood, quoted earlier in this text (as, for example, in her way of establishing a potential causal relation between seeing a little boy's genitals and her desire to be a boy). The psychoanalytical influence is perhaps also the reason why her autobiography has the most detailed accounts of childhood sexuality of all the women of her generation, although similar memories were not uncommon for the other women either.

CONCLUSION

We have distinguished here between three generations of sexual culture in the Soviet Union: the generation of silence, with the formative years being the late 1930s to 1960, the generation of learned ignorance, and the generation of articulation. The Russian sexual revolution can be said to have happened in two phases: the first as a behavioural change due to urbanisation and rising living standards; and the second, public revolution, taking place ten years later.

During the 1960s and 1970s there emerged a variety of sexual behaviours and ethics. Not only did the gap between the official ideology and private behaviour widen, but there emerged different 'semi-public' spheres of Soviet sexual milieu. This impression is confirmed by other informal accounts of the Soviet Union during late socialism. The physician Mikhail Stern talked about a 'sexual revolution' happening in the late 1970s: 'The current Soviet "sexual revolution" is not the result of forced urbanisation, but rather the manifestation of a search for natural and normal forms of sexual expression. So far these preliminary attempts have usually been characterised by cynicism and sexual license.'[53] Elena Zdravomyslova has recently described this period as a time of faked sexuality, *litsemernaia seksualnost'*.[54]

Far from presenting one stereotyped homogeneous Soviet experience, the autobiographies show evidence of quite different conceptions of sexuality that existed simultaneously, inside the same generation. These differences sometimes achieved the point of non-communication between different classes and sexual lifestyles, a lack of mutual understanding that is still at the core of the Russian cultural conflicts. They are partly generational and partly cognitive, due to different social milieus and varying access to printed sources. Some milieus in the second generation have experiences similar to those of the first generation, while others were already 'Westernised' in the 1960s.

In conclusion, we can speculate about the different structure and dynamics of the sexual revolution in East and West – in our research, between St Petersburg and Russia on the one hand, and Finland on the other. In Finland the 1960s gave rise to a public discourse, which led to state and school programmes of sexual education that consciously changed traditional attitudes to sexuality. Generalising, we can say that general ideology in Finland changed before sexual practice. In Soviet Russia, the sexual revolution – again generalising – can be said to have happened the other way around: sexual practice changed much before public ideology. In the late 1970s, many people were already living as though the sexual revolution had happened. But its spoken articulation, both private and public, only began a decade later, right at the end of the Soviet era. Indeed, in Russia today, the new public ideology is only now in the making.

Notes

Numbers in parentheses in this chapter identify the writers of the autobiographies, generally following the principle of oldest to youngest, so that the oldest woman is no.

1 and the youngest no. 24, while the oldest man is no. 25 and the youngest no. 45. The translations are mine. An earlier version of this chapter forms Chapter 6 of my book, *The Man Question* (2000).

1 Marina Liborakina, personal communication, Helsinki, April 1997.
2 Anna Rotkirch, *The Man Question* (Department of Social Policy, University of Helsinki, 2000).
3 Jukka Gronow *et al.*, 'Cultural inertia and social change in Russia. Distributions by gender and age group', paper, Department of Sociology, University of Helsinki, 1997.
4 Ekaterina Lachova, 'Vse my vhodim v "gruppu riska"', *Nezavisimaia Gazeta*, 10 April 1997.
5 Masha Gessen, 'Sex in the media and the birth of the sex media in Russia', in Ellen Berry (ed.), *Postcommunism and the Body Politic* (New York University Press, New York, 1995), 197–228; Igor Kon, *The Sexual Revolution in Russia. From the Age of the Czars to Today* (Free Press, New York, 1995).
6 Kon, *The Sexual Revolution in Russia*.
7 Osmo Kontula and Elina Haavio-Mannila, *Sexual Pleasures: Enhancement of Sex Life in Finland, 1971–1992* (Dartmouth, Aldershot, 1995); Elina Haavio-Mannila, Osmo Kontula and Anna Rotkirch, *Moments of Passion: Sexual Autobiographies from Three Generations* (Palgrave, London, 2002).
8 The total number of respondents was 2,081: Gronow *et al.*, 'Cultural inertia and social change in Russia'.
9 Kontula and Haavio-Mannila, *Sexual Pleasures*, and Elina Haavio-Mannila, J. P. Roos and Osmo Kontula, 'Repression, revolution and ambivalence. The sexual life of three generations in Finland', *Acta sociologica*, 39 (1996), 409–30.

The biographical material consists of 44 autobiographies (24 women and 22 men, born between 1923 and 1973) about love and sexuality, collected in St Petersburg during 1996 by the project 'Mosaic life. Upbringing, gender and sexuality in Finland, the Baltic countries and St Petersburg', directed by J. P. Roos. Middle-class authors with higher education are predominant, but there are also 16 autobiographies by workers (the criteria for workers were no education after school or only vocational training, and low income). Four biographies have the search for a homosexual identity as their central theme. Four of the authors have never had a sexual relationship, 13 have had over 20 sexual partners. The length of the autobiographies varies from 2 to about 70 pages.

10 Non-academic monographs on the late Soviet Union include Mikhail Stern, *Sex in the USSR* (Times Books, New York, 1979); Mark Popovsky, *Tretii Lishnii. On, Ona i Sovetskii Rezhim* [The Third Wheel: He, She and the Soviet Regime] (Overseas Publ. Interchange Ltd, London, 1985) (all critically presented in Kon, *The Sexual Revolution in Russia*, 279). Academic monographs about the same period include Igor Kon and James Riordan (eds), *Sex in Russian Society* (Indiana University Press, Bloomington, 1993); Kon, *Sex in Russian Society*; Sergei I Golod, *XX Vek i Tendentsii v Seksualanykh Otnosheniiakh v Rossii* [The 20th Century and Trends in Sexual Relations in Russia] (Aleteia, St Petersburg, 1996); Laurie Essig, *Queer in Russia: a Story of Sex, Self and the Other* (Duke University Press, Durham, 1999); and Rotkirch, *The Man Question*. Hilary Pilkington, *Russia's Youth and its Culture: A Nation's Constructors and Constructed* (Routledge, London, 1994) partly discusses Soviet youth and sexual morals.

For separate articles, see especially Gessen, 'Sex in the media'; Anna Temkina, 'Sexual scripts in women's biographies and the construction of sexual pleasure', in Marianne Liljeström, Arja Rosenholm and Irina Savkina (eds), *Models of Self: Russian Women's Autobiographical Texts* (Kikimora, Helsinki, 2000); Elina Haavio-Mannila and Anna Rotkirch, 'Generational and gender differences in sexual life in St Petersburg

and urban Finland', *Yearbook of Population Research in Finland*, XXXIV, *Population Trends in the Baltic Sea Area* (Väestöliitto, Helsinki, 1998).
11 Kon, *The Sexual Revolution in Russia*, 51–107, 267; see below for a more detailed description of each period.
12 *Ibid.*, 109
13 *Ibid.*; Popovsky, *Tretii Lishnii*, and Stern, *Sex in the USSR.*
14 Kon, *The Sexual Revolution in Russia*, 269, 212.
15 Stern, *Sex in the USSR*, 278.
16 Kon, *The Sexual Revolution in Russia*, 86.
17 Vladimir Shlapentokh, *Public and Private Life of the Soviet People. Changing Values in Post-Stalin Russia* (Oxford University Press, Oxford, 1989).
18 Boris Groys, 'Den ryska filosofins ansikte. Från Tjaadajev till Marx' [The face of Russian philosophy. From Chaadaev to Marx], *Ord & Bild*, 4 (1994), 21–30.
19 Yet another explanation for this kind of 'two-sided argument' can be found in the pragmatic goals of Russian sexologists. The position of Igor Kon and his followers in the Soviet Union resembled that of all sex research pioneers. For example, in the American 1950s the most effective argument adopted by Kinsey was that sex education could not destroy an innocence that anyway no longer existed (Gail Hawkes, *A Sociology of Sex and Sexuality* (Open University Press, Buckingham, 1996), 65). Similarly, in the Soviet 1960s, the main strategy the scholars could use was 'hard' scientific facts. The system was perhaps privately criticised for creating uncivilised, 'ugly' sex. The best way of potentially reforming the system might have been to show that Soviet sexual behaviour was actually something 'normal'.
20 This is not to deny that I am myself constantly caught by the two-sided argument. Reading the sexual autobiographies from St Petersburg, it first seemed to me – born in the 1960s and raised in a milieu of early, explicit and extensive sex enlightenment – that of all the civilisations on earth the Soviet Union must have been the least informed about sexual matters: cut away from agrarian traditions and nature, and without urban forms of knowledge transmission. Then I re-read excerpts from the sexual stories of Finnish people born in the 1920s and 1930s (Kontula and Haavio-Mannila, *Sexual Pleasures*), and was surprised by all the similarities. Then I analysed the accounts of sexual violence in the Russian texts and found them unique; and so on.
21 Kontula and Haavio-Mannila, *Sexual Pleasures*.
22 Barbara Clements, 'The birth of the New Soviet Woman', in Abbott Gleason, Peter Kenez and Richard Stites (eds), *Bolshevik Culture. Experiment and Order in the Russian Revolution* (Indiana University Press, Bloomington, 1985), 220–37; Gail W. Lapidus, *Women in Soviet Society: Equality, Development, and Social Change* (University of California Press, Berkeley, 1978).
23 Beatrice Farnsworth, 'Village women experience the revolution', in Gleason *et al.* (eds), *Bolshevik Culture*, 238–60.
24 Lapidus, *Women in Soviet Society*.
25 Alexandr Etkind, *Eros Nevozmozhnogo. Istoriia Psikhoanaliza v SSSR* [Eros of the Impossible: Pyschoanalysis in Russia] (Progress, Moscow, 1994).
26 Marianne Liljeström, *Emanciperade till underordning. Det sovjetiska könssystemets uppkomst och diskursiva reproduktion* [Emancipated to Subordination: The Emergence and Discursive Reproduction of the Soviet Gender System] (Åbo Akademis förlag, Turku, 1995).
27 Gronow *et al.*, 'Cultural inertia and social change', 290, 227–8 and 237–8. The age cohorts of the survey do not coincide completely with my periodisation of generations. The statistics I quote refer to people born 1922–41, 1942–61 and 1962–78, whereas I divide the biographies at 1945 and 1965. Therefore I do not take the decimals of the statistical percentages, but try to convey the overall generational differences evident from the survey material.

28 Valery Golofast, 'Three levels of biographical narratives', in Viktor Voronkov and Elena Zdravomyslova (eds), *Biographical Perspectives on Post-Socialist Societies* (Centre for Independent Social Research, St Petersburg, 1997), 140–3.
29 This can be interpreted as supporting the observation made by Mikhail Stern (*Sex in the USSR*, 199): 'Although sex may be a taboo subject among "respectable" people in the Soviet Union, those people who live on the fringes of society, who think of themselves as belonging to "the lower depths", talk about sex very openly and naturally.' This is also confirmed by one male autobiography (no. 29, born 1935) describing an extremely poor and promiscuous childhood. However, the biographies are too few to make any stronger statements about the 'loose behaviour' of the poor working class, which of course is also a prevalent social stereotype in Russia just as in the West.
30 Gronow et al., 'Cultural inertia and social change', 234–5.
31 One Estonian woman of the same generation (but born 1926 during pre-Soviet times) also interprets literally what she heard men saying about them 'making children'. She is astonished and wonders how these huge male hands can produce intricate small baby ears and fingers, and tells her mother she also wants to learn how to make children. The mother slaps her face, silencing her daughter.
32 Peter Gay, *The Bourgeois Experience: Victoria to Freud. The Education of the Senses, I* (Oxford University Press, Oxford, 1994).
33 Kontula and Haavio-Mannila, *Sexual Pleasures*, 163.
34 Gay, *The Education of the Senses*, 334–5.
35 Cf. Yelizaveta Lagunova, 'The educated Russian woman: Dominantes of destiny', in *Feminist Theory and Practice: East–West* (St Petersburg Centre for Gender Issues, St Petersburg, 1995), 115–21.
36 Lapidus, *Women in Soviet Society*.
37 That the Western 1960s debate was, at its core, about youth, with sexual and a little later women's liberation derived from the new generation's rejection of previous double moral standards, is demonstrated in the case of Sweden by Lena Lennerhed, *Frihet att njuta. Sexualdebatten i Sverige på 1960-talet* [Freedom to Enjoy: The Sexual Debate in Sweden in the 1960s] (Norstedts, Stockholm, 1994).
38 The decline and revival of Soviet sexopathology is well illustrated by the quantity of books published: 52 from 1917 to 1936, only 5 from 1937 to 1960, followed by 15 in the 1960s and 61 in the 1970s. (Before 1917, 126 Russian books on sexual research were published: Kon, *The Sexual Revolution in Russia*, 91)
39 Earlier, during the egalitarian and collectivistic ideology of the 1920s, *intimnost* had been the provocative word, considered to be degenerate and bourgeois. It was taken into use only during Stalinism. Svetlana Boym, *Common Places: Mythologies of Everyday Life in Russia* (Harvard University Press, Cambridge, Mass., 1994).
40 This seems to coincide with the spread of this foreign word in Finland too: Kontula and Haavio-Mannila, *Sexual Pleasures*, 63 and 68.
41 Kon, *The Sexual Revolution in Russia*, 85–106; cf. Peggy Watson, 'Eastern Europe's silent revolution: Gender', *Sociology*, 27, 3 (1993), 471–87.
42 Gay, *The Education of the Senses*, 278–327.
43 In Finland, by contrast, children from academic and educated families seem to have got more sexual enlightenment than children from workers' families and, especially, agrarian families, where sexuality was never mentioned (Kontula and Haavio-Mannila, *Sexual Pleasures*). However, this generalisation does not fit the experience of girls – as in Soviet Russia, girls from the upper classes were sometimes kept in the deepest ignorance.
44 The popularity of nineteenth-century art and literature is also described in the following anecdote of the 1970s, quoted in Stern, *Sex in the USSR*, 81:

A police patrol comes upon two lovers kissing in a Moscow street. One of the officers confronts the couple:
'Who taught you to carry on like that?'
  'Maupassant.'
'Sergeant! Run a check on this Maupassant fellow and bring him down to the station!'

45 The percentages who had *not* received any sexual information in their childhood home declined from almost 90 per cent in the previous generation to less than 80 per cent in this one, although information had still been given 'sufficiently' to less than 5 per cent in both generations. Here a decisive change occurs only for the next generation, where 'only' about half had no sex information in the family, and about 15 per cent sufficient: Gronow *et al.*, 'Cultural inertia and social change', 225.
46 *Ibid.*, 246–7.
47 Anna Rotkirch, 'Women's sexual biographies from two generations. A first comparison between Finland and Russia', in Viktor Voronkov and Elena Zdravomyslova (eds), *Biographical Perspectives*, 205–11.
48 Haavio-Mannila and Rotkirch, 'Generational and gender differences'.
49 Cf. Katerina Gerasimova, 'The verbalisation of sexuality: talks about sex with partners', in Voronkov and Zdramvomyslova, *Biographical Perspectives*, 215–21.
50 Marina Liborakina, *Obretenie Sily: Rossiiskii Opyt. Puti Preodoleniia Diskriminatsii v Otnoshenii Zhenshchin (Kulturnoe Izmerenie)* [Empowerment: The Russian Experience – Ways of Overcoming Discrimination against Women (a Cultural Dimension)] (Tshero, Moscow, 1996).
51 Anna Temkina, 'Sexual scripts'.
52 Golod, *XX vek*, 130.
53 Stern, *Sex in the USSR*, 282.
54 Elena Zdravomyslova, 'Hypocritical sexuality of the late Soviet period: sexual knowledge and sexual ignorance', in Sue Webber and Ilkka Liikanen (eds), *Education and Civic Culture in Post-Communist Countries* (London, Palgrave, 2001), 151–67.

6

FAMILY MODELS AND TRANSGENERATIONAL INFLUENCES

Grandparents, Parents and Children in Moscow and Leningrad from the Soviet to the Market Era

Victoria Semenova and Paul Thompson

The transformations from a Soviet to a market society, which had begun in Russia in the 1990s, raised a fundamental issue for the analysis of social change, which is our concern in this chapter: what happens to men and women when basic social structures and institutions, which have hitherto provided meaning and order in their lives, begin to change radically, fragment, even vanish from view? How do men and women develop new systems of meaning and order to make sense of their changing world? How far do they wish, or are they able, to make new kinds of life choices? And, in particular, to what extent do their own private resources, through their personal and family experiences, either constrain or encourage their adaptation to radical change?

We have discussed our sources – which combine a substantial survey sample with over fifty in-depth life-story interviews – elsewhere.[1] The theoretical perspective which we share is that the shaping and socialisation of human energy takes place primarily through the family. Hence, in understanding how men and women respond to radical change, one of the principal resources on which they are likely to draw are the models offered by their parents and grandparents. It should be emphasised, too, that we do not see familial influences as simple and unilinear. Families typically offer a choice of models, which can be drawn from a mother or a father, or a grandparent, or from other kin too. And, sometimes, parents especially may be taken as negative models of what not to do with one's own life. In each family the interpretation needs to be drawn out from a complex of subtle in-depth information, such as we have been fortunate to be able to use here. Nevertheless, we did start from the hypothesis that forms of childrearing would be crucial to occupational behaviour as an adult; and that – just as one of us had concluded from a comparative study of fishing communities in four different cultures – the ability to be adaptable or creative in adult work would be related to a childrearing which encouraged early independence rather than placing the primary emphasis on discipline and obedience.[2]

On the other hand, the range of choices possible is always shaped by wider social structures at a particular moment in time. Tamara Hareven has shown this especially cogently in her three-generational life-story study of the workforce of the giant textile Amoskeag mills at Manchester in New England, *Family Time and Industrial Time*.[3] Her Amoskeag study spans both periods of boom and the hard times of the Great Depression of 1929–33, a period of national social crisis in North America which can be compared in its impact with that of the final years of the Soviet system in Russia. Indeed, Glen Elder has demonstrated through his re-analysis of the longitudinal studies of cohorts born in the 1920s in the industrial city of Oakland, California, how such an overall crisis, in which all social classes suffered from unemployment or reduced working hours, cuts in pay, and material losses, can leave its mark for a lifetime on a whole generation.[4]

It is certainly possible to see in the Russia of the 1990s a psychic situation comparable with that described of Germany in the 1930s, when the combination of economic collapse, inflation and instability transformed the psychological mood prevailing in society, with individuals perceiving the situation as one of mounting chaos, driving many to the point of hopelessness and depression. There were, however, crucial differences between the impact of the Great Depression and responses to it, and the more recent crisis in Russia. In the Depression, the most spectacular sign of the crisis was unemployment, which shot up to a third of the workforce, while in Russia unemployment was still under 2 per cent in 1992. Although unemployment did begin to rise slowly thereafter, it was still below 10 per cent in 1996.[5] The catastrophic slide in living standards – which was 40 per cent over the first three months of 1992 alone – was not related to losing jobs, but to lower pay rates at state enterprises in combination with soaring inflation.

The popular response was also significantly different. Certainly in both instances many people looked for other work, thought of moving, tried to reduce their needs, and moved back towards home production, making their own clothes, growing and bottling fruit and vegetables. But one difference was the Russian enthusiasm, not just for home production, but for using this as a basis for bartering or sale. The spirit in which people looked for work was also distinctive. In the Depression in many parts of Western Europe and North America, because men had lost their jobs, it was the married women and children, who in the middle- and 'respectable' working-class households had until then stayed at home, who broke social taboos by seeking work to fill the resulting gap in income; or alternatively whole families migrated to other regions where work was known to be available. Both patterns clearly reflected direct responses to labour-market opportunities. In the 1990s in Russia, on the other hand, there was little geographical labour migration in process, and wives had been working throughout the Soviet period. Indeed, among Russian women in the 1990s, so far from a shift into the labour market, there was a growth in the numbers reported as housewives, rising by 1993 to one in every eight women. Hence, the main question for both men and women who wanted to maintain family income was not to seek out *some* kind of work, wherever it was, but whether to switch from their current employment to the small but growing – and better-paid – private sector. The available figures suggest that, in the early 1990s, the number of entrepreneurs was growing a hundredfold annually, and by 1993 8 per cent of the workforce was in the private sector. The move was principally among men: in 1994, 5 per cent of men were fully self-employed, twice the proportion of women.[6]

Russians were thus faced, it appeared, with opportunity as well as crisis; but our longitudinal survey analysis suggests that they were very hesitant to take that opportunity. Perhaps most strikingly, and in contradiction of the assumption of American social scientists like Margaret Mead that change is normally led by the younger generation,[7] the new generation was certainly not in the vanguard of the switch to private work. On the contrary, they had overwhelmingly stuck to the jobs which they took up on leaving school five years earlier, over half of them not changing jobs at all, and by 1993 a mere 4 to 5 per cent had switched to private sector employment. The behaviour of the young was indeed typical of all those in work in Russia in this period, for survey evidence suggests that between 1988 and 1993 no more than 15 per cent of the whole workforce was mobile.[8] How do we explain this willingness of the young to suffer progressive deprivation rather than adapting to change and seizing their chances? Could the roots of this social immobility be at least in part due to transgenerational influences, patterns of childrearing, and models of behaviour passed down within families?

It is with this question in mind that we must now turn to the more detailed evidence of the life-story interviews. We shall look at examples from both the majority who were not socially mobile, and the small minority who did move upwards. Let us begin by considering family attitudes to education.

FAMILY ATTITUDES TO EDUCATION

The interviews give an overwhelming impression, at all social levels and among both those who were occupationally mobile and immobile, of parents who inculcated the importance of education for success in life. And indeed they had good reason, for educational credentials were normally of crucial importance in finding a good place in the formal Soviet economy. On the other hand, by the latter decades of the Soviet period, social mobility had probably become much more difficult. Moreover, although the overall message may seem similar, there can be important social differences in the manner in which it was conveyed by parents.

In some working-class families one senses that the parental aspiration was unsupported by any understanding of how it might be achieved. Quite commonly the parental attitude to education was a passive belief that the state schooling system would provide what their children needed for life. Thus Evgenii Mamlin (b. 1933) was the son of a high-class shoemaker, who worked for theatres and also made shoes to private order. The family lived in a crowded communal flat in Moscow, four of them living in one room, and sharing a common kitchen with sixteen other families. Evgenii's father had been the least successful of his own family, for his siblings had become doctors and engineers, and he hoped that his children would do better through education and 'make their way in life', but in fact neither Evgenii nor his brother were able to progress beyond secondary school. Evgenii became an electrician. It is striking that he too wanted his daughter Galina (b. 1961) 'to make her way in life', but took no interest in what kind of education she should take. He simply saw education as an abstract 'way to the top'; and Galina has ended up as an engineer without the qualifications she needed. It does not seem very surprising in an instance like this that the pull of the working-class culture in which Evgenii and Galina in turn grew up proved stronger than the examples of aunts and uncles or parental injunctions to pursue education. (P-T 17 and 16, Moscow.)

This could again happen, even when the family was able to develop a more concerted educational strategy. 'Study, study, study', Vladimir Ivanovich (b. 1949) was told by his parents, a building foreman and a laboratory assistant living just outside Leningrad; and when he was an adolescent, a 'family meeting' was held, as a result of which an aunt helped him to study for qualifications in a bakery college in the city itself, both by securing him a place and by taking him into her household. Vladimir proved in fact to be a poor student, and ended up working as a mechanic in a diesel plant where an uncle already had a job, and where his own son has followed him. (P-T 36, Leningrad.) What went wrong here? Vladimir's interview shows him as clearly intelligent and a keen reader. Maybe it was more that the bakery was the wrong choice for him, and he and his son have identified more readily with the masculinity of work in engineering.

Interestingly, too, in one working-class family in which education clearly led to success, it was as much through luck as through design. Vladimir Birikov (b. 1954) was the son of an unskilled casual building worker and was brought up in a communal flat. His father showed only a general interest in his education: 'He never taught me to do something, considering that school should do that. He respected school and my schoolteachers, believed them more than me. But he never interfered in my school life, except to ask about my marks.' As a boy, Vladimir was interested in science at school, and he wanted to enter a craft college for radio electronics in Leningrad. But he failed the entrance medical examination because of poor eyesight. He was then told that he could study electronics at the oddly named Calculation and Credit College:

> Nobody knew what it was in 1970. Well, we went there. And we realised that it's a very interesting profession to deal with computers. It

was an absolutely new thing at that time and we were so amazed that there was no competition to enter it at all ... The majority of the pupils in this college were from the provincial towns ... We passed our exams and we entered it without any problems. It was very easy to do.

Vladimir, who now feels particularly fortunate in the rigorous teaching about computer hardware and software which he received at the college, was through this unplanned fortune set on the path to striking occupational mobility, rising to become chief accountant at a state factory. (P-T 26, Leningrad.)

For the children of middle-class parents, by contrast, encouragement to educational effort was much more specific, and the danger was rather that it could create anxiety in the child. Igor Smirnov (b. 1961) was the son of a military officer and party worker, in whose steps he was expected to follow, while his mother was a trained accountant. Igor had regular constructive help from his parents in his homework, and they also took a very detailed interest in his progress. This was not always easy for the child. Igor well remembers coming home from school with his first marks in Russian:

When I came home, my parents asked me, 'What is your first mark? We think it is a "5" ', but I had to answer, 'I got "3" '. My parents did not show me affection. They just said, 'It could happen like that, don't worry.' But for me, it was a rather unpleasant situation. I wanted my parents to be pleased with me.

(P-T 41, Leningrad.)

Equally important, middle-class families were much more likely to have their own collection of books, so that reading was part of their culture from childhood. Sometimes the children of successful Soviet functionaries also had more time to read because their parents employed a servant, for example, who would cook and clean for the children, relieving them of time spent on household chores. The memories of the daughter of one Leningrad functionary, whose grandfather was a factory engineer, focus on her schoolteachers, the family flat and especially on the books which she still has, including the volumes of poetry which her father sent back from the war front – one inscribed 'Is it possible to give such poems to the enemies? This is a reason for the struggle' – and the complete centenary edition of Pushkin: 'the quality of paper is very good, it is an academic edition, a very good one, I like them very much and I keep them'. It is above all her possession of the family books which seems to give her the confidence – despite her father's role in building factories with slave labour in the Gulag, which it is difficult to believe she had not understood by the time of the interview – to burst out at the end: 'It was certainly the real Russian intelligentsia which was exterminated, and the inheritor of it, who remains from it, is in front of you now.' (P-T 47, Leningrad.)[9]

A less dramatic, but parallel, self-identity is found in Valentin Aleksandrovich (b. 1933), the son of a ship repair yard engineer and director, who himself became a professional military engineer, and whose son Sergei is chairman of a cooperative. When Valentin was a boy his mother was working in a fish factory and they had to share their flat with two other families, but even so there was a bookcase with reports and biographies by his bed, 'so they were very interesting books for me as a schoolboy'. There were also books on Russian history, and novels by Tolstoy and others. Later, this 'home library' was divided among Valentin, his brother and their parents. In Valentin's family it was considered a 'tragedy' not to secure a place in the top local educational institute. Valentin – as it turned out, not unreasonably – was so confident he would succeed that when he went to the entrance examination he went wearing his winter coat, boastfully saying that it would be less trouble to leave it there now. 'When I enter the institute I don't want to have to bother about my things.' (P-T 11, Moscow.)

Some working-class Russian children in the Soviet era were well aware that, despite the relatively slight differences between families in material terms, a minority of children had these important familial cultural advantages. As one put it:

> We were all the same grey mice in identical brown uniform frocks, all of us. Our parents gave us to the state for our upbringing. In my childhood, children did not differ in their material wellbeing. But we were divided into us and them – those others, who were also educated at home. They differed from us, because they were taught professionally to draw, play music, and speak foreign languages. They had advantages in every sphere where they appeared: they were loved by everyone. The only thing which was left for us was good learning at school, because this was our only possibility to be equal with them.
>
> (P-T 6, Moscow.)

TRANSGENERATIONAL FAMILY MODELS

These examples already suggest the crucial importance of transgenerational family models. In the Soviet Union, as in the Western world through the same decades, a strong family culture most often implied continuity at similar occupational levels, rather than social mobility.[10] From the working classes we already have the Mamlins: over three generations shoemaker, electrician and engineer; the Ivanoviches: building foreman, engineer and engineer; and it would be easy enough to find other instances. The mechanics of this familial transmission are not clear in working-class families, for it seems likely, at least for children who were brought up in collective flats, that they were as much shaped by the culture of the neighbourhood group as by their own parents.[11] One can indeed see socialisation in such contexts as nearly realising the aims of Soviet political thinkers like Kollontai, who argued that a child needed to learn to think collectivistically through being brought up in a social environment. According to this view, parents spoiled their children by bringing them up at home. The function of the family would wither away under socialism, for its role could be better carried out under the auspices of the state.[12]

In such proletarian homes, parents were certainly often away at work for most of the day, and children spent as much of their time as they could out in the communal yard rather than in the crowded family room. Without a private kitchen, it was difficult to maintain the family meal as a focus of transgenerational talk. As the son of an unskilled building labourer, whose family shared their common stove with three other families, put it: 'I think we did not have a common meal ... Firstly, because there was no room to get together, the table wasn't big enough for five people to sit together. Secondly, everybody had a different routine ... everybody came back at different times.' The only exception was the rare special festive occasions, when everyone did eat and sit around talking openly together. (P-T 26, Leningrad.)[13] Equally important, parents, especially fathers, tended to be emotionally distanced figures of authority, whose potentially threatening role was symbolised, when they were absent at work, by the ultimate instrument of authority: 'the huge belt [that] hung on the wall'. (P-T 36, Leningrad.)

The belt could certainly be used by middle-class fathers too.[14] But some of the interviews suggest a much more subtle and intimate process of transmission of models of behaviour. A particularly striking example is provided by the three generations of the Smirnov family.

Igor Smirnov (b. 1961), now a party political worker and lecturer in a military college, was the only child of an army officer who also became a Communist Party official. Igor has modelled himself very closely on his father, and openly thanks him for the example he set him: 'I'm grateful to my father for it, and I try to imitate him.' He encouraged him to think of following him in his occupation, but not crudely. Father and son would go on clandestine visits to the military college:

> It seemed to me very romantic: this military college and the servicemen who wore uniforms and bore weapons. It influenced me, as I was from the family of an officer ...
>
> When I was a nine- or ten-year-old schoolboy he talked to me a lot about his occupation. But he didn't force me to be a soldier in order to preserve the tradition of the profession through the generations. He explained to me about the interesting aspects of his job, and why he liked it, that there were happy moments, as well as the difficult ones ... He made me interested in it.

Igor's father is not just a model professionally, but also the bearer of a family tradition of ordered behaviour. 'The most important thing about him is that he never makes a decision in a hurry. He is a very rational and very attentive person.' Igor sees this as both a source and a reflection of 'the spirit of order' in his family with which he grew up. During his early boyhood his father was away on active service, so he and his mother lived in the country with his grandmother, and her influence too has left a permanent mark.

> The key figure was probably my grandmother ... I think it was my grandmother's way of life, that she put such order at home. Everyone knew their duties and rights, and everyone knew exactly what had to be done. Everything was definite. And I became a member of that order of things.

Hence, when his father returned, they continued in the same spirit. 'We sought for order in our family. My father, my mother, and I, everyone was responsible for our life: everything was decided together. Everybody had information about the situation, in order not to make a wrong decision.' Igor still tries to live like that, both in public and in private. 'Even in my job I prefer not to hustle, not to make a quick decision, right or wrong: I try to think things over, to think quietly about everything and only after that to make a decision.' He chose his wife Luba with the same careful caution. He met her at a friend's party, and 'realised very soon that she is a very reliable person whom I could ask for advice and whom I trusted. I felt safe with her.' Nevertheless, he needed to test her out, so 'I began to watch how she would behave in different social situations', taking her to the theatre, to meet his friends and family – until finally in 1985 they married. They build their joint life on 'a sense of common labour ... and identity of views ... We try to give in if we quarrel.'

And already the family torch is being handed down to their three-year-old son. Igor wants as a father to inculcate in him a sense of ordered tidiness and, for the future, of public service. 'I want him to be able to solve any problem correctly. The most important thing for him should be not to betray his ideals and we will try to bring him up with the ideals that we ourselves live by.' Fortunately Igor can already spot signs that his son may prove a chip off the old block. Although he can be 'a mischievous boy', he recognises paternal authority: 'he is obedient to me and ... he does what he is told to do. But I am a serviceman and a commander and I'm used to the immediate execution of my orders.' Hence it is equally promising that 'he can be nasty if he is not pleased with something. Maybe he has inherited from me the features which are typical of commanders. He gives orders to his friends in rather a sharp way: in a way which makes even adults look out.' (P-T 41, Leningrad.)

AUTHORITY AND ITS MITIGATION: FATHERS AND GRANDMOTHERS

The emphasis on authority in parenting, which is stressed especially by fathers in so many of these memories, does seem to have been pervasive. The survey evidence shows very clearly that, in the late 1980s, Russian parents wanted above all to bring up their children as obedient and honest. Some 70 per cent chose these qualities among their top three from of a list of eighteen alternatives. A further 45 per cent chose love of home and country. Independence and tolerance were rated as being much less important. This contrasts sharply with contemporary American survey results, in which 75 per cent of parents put independence first, followed by 47 per cent who name tolerance.[15]

It could be argued that recent Russian attitudes were closer to those held much earlier by American parents in the 1920s, but were changing in emphasis. Certainly the in-depth interviews do include signs of change. Thus Petr Andrienko (b. 1923), a skilled metalworker, already contrasted himself favourably with his fierce, unaffectionate and powerful father, whom he remembers whipping his brother with horse reins for stealing. Although Petr did smack his two children: ' ... it was quite different. We were not strict with them ... I have never beaten them.' (P-T 31, Leningrad.) And, certainly among the younger generation, Sergei Vedunin (b. 1961), an electrician's son who started as a skilled worker himself, and is now a foreman-instructor in aircraft construction, seems very different from the distant and often harsh working-class fathers of earlier decades. He deliberately decided to be a different kind of parent, and to give all his time off to his children, reading and talking to them as well as making special furniture and sports equipment for them. (P-T 28, Leningrad.) Nevertheless, it would be hard to contest that the predominant model of Russian parenting, right through the Soviet era up to the present day, has sought to encourage social conformity and obedience, and it has normally been imposed with the ultimate sanction of physical punishment.

There is, on the other hand, one almost equally widespread mitigation of this system of childrearing, equally distinctive of the Russian family: the notably prominent role of grandmothers. There is again statistical evidence which suggests some of the structural reasons for this. Firstly there was the housing situation. Throughout the Soviet period, despite the massive construction of urban housing, the shortage of independent accommodation remained acute, so that whatever families may have wished, a high proportion continued to live in extended family households. In Russia the proportion of households with couples which also included grandchildren or other kin was reported as 23 per cent in 1970, 19 per cent in 1979, and still 17 per cent in 1989. This may be compared with under 2 per cent in the United States. The situation, moreover, especially affected younger couples in the childrearing years, of whom 39.6 per cent were living in extended family households.[16] We know that a high proportion of such extended kin must have been grandmothers because of the much higher mortality of men through the political upheavals and wars between the 1920s and the 1940s.[17]

The figures for the Moscow longitudinal survey of young adults born in the 1960s bear this out more directly. One-third of them had lived with grandparents during their early school years, and altogether three-quarters had had at least weekly contact with a grandparent.[18] In other words, the majority of the Russian younger generation was brought up with the possibility of grandparental influence. Still more strikingly, the figures also provide a measure of how influential these grandparents may have been. Only 6 per cent of the grandmothers had themselves received some form of higher education; but of the grandchildren of these well-educated grandmothers a full 60 per cent went on themselves to higher education, while a mere 5 per cent finished at the lowest level. This is a strikingly higher level of achievement than with the majority, of whom less than 10 per cent went on to higher education in the 1970s.[19] It suggests that grandmothers could be not only vital carers for children whose parents were both away at work, but also transmitters of family cultural traditions. And, indeed, we find evidence of both aspects of their role in the life-story interviews.

There is certainly a different tone about the memories of childhood in households where the grandmother was the principal carer. Sometimes this was because she had been called to the city on the birth of the grandchild, to provide support, cooking, shopping and childcare. In other instances where the father was not present the mother moved instead into the grandmother's household. Either way, these memories convey a special sense of security from the hostile environment, of cosiness, under the protective wing of a grandmother who could be relied upon to cook delicious food, to nurse them when they were sick, to listen to their sorrows. One middle-class memory (that of Alexander Ulianin, b. 1969) sums up the typical tone:

> In childhood I was never sent to kindergarten because I stayed with my granny and great-granny. They were the nearest and dearest persons to me in my tender years. They baked delicious cakes, read and told me stories of their lives and fairy-tales, and later accompanied me to school. Unlike my mother, they were always very kind to me and never punished me. All my achievements in childhood were due to them.
>
> (B1, Moscow)

It is very striking how much more often there seems to have been a confiding intimate relationship between the child and its grandmother than with the parents. To some extent this reflected the much more gentle discipline imposed by grandmothers, perhaps because they were under less immediate strain, or perhaps because experience had brought more tolerance. This, interestingly, has been observed as an equally notable aspect of grandparenting in the West, in instances when children have lost a parent.[20] These Russian grandmothers were remembered as rarely punishing but, rather, forgiving and essentially goodhearted: and this encouraged intimacy. And even boys brought up by their grandmothers often seem to show more emotional sensitivity, as though their upbringing had given them some usually feminine skills.

It was only a minority who were able to transmit more than this. In most families there was a double reason why the transmission of a particular family culture, beyond ways of cooking and caring and relating, was unlikely. The first was that most of these grandmothers came from a rural background which was of little relevance to children in a major metropolis like Moscow or Leningrad And furthermore, many of them were illiterate. This meant that, rather than grandmothers handing on everyday knowledge to their grandchildren, the process was often the other way round. As Sergei Vedunin summed it up:

> I loved my grandmother very much in childhood and spent a lot of time with her. She lived all her life in the village, and came to our home from her village to the big city just after my birth, and lived with us from then onwards. But this does not mean I can tell you something about my family. Granny was practically illiterate and told us very little about her past: she considered that there was nothing interesting in her life.
>
> I tried several times to take her to the cinema, but she did not understand anything, so I had to retell her all the movie once again. I understood that my attempts to 'educate' my grandmother were all futile. But nevertheless I tried to tell her various interesting things which I knew. That is, I told her more than she told me ...
>
> (P-T 28, Leningrad.)

The most striking exception to this pattern among working-class families was, significantly, that of Vladimir Ivanovich, a grandson who spent much of his childhood in the village with his grandmother, and who therefore learnt peasant skills such as sewing, gardening and looking after cattle. In this context he also learnt from her the village's oral traditions and fairy-tales, and he can still recount these survivals from a pre-revolutionary rural culture. And although he became a worker and moved to the metropolis, he still identifies with his peasant roots. He feels ill-at-ease in the urban environment, and spends as much of his free time as he can back in his grandmother's village, helping with the farmwork. He has even passed on something of this rural identification to his own children. (P-T 36, Leningrad.)

SUPPRESSING AND TRANSMITTING DANGEROUS FAMILY PASTS

A second and often still more powerful inhibition against the transmission of family culture was the extent to which personal and family past could be dangerous in Soviet Russia. The recurrent social and political purges and the systematic discrimination exercised against those whose families had been aristocrats, landowners, *kulaki* . or big peasants, businessmen or entrepreneurs, supporters of the wrong political cause or actively religious, meant that many, if not most, Russian families had kin and stories which they preferred to keep hidden from the knowledge of others, including not only neighbours, workmates and friends, but also their own children. The politics of forgetfulness was a basic part of everyday living in Soviet Russia.

One of the first points which strikes a Western reader of these life stories is the number of informants who mention with regret gaps in their knowledge of their family history. Sometimes these gaps could be linked with the deliberate changing or forging of family documents, which seems to have been common in the inter-war years. Changes were made to parents' names, or dates of birth; family photographs were destroyed or mutilated, as families at all social levels sought to hide their earlier occupations, their attachment to religion, their military service in the White Guards, or their links with people who had been politically repressed. As one informant from a middle-class family put it:

> The Civil War had mixed up so many people and their families, one could not say that they were ashamed of their relatives, but they were afraid, afraid that those relatives who may have been killed in the war or later on could bring a shadow over the family, a shadow of unhappiness. And therefore they never discussed the problem of relatives.
>
> And now, as a consequence of this, with some exceptions most people know none of their predecessors beyond their parents. When, for example, during my business trips we discuss such topics, you come to understand that most people do not know their relatives. They are not afraid to talk of them [now]. They simply do not know them.
>
> (P-T 11, Moscow.)

One of the most striking instances of this is Alina Dobriaikova (b. 1937). Her maternal grandfather, father of Praskov'ia, her mother, had been a village priest who disappeared in the revolutionary wars. Her maternal uncle Alexander, the priest's eldest son, sided with the peasantry in the Revolution, made a quick military career, and ended up as a well-off KGB officer whose flat was filled with old paintings, Chinese vases and other works of art looted from victims of his repressions. His younger sister Larissa more prosaically became a village doctor and married the head of a collective farm: but then in 1937 she and her husband were repressed and sent to the Gulag. Her husband died there, but Larissa survived, and later remarried. Praskov'ia got on in life too, falsifying her date of birth and her parents' occupations in her documents – as her brother had done – and became a worker-student, also joining the Party, and becoming a technical specialist in the Ministry of Oil. She was married twice.

Alina was brought up severely by Praskov'ia in the militant Party style. She was given little opportunity for play, not allowed to listen to music on working days, and the only books she could find at home were the collected works of Lenin and the great Soviet encyclopaedia. Above all, her knowledge of her family background was thoroughly censored. She was not told that her Uncle Alexander was in the KGB, and only guessed from the shoulder straps in his photograph. She did not even know of her Aunt Larissa's existence until she suddenly appeared in the family in 1947, and it was only through her aunt that she discovered that her grandfather had been a priest.

The most drastic concealment, however, was over Alina's own birth. Her real father was her mother's second husband, who was shot when she was a few months old: it is still not clear why, but the manner of his death certainly gave the family a severe stigma. Her mother then gave Alina the patronimic of her first husband and her own family name. So all her life she has lived with alien patronimic and family names, as if her father had never existed. Her mother destroyed her birth certificate and created false documents for her daughter to match her own.

> As a teenager I had a Komsomol card in one name ... But later, when I needed a passport, there was a discussion in my family and they decided that with the help of somebody from the KGB I should change from my father's name ... My mother went somewhere, and then later she told me that now I could enter any prestigious institute. I did enter an institute without any difficulties, but several times they requested me to rewrite my biographical data. I was really puzzled by this. Every time I needed to fill in an official form I had to run back home and open a wardrobe where there was a crib-sheet showing how to write it in the proper way.

Alina became thoroughly confused between her real and her fictitious biographical data. It was only much later in life, through stories told by relatives, that she came to realise that the man with large eyes in the family photo album had been her own father. In this family, as in so many others through the Soviet years, secrets and deception, even in privacy, had become part of the everyday way of life. (P-T 6, Moscow.)

There was, in short, an immense swathe cut through the transmission of Russian family culture in the inter-war years, which clearly fundamentally reduced, and sometimes completely interrupted, the process of handing down family cultural capital from generation to generation.

This appears to have been as true of virtuous Communists as of those outside the establishment. Thus Igor Smirnov (b. 1961), Party political worker with the military like his father, remarked: 'We prefer not to talk about our relatives, who they are.' Igor did not know his maternal grandfather's occupation. And of his grandmother, with whom he and his mother lived as a child, and whom he greatly admires, he said:

> My grandmother was brought up in a noble family, she was a well-bred person ... an educated person ... Unfortunately she never told me sincerely about her life. Probably she thought it useless or unimportant. She never told me about it. So I got my image of my grandmother's youth and life through my mother's stories, which were rather short ones.
>
> (P-T 41, Leningrad.)

Similarly, Valentin Alexandrovich (b. 1933), whose parents were leading Communists in Murmansk, knew nothing about his maternal grandparents, even though his mother had been the subject of a biography as an exemplary pioneer and a heroine of Communism. 'I don't know the dates of their life, simply because nothing has survived about them, and their youngest daughter [i.e. his mother] got no heritage from them except for her mother's golden cross and marriage ring.' In the photographs of his grandmother and grandfather taken as a couple, his grandfather's image had been deliberately cut out. Valentin only knows that he was in the military, like himself.

> So his image was cut away from all the pictures ... But actually I can say nothing about it, because this issue was never discussed in our family ... They were simply afraid that memories about them would cause troubles for the rest of our family. They were very afraid of it, and it was never discussed at home ...
>
> Because it was never discussed, I suspected there was a mystery about their deaths, there had been certain events which my parents preferred not to tell me about.
>
> (P-T 11, Moscow.)

For these families, secrecy was necessary about the grandparental generation. It had been still more difficult for those, usually of an older generation, whose parents themselves had the questionable history. Petr Andrienko (b. 1923) became a skilled worker in Leningrad, a factory mechanic. He was a straightforward proletarian: 'I have never been master of myself, I was a simple worker.' But his father had been the leading figure in his village in Siberia, the shopkeeper, literate, and originally quick to seize the post-revolutionary chances of the New Economic Policy by buying farm equipment for his holding. At that moment the family were wealthy people. 'The storehouse had plenty of bread and they had a lot of cattle and they had their own houses.' But all that was ended by collectivisation. 'They took the cows and everything that one had in the household to create the collective farm's property.' Eventually in 1931 the family were evicted from their home, put in a cart along with some of their things, driven to the railway station and deported to another region. After a while they were allowed to return to a primitive cottage in the village, but three years later they were subjected to renewed repression. One brother was briefly arrested, and their father was taken from them permanently: 'I don't know when he died, because he was arrested as an "Enemy of the People" ... and we have known nothing about him since it happened.'

All three brothers lived their lives as 'simple workers'. Petr always knew why, and he had to keep it a secret.

> I was not able to tell the truth about myself, because I had to fill in a questionnaire when I took the job at the factory. There were questions

about your relatives: were they repressed or not? ... That made me very downcast. You could not tell people that your father was repressed and that he was an 'enemy of the people'. There was – my brothers tried to get educated, but they were not allowed to enter the institutes ... I didn't feel absolutely secure even with my job in the factory. Even now I don't feel secure. We were so put down, that even now I'm afraid of saying anything about it. And no doubt it is better to keep silent about it.

(P-T 31, Leningrad.)

In Petr's family the secrecy was maintained in public, but not in private. He has vivid recollections of stories told by his father's father. It is difficult to know how far there were families throughout the Soviet era in which grandparents continued to tell a fuller family story, because by the time of our interviews they were at the end of their lives and it may have seemed more urgent to them that the story should not be lost with their own death, and also because by then they had less to lose by telling. No doubt this kind of family storytelling also seemed in general much less dangerous by the 1980s. But the leapfrogging of information from grandparent to grandchild does seem an important minority pattern. In Petr's family the transmission was in the male line, but this is rather uncommon. Much more often the transmitters were grandmothers, both because they were more likely to have survived, and because as carers they more often achieved a special intimacy with their grandchild.

Thus Vladimir Ivanovich (b. 1949), a Leningrad mechanic, was largely brought up by his maternal grandmother while his mother, Antonina, was at work as a laboratory assistant. Vladimir as a child talked more often and more intimately to his grandmother than to his mother, and often she would tell him 'tales of her life'. There are striking differences between the stories which they gave us. For example, Vladimir's mother said that her fifth sister died of pneumonia in 1943; but Vladimir knew better, and said that 'she lost her bread card during the siege, and, well – she committed suicide'. Vladimir also knew that, before Antonina's father became a medical assistant at a power station, the family had been village *kulaki* – perhaps combining medical practice with shop-keeping – and they had escaped victimisation because 'they were defended by the people ... I was told about it'. Antonina told us nothing about this at all, beginning her story after the Revolution, when her father was already working at the power station. She said that she had no memories of her grandparents. (P-T 36 and 37, Leningrad.)

There is a parallel pattern of transmission in the Birikov family. Ivan (b. 1926), a Leningrad fireman, describes his father Ermak as 'a peasant ... He worked as a team leader ... but he was not very satisfied with the collective farm's way of life. So he took a job as a miner.' Ivan says that he has no memories of collectivisation, and that 'nobody told me anything about that time'. But it was quite different for his son Vladimir (b. 1954), who rose to become a factory chief accountant. He was very close to his grandmother as a child – 'she loved me the best, I think, among all her grandchildren ... we had a lot in common' – and deliberately drew out her memories, understanding how old people like to talk about their earlier lives. He also spent many holidays as a boy in the village, where he talked to other people about his family. So Vladimir has quite a full picture of his grandfather before the Revolution as a *kulak*, a 'severe ... very strong man ... a very hard working master', who then was head of a 'wealthy' household. This puts a different slant on his subsequent dissatisfaction with the collective farm. Vladimir has also discovered – as Ivan must also know, but chose not to tell us – that, after working as a miner, his grandfather returned to the village, and in 1940–3 he was village headman under the German occupation. He was later arrested for this, imprisoned for ten years, and only released after Stalin's death. But even Vladimir feels that he has not got to the bottom of this part of the story. 'How did he manage to survive under German occupation? Well, people tell different stories.' (P-T 26 and 27, Leningrad.)

Thus, despite these inhibitions, in a minority of families a transmission of family stories was taking place from the grandparental generation. And at the same time, especially when the grandmother was a well-educated, middle-class woman from a pre-revolutionary family, other significant aspects of the family's cultural inheritance were also handed down. A good instance is provided by Aleksei Novikov (b. 1961), an academic lecturer in geography who edits his own specialised journal. Both his parents were lecturers too, in the same aviation institute in Moscow, following on from all four of his grandparents who had been pioneering Russian aviation engineers, while his great-grandparents had been high-ranking and well-educated pre-revolutionary merchants and factory owners. Aleksei says of his childhood:

> There are two homes in my memories, and they are of equal importance for me, my parents' home and my grandmother's, and I cannot separate them. In spite of the kindergarten which I attended occasionally, family takes a much greater part in my recollections. Either my grandfather was engaged with me, after he retired on a pension, or my grandmother, or my great-grandmother while she was alive. In general my reading was defined not by my parents, but by my grandparents ... They had a library. They simply stuffed me with books, mostly old-fashioned from my point of view: Russian classics – Pushkin. Very often they read books aloud, and all the family would gather to listen ... They were very well aware of everything concerning books, music, and they liked to stage Russian plays at home.
>
> (P-T 3, Moscow.)

Another interesting case is provided by the family of Zhenia Zhurnalistova (b. 1966), a teacher. She had two grandmothers of different cultures who offered two types of cultural inheritance. On her father's side was grandmother Agaf'ia, who came from an impoverished and illiterate peasant family, but who after the

Revolution had seized the chance of education and become a teacher. She was a convinced Communist. In contrast, on her mother's side was grandmother Galina, who came from an educated, land-owning background, but who had not been employed since the date of her marriage. Zhenia recalls that in her childhood:

> ... we lived together with two grandmothers. But the relations with them were quite different. I didn't like my grandmother Agaf'ia, although she stayed with me more often. She would give me books about pioneers, which I didn't like. She could shout at me without any apparent cause, and speak to me with unjust and sharp words. And she always corrected how I spoke in a didactic fashion.
>
> One could never imagine that sort of thing with my other grandmother, Galina. She was quite the opposite. She created an atmosphere of love and kindness in the family.

It was from Galina that Zhenya first heard biblical stories, and in Galina's library that she found the books from which she later developed an interest in occultism. (B6, Moscow.)

On one level one can see this as a contrast between two different types of personality linked to different educational approaches: influence on the one hand through kindness and example, on the other through severity, instruction and discipline. But in the Russian context they also symbolised adherence to two kinds of family culture. On the one hand was the aggressive revolutionary culture of class hatred, on the other the kindness and gentleness of a privileged elite which typified the culture of gentry covertly surviving from the pre-revolutionary era.

Alexander Ulianin (b. 1969) was born into a still more remarkable example of a transgenerational intellectual family, and brought up with his parents, grandmother and great-grandmother. For his first three years they still shared a single room in a communal flat. His great-grandmother Antonina (1895–1975) had been the wife of a Byelorussian landed gentleman and army officer, who had been killed fighting on the Bolshevik side in the Civil War although, because for a long time no witnesses to this could be found, all his photographs were removed from the family album, and his name replaced in his daughter's documents by that of her stepfather, Antonina's second husband, who was also from the landed gentry but able to prove his war service on the Bolshevik side. Alexander's grandmother Lydia (b. 1914) was a powerful personality, who had recovered her social position by migrating to Moscow, becoming a textile worker and then a worker-student, and rising to become a prominent geologist. She sealed this position by marrying in succession two high-ranking geologists, and both of her two elder children followed in the same profession. Her daughter by her second marriage, Alexander's mother, Irene (b. 1940), also became an academic scientist, a biologist.

Alexander himself was clearly a precocious child. He recalls:

> I learned to read from my grandmother and great-grandmother in the main. My mother also taught me to read, but most of the time she was not at home, so we spent time with grandmother and with great-grandmother when she was still alive ... From time to time I would attend kindergarten, but in all I spent there no more than half a year. At the age of three I could already recite from memory verses from the Russian classics, to the surprise of our guests. And I remember that, when we would go with my grandmother to the shop and stand in the queue, I liked to surprise the other people queuing by reciting Pushkin's and Lermontov's verses.

One might say that Alexander has not entirely fulfilled this early promise, for he did not do well at the commercial institute where he first studied, and went into the army for his military service – which could have led to his following another family tradition, from the grandfathers he never knew – but he did not sustain that either. Although he is now in post-graduate education again and could possibly become a lecturer, his chosen specialism is sport, and he is more attracted to the idea of earning a living as a jockey and private coach. He spends much of his time with his newly married wife at the racecourse. But that might also perhaps be seen as reflecting a less conventional aspect of his transgenerational inheritance, for he had heard many stories from his grandmother Lydia of her annual geological expeditions with her husband, which were a regular part of her earlier life. These included tales of many exotic adventures, ranging from commanding mineral-prospecting gangs made up of convicts, to riding mountain rivers on rafts. As Lydia herself put it, 'as far back as I can remember, our family has always been on the move'. (B1, Moscow.)

FORMS OF FAMILY SOCIALISATION AND ADAPTABILITY TO CHANGE

This leads us back to the question of change and adaptability with which we began. We have already suggested that the strength of transgenerational family influences can inhibit change, and so family characteristics which are an asset in a relatively stable context may become a disadvantage in periods of rapid change. We can see the inhibiting power of family tradition, for instance, in the case of the family of Viacheslav Offitserov (b. 1968), whose grandfather, father and sons have all been military officers. Influence in this family, as with the Smirnovs, is definitely passed primarily through the male line, and the mother sees her principal function as keeping a 'sweet' home for her men. Both Viacheslav and his brother Boris, who are twins, were sent to a prestigious military school and then on to a military institute chosen by their father. He took a close interest in their education from childhood, and used his personal networks to further their careers. By the time that they were young adults, however, it was clear that changes were taking place in Russia, and that social prestige had begun to depend as much on income as on occupation itself. They could see that they might do better by leaving the army. But that choice implied a serious conflict with their father. Eventually Boris decided to make a break and become a business entrepreneur. He opened his own small shop. His father then refused to speak to him for months. Viacheslav, the first-born twin, initially felt unable to make such an open protest against his father's control of his destiny. At first he simply used his leisure time to help his brother in the shop, trying to manage two careers in parallel. But eventually he too abandoned the army, and now he and his brother are working together full-time in their small cooperative. (B23, Moscow.)

It is interesting to contrast this narrative from a traditional, male-dominated authoritarian family with what happened to Alexander Ulianin. His primary socialisers were all women. He decided to abandon the high intellectualism of his family, specialise in the more low-brow field of sport, and spend much of his time in the gambling atmosphere of the racecourse with his new wife. In his case his choice was met in the family with understanding; and in particular, his grandmother Lydia turned out to be the most supportive of his decision. While Alexander's parents expressed their tacit consent, his grandmother actively defended his choice and continues to support him morally. Lydia's attitude fits closely with her own experience, which she has conveyed over the years to her grandson, of a life of continual change and adaptation, always 'on the move'. She and her mother had been reduced from their comfortable gentry status to a situation of post-revolutionary poverty and insecurity in which they were often shivering and close to starvation. 'The whole family huddled in two rooms, for they could not afford to heat the whole house ... On the roof of the next-door house my grandfather lured pigeons and caught them to feed the family.' It was her willingness to change, to migrate first to the countryside and then back to Moscow, and to transform herself into a worker-student, which enabled Lydia to recover some of her lost social status over the years that followed. Adaptability had been the key to her own success in life and, as a grandmother, perhaps this was the most important message which she transmitted to her grandson. (B1, Moscow.)

FAMILY UPBRINGING AND ENTREPRENEURSHIP

To what extent do those who move like 'sputniks' out of the orbit of their parents' occupational spheres, and plunge into the risky and socially suspect world of entrerpreneurship, make this choice with some support, or even encouragement, from other kin in their families? We cannot hope to answer this question with our present evidence alone, but some of the pointers are interesting.

Current research suggests that, typically, the new post-Soviet entrepreneurs of the early 1990s were in early middle age, most often in the age range 35–45 (that is, born in the 1940s and 1950s), and that they have moved into business from positions of power as Party officials in the former *nomenklatura* structure.[21] We have nine life stories, all but one of them from younger and still-tentative entrepreneurs born in the 1960s and still in their late twenties.[22] It is interesting to find, however, that the two older instances of the new entrepreneurship, both described below, do both come from a Party background, although the second of these is of a very different type.

Dmitrii Iakovlev (b. 1954) seems an instance of family reversion, for his grandparents were prosperous Siberian fur traders who moved to Moscow. It is important to notice that, in each generation, because of the early deaths of men, and in his mother's generation the political repression of both her brother and brother-in-law, the family was dominated by women. Rather unusually, they succeeded in remaining in the upper floor of their original family house, at various stages selling off their antiques and furs for money, and finally burning the remnants of their old furniture to keep warm during the war years. But the next generation all succeeded in becoming professionals. Dmitrii's mother was a history teacher. Dmitrii himself entered the Moscow aviation institute and then launched himself rather pragmatically into a career as a Party political worker. As soon as he saw the wind changing, however, in the late 1980s, using his divorce as a pretext with his Party colleagues, he shifted into trade-union work, which gave him more freedom, and from there moved to head a commercial tourist company which the Moscow trade-union committee had established. Finally he set up his own firm, specialising in apartment repairs in Moscow, in which he has some hopes of obtaining a monopoly. In the current fluid legal situation he sees his former Party networks as a crucial asset for developing his business. He explains:

> If you need to open a foreign currency account, you have to get it registered at the Ministry for Foreign Economic Relations; to avoid taxation, you should get it registered at the Finance Ministry, and so on ... When I needed to open my foreign currency account in this country, I made it quite simply by taking advantage of all my former connections ... If you know the legislation and can explain what you want intelligibly, all of them will always give their consent to 'mutual interest' ... In short, I knew how to create a structure capable of bringing profit: that's the structure I've created.

Apart from the pleasure brought by regular journeys abroad, Dimitri now has time also to enjoy his unusual recreational pleasures – his swimming pool, his tennis court, sauna and skiing. He has been able to find work in the firm for his ex-wife and two other kin, and he has been helping his son into a private legal career. (P-T 7 and 8, Moscow.)

Sergei Valentovich (b. 1961) is a very different case. He also comes from a family of successful professionals who rose as good Communist engineers, but in this case the male tradition was clear, and in fact Sergei's career has been shaped by his reaction against the example of his father, who worked in a secret military factory. Sergei wished to avoid being tied down by such discipline and regulation. After graduating as a military engineer in the family tradition, he decided on a complete break with the life his parents stood for. He left home and took a part-time job as a poorly paid watchman, originally in order to give himself the time to develop as a creative musician. He studied music successfully at the Institute of Culture. At the same time he began reading underground literature, although he never became an active dissident. Then, in 1987, as soon as the decree legalising the setting up of private cooperatives was passed, Sergei and his wife decided to set up their own. After discussing a range of possibilities, from growing ecological flowers to teaching children music, he eventually developed a successful venture specialising in ecology and chemical analysis on a contractual basis. Ironically, Sergei still has to work so hard that he has had no chance to become the composer he once dreamed he might be. Nevertheless, he feels a sense of achievement in the results of his hard work.

> I simply cannot stand it when somebody orders me about. We have obtained inner freedom, and that feeling of freedom is quite strong. We understood that the old system was being destroyed because we ourselves took part in it. And that was not through writing letters, or listening to Radio Liberty, but due to our own activities. We were able to prove that, even without state donations, without credits or accommodation, a private company could survive and prosper.
>
> (P-T 10, Moscow.)

We have other evidence from interviews with seven other younger entrepreneurs. All but one are from professional families. It is immediately apparent that their careers have involved considerable changes of direction in their search for suitable work, and also that their present jobs have no direct connection with their education. This is in itself partly a reflection of the structural situation in Russia, in which the economy has changed much more quickly than the education system. It is therefore not entirely surprising that they all tend to describe their career paths in terms of opportunities brought through personal networks.

It is also notable that, with the exception of Dmitrii, who is older and probably more typical in general of those who became successful entrepreneurs in Russia in the 1990s, none of them are as yet really successful financially. They are independent and self-driven, but at the expense of much longer hours than in state-sector work, less security, and as yet no significant riches. They are simply making a living, with hopes for a better future. This is no doubt one reason why, when talking about their work and their motivation, they all emphasise above all their wish for 'personal freedom' and 'independence'. Sometimes they speak almost with the rhetoric of pioneer American settlers: 'It was a chance to be a free man'; 'I don't like bosses, I can't stand being ordered about'; 'the whole idea was to get free'. Leonid (b. 1966), a Moscow technical insitute graduate who first tried hairdressing, and then went on to the new commodity exchange where he is co-owner of a broking company, explicitly sees himself as 'an internal migrant', but still with better chances than those who emigrate to the United States:

> I was an employee, merely a hired worker, but the salary wasn't bad. Financially I've gained nothing so far ... What I've gained is independence and prospects. I wanted to be independent, to realise my ideas. I've got a good stock of commercial ideas ... Now everything depends on me ... I'm just walking on air from happiness. I'm starting life anew.
> (P-T 9, Moscow.)

It is interesting to contrast their attitudes with those of Stepan Malakov (b. 1966), a skilled worker who had recently married when he returned from his service in the army and decided to try to make more money by working in the cooperative sector. Through his friends he found work first in a cooperative café, and then at a private detection agency, but he did not keep these jobs for long. He could not accept the competition and individualism inherent in private enterprise: 'I made up my mind to return to the plant, to my collective: there you may be certain that anyone will help you with a request ... After all, we manufacture helicopters there, which are necessary for the whole country. There you feel you're needed.' (B53, Moscow.)

The drive for independence can imply either ruptures or positive transmissions in familial influence and support. It is immediately obvious that, precisely because they depend so much on networks, some of these entrepreneurs are creating the nucleus of new family firms powered by their own generation. Some are working with friends; but Alexander and Sergei are both working with their wives, and Dimitri already has three relatives in his firm. And in terms of transgenerational connections, the patterns are also very varied. There are, among our nine entrepreneurial examples, three clear cases of strong parental opposition. Two of these instances are of fathers who opposed their sons, and one of a mother who opposed her daughter. It is probably significant that, in the only two families of future young entrepreneurs in which fathers were fully present and influential, in each case the sons had to explicitly reject parental example in the face of open opposition from their fathers. Of the remainder, in three other homes there was no father present during childhood, in two the parents were in dispute and unable to control their child, and in Alexander's family the primary influence was his grandmother.

It does also seem likely that there was an important difference in the message given by parental upbringing between male-dominated and female-dominated households. It looks as if fathers were much more likely to instil the need for disciplined obedience, entailing the following of a particular path, while women as carers conveyed a more open message. Thus Dmitrii remembers how he was brought up, as a fatherless child, 'to stand on his own feet'. Even the one instance of opposition between mother and daughter is striking in its ambivalence. Anna (b. 1967) is an unusual instance of a young entrepreneur from a working-class background. She was also brought up without a father, and followed her mother, who was a furrier, into the clothing industry, studying at a textile institute, beginning work as a dressmaker in a state firm, and then becoming a designer at a prestigious atelier. Subsequently she joined a tailoring cooperative, and she now runs a private fur atelier herself. Anna's mother was extremely hostile to her move into the private sector, even accusing her of being an 'enemy of the people'. Nevertheless, Anna believes that her own very rational and businesslike way of working comes from her mother's example: 'Seeing my mother work, I have since childhood acquired the habit of doing everything accurately and thoroughly.'

Nevertheless, it is Grigorii Osipov (b. 1965), a third fatherless child, now in independent farming, who expresses most strongly of all his debt to this more open and adaptable form of childrearing, which seems so often to have helped shape these future Russian entrepreneurs:

> Even when I was still entering the agricultural institute – that was before *perestroika* – I was well aware that I'd never be able to work in this [Soviet state] system: I would either be a thief, or I would try to change something and get it in the neck. I grew up in freedom, was brought up in this way – freedom and insubordination are in my blood.
> (B34, Moscow.)

CONCLUSION

It does not seem, in short, that the family socialisation typical of Soviet Russian families with intact parental marriages encouraged the development of adult independence, adaptability and creativity. These were not the values of the majority at any social level in the Soviet era, and surveys suggest that, even in the 1990s, Russians identified themselves primarily in terms of collectivities, of family and community, rather than in terms of professional achievement.[23] During the Soviet period, it was typical for working-class families to leave their children to be socialised by their peer group in the communal yard, while parents saw education as a responsibility of the State. These attitudes were, moreover, encouraged by Soviet political ideology. Middle-class parents were much more actively concerned with education, and those whose families came from an intellectual tradition often had homes 'stuffed with books' to inspire their offspring, some eventually becoming successful academics. Typically, however, especially where fathers were involved, middle-class upbringing was severe, based on instruction and discipline, and dedicated to inculcating the values of order, tidiness and service: 'everything was definite'. Perhaps most severe of all was the puritanical instructionalism of those parents who were Communist militants.

On the other hand, the very stresses of the period meant that an alternative model of upbringing was also relatively common. Because most Soviet mothers were in full-time work, and very many fathers were absent through divorce, death, travel for work or military service, many children were brought up primarily by their grandmothers; and as carers, grandmothers were typically recalled as rarely punishing, bringing their influence through gentleness and intimacy. It is not a coincidence, we believe, that when we turn from the childrearing and family relationships of the majority to those of the new entrepreneurs who were adapting to the advent of a market society in the 1990s, we find that only two out of nine came from intact nuclear families in which the fathers were fully present and influential, and these two had to defy their fathers in order to innovate. In the others, usually because the parental marriage was dissolving or dissolved, it was mothers and grandmothers who were the primary influences. Some of these grandmothers, moreover, had themselves learnt the need for adaptability in surviving the still greater turbulence of the years from the October Revolution to the Second World War. Paradoxically, then, if there is a lesson for the future from these family histories it is that, rather than from the conventional, intact nuclear family, it is from extended and split families headed by mothers and grandmothers that the younger generation is most likely to have imbibed the flexibility of attitudes and belief in independence needed for success in the capitalist Russia of the twenty-first century.

Notes

Interviews referred to in this chapter are drawn from two research projects, described in the Introduction and identified here by the initials of the researchers (P-T: Pahl–Thompson; B: Bertaux) and sequence numbers.

1 See Chapters 1 and 3, this volume.
2 Daniel Bertaux and Paul Thompson (eds), *Between Generations: Family Models, Myths and Memories*, International Yearbook of Oral History and Life Stories, 2 (Oxford University Press, Oxford, 1993); Paul Thompson, 'Women, men, and transgenerational influences in social mobility', in Daniel Bertaux and Paul Thompson, *Pathways to Social Class: A Qualitative Approach to Social Mobility* (Clarendon Press, Oxford, 1997), 32–61; Gill Gorell Barnes et al., *Growing up in Stepfamilies*, (Oxford University Press, Oxford, 1997); Paul Thompson, 'The family and childrearing as forces for economic change: towards fresh research approaches', *Sociology*, 18 (1984), 515–30; Paul Thompson, *Living the Fishing* (Routledge & Kegan Paul, London, 1983). In these works our aim has been to understand both the processes of family transmission and its impact on the lives of successive generations. For two interesting interpretations which focus much more on the narratives, see Victoria Semenova, 'The message from the past: experience of suffering transmitted through generations', and Gabriele Rosenthal, 'Social transformation in the context of familial experience: biographical

consequences of a denied past in the Soviet Union', in Roswitha Brecker, Devorah Kalekin-Fishman and Ingrid Miethe (eds), *Biographies and the Division of Europe: Experience, Action and Change on the 'Eastern Side'* (Leske and Budrich, Opladen, 2000), 93–158.

3 Tamara Hareven, *Family Time and Industrial Time* (Cambridge University Press, Cambridge, 1982).

4 Glen Elder, *Children of the Great Depression: Social Change in Life Experience* (University of Chicago Press, Chicago, 1974). On the Depression in North America and intergenerational family relationships, the outstanding research has been by Elder, combining in-depth and quantitative information from the Oakland, California, longitudinal cohort study of children born in the 1920s.

5 Percentage of population aged 16–60: *Rossikski Statisticheski Sbornik, 1994* [Russian Statistical Report for 1994], (Goscomstat Rossii, Moscow, 1994); *Korotkyi Statisticheskyi Otchet* [Short Statistical Report], (Goscomstat, Moscow, 1997), 50.

6 The percentage of women reported as housewives in the longitudinal survey rose from 3 per cent in 1988 to 12 per cent in 1993: Ludmilla Kokliagina and Victoria Semenova (eds), *Doklad o Tret'em Etape Longit'iudnogo Issledovaniia Puti Odnogo Pokoleniia* [Report on The Third Wave of Longitudinal Survey: Paths of One Russian Generation] (ISAN, Moscow, 1993). For the percentage of the workforce in the private sector: *Economicheskie i Sotsialjnye Izmeneniya: Monitoring Obshhestvenogo Meneniia* [Economic and Social Change: Public Opinion Monitoring] (Aspect Press, Moscow, 1997); information for a transnational sample of 5,000 men and women aged 16–65, conducted in June 1994, kindly communicated by Eva Fodor, ESRC seminar, London, December 1994. The figures of fully self-employed were much higher elsewhere in Eastern Europe than in Russia, most notably in Poland and Hungary (25 per cent and 14 per cent of men respectively). Even in 1999, estimates suggest that the private sector accounts for around 20 per cent of employment in the major cities, but significantly less in the country as a whole: Simon Clarke, *New Forms of Employment and Household Survival Strategies in Russia* (ISITO/CCLS, Coventry and Moscow, 1999).

7 Margaret Mead, *Culture and Commitment: a Study of the Generation Gap* (Bodley Head, London, 1970).

8 Michail Titma (ed.), *Sotsial'naia Differentsiatsiia Vozrastnoi Kogorty* [Social Differentiation of an Age Cohort] (ISRAN, Moscow, 1998), 64; information from Eva Fodor (see note 6 above). There was much higher mobility reported from Poland and Czechoslovakia.

9 This is an incomplete pilot interview without full details on occupations.

10 Pierre Bourdieu, *Distinction: A Social Critique of the Judgement of Taste* (Harvard University Press, Cambridge, Mass., 1984); Paul Thompson, 'Women, men and transgenerational influences in social mobility', and Daniel Bertaux and Isabelle Bertaux-Wiame, 'Heritage and its lineage: a case history of transmission and social mobility over five generations', in Bertaux and Thompson, *Pathways to Social Class*, 32–97.

11 See Victoria Semenova on the *kommunalki*, Chapter 3, this volume.

12 A.M. Kollontai, *Sem'ia i Communisticheskoe Gosudarstvo* [The Family and the Communist state] (Communist, Moscow, 1918).

13 Interview P-T 26, Leningrad.

14 E.g. interview P-T 11, Moscow (father military engineer).

15 Yu. Levada (ed.), *Prostoi Sovetskyi Chelovek* [The Ordinary Soviet Person] (Mirovoi Okean, Moscow, 1993), 99–100, 252.

16 M.S. Matskovski (ed.), *Sem'ia v Krizisnom Obshchestve* [The Family in a Crisis Society] (Institute of Sociology, Moscow, 1993), 19–20.

17 *Demograficheski Ezhegodnik SSSR, 1990* [Annual Demographic Report on the USSR for 1990] (Finansy i Statistika, Moscow, 1990), 27.

18 Kokliagina and Semenova, *Doklad o Tret'em Etape*.
19 *Ibid.*; *Economichesteskie i Sotsialjnye Izmeneniya* [Economic and Social Change: Public Opinion Monitoring] (Aspect Press, Moscow, 1997).
20 Gorell Barnes *et al.*, *Growing up in Stepfamilies*, 61–4; Paul Thompson, 'The role of grandparents when parents part or die: some reflections on the mythical decline of the extended family', *Ageing and Society*, 19 (1999), 471–503.
21 L.V. Babaeva, *Sotsial'no-stratifikastionnyi Protsessi v Sovremennomn Obshchestve* [Social Processes in Modern Society] (Institute of Sociology, Moscow, 1992). For an analysis of the social attitudes of current Russian entrepreneurs, based on ten in-depth interviews with senior businessmen mostly in their thirties, see Johan Bäckman, ' "New Russians" and social change', in Markku Kivinen (ed.), *The Kalamari Union: Middle Class in East and West* (Ashgate, Aldershot, 1998), 15–35.
22 These consist of three from the Pahl-Thompson transgenerational families and six from the Bertaux families; all but one are from Moscow.
23 Vladimir Yadov, *Krisis Indentichnosti* [The Crisis of Identity] (Institute of Sociology, Moscow, 1995).

7

'COMING TO STAND ON FIRM GROUND'

The Making of a Soviet Working Mother

Anna Rotkirch

THE UNLIKELY PRIZE CANDIDATE

Among the works included in the shortlist for the prestigious Russian Booker literary award in 1998, one appeared particularly surprising with regard to genre, author and content. The jury had unanimously agreed to include the autobiographical text of Aleksandra Chistiakova, an elderly woman from the Siberian town of Kemerovo. This life history had been published with the title *Ne mnogo li dlia odnoi?* – 'Enough for one?' – by the journal *Den' i Noch'* (Day and Night), published in Krasnoiarsk. The book was edited by the journalist Vladimir Shiriaev.[1]

The extent of Shiriaev's involvement remains unclear. The text appears to be drawn from diary excerpts, as suggested by the opening sentence – 'I decided to keep a diary. But first I will describe my life so far. I am already twenty-four years old ... ' and the last page – 'Now it is already winter and New Year is approaching ... This is how we live, the two of us, Stepan and I. Today I came from visiting my mother, where I was for two days. He is sleeping now, the rugs are rolled away ... When he insults me, I no longer want to live. I will for the rest of my life be disappointed with my fate.' Shiriaev is said to have 'recorded' the text (the verb used is *zapisat*, which can be understood to mean both 'to record', as in recording an interview, and 'to write down'). It is possible that he selected and transcribed the diary excerpts, or that Chistiakova read them to him. He also interviewed her directly to complement the entries. He may indeed have chosen the title and added the very last sentences, which are both more abstractly reflective than the main text.

Language corrections may also have modified the original language of the diary. This published version of Chistiakova's life-history text has none of the frequent spelling and punctuation errors found in other working-class women's autobiographies of the same generation.[2] Chistiakova tells us that she was never very good in Russian at school, but that she loved writing poems. Her writing often has a real literary quality – for instance, when Aleksandra recalls how for the first time she talked with her childhood love and he 'looked at me like on some map that he wanted to study'.[3]

In this chapter I will use Chistiakova's life history as a case for exploring the experiences of the first generation of Soviet women. I am interested in the gendered aspects of Soviet social mobility and everyday life: in how professional work was intertwined with unpaid care work, and how kinship networks competed with marital loyalties. From the point of view of the analysis here, therefore, possible grammatical corrections to Chistiakova's original diary do not matter. But precisely because of this uncertainty with regard to authorship, the Russian Booker jury had in advance agreed that Chistiakova could not be awarded the main prize.[4]

Enough for One Woman? was thus no conventional literary work. In addition, its narrator represented one of the lowest social groups in Soviet and post-Soviet Russia, elderly women of the countryside. The life history depicted famine, unhappy love, a drinking husband, illegal abortions, hard work and extreme physical and emotional suffering. These topics are easily put into the category of being frustratingly banal, commonplace and intellectually worthless. Thus the prestigious literary weekly *Literaturnaia gazeta* wondered what a *derevenskaia starukha*, or countryside hag, was doing in the Booker shortlist, and suggested that the jury could as well give money to the beggars on the street. Another journalist predicted that this trivial story would interest only 'Western feminists'.[5] The latter assessment was, as this article shows, not totally wrong, but it was intended as an insult belittling the possible domestic relevance of the work. Chistiakova documents the repetitive, boring and 'feminine' aspects of everyday life, or *byt*, which in Russian history of ideas has usually been understood as provokingly trivial, degrading and amoral.[6]

However, many commentators wholeheartedly supported the jury's decision to include Chistiakova among the six best literary publications of the year. During the 1990s, post-socialist Russian literature had witnessed a veritable autobiographical boom, ranging from the publication of previously censored and unpublished diaries from Soviet times to memoirs written by more or less famous contemporaries. The boom included the spread of life-history interviews and of biographical methods in the social sciences.[7] Several of the published memoirs were written by women, although mostly these were women with higher education.[8] The publication of Chistiakova's autobiography clearly formed part of this general movement to rediscover and preserve personal memories of everyday life under socialism. It was, however, unique in voicing the experiences of a poor working woman. The previous year had seen the full publication of perhaps the closest analogue to Chistiakova's work – the autobiographical notebooks of Evgeniia G. Kiseleva, 1916–90. The general outline of Kiseleva's life is close to Chistiakova's, including migration from the countryside to industrial work, two children, male betrayal, emotional abandonment, alcoholism and violence. Kiseleva's three notebooks form a longer text, with emphasis on everyday social relations and emotions, written in an incoherent and detailed, 'naïve', style. Kiseleva was less well educated, and was also a less qualified worker, than Chistiakova. Evidently Kiseleva's everyday life had also been even more violent. As Kozlova and Sandomirskaia point out, Kiseleva's way of life approaches 'the borders of social existence', with few indications of self-control, long-term planning, division between work or free time, or basic knowledge of history.[9]

Chistiakova's text has almost nothing in common with the testimonies of the times that have characterised both men's and women's published autobiographical writings in Russia.[10] Nor does it follow the official Soviet autobiographical format of social success and political correctness. Due to its diary basis, it avoids any clear divisions into 'professional' and 'intimate' biography.[11] The political system is also only indirectly present in this intense, highly personal document. Like in most autobiographies written by 'ordinary' people, political events and legislation are referred to only if they affect the everyday life of the author and her family — the announcement of the beginning of the war on the radio; the difficulty of finding a doctor who agrees to help when you are bleeding to death from an illegal abortion. (By contrast with Chistiakova's narrative, Kiseleva's notebooks often praise the Soviet leaders. These mentions refer to television news or to letters Kiseleva writes to the authorities. Their style is highly hagiographic, the socialist leaders taking the place previously reserved for the Tsar, the Almighty and the Virgin Mary: 'I certainly don't want Leonid Il'ich [Brezhnev] to die. He is already old; I want him to be immortal.'[12])

As the president of the Booker jury, professor of literature Andrei Zorin, noted at the time, *Enough for One Woman?* was written in 'the language of a person standing on the threshold of illiteracy'. Zorin was fascinated both with the life history itself and with the unexpected literary perspective it opened up. Most of Russian fiction in the late 1990s had been overtaken by 'sweet-languishing erotica, mystical symbols and belated experiments with flows of consciousness'. By refreshing contrast, the often horrendous events in this autobiography were rendered with laconic detachment. In Zorin's view, it also showed how 'radical naturalism in its extremely exaggerated outpouring approaches the esthetics of absurdity'.[13]

Below, I will use the 'naturalist absurdity' of Chistiakova's life and text to discuss what it could be like to live through Soviet Russia as a woman of the first Soviet generation. We will see how the formative experiences of this female generation were combined in the *working mother*, the gender contract that has dominated Russian society since the forced industrialisation of the Stalin period.

By gender contract, I here understand a dominant form of gender relations in a specific society. The gender contract is no legal, formal agreement — rather, it denotes a prevailing view about how the relations between the sexes should be shaped. The gender contract may be both tacit and explicit, and it is shaped by social institutions and discourses. It especially reflects how family life is organised and under what conditions men and women can enter the public sphere and professional life. The gender contract can be approached from various angles. Yvonne Hirdman has shown how the gendered system of work is perpetuated in an asymmetrical and hierarchical way on the symbolic, the institutional and the individual levels of gender contracts. In Soviet society, we can also distinguish between the official, the everyday and the illegitimate gender contract.[14]

Many traits of the Soviet gender contract are already familiar from previous research. The specific contribution of this chapter is to redefine the concept of Russian gender traditionalism by introducing the notion of selective traditionalism. Chistiakova's detailed memories will also help us go beyond the stereotype of the 'strong Russian woman'. Both Western and Russian accounts of Russian working women have shown a 'remarkable measure of agreement ... resulting in admiration for the stoicism of Russian women mixed with frustration at their apparently willing acceptance of a subordinate role'.[15] Women in the Russian countryside and Soviet factories are easily lumped together to form a monolithic image of the strong woman who is also passive and self-sacrificing, a woman whose life is 'to labour, to bear and to endure'.[16] Her partner, the Russian man, is described just as stereotypically as a brutish drunkard. As with most stereotypes, these images are not totally untrue. Nevertheless, I would like to point to their structural underpinnings, and also to put some real flesh and blood on them, through discussing the forms of organising everyday life between genders and generations in Soviet Russia.

TURNING POINTS AND GENERATIONAL FORMATION

Born in 1922, five years after the October Revolution, Chistiakova belongs to the first generation born and raised in Soviet Russia. As it turned out, her generation was also the only one that lived through the main events of the life course under the Soviet regime. When the Soviet Union fell apart in 1991, Chistiakova had already been retired for more than a decade, her husband had returned from jail, and both her children had tragically died. The formative years of this generation were in the late 1930s, the period when Soviet society, including the Soviet class and gender order, was established. This generation benefited most dramatically from the educational and professional opportunities of Soviet society, as well as from the relative calm and material prosperity of late socialism in the 1960s and 1970s.

Obviously, many people of this generation also died in famines and camps or were denied education and professional self-realisation for political reasons. However, I will here focus on the constructive and 'positive' effects of the Soviet system. This is due to the interesting tendency of generational consciousness to feed on specifically positive experiences. Generational experiences appear to follow two criteria: they should happen at about the same time for the whole generational cohort, and they should help to build a positive self-image of that generation. Indeed, formative experiences are usually by definition positive in the sense of empowering, constructive, opening up ways of social advancement and creating new life-styles. Illness and death are individual turning points, but not the stuff that generations are made off. Tragedies that do affect a whole generational cohort simultaneously – such as economic depression, famine or war – tend to become formative generational experiences mainly through the way that they present opportunities for upward social mobility and create meaningful collective memories.[17]

I will discuss some of the major turning points in Aleksandra Chistiakova's life history, in order to highlight the formative experiences of the first Soviet generation. First, however, I will present a chronological overview of Chistiakova's life.[18] Table 7.1 shows the main events of her life course on the left, with individual turning points marked in bold. To the right are some of the major events in Soviet history that directly affected Chistiakova's life.[19]

Table 7.1 Chronology of Aleksandra Chistiakova's life history, with turning points marked in bold

Year	Chistiakova's life history	National events
1918		Family law of Soviet Russia passed [20]
1920		Abortion legalised
1922	**Birth of Aleksandra (A) in Maloitatka; A is the fourth daughter in the family**	
ca 1926	Mother sick with tuberculosis; birth of younger sister Tamara	
1928	**A starts school in Itata**	First five year plan
1929	Birth of A's brother	Forced industrialisation and collectivisation of agriculture
1932	Family moves to Tiazhin	Nationwide famine
1932	A in 3rd grade; mother sick again **A's parents divorce; the family splits up; A begs for food with her sister**	
1933	A's first love	
1936	A stays with elder sister; enters 4th grade	Abortion criminalised

Year	Chistiakova's life history	National events
1939	A joins mother and younger sisters in Taiga	World War Two begins
	A finishes 7th grade and enters professional education	
	A to Novosibirsk for training at construction site	
1943	A to Kemerovo, attends chauffeur courses	
	1st marriage and divorce	
1944	**2nd marriage, to Stepan Chistiakov, b. 1927**	
	1st pregnancy; Stepan sentenced to 3 years' jail	**End of World War Two**
1945	Stepan freed in post-war amnesty	
1945	**Birth of 1st son, Vladimir (Volodia)**	
c. 1947	2nd pregnancy, illegal abortion	
	Stepan unemployed, then tractor driver	
c. 1948	A looks for wage work after prolonged child-care leave	
	A employed at railway station	
1949	**Birth of 2nd son Anatolii (Tolia)**	
	4th pregnancy, illegal abortion	
1953		Death of Stalin
1955		Abortions legalised again
1958–60	**A builds a new house**	
c. 1961	**Stepan kills his own mother**	
	A rescues him from death sentence; Stepan jailed	
c. 1963	Volodia's army service	
c. 1967	Tolia's army service	
1968	Volodia marries	
	Tolia dies in accident in the army, 13 June	
1975	Stepan freed from jail	
1977	**A retires**	
c. 1978	**Volodia dies in accident**	
1991		Dissolution of the USSR
1997	A living with Stepan, active in community life	

Aleksandra's own mother was born during the last years of the nineteenth century into a poor village family in Siberia. Aleksandra's grandmother had been forced to send her daughters to work after becoming a widow. 'My mother was always praised for her cooking. She learnt that in the homes of the rich. After her father had died she worked as a nanny from the age of seven, then as a servant, that's how she learnt. And at seventeen she was already married.' Aleksandra's father also grew up in a poor agrarian family with too many mouths to feed. 'They were divided, each got a spoon and a cup, an old cow and an old mare.'[21] The couple settled down in the small town of Maloitatka and had six children altogether: five daughters, of whom Aleksandra was the fourth, and a younger son.

Aleksandra's first childhood memories – recorded in her diary at the age of 24, in 1946 – are those of a large, happy family. When their parents were away working in the fields, the three elder sisters took care of the house. The most joyful memories are of the whole family making *pelmeni*: 'Mother is making the dough, father rolls the meat, while we all put them together, and we were always singing while doing this.'[22]

Then Aleksandra's mother fell ill with tuberculosis. At first, her father reacted with appropriate concern: he sold the family's cow and sent his wife to be treated at the nearest hospital, in Tomsk, where she was temporarily cured. In 1928, Aleksandra's older sisters started school in the nearby town of Itata, and she persuaded her parents to let her start school earlier in order to be able to join her sister Katia, who was two years older and very close to her. The father, whose current occupation we are not told, was 'assigned' work in various small towns, and the family moved twice, so Aleksandra attended the third grade in Tiazhin. During these years her mother's illness continued. She also gave birth to two more children. While Aleksandra's mother was once more hospitalised, her father started drinking heavily and spending time away from home. When their mother returned, the children had stopped attending school, their clothes were in rags, and their father was having an affair with 'some dairymaid'. In 1932 the mother divorced him, and he disappeared, receiving no further mention in Aleksandra's life history.

After the divorce, Aleksandra's mother returned to live in Maloitatka with her own mother and brother, who was also Aleksandra's godfather. Soon afterwards, their house burned down and they all found themselves homeless. The eldest sisters had already married, but the middle children, Aleksandra and Katia, were sent to work in other people's homes – Aleksandra as a nanny, Katia as a servant – in a repetition of the childhood experiences of Aleksandra's mother. The two youngest children were left in the care of their grandmother and uncle. We are not told why or where Aleksandra's mother went. 'Mother left alone,' Aleksandra notes, in her only comment on being abandoned by both her father and her mother during the same year.[23]

Next autumn, famine hit. Katia and Aleksandra had to go on the streets begging for food. The nationwide famine of 1932–3 is nowadays estimated to have killed between three and seven million people. The tragedy was suppressed by the authorities and could only occasionally be referred to – as 'the well-known events' (*izvestnüe sobytiia*).[24] Chistiakova does not use the dangerous word 'hunger' (*golod*), but merely mentions 1932 as a 'year of bad harvest' (*god neurozhainyi*). She describes her own hunger and poverty openly, but does not mention other people dying of hunger.[25]

At this point there comes the first terrible memory to be described in detail. Aleksandra's uncle asked her to visit him, and she went to her grandmother's house in the hope of finding food, since 'they had everything, meat and grease and milk and much potatoes also'. Instead, he asked her to travel with him to the town where her mother was. (These small towns that the family moves between – Itatka and Maloitatka, Taiga and Tiazhin – all lie south of Tomsk, but are separated by hundreds of kilometres and several hours by train.) Evidently the uncle wanted to return Aleksandra's young brother to their mother. However, they could not find her, and when they returned by train the uncle refused to pay for Aleksandra's ticket, pretending he did not know her. The young girl was thrown out of the train and almost froze to death before she managed to get home. She did not cry, although her 'heart was pressed together'. After making it to her grandmother's house, she was put on top of the stove to warm herself, received 'a piece of bread and three cooked potatoes', and fell asleep. But when her uncle came home, he yelled at his mother for letting Aleksandra in. Aleksandra stood up and left the house without a word. Her grandmother did not apparently dare to say anything in her support. Outside, she could no longer hold back the tears and cried out loud.[26]

Parallel to such memories of abandonment and suffering run Aleksandra's memories of her first love, for Shura, a young man in her grandmother's village, her frequent attempts to travel there in order to meet him, and the problem of not having a pretty dress to put on. This dress problem also appears in Kiseleva's notebooks,[27] and reminds us of what kind of status symbol a factory-made dress was in the Siberian villages of the early 1930s. Although 80 per cent of Soviet citizens lived in the countryside, this part of the population received only 30–40 per cent of all textiles, shoes and soap – products that were also scarce in the cities. The peasants were severely underpaid and faced higher prices than urban citizens. According to one estimate, a peasant had in theory to sell 1630kg (or 100 Russian *pud*) of bread in order to buy one pair of boots.[28]

By then, Aleksandra was staying with her elder sister, and in 1939 she was reunited with her mother and younger siblings in Taiga. The family seems to have escaped the famines of 1936. Things slowly improved, if only in comparison with the collapse and chaos of the beginning of the decade. Aleksandra was the first generation of her family to finish seven years of school. While less than 10 per cent of Russian children had enrolled in grades five to seven in the 1920s, the proportion grew during Aleksandra's childhood to almost two-thirds in 1939.[29]

At the outbreak of World War Two, Aleksandra was seventeen years old and had just begun to work at a construction site. She started in outdoor production but was soon transferred to indoor work. News reached her about the infidelity of Shura, her childhood sweetheart, and when he soon afterwards married somebody else, she also quickly got married. However, her first marriage ended 'within a month', because it turned out that her husband was already married to somebody else and had a daughter. Such parallel marriages – whether officially registered or not – were not uncommon due to the migrations, evacuations, sexual licence and general instability of the war situation. Kiseleva's biggest sorrow was the loss of her first husband during the war, and when she found him again he had remarried. She scolds him for subsequently 'remarrying' several times without officially divorcing his first wife, while Kiseleva herself also lived in a second 'marriage' without first being divorced.[30]

By the time of her first short marriage, Aleksandra was already the object of attention from a 'countryside boy with curly hair ... but I did not like him at all, everything in this boy showed that he was rude and lacked manners'. The boy was five years her junior and called Stepan, or 'Stepa', Chistiakov. Notwithstanding this version of Aleksandra's first impression of Stepan – written in 1946, after they had been married for some years, by which time she already had many reasons to regret her choice – she soon decided that she could make him change his ways and would always stick to him. 'At this time Stepan Chistiakov crashed a car. I somehow started to pity him.'[31] He moved into her apartment after one of many quarrels with his sister and mother. Soon she was pregnant. It is not clear from the account at which point the Chistiakovs officially registered their marriage, although they probably did so at the beginning of their life together. From the mid-1930s to the mid-1950s, Soviet family policy was at its strictest, discouraging divorce, reintroducing the stigma of born-out-of-wedlock children, and protecting the rights of married men as opposed to those of unmarried mothers.[32] Nevertheless, it remained more liberal than the average family policy of capitalist Europe, especially the Catholic countries.

Stepan was a heavy drinker, and incapable of the kind of tenderness and attention Aleksandra longed for. Chistiakova's relatives soon understood that this marriage was the mistake of her life. Nevertheless, she stuck to her husband – and was evidently still living with him when the publication of her life history made her famous all over Russia.

At the very beginning of their life together, Stepan was sentenced to three years in prison for causing accidents at work when drunk. Miraculously, he was soon set free 'by uncle Kalinin in honour of Victory': that is, in the post-war general amnesty. From Kemerovo the couple moved to the village where Stepan's mother lived, sharing an apartment with Stepan's sister and another mother with two children. At the age of 23, Aleksandra gave birth to a son, Vladimir, known as Volodia. She notes how it was her mother-in-law and a friend of Stepan's, not the new father himself, who fetched her from the hospital. 'That is when my suffering began. My husband drinks, leaves with his mates, and I am sad. Volodia sucks my breast and screams the whole night, and sometimes the whole day. I cannot understand that he did not die of it.' [33]

After the war, Stepan's father returned from the front, but moved out soon afterwards, disappearing from the life of the family for the next fifteen years. Aleksandra's mother-in-law obtained a better dwelling from the *sovkhoz* and moved in there with her own daughter, Stepan, Aleksandra and little Volodia. They continued to live, on and off, with Stepan's mother for several decades.

Partly because of her baby's constant screaming, Aleksandra decided to stay at home with him for a few years. Her mother-in-law moved out after a quarrel about milk: as Chistiakova explains, her mother-in-law had taken all the milk to the house of her other son, so that Stepan had none. Such shortage of basic products was no exception. In the 1930s and 1940s, peasants often had worse access to bread and milk than they had had in the 1920s. It was only at the end of the 1950s that the production of dairy and meat products would return to the level of Aleksandra's childhood.[34]

When Volodia was a bit older, Aleksandra found herself a new job as a watchman at the railway station. Having registered as a worker, she immediately received a bread card of 800g for her and 400g for her son. This day, as we shall see below, was one of the happiest of her whole life. Also, in a longer perspective, family life settled down, and Aleksandra could often feel on 'firm ground'. She enjoyed work and its advantages – for example, she could take home coal from her work for heating the house. Stepan took care of the household when she had night shifts. The house was tidy: the floors shone 'like an egg yolk', and the baby was clean. Her mother-in-law was so impressed by these improved living standards that she wanted to move back in with them once again.[35]

In 1949 Stepan and Aleksandra's second son, Anatolii (Tolia), was born. Between and after these births Aleksandra had at least two illegal abortions, of which the first was almost fatal.[36] Stepan was still drinking more or less heavily, but there were moments when they lived as proper cultivated citizens and 'went to the cinema, or read books'. Aleksandra regularly received appreciation for and reward from her work on the railway.

But it is also at this time that we get the first close account of one of Stepan's jealous rages. The reason we are given for the outburst is that her mother-in-law had told him that Aleksandra had mentioned her earlier suitors when the two women were blaming each other for Stepan's drinking. When Stepan heard about this, he hit his wife on the head and tore her clothes to pieces. That time she fled to her sister, who advised her – as she always did – to leave her husband. Instead, Aleksandra wrote him a letter threatening to kill herself if he ever beat her again. He asked her to forgive him, and she did.[37]

At the age of 35, Aleksandra started having health problems in the form of complicated neural inflammations. She was ill for several months at a time, but recovered after several stays in special sanatoria, organised and paid for by her workplace. Then, at the end of the 1950s, Aleksandra embarked on one of the big projects of her life, that of constructing a house for their family. Detailed descriptions follow of how much workers should be paid, how to organise the transportation of roof tiles, etc. Obviously she had the organisational and most of the economic responsibility for the construction. Stepan also had health problems, and Aleksandra pushed him to obtain sanatorium trips from his workplace. At regular intervals Aleksandra also saved him from the consequences of the accidents he caused at work – once by proving that he could not be blamed for sinking a tractor in a marsh, as the boss had only seen the tractor but not Stepan actually driving it! Almost as frequently she tried to influence his employers to improve his behaviour, or at least to tell her how much money he should be bringing home. Tolerance for drunk-driving was obviously quite high at Stepan's workplace. When Aleksandra once called there as an outsider and asked, 'Please tell me, how is Chistiakov working these days?', the immediate cheerful response was that comrade Chistiakov was working very well.[38]

Then the first of a series of absolute tragedies hit. At a party, Stepan once again became jealous, and a heavy beating followed. When Aleksandra woke up, she found herself in hospital, while her mother-in-law was 'in the morgue'. For having killed his own mother, Stepan was initially sentenced to execution. Aleksandra then travelled, on her own and for the first time in her life, to Moscow to defend him. She succeeded, and Stepan's death sentence was changed to fifteen years in prison.

While Stepan was serving his sentence, their younger son, Tolia, died during his army service. Aleksandra was told that he accidentally became stuck under a crane.[39] In the mid-1970s, Stepan returned home from prison. Their older son, Volodia, had married and had two children (although Aleksandra believed the gossip about only the second being his biological child; she was not exactly fond of her daughter-in-law). Volodia had been persuaded by his mother to study at a professional high school and become a mountain engineer. His family, therefore, lived in what to Aleksandra's eyes was luxury: they had three rooms and a kitchen, a piano, and a Chinese table service for twelve persons. But then, in the late 1970s, Volodia too was killed in an accident, after attempting to climb into his apartment from a neighbour's balcony. The role of alcohol in this accident is not mentioned, but the reader knows that Volodia had for several years been both smoking and drinking.[40]

'Is this destiny? Or not knowing how to live otherwise? I still do not know', ends Aleksandra Chistiakova's published life history. As I have mentioned, such sweeping reflections are not typical of the whole text. Instead, we have frequent allusions to tears, to when it is of no use crying and yet one does so nevertheless. We also have recurring laments in the form of poems and letters written to Stepan: 'Everything good and sane in my organism I gave to you ... I did not have enough strength to re-educate you, I hope you are satisfied with the state you have pushed me to.'[41] The diary excerpts are also full of lengthy quotations of both Aleksandra's and other women's laments in connection with the deaths of relatives and children. However, it is crucial to remember that such rhetorical use of self-sacrifice and passivity does not imply actual passive behaviour.

The formative experiences of Aleksandra's generation of Russian women coincided, as we have seen, with the formation of the Soviet Russian gender contract. I will now approach this 'contract' as it was lived out by Aleksandra and her families. First, I will discuss the gender contract from the perspective of change and continuity in Russian women's work. Next, I will look more closely at women's care arrangements in the pattern of extended mothering; love stories and selective traditionalism in perceptions of masculinity and femininity; and finally at Aleksandra's encouraging experiences of professional life.

THE GENDER CONTRACT OF THE WORKING MOTHER

As in many workers' autobiographies, Aleksandra's transition to adulthood took place as she entered paid work.[42] In connection with her frequently interrupted years in school, Chistiakova recalls the young girl's eagerness to learn and her joy in studying. At the age of seventeen she received some marriage proposals, but turned them down and travelled alone to Novosibirsk in 1939. Through the Komsomol organisation she became a trainee at a construction site. Of the newcomers, twelve were men and three women. All the women were sent to the same work, which included outdoor digging. 'My girlfriends quit, but I decided to endure it.' Chistiakova also proudly remembers how she introduced the habit of reading the newspaper during lunchbreaks, one paradigmatic way of implementing active Soviet citizenship. Soon she was transferred to the storage room and white-collar work. As it was wartime and one of the supervisors was away at the front, she received much responsibility and work 'up to the ears ... I knew what to do in the household of one home. But this was a whole organisation!' She was also unprepared for the level of stealing that went on; everything from building materials to the cups from the canteen kept disappearing, until she learnt to demand receipts for everything. 'Probably the chairman of the local committee himself took them', she reflects about some lost curtains.[43] By this time, the black market had become an integral and parasitic part of the Soviet economy.[44]

After her training, Aleksandra's first permanent job was at a construction site, where she handled a transport vehicle together with a male chauffeur. Again, we are told how she succeeded in working in a male environment as a worthy stand-in for the men who were away fighting. She boasts about being approved of by the men – including those who were known to dislike female colleagues.

> I was so glad that, being so young, I could stand in for a man and that they did not laugh at me, like at the other girls, whom the steamers hunted. Sometimes I worked two shifts in a row and nobody knew about it.[45]

Eventually, Aleksandra was moved from Novosibirsk to Kemerovo, where her workplace provided her with an apartment of her own – a happy event, since most of her co-workers went to live in a workers' dormitory. She worked briefly as an operator at the station, but as she did not like it she applied for chauffeur courses. Once more, her gender created doubts about her competence and suitability, but she managed to win the argument. 'I pointed out that, as I will not be taken to the front, I should substitute for a man at the home front. And I succeeded.'[46] After quitting this workplace during her first pregnancy, at 29 Aleksandra was employed by the railway, and remained there until her retirement at the age of 55.

The young Aleksandra was thus part of the fast migration (if not flight) from the countryside to the cities and from agriculture to industry. During the first five-year plan, from 1928 to 1932, women moved into industrial work at a tempo unpredicted by Party politicians. The number of women in industry doubled within a few years, as they entered especially textiles and the railways, but also the iron and mining industries.[47] Aleksandra's career included several typical traits of women workers in the Soviet Union. In her first workplaces, she was one the women who did heavy industrial work 'as men' and together with men. In such heavy, male-dominated work, Russian women tended to encounter more sexist attitudes, sexual harassment, and a higher gendered wage gap.[48] Through her next work, on the railways, she again entered a previously male-dominated sector: before the Revolution, very few Russian women worked there, and in 1927 they constituted less than 9 per cent of railway workers. But in the following fifteen years women railway workers made fast progress, both in numbers and symbolically. The number of women in the railway sector rose rapidly in the early 1930s, and Soviet propaganda celebrated the first woman to become a fully qualified engine driver – Zinaida P. Troitskaia in 1935.[49]

For these reasons, it is often stressed that the decisive break with regard to women workers in Russia came not with the Bolshevik Revolution but during Stalin's forced industrialisation from 1928.[50] The lives of Aleksandra's grandmother in the 1890s and of her mother in the 1920s were quite similar: both were illiterate, agrarian women who worked long days and bore many children. The change came with Aleksandra's generation, although this change was of course not that women suddenly started working. In Aleksandra's family, women had always worked – in the fields, in households and in other people's homes. Indeed, if it makes any sense at all to use the expression 'traditional womanhood' in Russia, the term should refer to women raising children *and* working. The change of the 1930s consisted in the speed of women's education and entry into the workforce, especially the sharp increase in factory work and the wages this (unlike most agrarian and *kolkhoz* work) brought – money the women could freely dispose of. If one of the spouses in a Soviet family had control over all the family's income, it was usually the wife.

The type of gender relations that the Soviet state offered and forced women into from the early 1930s has been called the *contract of the wage working mother*. All women were supposed to do wage work and have children, while the socialist state was supposed to provide improved versions of traditional domestic work by establishing state canteens and nurseries. However, any abolition of the family or housework was no longer on the agenda when Aleksandra came of age, as it had briefly been in the 1920s. Stalinism reintroduced the concept of the tidy, well-kept home, the woman as its creator and the husband as a somewhat distant but authoritative person. Especially in the post-war period, Stalinist socialism emphasised soft, subdued femininity and moderate consumerism as part of promoting middle-class values.[51]

The woman who both mothered and worked for a wage quickly became the official, everyday norm – a part of the symbolic level of the Soviet gender contract that lasted well into post-socialist Russia. For instance, Chistiakova feels a need to justify her decision to stay at home with her first child for a while in the late 1940s: 'I did not work any longer. Where would I go from such a [screaming] child? Who would agree to look after him? And my work was inconvenient, over eight kilometres away. I thought that as I am married, and with a small child, no-one will judge me if I quit. Even more so as the war was over.'[52]

Later, Aleksandra made an appeal to the shared identity of women workers when she wanted to find out about Stepan's salary.

> The woman screamed to me that she did not have time to answer all the wives. Then I asked in an even quieter voice: 'Have you worked here for a long time?' She answers: 'Yes.' 'Know then that as long as this quarry exists I have called you for the first and maybe the last time. I'm a woman like you and I work like you. I bothered you because I want to learn what a conscience my husband has.' She listened to me, and now answered amiably that Chistiakov earned one thousand one hundred and fifty.[53]

The Soviet contract of the working mother has been described as a way of life where women were 'married to the state'. In this view, not the bourgeois male breadwinner but the patriarchal socialist state supported and exploited women's labour. Indeed, socialist social policies are even understood as intentionally undermining the patriarchal role of men in the family in order to gain increased control over both men and women. According to Marina Kiblitskaia, this 'marriage' was first and foremost based on women's sense of duty towards wage work, a duty that for the first Soviet generations often grew to a strong commitment and emotional attachment to work. Chistiakova's memories do show how the state – as mediated by the work collective – did indeed provide her with many things she expected but failed to get from her husband: appreciation, happiness, friendship, rest, truthfulness, rewards and gifts. The expression 'married to the state' also captures the important point that Soviet men were little symbolised in the Soviet gender contract. The relation focused on women, as they were held responsible for child rearing and social reproduction.[54]

However, the concept of being married to the state ignores two crucial aspects. First, and most obviously, it ignores the physical and sexual dimensions of gender and marriage – in this case, especially Stepan's continual beating of

Aleksandra and his relatives and all the consequences this had for family life. Second, the expression is constructed in opposition to the male breadwinner model, so that the state supported women 'instead' of her being provided for by her husband. For instance, in Sarah Ashwin's anthology *Gender, State and Society in Soviet and Post-Soviet Russia*, the frequent references to 'the traditional family' are either little defined or referring to a bourgeois nuclear family. Ashwin writes how 'the [Soviet] authorities sought to forge an alliance with mothers through their definition of motherhood as a noble and rewarded service to the state, rather than as a private matter proceeding from the relationship between husbands and wives', thus contrasting the state's alliance with the mothers with the 'private matters' of an isolated heterosexual couple; while Marina Kiblitskaia introduces the 'pre-revolutionary figure of the male breadwinner', in contrast to which Soviet women 'were supposed to look to the state and their work for support, not individual men'.[55] This is a crucial mistake, since the majority of both men and women in pre-revolutionary Russia did not live in nuclear but in extended family households. Most Russians have always, 'traditionally', worked both inside and outside the home and under the dictate of somebody else – first the landlord and the Tsar, then the socialist state. Hierarchical networks between women – in-laws and servants – were an integral part of daily coping. Aleksandra's mother and grandmother were used to their fathers and husbands being away fighting, drinking or at seasonal work. And even if present, they were not automatically reliable sources of either income or support.

Finally, the notion of 'marrying the state' completely ignores the vital importance of informal social networks in keeping up the Soviet gender contract. As we shall see, Aleksandra was in many senses as much 'married' to her mother-in-law and to her own mother, as she was to Stepan or to the state.

EXTENDED MOTHERING

The rapid move into industrial paid work described above went hand in hand with a drastic drop in the numbers of births. Together, these two tendencies formed the greatest change for Aleksandra's generation, compared to those of her mother and grandmother.[56] While forced industrialisation affected both sexes, the changes in reproductive behaviour were obviously more directly connected with women's lives. Indeed, a shorthand for the term 'gender contract' would be 'who takes care of the children?'.[57] The answer to this question was increasingly hard to provide, as mothers worked further away from home and as state childcare and other basic services were not adequately developed. Becoming a Soviet working mother implied developing intricate networks of predominantly female caring work.

For the smaller number of children being born, the pattern of extended mothering was essential. Victoria Semenova and Paul Thompson describe the crucial role of grandmothers in chapter 6 of this volume. Extended mothering –

the norm in most non-European cultures – takes care of children and household tasks through a large network of mainly female kin. The biological mother and her own mother and sisters, or mother-in-law and sisters-in-law, form the core, collecting around them other kin, friends and neighbours.

Aleksandra herself had been raised mainly by her biological parents until they divorced. She was born in the village of her maternal grandmother, and that is where her mother returned after she had left her unfaithful and drinking husband. In this and subsequent crises – the loss of their house, the famine – the mother relied on the help of her kin. So did Aleksandra when she had children of her own. After the birth of her first son, Volodia, Aleksandra's mother arrived and, obviously grasping the complicated marital situation, returned home with her young grandson. Her younger sister sent Aleksandra a letter – because the mother could not write herself, perhaps – urging her to leave Stepan and join her mother again: 'Leave it all! The precious thing in your life – that is Volodia, and Volodia will always be with you. Don't look at that house, you did not build yourself a house but a tomb. Leave it all, come here.' Similar invitations were accepted by other young Soviet mothers. One woman from Leningrad, born in 1923, the same year as Chistiakova, recalls how her mother persuaded her to leave her first husband: 'When I argued that he was the father of my child, [my mother] said: "The father is not the one who conceives, but the one who brings the child up ... " That is how I became a single mother.' But Chistiakova tells us that she felt uneasy about how people would react to her if she left her husband, and especially unsure about how her mother would react. 'I should not involve other people in my life.' Getting Volodia back was not easy, and Aleksandra had to send many demanding telegrams before he was returned. Aleksandra's mother clearly was 'not at all happy with my life'.[58]

The help from her maternal kin nevertheless continued. As Aleksandra was expecting her next child she travelled to her mother's town in order to give birth there. She then took her youngest sister back to Kemerovo as a nanny, and this sister eventually stayed in the city and married one of Stepan's friends. Most probably Aleksandra's relatives would have taken care of her children if something fatal had happened to her. Still, Stepan's maternal relatives were the ones directly involved in her everyday life. Following the usual Russian custom, Aleksandra moved in with her mother-in-law, whom she simply called 'mother'. In the beginning of her marriage, she also lived together with Stepan's sister.

Aleksandra's house project in the late 1950s should be seen against this background – it is a general desire to live 'at least these years like people live',[59] but it is also an attempt to live separately from Stepan's relatives. The couple's relations with his mother were never easy, and we have seen how she moved in and out of their house depending on her own income and her relations with other kin. For instance, in the late 1940s Aleksandra's mother-in-law had started drinking too much, and after the neighbours complained about her behaviour Stepan threw her out of the house. Aleksandra, although not very attached to her mother-in-law, complained about the loss of helping hands: 'We were left alone, but things did not get easier for me because of that. Earlier, at least, mother helped, so that I was not completely alone.'[60] Some years later, in 1952, Aleksandra, Stepan and his mother bought and fed a cow together. At last they had enough milk for everybody. Then, suddenly, the mother-in-law sold the cow and kept all the money for herself. Stepan and Aleksandra were upset and decided 'no longer to think about her as a mother'. But as winter approached, Aleksandra knew the old woman had no fuel, and took her back again to live with them.[61]

At an earlier point, when her two sons were still young, Chistiakova recalls hiring a nanny because her mother-in-law was wage working at the time. She almost presents this absence of her mother-in-law as a reason for aborting her fourth pregnancy:

> I was pregnant again. Again sorrow was on my head. Tolia is still small, no help at all from my husband, nor from his mother. She had begun to work at a sauna, she had begun to earn money. She began to eat separately, I had to take a nanny. I took a young girl.
> I made an abortion again.[62]

From the traditional Russian agrarian pattern of early marriage and many children, Soviet Russia moved in the 1930s to a pattern of somewhat later marriage and few children. In Aleksandra's generation, women with four or five children were already seen as exceptional. How much did this reflect desired birth limitation and to what extent was it a necessary response to harsh conditions? Unfulfilled dreams about a second or third child were found in many Russian women's lives.[63] In any case, the smaller number of children was a clear generational marker for Aleksandra's generation. Abortions were illegal for the first half of their reproductive years (1936-1955), the part of the life course during which most women give birth to children. This notwithstanding, her generation of Soviet mothers soon found ways to terminate unwanted pregnancies, and Stalin's anti-abortion legislation did not succeed in raising the number of births.

These patterns of extended mothering contrast sharply with the prevalent American and Northern European family pattern, where the biological parents are considered more central than a larger, female community. Extended mothering also constitutes one of the long-term continuities in Russian history, and continues well after Chistiakova's generation. When her son Volodia had his children, he and his wife took it for granted that Aleksandra would look after them. She grunted over this as the parents offered little compensation (for instance, once they brought her back nothing but 'two oranges' from a romantic trip they had made to the Black Sea). Nevertheless, she eagerly advised Volodia to leave his wife, keep his children and move back in with her: 'There's room, and I don't raise them any worse than she does.'[64]

THE ROLE OF BIOLOGICAL PARENTS

Extended motherhood made grandmothers a functional necessity, whether the parties involved liked it or not. In Chistiakova's life, we see how this feature of Russian family life formed part of the close urban–rural interaction in Soviet society. Forced industrialisation, the destruction of agricultural trade and the imposition of state distribution contributed to the peculiar Soviet phenomenon in which villagers travelled to the cities to buy food. At the same time, city residents used the countryside as a source of extra food and childcare provision; for importing nannies and grannies or exporting children to them. As the mother-in-law moved in and out with the Chistiakovs, so did Aleksandra's whole family appear to have moved in and out of an industrialised and monetarised way of life. This had already been typical of late nineteenth-century Russia. 'The patterns of migration reinforced the town–village nexus so that even where peasants became year-round factory workers, their ties with the village persisted, and the industrial system in Russia was permeated with the institutions, habits and customs of a recently enserfed peasantry whose communal tradition retained its vitality.'[65] It was only implemented on a grander scale in the 1930s and 1940s.

Some scholars like to present extended mothering as something completely different from current Western conceptions of motherhood. For instance, one overview of the research into contemporary transnational motherhood experienced by domestic servants in Europe quotes the relativist view that, because the child has several female caregivers, a prolonged absence of the mother (or father) is not as dramatic as it would be for a Western child, accustomed only to its biological parents. Other approaches have been more concerned about the emotional costs of both parents and children facing prolonged abandonment.[66] In any case, it is worth inquiring about the mother–daughter relation in Chistiakova's life history, and considering why she herself writes so little about it.

When Aleksandra was in her mid-thirties, she decided to write to the newspaper with a poem praising her mother. The poem was not published by the newspaper, but is included in her life history. Its rhymed verse depicts a touching image of a sweet, poor, illiterate mother with six children. All of the children now have their own families, but they lovingly gather around their mother every New Year's Eve. The children had always understood that their mother had a hard time coping, the poem claims: 'one needs means to clothe children, and where could she find them?' Still, the mother had succeeded with her wise education. 'Raising children does not demand luxury, but a wise approach and words', the poem ends.[67]

Chistiakova's verse is far from the empty glorification common in Soviet printed maternal praise. Nevertheless, the reader feels a bit uneasy recalling that this mother left all her children for one or more years during the worst times of hunger. The maternal – and paternal – abandonment in Aleksandra's youth is, as we have noted, never commented or reflected upon in the published text. It is difficult not to interpret this silence as one of suffering, a suffering that is then echoed in the numerous complaints about emotional abandonment in other close relations. This is because extended mothering does not, in my understanding, mean that all caregiving women are equally close to the child, or that the child and/or the mother do not suffer as a result of separation. What it does imply is a shared female responsibility for childraising and household work that does not systematically involve men.

What, then, was the place of men in the pattern of extended mothering typical of the Soviet working mother? In Stepan's family, as well as in Aleksandra's own childhood and adult families, men were not around or not to be trusted – including male blood relatives such as the treacherous uncle of the famine years. Aleksandra's mother, Stepan's mother and his sister had all divorced, although some of Aleksandra's sisters had husbands who did stay around. Men could provide support in the form of both money and care, but even then they were not as functionally necessary as the networks of extended kin. In her diary, Aleksandra often complained about Stepan's bad influence on the children and his refusal to assume a paternal role with them: 'You're one big misunderstanding, not a father!'[68] But otherwise she mostly remains silent about his emotional relationship with the children. At one point, she complains that he did not ask about the children when she visited him in prison. She presents us with only one indication of fatherly involvement, but one that is all the more touching. In the court during his trial for manslaughter, Stepan looked at his youngest son and started to cry, and then a little later he asked his older son to sit closer so that he could see him better.[69]

LOVE AND SELECTIVE TRADITIONALISM

As extended motherhood co-existed with a relatively frail marriage institution, it is worth looking more attentively at the depictions of heterosexual love in Chistiakova's life history. They appear to follow two quite common themes in Russian women's autobiographies: the story of the first and sweet love (with a tragic ending), and the story of the unhappy relationship the woman nevertheless decides to stay in. The first story is obviously not unique to Russian culture, although the status of pure and unhappy love appears to be especially prominent in Soviet Russia.[70] Kozlova and Sandomirskaia trace this characteristic to the traditional agrarian life course where the few years of non-married young courtship provided the only time of unregulated, joyful living and bittersweet memories.[71]

The second love story – the story of the Chistiakovs' marriage – is what probably most irritates its readers. Andrei Zorin found that the text had an 'intonation of resigned agreement with fate', and that 'the semi-question put in the title sounds as almost the only outburst of protest in the whole book'.[72] Of course, Chistiakova does protest – against her workload, against ignorant doctors, against fate, and most of all against Stepan's behaviour. But her protests have little credibility, as she always forgives him:

Oh sorrow, my sorrow! Even if I am away from him I know everything he is doing. Sometimes this thought came to me: if I only could stand up [from the sickbed] and then I should think it well over, should we live together or part? He is no friend to me, he has no feeling of pity for me ...

Again my partner started drinking. He's one day drunk, a second day, on the third I resolutely tell him: it's the vodka or me. Chose as you like, but there is no way I can accept your drinking.[73]

Aleksandra posed such questions in the second decade of her marriage. So why doesn't she leave him, the reader asks, and the author almost revels in her misery and self-denigration: 'I didn't have enough courage to divorce him, and I had to think about the upbringing of the children. How will they manage without a father? No, once you've started, you can't back out.'[74] She uses the Russian proverb, 'You have taken the rope, so you must pull.'

Interestingly, Chistiakova does not appeal to the good and/or the attractive sides Stepan probably did have. While her teenage first love was said to be 'like a flower, enchanting me', making her want to 'hug him and even kiss him',[75] Stepan is seldom pictured as being romantic. We get only a few glimpses of something: of how he used to call her his queen, or how once, after she had refused to sleep with him for several nights, a scene of tender reconciliation took place. 'Once at night he came to our bed and called me quietly: "Sasha, hey, Sasha". "What is it?" I answered. "Stop tormenting me, come to me." I was silent, but he took me in his arms and carried me like a child. He caressed me and was content that we had come back to each other.'[76]

Perhaps there were more such scenes, and perhaps Chistiakova, who can openly describe do-it-yourself abortions and illness, did not want to record sexual passion. Be that as it may, her obstinate attachment to her husband can well be regarded as an active attitude to life – contrary to what her rhetoric of weakness and self-sacrifice implies. Keeping her marriage, against the advice of her closest kin and her own better knowledge, even just keeping her husband alive, demand enormous efforts, from trying to get hold of Stepan's salary before he drinks it away, to saving him from a death sentence by travelling alone to Moscow to defend him, replacing an inefficient lawyer. Obviously one cannot recommend this marital strategy for everybody, but does that make it less of an absolute protest?

Nevertheless, the limits of my understanding are reached at the point where Chistiakova recommends her own way of life to the next generation of Russian women. When her daughter-in-law told her that her son, after receiving a work bonus, had been drinking and stayed away the whole night, Aleksandra retorted:

'Is that all?'
'Is that not enough?'
'It's not enough to worry a mother ... Look at your drunkard husband – your apartment is furnished like a high boss's and you've

only just started living together ... I don't say that it's good that he was drinking, that's not right, but you should live in peace with your family ... '[77]

Similarly, when Aleksandra's young friend complained that her boyfriend was drinking and told Aleksandra that she had written about this to her own mother, Aleksandra immediately advised the young woman to send a telegram home saying, 'Dear parents, everything is fine' – supposedly in order to protect her mother's health.[78]

In her obstinate devotion to her husband, Chistiakova is obviously not representative of her generation, in which Russian women did initiate divorce – all the more often once it had again become easier in the mid-1950s. But she does espouse a trait typical of the Soviet gender contract when it comes to her view of masculinity and femininity. ' "You're a man, aren't you", I said, "you look strong and brave, but your little soul is worse than a weak woman's." '[79]

At another time, Stepan had a very bad headache, and Aleksandra tried to organise for him a trip to a sanatorium, but he resisted getting his medical certificate and said he preferred to die.

'Who will you surprise', I said, 'if you go into the moist earth in these years. It's never too late to die, but in order to live as a human being, that's where you need willpower. You're a man, but you have no willpower, and that's very bad. I'm even sometimes ashamed of you, that you're so weak. And then you also drink vodka.'[80]

Such statements are typical, are frequently found in Soviet and post-Soviet talk, and have been labeled Russian 'gender traditionalism'.[81] In family life, the husband is supposed to be strong and authoritative and the wife soft and submissive, so the tradition goes. This perception of gender had deep roots in Tsarist legislation and Bolshevik ideology. It also formed an integral part of the contract of the Soviet working mother, who was supposed to put the needs of her husband and children before any personal ambitions. Both men and women generally appreciated gender equality at work but not at home, and this was (and still is) true also for many career women in Russia.[82]

However, one should be careful not to confound this lip-service to 'tradition' with traditional practices. Soviet-style gender traditionalism often implied a normative *longing* for a certain kind of fixed, stable relation, thought of as 'natural' and 'normal'.[83] Men longed to be able to control women's reproductive and professional behaviour; women longed for emotional and practical support from men. In Chistiakova's text, we see a clearly strategic use of traditions: among traditional values, only those that would have suited her situation are appealed to, but others not. For instance, in Russian tradition the daughter-in-law should obey the mother-in-law. Aleksandra clearly did not always do this, and nowhere in her quarrels with Stepan's mother is this tradition alluded to.

Kozlova and Sandomirskaia correctly underscore that such unattractive traditions simply disappeared: 'Traditions force the fiancée to submit to the mother-in-law, to perform certain domestic duties and generally to "show respect". When the crust of habits falls apart, fiancées stop obeying. This submission is not replaced at all by some other level of relations, it simply ceases to exist. The conflict becomes grimmer and less controlled.'[84]

This perceptive comment, however, does not prevent Kozlova and Sandomirskaia's analysis from assigning women a more 'traditional' role with regard to their male partners. Thus they suggest that destruction of traditional female and male sociability followed a different pattern: 'The woman tries to follow a traditional morality in marriage. For the men this model has been destroyed. Women reproduce traditional values, providing the functions of protecting community life. For instance, men drink away their salary, but, because of the garden, fowls and domestic supplies, the family's life continues.'[85] But this view of male traditional behaviour is mistaken in its implicit reference to a male breadwinner that was never widely represented in Russia (nor in most other countries).

The interpretation also obscures the rational and pragmatic 'tradition work' which Soviet Russian women performed. For instance, Chistiakova tells us that Stepan used to complain about how she spent their income. Her reaction is not to oppose the 'tradition', but to challenge him to live up to it: 'Many times we quarrelled over money. I said: "Maybe indeed I cannot handle money; then stop drinking and take command yourself. But don't yell at me in front of the children."'[86] In a situation where she organised and to a large extent financed everything the family did, Aleksandra had no reason to question the principle that a man should be in charge of the household money. But on the other hand, as we shall see, she was quick and effective in overriding Stepan's 'traditionally male' attempts to decide over where she would work.

WORK – THE FRIENDLY FAMILY

Chistiakova complains that her first, harsh construction work destroyed her looks: 'I had become so terrible that if anybody I knew had seen me they would not have recognized me. My face was wind-torn and my cheeks were peeling, as if I had frozen them a couple of times.'[87] But that is the only negative comment ever connected with her work. Only a couple of times does she discuss her work with the lamenting style that characterises the descriptions of her social relations, and that is when she felt excluded from work due to illness or retirement. Generally, work is the only constant source of pride, success and self-esteem in her life. As we have seen, her mother, father, sisters, relatives, children, mother-in-law and husband – all betray her at some point. But her workplace never did. It fed her, it healed her, it even remembered her birthday – and women's day on the 8 March – which her husband and sons all tended to forget. When

Aleksandra attempted to improve her working conditions, she succeeded in getting both more pay and two additional employees – very much unlike her numerous attempts to improve her husband.

The story of how Aleksandra found herself a new workplace after the birth of her first son is worth quoting at length here:

> All three of us [Stepan, his sister and Aleksandra] were unemployed. I went looking for work. I learnt that they needed motorist women for the mine. I came home and said to him, I'm going there to register. My husband said: 'When you die, that's when you go to lie below the earth.' I said 'I went to the canteen, they need a cashier woman.' So again he says: 'I can swear enough at home, better than everybody swearing at you in the canteen.' Then I decided: 'I won't ask him because then you never get a place.'
>
> I am going to the mine station. I meet a weigher, Galia, a nice young woman. I boldly ask her: 'Do you need a switchman or a weigher?' ... I wrote an application, and the foreman signed me on at once: 'Register as a watchman in the Butovskaia station in place of Shishkina.' ... The head of the administration also signed ... On the way home I stopped by the buffet Severnyi, bought two and four hundred [grams of] bread, and for the meat units on the food card I bought sausage. At that time I was shining from joy and pride at having come to stand on firm ground again. I walked so that probably no-one could have caught up with me. I wanted to surprise Stepan and entertain my beloved son. Stepan was actually glad when I told him that I would be a watchman on the station to the Butovskaia mine.[88]

Applying the fairy-tale structure of three attempts, Chistiakova here describes both the potential tensions between husband and wife caused by her wage work, and her enormous personal happiness. Aleksandra's retirement was even more loaded with emotions and proud memories. In the spring before her 55th birthday, she travelled on a holiday and health trip organised through her work. She knew it would be her last.

> In Piatigorsk it was spring, very good care. We travelled with the guide to Kislovodsk and Essentuki, and the food was marvellous. I gathered strength for the whole rest of my life. I knew that I would soon retire and I will not dare to provoke the administration, although I will pay the trade union fees. I often thought about my retirement. I trained the new switchman as well as I could.
>
> One night I was lonesome and wrote again:
>
> ... I do not wish for this, my friends

My heart is aching too

Retirement – there it all ends

And no-one visits you.[89]

After listening to this poem, her colleagues assured her that they would not forget her. Indeed, on Aleksandra's birthday they did show up, organised a party at the station, dressed her in new clothes from top to toe, and awarded her a premium of 100 roubles together with an honorary diploma as a veteran of work. The whole evening was perfect, with music, songs and dancing, and 'Stepan restraining himself, so as not to show his bad side'.[90] This is one of the few times he ever gets credit for not ruining everything. In this final turning point of her professional career, Aleksandra was celebrated by her work collective almost like a bride – witness the new clothes – and the importance of the situation even made her husband behave properly.

CONCLUSIONS

Aleksandra Chistiakova's published life history illustrates the dramatic change which Russian gender relations underwent in little more than a decade, from the end of the 1920s to the post-war situation. In one generation, Soviet women experienced uniquely rapid social and gendered mobility. They achieved the means to decide about their education, spouse, numbers of children and the use of their own money in a way that was limited, but still unprecedented, for the Russian majority.

I have focused here on the formative experiences of a female generation, consciously emphasising the positive and constructive experiences. We can see Aleksandra's pride and joy in work as constitutive of the generation of the Soviet working mothers who gained financial independence, but who also enjoyed bringing home an especially good dinner for their husband and children. Chistiakova's story is one in which the state's relation to women is basically supporting and empowering. It is through her education and her work collective that she 'comes to stay on firm ground', can fulfil her dreams of building a proper house, can cure her illnesses, and can keep her family life at least partly under control.

Aleksandra's happy depictions of her workplace in the 1940s almost echo the situation of contemporary Western culture, where work is said to feel like home should feel, while home feels like work.[91] Nevertheless, her life history can also help us guard against the nowadays quite common view that socialism made women 'neglect' and 'sacrifice' their private and personal lives.[92] The same lesson can be drawn from the life history of Evgeniia Kiseleva, which I have partly discussed in relation to Chistiakova's fate. Kiseleva always worked in low-esteemed service jobs and her life trajectory did not move towards an established and respectable working-class lifestyle as Chistiakova's did. In Kiseleva's case, the professional, private and public spheres do not appear to be separated from each other at all: she lives in a traditional world 'where everybody knows each other'.[93] Also for more generalisable data and with regard to the educated middle-class, Soviet Russian private relations appear to have been *more*, not less, intertwined with professional relations in comparison with Western Europe.[94] These findings contradict any easy assertions about what Soviet people neglected, although they do lead us to interesting further questions about the varying meanings of 'the private'.

Chistiakova's family life did not suffer as a result of her working life. On the contrary, it benefited from the now-extinct Soviet social policy that provided inexpensive, week-long trips for exhausted women or alcoholic men, and summer camps for children of all classes. Support from the state and the work collective can strengthen family life instead of undermining it. This should not make us forget the countless instances where the Soviet system on the contrary destroyed family life by imposing bureaucratic obstacles to professional self-realisation or by causing death by famine and political repression. Neither should this lead to any hasty conclusions about socialist achievements. As Irina Osokina has stressed, the feeling of material improvement many of this generation of men and women experienced was until the 1960s an actual improvement only in comparison to their youth in the early 1930s – and that period was in many ways worse and poorer than the 1910s or the 1920s.[95]

The Soviet system did not invent Russian women's harsh work, it did not even invent women's industrial work. Rather, it implemented female wage work on a massive scale, and presented the majority with new educational and professional opportunities, increasing women's economic and marital independence. As in many other tales of the modernisation of patriarchal agrarian societies, most women had relatively more to gain than most men. The gender contract of 'the Soviet working mother' was indeed in many respects an affair between women and the State. A man could lose his influence over his wife's choices, as she simply agreed with the employer without telling him first.

For this reason, it is sometimes claimed that Soviet ideology and everyday life presupposed a male breadwinner. According to this view, family life and traditions would follow the model of the male as the head of the family, notwithstanding egalitarian Communist rhetoric. There are several indicators that support this conclusion: the existence of a gender gap in wages; the nuclear family propaganda from Stalin to Brezhnev; the high tolerance for abusive and violent male behaviour; and the speed with which the male breadwinner was reintroduced in post-socialist Russia.

However, this argument tends to overlook the historical fact that both the bourgeoisie and its cultural values, including its gender values, rooted themselves comparatively late and only partially in Tsarist Russia.[96] In Soviet times, support of the male breadwinner ideal is not monolithic, but varies according to gender and class. For instance, a recent study shows how explicit propaganda for a male breadwinner and head of the household is most often found among educated men of the Russian middle class, while male manual workers tend to talk less about differences in sex roles and duties. Allusions to the male breadwinner also serve different strategic aims when uttered by men and by women. It is in the collective interest of men to support the idea of submissive women. When women subscribe to apparently misogynistic ideas, it often expresses a longing – a dream of a second breadwinner in addition to the female, and a dream of a supportive and reliable husband. We need to take better account of the ways in which Russian women have made rational and pragmatic use of their 'traditional' habits, discarding the ones that restricted their freedom of movement and repeating the ones that could have increased their amount of received help, support, love and understanding.

Notes

1 Aleksandra Chistiakova, *Ne mnogo li dlia odnoi?* [Enough for One Woman?] (Den' i noch', Krasnoiarsk, 1998). I want to thank Natalia Kolesova, Marianne Liljeström, Arja Rosenholm, Kristina Rotkirch, Marja Rytkönen and Irina Savkina for their useful help and commentaries in reading this autobiography.
2 See the autobiography of Evgeniia Kiseleva published in N.N. Kozlova and I.I. Sandomirskaia, *Ia tak tak khochu nazvat' kino. 'Naivnoe Pis'mo'. Opyt lingvo-sotsiologicheskogo chteniia* [That's what I want to call the movie. The 'naive letter'. The experience of a linguo-sociological reading] (Gnozis, Moscow, 1996), in which ordinary words are spelled the way they are pronounced, *ftoroi* instead of *vtoroi* [second], or *harasho* instead of *horosho* [good]). Another autobiography of a Russian woman worker born in 1925 is discussed in Anna Rotkirch, *The Man Question, Loves and Lives in Late 20th Century Russia* (Department of social policy, University of Helsinki, Helsinki, 2000).
3 Chistiakova, *Ne Mnogo li dlia Odnoi?*, 35.
4 Andrei Zorin, *Kak ia byl predsedatelem* [When I was chair], *Neprikosnovennyi Zapas*, 4, 6, (1999).
5 Zorin, *ibid.*; Irina Savkina, personal communication, Tampere, 1998.
6 Svetlana Boym, *Common Places: Mythologies of Everyday Life in Russia* (Harvard University Press, Cambridge, Mass., 1994).
7 Kozlova and Sandomirskaia, *Ia tak tak khochu nazvat' kino*, 7; Elena Zdravomyslova, 'Male life histories from St Petersburg', paper presented at the 4th European Conference of Sociology, RN1: Biographical Perspectives on European Societies, Amsterdam, 18–21 August 1999.
8 Marja Rytkönen, 'Narrating female subjectivity in the autobiographical texts of Elena Bonner, Emma Gertejn and Maiija Pliseckaja', *NORA Nordic Journal of Women's Studies*, 7, 1 (1999), 34–46.
9 Kozlova and Sandomirskaia, *Ia tak tak khochu nazvat' kino*, 87, 73–5. Among autobiographical publications of poor and marginalised groups we also find the collection *Rasskazhi Svoiu Istoriiu* [Tell Us Your Story] (Fond Nochlezhka, St Petersburg, 1999). Although extremely valuable and interesting, most of these stories are quite short and centre on the social marginalisation of the narrators in the 1980s and 1990s. This general scarcity of (published) non-middle-class women's autobiographies is evident, for example, in Jane McDermid and Anna Hillyar, *Women and Work in Russia 1880–1930. A Study in Continuity through Change* (Longman, London and New York, 1998), which aims to make extensive use of Russian women worker's memoirs, but does not feature any autobiographical accounts by ordinary Soviet women, partly

because most women workers were still illiterate in the 1920s. For published oral histories of rural and working women of the same generation as Chistiakova, see Marina Malysheva and Daniel Bertaux, 'The social experiences of a countrywoman in Soviet Russia', in Selma Leydesdorff, Luisa Passerini and Paul Thompson (eds), *Gender and Memory*, International Yearbook of Oral History and Life Stories, IV (Oxford University Press, Oxford, 1996), 31–44; and Anastasia Posadskaya-Vanderbeck and Barbara Alpen-Engel, *A Revolution of Their Own: Voices of Women in Soviet History* (Westview Press, New York, 1998).

10 Sheila Fitzpatrick, 'Lives and Times', in Sheila Fitzpatrick and Yuri Slezkine (eds), *In the Shadow of Revolution: Life Stories of Russian Women from 1917 to the Second World War* (Princeton, Princeton University Press, 2000), 3–17.

11 See Marianne Liljeström, chapter 11, this volume.

12 Kozlova and Sandomirskaia, *Ia tak tak Khochu Nazvat' Kino*, 156–7.

13 Zorin, *Kak ia byl predsedatelem*.

14 Yvonne Hirdman, *The Gender System: Theoretical Reflections on the Social Subordination of Women* (The Study of Power and Democracy in Sweden, English Series, Report 40, Uppsala, 1990). The Soviet gender contract of the working mother has been described in Anna Temkina and Anna Rotkirch, 'Soviet gender contracts and their shifts in contemporary Russia', *Idäntutkimus: Finnish Journal of Russian and Eastern European Studies*, 2 (1997), 6–24.

15 McDermid and Hillyar, *Women and Work in Russia*, 3–4.

16 *Ibid.*, 9.

17 Tommi Hoikkala, Semi Purhonen and J.P. Roos, 'The baby boomers, life's turning points and generational consciousness', in Bryan Turner and June Edmunds (eds), *Generational Consciousness, Narrative and Politics* (Rowman and Littlefield, London, 2002: 145–64). As these authors stress, there is also a significant difference between the generational consciousness of the elite and that of 'ordinary' people. Here I will ignore this distinction and discuss 'formative generational experience' in the meaning of the key social events and structures facing a certain age cohort (not as how the members of this age cohort would define their generation themselves).

18 I refer to Chistiakova as the author of her life history and in the present tense, while I use Aleksandra and the past tense to denote the actions of the protagonist of the life history; e.g., 'Chistiakova recalls how happy Aleksandra was to start school'.

19 For this way of presenting the individual life course together with main historical events, see Daniel Bertaux, *Les récits de vie*, Nathan, Paris, 1997.

20 The original family law of the Soviet Russian generation is world-famous for its gender equality. Marriage required the mutual agreement of the future spouses, and divorce could be obtained if both or either of the spouses so desired. The spouses had no right to each other's property, the wife had the right to keep her own surname, and the status of children born in and out of wedlock was formally equal. The abolition of large private properties also diminished economic inequalities between men and women. For a collection with English translations of early Soviet family legislation and principles, see Rudolf Schlesinger, *The Family in the USSR: Changing Attitudes in Soviet Russia – Documents and Readings* (Routledge, London, 1949). For an overview of Soviet family policy in this period, see Wendy Z. Goldman, *Women, the State and Revolution: Soviet Family Policy and Social Life, 1917–1936* (Cambridge University Press, Cambridge, 1993).

21 Chistiakova, *Ne mnogo li dlia odnoi?*, 34.

22 *Ibid.*

23 *Ibid.*, 35.

24 Between 1928 and 1932 the previous system of trade and distribution of food and basic goods practically broke down, as the remaining private companies and trade relations were destroyed. Furthermore, the Soviet State imposed heavy production

quotas for the countryside, quotas which had to be met irrespective of the harvest. In addition to the national famine of 1932–3, bad harvests easily led to local famines later in the 1930s too. Elena Osokina, *Za Fasadom 'Stalinskogo Izobiliia'. Raspredelenie i Ryno Snabzhenii Naseleniia v Gody Industrializatsii 1927–1941* [Behind the Façade of 'Stalin's Time of Abundance': Distribution and the Market for the Population during the Years of Industrialization 1927–1941] (Rossiiskaia akademiaa nauk, Institut Russkoi Istorii, Rosspen, Moscow, 1999), 114–20. An English version of this has appeared as Elena Osokina, Kate S. Transchel and Greta Bucher, *Our Daily Bread: Socialist Distribution and the Art of Survival in Stalin's Russia, 1927–1941* (M.E. Sharpe, Armonk, 2001).

25 Chistiakova, *Ne mnogo li dlia odnoi?*, 35. By contrast, Evgeniia Kiseleva uses the word 'hunger' in 1933 in her life history, written in the 1970s. Kiseleva escaped by being employed in a canteen, and remembers stealing extra bread to help the hungry miners (Kozlova and Sandomirskaia, *Ia tak tak khochu nazvat' kino*, 227–9).
26 Chistiakova, *Ne Mnogo li dlia Odnoi?*, 36.
27 Kozlova and Sandomirskaiia, *Ia tak tak khochu nazvat' kino*, 156.
28 Osokina, *Za Fasadom 'Stalinskogo Izobiliia'*, 115–17.
29 Gail Lapidus, *Women in Soviet Society: Equality, Development, and Social Change* (University of California Press, Berkeley, 1978), 140.
30 Kozlova and Sandomirskaiia, *Ia tak tak khochu nazvat' kino*, 70.
31 Chistiakova, *Ne mnogo li dlia odnoi?*, 41–2.
32 Lapidus, *Women in Soviet Society*, 111–14.
33 Chistiakova, *Ne mnogo li dlia odnoi?*, 42.
34 R.W. Davies, Mark Harrison and Stephen Wheatcroft, *The Economic Transformation of the Soviet Union, 1913–1945* (Cambridge University Press, Cambridge, 1994), 21, 41.
35 Chistiakova, *Ne mnogo li dlia odnoi?*, 44.
36 Chistiakova recalls how she first lay silently bleeding for one whole night, without complaining and without her husband or her mother-in-law noticing anything. When her mother-in-law understood the situation, no doctor willing to help Aleksandra could be found. However, Stepan returned home from work and brought her milk and sugar. His care and the sweet milk gave Aleksandra power 'to continue fighting and not give in to death'. For a discussion of the symbolism used in this story, see Rotkirch, *The Man Question*, 99–101.
37 Chistiakova, *Ne mnogo li dlia odnoi?*, 45–6, 50.
38 *Ibid.*, 56.
39 *Ibid.*, 68 and 74.
40 *Ibid.*, 81.
41 *Ibid.*, 46.
42 Cf. Mary Jo Maynes, *Taking the Hard Road: Life Course in French and German Workers' Autobiographies in the Era of Industrialization* (University of North Carolina Press, Chapel Hill, 1995), 102.
43 Chistiakova, *Ne mnogo li dlia odnoi?*, 40.
44 Osokina, *Za Fasadom 'Stalinskogo Izobiliia'*, 11. Osokina calls the period between 1936 and 1941 a 'union' between State distribution and (legal or illegal) market provision. Evgeniia 'Zhenia' Kiseleva was at the same time employed in a food shop selling fish. She stole some fish and was caught by her boss, who yelled at her. 'I was all burning [with shame], I thought probably you have to cheat people ... I counted wrongly, where it was 200g I said 300g, where 500g I said 700g ... "What do you do, Zhenia, after the shop has closed – you will come to my office." I could not wait for the end of the working day. I entered trembling after work, but he stood up from his table, tapped me on the right-hand shoulder, and said "Ah-ah-ah, I think that is how one should work, that is how" ... Until 1941 I worked in the shop, both honestly and cheating people.' (Kozlova and Sandomirskaia, *Ia tak tak khochu nazvat' kino*, 219.)

45 Chistiakova, *Ne mnogo li dlia odnoi?*, 40.
46 *Ibid.*, 41.
47 Lapidus, *Women in Soviet Society*, 99; McDermid and Hillyar, *Women and Work in Russia*, 202. Soviet women did not become domestic servants as often as in Western Europe, where it was a typical form of female urban migration: Malysheva and Bertaux, 'The social experiences of a countrywoman', 39; Lapidus, *Women in Soviet Society*, 108.
48 McDermid and Hillyar, *Women and Work in Russia*, 201.
49 *Ibid.*, 202.
50 Lapidus, *Women in Soviet Society*, 95–122; McDermid and Hillyar, *Women and Work in Russia*, 3.
51 On Soviet gender ideology of the 1920s and 1930s, see Barbara Clements, 'The birth of the New Soviet Woman', in Abbott Gleason, Peter Kenez and Richard Stites (eds), *Bolshevik Culture: Experiment and Order in the Russian Revolution* (Indiana University Press, Bloomington, 1985), 220–37; and Goldman, *Women, the State and Revolution*. On post-war conceptions of gender, see Vera Dunham, *In Stalin's Time. Middleclass Values in Soviet Fiction* (Cambridge University Press, Cambridge, 1976).
52 Chistiakova, *Ne mnogo li dlia odnoi?*, 42.
53 *Ibid.*, 49.
54 The expression 'married to the state' is found in Marina Kiblitskaya, 'Russia's female breadwinners: the changing subjective experience', in Sarah Ashwin (ed.), *Gender, State and Society in Soviet and Post-Soviet Russia* (Routledge, London, 2000), 55–70.
55 Sarah Ashwin, 'Introduction' to *Gender, State and Society in Soviet and Post-Soviet Russia*, 11; Kiblitskaya, 'Russia's female breadwinners', 65. See also Sergei Kukhterin, 'Fathers and patriarchs in communist and post-communist Russia', *ibid.*, 71–89, for a better-argued but still problematic perception of what the 'traditional' Russian family and patriarch was.
56 As in most countries, the drop in birth rate in Soviet Russia did not totally coincide with industrialisation. In Russia, the decline in the birth rate was under way in urban areas by the end of the nineteenth century. It then accelerated during the first decades of Soviet power. By the 1970s, the average number of children per family was 2.24 in the countryside and 1.64 in the towns: Ellen Jones and Fred W. Grupp, *Modernization, Value Change, and Fertility in the Soviet Union* (Cambridge University Press, Cambridge, 1987).
57 Temkina and Rotkirch, 'Soviet gender contracts'.
58 Chistiakova, *Ne mnogo li dlia odnoi?*, 44–5. The quotation from the Leningrad woman's autobiography is from Rotkirch, *The Man Question*, 126.
59 Chistiakova, *Ne mnogo li dlia odnoi?*, 42.
60 *Ibid.*, 48.
61 *Ibid.*, 51.
62 *Ibid.*, 45.
63 E.g. Valentina Belova, *Chislo Detei v Sem'e* [The Number of Children in the Family], (Statistica, Moscow, 1975), 109–41
64 Chistiakova, *Ne mnogo li dlia odnoi?*, 80.
65 McDermid and Hillyar, *Women and Work in Russia*, 34.
66 Emma Lutz, ' "At your service, madame!" The globalization of domestic service', *Feminist Review*, 70 (2002), 89–104.
67 Chistiakova, *Ne mnogo li dlia odnoi?*, 55.
68 *Ibid.*, 52.
69 *Ibid.*, 67.
70 Rotkirch, *The Man Question*, 58–77.
71 Kozlova and Sandomirskaia, *Ia tak tak hochu nazvat' kino*, 73.
72 Zorin, *Kak ia byl predsedatelem*.
73 Chistiakova, *Ne mnogo li dlia odnoi?*, 52, 54.

74 *Ibid.*, 55.
75 *Ibid.*, 37–8.
76 *Ibid.*, 55.
77 *Ibid.*, 76.
78 *Ibid.*, 76–7.
79 *Ibid.*, 50.
80 *Ibid.*, 56.
81 Peggy Watson, 'Eastern Europe's silent revolution: gender', *Sociology*, 27, 3 (1993), 471–87; Kiblitskaya, 'Russia's female breadwinners'; Kozlova and Sandomirskaia, *Ia tak tak hochu nazvat' kino*, 72–7.
82 See, e.g., Lynne Attwood, 'Young people's attitudes towards sex roles and sexuality', in Hilary Pilkington (ed.), *Gender, Generation and Identity in Contemporary Russia*, (Routledge, London, 1996), 132–51; Anna Temkina, 'Women's ways of entering politics', in Anna Rotkirch and Elina Haavio-Mannila (eds), *Women's Voices in Russia Today*, (Dartmouth, Aldershot, 1996), 33–48.
83 Watson, 'Eastern Europe's silent revolution', 472.
84 Kozlova and Sandomirskaia, *Ia tak tak Khochu nazvat' kino*, 77.
85 *Ibid.*, 72.
86 Chistiakova, *Ne mnogo li dlia odnoi?*, 54.
87 *Ibid.*, 39.
88 *Ibid.*, 44.
89 *'No mne ne chochetsia, druzia, i serdtse moe zhmet, uidesh na pensio – konets nikto uzh ne pridet.'* This is the third of four verses; *ibid.*, 79.
90 *Ibid.*, 80.
91 Arlie R. Hochschild, *The Time Bind, When Work Becomes Home and Home Becomes Work* (Metropolitan Books, New York, 1997).
92 Kiblitskaya, 'Russia's female breadwinners', 56, 60.
93 Kozlova and Sandomirskaia, *Ia tak tak Khochu nazvat' kino*, 58.
94 Markku Lonkila, 'The social meaning of work: the teaching profession in post-Soviet Russia', *Europe-Asia Studies*, 50, 4 (1998), 699–712.
95 Osokina, *Za fasadom 'stalinskogo izobiliia'*, 236.
96 For the relatively late arrival of the bourgeois gender role, see, e.g., Laurie Engelstein, *The Keys to Happiness: Sex and the Search for Modernity in Fin-de-siècle Russia* (Cornell University Press, Ithaca, 1992), 4.

8

THE STRENGTH OF SMALL FREEDOMS

A Response to Ionin, by Way of Stories Told at the *Dacha*

Naomi Roslyn Galtz

In 1997, while pursuing fieldwork in Moscow, I had the great pleasure of becoming acquainted with several members of the Moscow Institute of Sociology who – through their work on the landmark collection, *Sud'by Liudei* [The Fates of People][1] – helped to firmly establish a role for life-history approaches in post-Soviet sociology. In one of our discussions, these colleagues shared an article which had recently occupied their attention, 'Freedom in the USSR', by the political scientist L.G. Ionin.[2] They mused that, in certain respects, this article provided a perfect companion piece to *Sud'by Liudei*.

The connection was a curious one. *Sud'by Liudei* grew out of a central project gathering multi-generational life histories; Ionin, author of 'Everyday Life', did not participate in the project, nor is he a proponent of life-history approaches more generally. My colleagues proposed that, nevertheless, there was some basic link between Ionin's project and their own. They suggested that both works were capable of provoking a more perceptive, wide-awake consideration of the Soviet experience, and that both had particular value for Western scholars attempting to configure the details of living through the Soviet years.

The present article evolved from something of a challenge put to me by my colleagues: to place Ionin's propositions into dialogue with my own research at that time, which was grounded in theories of space and place, and which involved gathering memories, impressions and life histories among members of *dacha* (or summer home) communities outside Moscow in 1997 and 1998. The chapter proceeds in several parts: first, a consideration of the Ionin argument and its resonance in contemporary Russia; second, an introduction to the space of the Russian garden comradeship (*sadovodcheskoie tovarishchestvo*); third, the close analysis of one *dacha* life story. In conclusion I approach the question: what can stories told by way of the *dacha* tell us about Ionin's thesis? and by extension, what can they suggest about the study of freedoms in Soviet Russia?

(THE STRENGTH OF) IONIN'S THESIS

'Freedom conjugated with a ban'[3] is how Ionin summarises and evokes a particular incarnation of liberty during the Soviet years. In contrast to truncated political and public realms, he proposes, the realm of the private flourished in Soviet life; moreover, the freedoms experienced in this private realm gained a particular depth and resonance – were gracefully cloaked in a sense of intimacy – precisely because of their location in a wider system of falsity and prohibition. Thus, rather than widening the experience of freedom, post-Soviet democracy – with all the proliferations in choice and opportunity which it inexorably entails – actually spells the partial collapse of the sensation of freedom, the special ability to self-reflexively experience autonomy.

Ionin's argument is predicated on the idea that the existence of freedom within any society should be monitored at the level of experience – it is phenomenal, context dependent, and best captured in relativist approaches. If we jettison the idea that Soviet citizens were limited to 'truncated, partial, castrated' realms of experience,[4] we discover – according to Ionin – that they enjoyed a particularly full type of freedom. To this end he uses as a prefacing quote, and as a literary anchor point, the following lines from (forced émigré) poet Joseph Brodsky:

... While coaxing a beauty,

along the prison walls where you did three years,

to rush along, splashing mud, in a taxi,

with a bottle of wine in a string bag – that's freedom![5]

Here, the proximity of the prison, the sense that prerogative force girds experience (and may intrude on it), opens a space for the eruption of freedom, an experience which seems both to emanate from, and to lodge in, scattered artifacts of the mundane: a taxi ride (to see friends?), a bottle of wine (to be shared among friends, brought in a string sack – also called a 'perhaps bag', *avos'ka*, carried perpetually *just in case* something interesting might appear on sale). By marshalling these lines of poetry as evidence, Ionin does not seek to fetishise political repression. Rather, he introduces them, it appears, to map the extreme of a more general condition, in which the hindering of entry into a variety of quasi-public spheres of experience (literature, religion, travel, even criminality) actually produced a heightened experience of autonomy as individuals struggled to appropriate and re-create these spheres within their private lives (for example, most famously, through the private circulation of manuscripts, which would otherwise be openly published and purchased). This kind of freedom, for Ionin, is therefore dependent not only on the specifics of Soviet government – with its restrictions and its 'ersatz'[6] public realms – but on what he sees as a particularly Russian movement between the public and the private, or everyday (*povsednevnost'*).

In this, Ionin's proposition differs from Isaiah Berlin's more classic observation that daily personal freedoms merely *may exist* concomitant with life in an authoritarian regime, if the regime maintains an acceptable detachment from private spheres.[7] Embedded in Berlin's observation is the idea that public and private spheres are clearly distinguishable and operate independently of one another.[8] Ionin, on the other hand, sees these spheres as discrete, but links their operation dialectically. To highlight this linkage, and to avoid the idea that Ionin is 'simply' pointing to the persistence of private freedoms in a politically restrictive system, I will refer at points to what I have dubbed 'small freedoms'. While *freedom*, according to liberal theory, is cohesively engendered across a given population through a framework of inviolable legal protections, *small freedoms* – following Ionin – arise in fragmentary ways, atomistically, in the course of daily life, and they are spiked with meaning by their position within wider systems of impossibility.

The idea of the small freedom has enjoyed a certain currency over the last decade of scholarship and retrospection on Soviet Russian life.[9] Of course, Vladimir Shlapentokh's classic study showed that people in late Soviet society had shifted their interests and investments to the personal sphere.[10] More pointedly, Svetlana Boym has argued that, in the Soviet 1960s, the life of small circles of intimates took on depth of meaning as retreats from, and re-creations of, a politically risky 'public li(f)e'. (The theme music for this phenomenon was Okudzhava's 'Arbat', representing a cult of 'minor everyday epiphanies on the street corners'.[11]) In his 1996 exploration of gay and lesbian culture in Russia, David Tuller concludes that the very strictures of the Soviet system promoted a flexibility and creativity in the definitions of sexual identity that are to a large degree absent in US gay culture.[12] And at a 1996 conference on private life in Russia, discussion of the late Soviet period was permeated by a nostalgia for the depth of fragmentary experience in Soviet times; indeed, the single toast raised at the concluding event suggested that, while Americans had mastered the professional, organisational side of life, they might do well to learn from their Russian counterparts, schooled in the Moscow kitchen,[13] how to live more fully in the personal.

More importantly, the sense that a certain group of graceful, nuanced freedoms is dissipating in the presence of a louder, more uniform and putatively Western-inspired freedom (singular) represented a recurring motif in daily conversation in Moscow as I encountered it in 1997–8. Much of this informal talk, not surprisingly, concerned economic change, and 'market freedoms', in a discourse inseparably bound with the evaluation of political freedom. For instance, people might express how they missed the bureaucratically ordered disorganisation of workplaces which allowed them to skip days, engage in personal transactions on the job, etc., even though this very disorganisation was simultaneously a source of severe limitation in public life. Some of this talk was rooted at the most literally material, tactile levels: the sense that mundane objects gained depth of meaning in the years of shortage because of the troubles gone through to procure them, the sense that the dizzying array of *stuff* available now makes it more difficult to be inventive. As one acquaintance joked: 'I'm Russian! If you give me everything to work with, I can't make anything out of it. But give me nothing to work with, I can make miracles!'[14]

This daily discourse is distinct in its logic from the (understandably) more pervasive calculations of gain or loss ('Maybe we weren't free before *perestroika*, but food was always cheap'). And though in an analytic sense the daily expressions described above do not sit in an orderly way under the heading of 'freedom conjugated with a ban', they cluster easily around the pieces of poetry Ionin quotes from Brodsky; they evince a similar wry warmth towards small freedoms – ephemeral moments of private life, choices spiked with meaning by their location in systems of limitations. And they express something that can never fully be apprehended by an outsider, but which must be looked at, accounted for, broached, if we are to work towards a more honest understanding of social forces in the post-Stalin years.

It is not my intention to assess the political implications of Ionin's propositions,[15] or to assess whether or not they represent an original contribution to theories of freedom. I propose, rather, to approach a more basic issue: what happens when we place his thesis into dialogue with a life history? After all, though Ionin advocates anthropological understandings, he himself works from the realm of the abstract, marshalling largely personal evidence – and hence, evidence from a very particular social location and social stratum.

Moreover, Ionin sees the small freedom as arising from a particular set of tensions generated by the Soviet political system, and he thereby forecloses on other sources of tension or prerogative force which might gird the experience of freedom. In this respect, his use of the quote from Brodsky is symptomatic. Gender and class also figure in this quote, through the presence of the 'beauty' and the taxi driver, but Ionin does not point us to them or question how gender and class location shape the experience of freedom. He assumes that the line of the prison wall is the horizon for the emergence of the experience of freedom. It is possible, then, that Ionin *may not be going far enough* in mapping the uneven territory of small freedoms.

I venture to explore Ionin's propositions by way of a very particular case – or, more clearly, by way of a space: a workplace-based 'garden comradeship' (*sadovodcheskoie tovarishchestvo*)[16] founded in the last years of Brezhnev, and one woman's life experiences with her *dacha* there. I chose this site, and this respondent in particular, as representative of a curiously understudied social stratum: the ranks of the technically trained who fared well under Brezhnev, the closest thing to what one might call a late Soviet-era middle class. Not only were the workplaces involved in the *tovarishchestvo* I studied representative of this stratum (a chemical research lab, a federal economic planning bureau, etc.), but the people who received *dacha* plots were likely to be solidly placed within their own organisations, owing to the formulae for assigning membership. Thus, where the Ionin argument depends on the vantage point of a more marginalised, creative intelligentsia, this exploration turns to a group with whom many in the creative intelligentsia would have no truck – Soviet society being in its own cultural ways rigidly stratified.

THE SETTING

Although it may seem an odd choice of inquiry, the garden comradeship *dacha* is uniquely suited as a space for examining freedoms within daily life in the Soviet years. In part, this is because the *dacha* touches on issues of ownership and proprietary relations, which have long been considered central to the study of freedom.[17] More centrally for present purposes: the plot, or *uchastok*, within the *tovarishchestvo* represents a supremely *private* space (devoted to family, rest, hobbies and the fulfillment of personal economic needs), and yet it is a place where experience is particularly clearly and transparently girded by state restrictions and economic impossibility. Therefore it is necessary to begin with something of a description of the space itself, in order to begin to appreciate the quality of experience and life stories told around and at the *dacha*, and to set the stage for re-engaging Ionin.

Eleven major rail routes stretch radially out of Moscow from nine stations. Around these lines, ringing Moscow far beyond the ends of the *oblast'* (region) boundaries, cluster millions of *dachi*, a sizable number of which were built within *sadovodcheskie tovarishchestva*. A *tovarishchestvo* was formed when members of a workplace, acting under the auspices of labour or professional union organs, presented a request for the designation of lands (*zaiavlenie na otvod zemli*) to city or regional executive committees. Usually the impetus for this came from within the workplace, when potential *dachniki* – in an age-old tradition, hardly limited to Russia[18] – hankered for a place outside the city. Once lands were provided, at the end of a fairly long, bureaucratic process, the *tovarishchestvo* would mark out equal plots and confer them to individual workers by queue. In accordance with guidelines set in the *tovarishchestvo* charter, a worker's tenure, work record, age, community service and similar factors went into deciding the place in the queue. Collective gardening associations have existed in this basic form since the late 1940s, with interest and access to membership growing steadily – so that, if in 1951 there were 40,000 members of *sadovodcheskie tovarishchestva* in Russia, by 1983 there were over 4 million.[19] The late 1970s and 1980s saw the development of a *dacha* 'boom', prompted by increasing deficits in fruit and vegetable supplies, increasing concerns about the chemicals used in Soviet agriculture, a certain vogue (or *moda*) for *dacha*-going and gardening, and a raft of measures taken in 1977 which facilitated development and access to *tovarishchestva*. In 1978–9 alone, lands allotted to *sadovodcheskie tovarishchestva* increased by 62,000 hectares, eight times the jump of the previous year. An estimate from 1981 indicates that approximately 3 million plots were in use in the Russian Republic, from which were gathered 500,000 tons of fruits and berries. That summer, nearly 15 million individuals would reside at garden plots (*uchastki*), a figure more than that for all the union-run sanatoria put together.[20]

Unlike the institution of the *Dachno-stroitel'nyi kooperativ* (DSK), which has been in place longer, entails a different relationship to property, and was used more clearly in the service of elites,[21] the express purpose of the *tovarishchestvo* was to promote not the construction of *dachi*, but the development of fruit and vegetable gardens. Most of my *tovarishchestvo* respondents, in fact, would chafe at my discussion of their stories in connection with the topic of '*dacha*'. Indeed, there exists something of a universal hand gesture for insisting the opposite: the showing of nails with hands curled and turned out – a demonstration that too much work goes on here for this to be a *dacha* (coded as a space for rest). And yet these *dachi* serve, just as '*dachi* proper' do, as a space outside the city to socialise, take kids for fresh air, and so on. In any event, the act of being there is always the act of being *na dache*.

During the late Soviet years the *tovarishchestvo dacha* represented one of the most intriguing spaces imaginable. The space was intriguing, first, in a straightforward, physical sense. Most *tovarishchestva* were granted virtually non-arable lots, in order not to 'waste' cultivatable soil, as well as in the hopes that personal labour would be invested to recover parcels of land which would otherwise be lost.[22] For instance, the *poselok* (tract) near Dmitrov where I conducted interviews for this article was situated on a former peat processing site – the stripping of peat having left the soil loose and spongy, sodden with water like swampland, as well as mineral-poor. The *poselok* is bounded on two sides by drainage canals, and several of the plots granted to individual tenants originally sloped down to these ditches at precipitous angles; 150 truckloads of earth had to be brought in to level out the plots and replenish the soil.[23]

Though large projects such as the trucking of soil were generally coordinated by the *tovarishchestvo*, each tenant was responsible for the arduous preparation of his or her plot (*uchastok*), leading some members to relinquish their plots to co-workers in the queue, and others to become engaged in something of a competitive camaraderie, seeking to outfit their plots as professionally and creatively as possible. Though the elaborateness of plots varies, each respondent at the Dmitrov *tovarishchestvo* reports investing at least one full season of work before the ground was ready for a diverse horticulture. One *dachnitsa* – whose plot is one of those running down to a canal – dealt with the extreme sloping not simply by adding soil, but by arranging her garden in a series of terraces, each carefully supported and enclosed by corrugated metal barriers. At first the choice of terraces would seem obvious; but when one takes into account that both husband and wife were working full time, travelling to the *tovarishchestvo* mainly at weekends, the neat terracing of the land emerges as a remarkably ambitious, labour-intensive solution.

In addition to the vagaries of the land itself, the space took shape through an interplay of administrative constraint and personal initiative. For instance, in accordance with the republic-wide *typovoi ustav* (a standard charter used as the basis of charters for individual *tovarishchestva*),[24] each lot consisted, with relatively little variation, of 600 square metres of ground.[25] These size constraints were not particularly prohibitive, considering that each plot was meant to provide supplemental produce for one family only. But the chart-like regularity with which plots were demarcated tended to exacerbate natural variations in the land (orientation to the sun, shade from trees on neighbouring plots, etc.), and this, in conjunction with a number of building and zoning codes (permitted size/height of buildings, required distances between living spaces and compost/toilets, required distances between structures on adjoining plots) served to demand – and foster – considerable ingenuity on the part of tenants in utilising the space. (Often that ingenuity was dedicated to getting around regulations – gardening out onto the strip across the road, leaving out the dimensions of outer walls in the calculation of building size, etc.)

Yet more ingenuity was required to find the resources to build and outfit both house and garden in the late, deficit-ridden years of the Soviet regime. Members of *tovarishchestva* were eligible to take bank loans on fairly favourable ten-year terms in order to cover costs of building.[26] At the Dmitrov site, where most *dachi* were erected in 1981–3, tenants describe few initial difficulties in erecting a basic building, whether this was a caravan-like 'household block' (*khozblok*), or a modest two-storey home. However, stories grow and multiply around particularities in interior design, the building of *bani* (Russian baths) or garden buildings. It is in discussion of these flourishes that one encounters repeatedly the canny Soviet term *dostavat'* – to get, to obtain (paramount importance lodging in the fact that this verb is in the imperfective, signifying a process that can never be complete).

Interestingly enough, the tenant described above as having established a terraced system of gardens stalwartly refused over several conversations to describe how she obtained the corrugated sheet metal used as embankments; she would merely shake her head and snort, saying something such as 'Oh, now that's a history,' or 'there's a fairy tale'.[27] Yet one gets the sense that there was really nothing particularly irregular in the way she procured the metal sheeting. The material may have been left over from a construction site, or obtained by a friend. Her silence on this point, however, served to convey an overall sense of how her place was built, regardless of the concrete history of any one item. And it operates, too, as a spell, preserving a mystery around the machinations gone through in the Soviet years, in accordance with a self-fulfilling logic – impossible to ask about, unnecessary to explain to anyone who knows about the word *dostavat'*.

As a net result of the vagaries in the land, administrative constraints and difficulties in obtaining building supplies and materials, the cultivation of these plots represents a concerted transformation of geographical *space* into social *place* – that is to say, into places, in the plural, humanly marked by the most intimate and intricate of labours.[28] What is more, we can begin to divine in the physical contours of the space an emergent argument along the lines of Ionin's: there is a curious link between prohibition and possibility in the way the houses and the plots take shape; they seem self-consciously to be constructed *in tension with*; the presence of limitation itself allows for the sense of a 'carving out'.

This sense only increases when we look at the *dacha* not only as a physical space but as a symbolic one – that is to say, a space in the system of authority, power and governance. The city planning literature in Russia of the 1960s–80s largely ignores, or predicts the imminent demise of, the ever-increasing number of *dacha* and gardening communities which spiralled out from Moscow and other Soviet cities. At the same time, shortfalls in the agricultural and consumer product sectors pushed the state to encourage the growth of the '600-square-metre' brand of garden. As a 1965 resolution of the Soviet of Ministers laconically puts it:

> The Soviet of Ministries of the Russian Republic [have] observed that over the last several years local soviet, agricultural and labour organs have allowed their attention to the development of collective gardening among workers and civil servants [i.e., not farm workers] to wane. Besides this, the production of potatoes and vegetables in collective gardens serves as an important supplementary source of these food crops.[29]

The note of alarm – and the perceived link between homegrown foodstuffs and a satisfied populace – becomes ever more clear in a series of such decrees, extending to the very end of the Soviet system.

A similar tension or paradox of this sort is at work concerning the property status of the garden plot. In one sense the *tovarishchestvo* plot served as a neat proxy for private property: land could be utilised, within certain limits, in accordance with the tenant's wishes; proprietorship was lifelong, and plots could be passed down to heirs (subject to a vote by the *tovarishchestvo*, which had to approve the heirs as members). The house, meanwhile, actually was private property (*chastnaia sobstvennost'*) in the Soviet legal sense of the term. All the same, tenants could, in principle, be evicted from their plots if they overbuilt, failed to garden on their land, or otherwise violated the spirit of the *tovarishchestvo*, and homes could be dismantled, 'reduced', etc. if they exceeded the following size limits: approximately 20 square metres of living area, with a 10-square-metre veranda, and the option of 3 square metres of root cellar.[30] In this sense, the plot represented a fragile and incomplete form of property, always liable to incursion by the 'state'. (Here I place the word state in quotes because it is important that it be imagined not in its faceless bureaucratic form, but in the guise of the most concrete, familiar and everyday figures of Soviet life – for instance, the overly inquisitive *tovarishchestvo* president who dropped in on her neighbours to track their compliance with state and *tovarishchestvo* norms.) But from this set of tensions emerged a fairly unified experience of the space: the plot was *svoi*, one's own.[31]

In its symbolic configuration, then, the pleasures and freedoms offered by the space of the *dacha* seem to represent a full incarnation of Ionin's proposals. Here, frozen at the structural level, neatly ensured by seemingly conflicting sets of legislation and administrative procedure, is the precarious (yet sturdy) emergence of a cosy space, bounded by prohibition and impossibility: an excellent case of 'conjugation with a ban'.

But even if we can spy this as an operative logic at the structural level, it is still not clear that this is a durable description of lived experience. In other words, it is important not simply to 'read', or 'read into' the landscape an operative logic – one which will doubtlessly be conditioned by our own preconceived ideas of how things work – but to grapple with the logics of practice. And in particular, I am interested here in the practices of a group far different from Ionin's – or Brodsky's – milieu, or the milieu that most Western scholars have sought out in Russia. This is where I turn to the case of Raisa Alexeevna.

STORIES TOLD AT THE *DACHA*

Raisa is a short, roundish woman, 63 years old, with a brisk and easy manner. We met at a book and magazine stall, where I was seeking back issues of the gardening magazine *Priusadebnoe khoziaistvo* (Personal Agriculture). Raisa, who was browsing at the stand, stepped in to say that she had collected all issues of the journal since it began publishing in 1981 and could show them to me. This began our relationship, as well as my connection to the *tovarishchestvo* at Dmitrov: Raisa is the one who first invited me there and provided crucial initial introductions to other members of the community.

Like many members of the Dmitrov *tovarishchestvo*, Raisa is a pensioner, born in the 1930s. She studied to be an economist/planner (something akin to the American notion of an accountant) in the early 1950s at a Moscow technical institute, then worked as an economic planner in a federal office continuously from her graduation until her retirement three years ago. When her workplace joined the Dmitrov *tovarishchestvo* in 1981, she and her husband enthusiastically (she more so than he) embraced the idea of getting a plot. Before undertaking this work, she had no links to farming; neither of her parents had been peasants, and she had no *dacha* experiences when growing up. When I ask her about this sudden pull to gardening she describes it as a 'natural' thing, tied to age,[32] and tied to the fact that many people were taking plots at that time. It seems the case that the opportunity for a plot opened up just as a vague desire was taking shape in her life, fed by the heightened interest in gardening in the Russian media and among her friends.

Though she never specifically describes it this way, the *dacha* also seems to represent a way to stay connected with her daughter. In a fairly typical pattern, her daughter and son-in-law have put up much of the funding for the development of the plot; they use the *dacha* as a place to relax, visit with their parents, swim (in a nearby lake or the Moscow–Volga Canal) and sunbathe. Though her daughter has little interest in gardening, she is a great partisan of the *dacha*; she takes a proprietor-like pride in the fact that the Dmitrov environs are still rural enough for nightingales, hedgehogs and even beavers. Interestingly, in one of our interviews Raisa describes the *dacha* as a project undertaken 'together with my daughter (*my s dochkoi*)' rather than with her husband.[33]

Raisa's plot sits on flat ground at the end of a row of *dachi*, near the entrance to the *poselok*; on one side it is bounded by the access road, and beyond that by a thick birch and pine forest. The first season they came to the *poselok*, she and her husband pulled out wild bushes, mowed (with a scythe) and filled the plot with trucked-in dirt and sand. (On one of our walks through the *poselok* she pointed out an unclaimed plot, overgrown with weeds, with at least an inch of standing water. 'It's hellish labour. This was the kind of swamp we had, this is the kind of overgrowth.' And then, as if on cue in an overdrawn movie, a very unattractive two-inch bug, a pest known as a *medved'ka* – a 'little bear' or mole cricket – slithered out of the weeds at the edge of the field, and Raisa sighed and crushed it with her foot.)

In that first year, in addition to clearing and draining the plot, they erected a sturdy shed, built up the land at one edge of the plot, and planted several fruit trees there so that the roots would not rot; and they started beds of potatoes, beets and a few other essentials. In the second year, they put up the *dacha*. This was mostly the labour of Raisa's husband and their daughter, working from a pre-fabricated kit. The *dacha* is tidy in the utmost – a small, box-shaped house, with a sharply peaked roof and modest windows. It looks like one of any of dozens of projects published in the 1970s, 1980s, and early 1990s in building guides for popular consumption. Inside the *dacha*, the ground floor consists of a small closed-in verandah with two old refrigerators and a cupboard, a cosy dining nook and a bedroom; the upper floor is smaller, due to the slope of the roof, and only semi-finished; it is fitted out with two narrow beds for Liuda, the daughter, and her husband, as well as (from this year) a miniature portable toilet.

One of Raisa's dissatisfactions is that she 'stuck too closely' to the building guidelines when they planned the *dacha*. She tells the story of a neighbour who over-built and then 'threw out the *tovarishchestvo* president' when she came to make a complaint. This is not a confirmable story – certainly the *tovarishchestvo* president would have been able to take action if so inclined. But it speaks to the fact that there was an unknown quantity of slack in the rules for building and development. Raisa regrets that she didn't risk more; indeed, her *dacha*, with a combined living space of about 25 square metres, is small compared to many of the other *dachi* at the *poselok*.

By their third year, Raisa and her husband began to keep chickens and rabbits. This was an endeavour in the order of a hobby (probably inspired by reading *Priusadebnoe khoziaistvo*). As a family, they did not lack the funds to buy eggs or meat; and they did not sell the animals as many *dachniki* did, quite legally, throughout the 1980s. Instead they ate or gave away the eggs, and used the rabbits for fur, commissioning two short coats to be made from them, one for Raisa and one for Liuda. Later they turned the henhouse into a dark but comfortable summer kitchen.

After sixteen years of tending, the plot has taken on full form, every corner developed, every spot having gone through several incarnations. The apple trees and summer kitchen fill the left side of the plot at the back. In the back to the right sit two long wood-and-plastic sheeting greenhouses for the tomatoes and cucumbers; in front of these, plum and quince trees, with flowers planted around their roots. The middle of the plot is laid out in a series of narrow beds with potatoes, strawberries, garlic, onion and herbs – including basil, coriander, dill, tarragon, valerian and curly-leafed parsley. (When the strawberries have gone over, Raisa digs up the rows and re-plants with more garlic and herbs, getting twice the use out of the bed.) Further up, to the right of the house and in front of it, she set in a series of flower beds, with a decorative border made of inverted glass bottles, pounded flush with the soil, to look like upholstery tacks. Here she grows climax, iris, phlox, peonies, tulips, gladioli and tiger lilies. Along the fence on both sides of the plot are berry bushes – red- and blackcurrant and gooseberry to the right, and *oblepikha*, a semi-tart, orange northern berry which grows voraciously, clustered thickly and high along the left. (Raisa gives a rapid tour of these numerous cultures, saying in her very firm, clipped way: *Eto luk, Eto pomidor, Eto zemlianika* – HERE's the onions, HERE's the tomatoes, HERE's the strawberries – motioning quickly to right and left. She pauses only over her new acquisitions, for instance the column-form apple trees she is experimenting with, purchased at a former *kolkhoz* which now caters to an upmarket *dacha* clientele.)

Finally, under the *oblepikha* berries, sandwiched between a permanently parked old car where the cat suns himself and a greenhouse full of sweet peppers, is a little area devoted to recreation. This space has been forged over the last two years, mostly by the daughter, Liuda. She laid a sand floor about 1.5 by 2 metres square, and dug out a pit for cooking *shashlyk* (a type of kebab), the social equivalent of a barbecue. Her father helped her line the pit with bricks and set in little benches by it; then, this summer, Liuda and Sasha brought in four white plastic deckchairs, with a matching table and a large bright beach umbrella. (In one of my favourite photos of the plot, this bright, striped umbrella incongruously pushes its head up over a swathe of garden greens.)

'That's theirs. Liuda laid the pit', Raisa notes dryly when giving her tour. The recreation area is a cause for constant light joking in the family; the 'kids' threaten to take over more land for a lawn and sunbathing area, causing Raisa to worry about her plans for new flower beds or trees. This, too, is an issue familiar to the point of stereotype at *sadovodcheskoie tovarishchestvoa*: children with more disposable income seek to turn their parents' *dachi* into spots for relaxing, like country cottages. Raisa is not at all dismayed by the tendency; she does not assert the need to work, or bemoan the laxity of recent generations. But still, the pervasive work ethic of the *tovarishchestvo* acts as a backdrop; against it, the presence of an area for rest is something to be explained. (So, for instance, as we walked by a *dacha* which belonged to the daughter of a deceased co-worker, Raisa felt the need to interpret the meaning of a blank lawn: 'They planted nothing *on purpose*. For them, it's like a place to rest.')

On a typical summer weekday, Raisa is alone at the *dacha*. Her husband, though also retired, picks up extra money by working two days on and two days off as a handyman. Generally, he spends his days off at their one-room apartment in the city. Liuda and Sasha come most weekends, and bring Liuda's father with them if he is free. (On workdays the collective has the feel of a women's zone, as men are more likely to commute in for the weekends, leaving their wives and/or mothers to tend the plots. Raisa moves about the garden freely in just a shirt and a pair of underpants.) Depending on the weather, Raisa is likely to stay at the *dacha* from early May, for planting, until the end of September, when the last two jobs are hastily done: digging up potatoes and gathering in the prodigious *oblepikha*.

She breaks this up with stays in the city as she wishes, taking rides home with Liuda and Sasha. Unlike other retirees I have spoken with, she does not regularly ride back into Moscow to collect her pension; rather, she lets it automatically roll over into a savings account.

If one had to pull a central thread from Raisa's story it would undoubtedly be the setting of a stage for her retirement. She took the *dacha* when she was nearing retirement age and pursued it as a beloved hobby with the free time which entered her life when her daughter became self-sufficient. Now the *dacha* acts as something of a homestead: the family as a whole invests resources into it, the children come here at weekends, or they retreat here on weekdays to recover from colds and stressful days at the office. In Raisa's mind, this would also be the perfect space in which to look after a grandchild.

This idea of the *dacha* as a stage for her retirement has led her to dream of other, yet more suitable options – something closer to the city, a community equipped with phone lines and gas mains. So, when TV ads in 1991 invited applicants for a sort of communitarian settlement, she called for more information. Eventually she invested the equivalent of approximately £500 in the venture, as a membership fee. For this money she received a beautifully made architectural plan of her dream home, as well as a present from the organiser on International Women's Day (a pair of leather boots). Raisa keeps the bound architectural plan carefully folded in an old school satchel of Liuda's and likes to take it out from time to time: it shows a fabulous three-storey structure, with two symmetrical dwelling units, one for herself and her husband, one for 'the kids'. The two units meet in the centre, in a two-storey hothouse-conservatory.

It is not clear how Raisa envisaged financing such a home, nor is it clear that such a home was ever meant to be built. In any event, by 1992, the venture began to encounter difficulties tied to its attempts to procure land, and in 1993 the organiser died under mysterious circumstances. Though there was clearly corruption in the organisation, Raisa is not particularly bitter about the experience. This project having failed, she is more cautious in her attempts to find a new home for her retirement, but dogged none the less. Her plan is to sell the Dmitrov plot, take out a mortgage and erect a modest-sized, three-bedroom home. Eventually, she would rent out her one-room apartment in the city in order to earn extra money.

In the end, then, the most striking feature of Raisa's story is the way it seems to unfold, driven by internal factors, with little disjuncture in the narrative between pre- and post-Soviet periods. The Soviet system presented certain opportunities (once she paused in the middle of a walk through a field to say, 'this was a great gift from our government') as well as certain barriers to her plans (for instance the building codes). And she remarks on these as normalised, routinised opportunities and constraints,[34] no different from the range of financial and organisational opportunities and constraints she encounters now, in a market economy, under conditions nearer to liberal democracy: getting a mortgage, finding suitable land, and so on.

At least in part, the pragmatic way she negotiates both opportunities and barriers must be tied to the fact that Raisa has fared well – solidly and moderately well – both during the Soviet years and beyond. Until her retirement, she held a secure mid-level position in a federal bureau. Now, during the dislocation of economic transition, though the family does not enjoy a lavish lifestyle, she is protected both materially and psychologically by a close-knit family network. In short, while Raisa was not a member of the Soviet elite, and is not now a 'New Russian', there is a solid middle-class ease which surrounds her sense of freedom and choice in her private life, and it is expressed in the way she uses the space of the *dacha*.

RE-APPROACHING THE THEORETICAL

Ionin's main concept – which I have dubbed here the 'small freedom' – resonates both with a number of moves being made currently in scholarship on Russia, and, more importantly perhaps, with a particular brand of nostalgia operative in daily talk in Russia in the late 1990s. What I have attempted to show is that the space of the *tovarishchestvo* is bounded in some ways by precisely the formula Ionin identifies: heightened possibility within restrictiveness, 'freedom conjugated with a ban'. And yet this is not a uniformly useful formula when examining the experiences of *tovarishchestvo* members, as is neatly exemplified by the story of Raisa Alexeevna.

Nearly all the people I interviewed and spoke with at the Dmitrov *tovarishchestvo* place a real importance on the role of the *dacha* in their lives. They speak of a sense of control and mastery in determining the course of a garden or the shape of a house. Or they find a singular sense of peace and security in the perfect routinisation of life there. Or they simply say they could not live as fully as they do without the access to fresh air and extra food the *dacha* affords. In each story, certain of these feelings are held in tension with the vagaries of the Soviet system. But they are also held in tension with narratives of urbanisation and pollution, narratives of ageing, and – more recently – narratives of the market economy. Taken together, the stories reveal something more pragmatic, less complete, less exotic, and ultimately less redemptive of Soviet restrictiveness than

Ionin's formulation. This is not to say that each and every one of my respondents would not recognise the condition Ionin describes so persuasively; it would seem there is no *dachnik* in Russia who cannot, for instance, find something noteworthy in the forced inventiveness of a Soviet gardener. But for many, the idea of heightened freedom within limitation is simply an available social formula that can be recognised and appropriated in discussion, but which is not cohesively reflective of experience.

One has to be careful where to step from here in drawing conclusions. The strength of Ionin's work is that it operates as a fantastic opening-up of the sociological imagination, an attempt to refigure our understanding of the relationship between personal experience and formal mechanisms of power and control during the Soviet years. On one level, then, I have simply tried to lay alongside his proposition another such opening of the sociological lens, with a much more mundane (but, ironically, possibly more controversial) suggestion: if the prohibitions and ersatz nature of the public realm enhanced, for some, the content of fragmentary experiences of freedom, for others the experience of freedoms in the late Soviet years was a more dully straightforward proposition. (Though this is by no means to imply that *freedom as a political condition* was a dully straightforward proposition.) People such as Raisa Alexeevna took their jobs very seriously, as well as their public lives and their civic responsibilities. And they also took seriously the personal opportunities afforded to them through those spheres – opportunities such as participating in a garden comradeship. Rather than a flight from an ersatz public realm, then, the *dacha* in stories such as hers represents a relatively smooth linkage between private and public realms. Moreover, in the stories of Raisa and others, barriers to enjoying the *dacha* which arose in the Soviet period do not figure as being significantly different from barriers which arise under conditions of market economy: they seem to negotiate these barriers in similar ways and with similar feelings of competence and/or stress. And though we cannot ever assume one-to-one correlations between class location and experience, it seems likely that their experiences with the garden comradeship *dacha* are linked to their position within the strata of engineers, chemists, economists and other technically trained people that contributed to the growth of a middle class during the late Soviet years.

If this is a worthwhile speculation, it would seem to beg a series of other questions – ones regarding age, gender, national identity, region and so on. That is to say, it would lead us to question the formulation of a cohesive Soviet experience of freedom, minding the ways that more complex forms of social location inflect experience. At the very least, it would remind us to use extreme caution in applying voices and sources from one social group to another, especially as the experiences of certain groups – the late Soviet middle class included – have yet to be adequately explored.

In suggesting this, I am also suggesting that a formulation such as Ionin's would most properly be explored in a *comparative framework*, despite his argument that the experience of freedom he describes is unique to Soviet Russia. If we conceptualise a more sociologically variegated landscape of the experience of freedoms, Ionin's suggestions begin to link implicitly with other important discourses, for instance the debate on active re-appropriations of consumer culture by 'dominated' consumers.[35]

If stories told at the *dacha* do anything, then, they remind us that a good deal of opening-up and parsing of life histories lies ahead, if we are to better theorise the content of experience in the Soviet years. And in this sense, Ionin's work represents the ultimate argument for the importance of life stories.

Notes

Research for this article was supported by grants from the Fulbright–Hays Foundation and from the International Research and Exchanges Board (IREX), with funds provided by the National Endowment for the Humanities and the United States Department of State, which administers the Russian, Eurasia and East European Research Program (Title VIII). I am grateful to the following for reading and commenting on drafts: Victoria Semenova, Elena Meshcherkina, Paul Thompson, Anna Rotkirch, Pat Preston, Michael Kennedy, Pauline Gianoplus, Daina Stukuls and other members of Contiguities and Transpositions for a Sociology out of Eastern Europe (CATSEE) at the University of Michigan's Department of Sociology.

1 Victoria Semenova, Ekaterina Foteeva and Daniel Bertaux (eds), *Sud'by Liudei: Rossiia XX Vek. Biografii Semei kak Ob'ekt Sotsiologicheskogo Issledovaniia* [The Fates of People: Russia in the 20th Century. Family Biographies as an Object of Sociological Research] (Institut Sotsiologii RAN, Moscow, 1996).
2 L.G. Ionin, 'Svoboda v SSSR' [Freedom in the USSR], in L.G. Ionin, *Svoboda v SSSR: Stat'i i Esse* [Freedom in the USSR: Articles and Essays], (Fond Universitetskaia kniga, St Petersburg, 1997), 9–36.
3 Ionin, 'Svoboda v SSSR', 35. 'Conjugated with a ban' is an excellent rendering of *sopriazhennyi s zapretom*, from a translation of the essay made by British translator George Blake. The translation was supplied to me in manuscript form in 1997; I have been unable to ascertain if it has been formally published.
4 *Ibid.*, 24.
5 As quoted from Blake by Ionin.
6 *Ibid.*, 15.
7 Isaiah Berlin, *Two Concepts of Liberty: An Inaugural Lecture* (Clarendon Press, Oxford, 1958), 14.
8 Berlin sees this separation as an historically contingent phenomenon, operative in Western culture since the Renaissance or the Reformation (*ibid.*, 14).
9 I use 'Russian' generally in the sense of *rossiisskii* as opposed to *russkii* – that is to say, as a way of indicating members of a community coextensive with geographical Russia, whether or not of Russian descent.
10 Vladimir Shlapentokh, *Public and Private Life of the Soviet People: Changing Values in the Post-Stalin Russia* (Oxford University Press, Oxford, 1989).
11 Svetlana Boym, *Common Places: Mythologies of Everyday Life in Russia* (Harvard University Press, Cambridge, Mass., 1994), 94–5.
12 David Tuller, *Cracks in the Iron Closet: Travels in Gay and Lesbian Russia* (University of Chicago Press, Chicago, 1997).
13 Throughout the Soviet years, the Moscow kitchen represented a warm, safe space where news, literature and politics could be discussed freely among a small circle of friends. Symbolically, it figured simultaneously both as a hearth and as a bunker.
14 Personal communication with Natalia T., 13 April 1997.

15 Though it would be a disservice to Brodsky to ignore them; after all, Brodsky can be seen as a connoisseur of 'Soviet freedoms' only at certain fleeting, poetical and warmly ironic moments. For Brodsky's literally and figuratively more prosaic stance, see, e.g., his 1993 open letter to Vaclav Havel, 'Letter to a President', in *On Grief and Reason* (Farrar, Straus and Giroux, New York, 1995), 212–22.

16 This might also be called a garden collective. The *tovarishchestvo* is similar to a cooperative, though, as discussed below, the *dacha* Building Cooperative (DSK) was a legally distinct form.

17 See, e.g., Richard Pipes, *Property and Freedom* (Alfred A. Knopf, New York, 1999).

18 In any event, since at least the thirteenth century outbreaks of plague spurred on periodic exoduses from European cities to a more 'healthful' countryside. Lewis Mumford, *The City in History: Its origins, Its Transformations, and Its Prospects* (Harcourt Brace, New York, 1961), 487.

19 K.B. Yaroshenko, *Kollektivnyi Sad – Pol'za Mne i Obshchestvu* [Collective Garden – good for Me and Society] (Znanie, Moscow, 1983), 11. These figures, as far as I can gather, relate only to urbanites.

20 N.E. Soispatrova, *Grazhdanskie prava chlenov sadovodcheskogo tovarishchestva rabochikh i sluzhashchikh RSFSR: Aftoreferat dissertatsii na soiskanie uchenoi stepeni kandidata iuridicheskoi nauki* [Civil rights for non-agricultural workers involved in garden collectives], (dissertation abstract 623.211.332, Vsesoiuznyi iuridicheskii zoochnyi institut, Moscow, 1981), 2.

21 The best published source on the DSK form is D.M. Vatman, M. Lipetsker and V. Khinchuk, *Kooperativy: Kvartira, dacha, garazh* [Cooperatives: Apartment, *dacha*, garage] (Iuridicheskaia literatura, Moscow, 1982). The idea that the *DSK* required more resources than a garden cooperative is part extrapolation, part 'common wisdom'. This is an issue that would bear further exploration in an expanded study. For a fuller statistical and juridical picture of the development of the *sadovodcheskoie tovarishchestvo*, see Naomi Roslyn Galtz, '*Space and the everyday: an historical sociology of the Moscow dacha*' (Ph.D Dissertation, University of Michigan, Ann Arbor, 2000), 279–93.

22 See Soispatrova, *Grazhdanskie prava chlenov sadovodcheskogo tovarishchestva*, 2–3. The problem would only be exacerbated in Gorbachev's land handouts at the end of the Soviet era, which resulted from a national inventory of usable versus unusable areas. See Stephen K. Wegren, *Agriculture and the State in Soviet and Post-Soviet Russia* (University of Pittsburgh Press, Pittsburgh, 1998), 47–8.

23 Grigorii Nikolaevich, former president of the Dmitrov *tovarishchestvo*, interview, 13 November 1997.

24 For the *typovoi ustav* of the Russian Republic, see Yaroshenko, *Kollektivnyi sad*, 53–64.

25 Hence the name of the popular weekly gazette devoted to gardening and *dacha* life: *Vashi shest' sotok*, or 'Your six hundredths [of a hectare]'.

26 M.S. Gudzen'ko and M.V. Shul'ga, *Podsobnoe Khoziaistvo Grazhdan* [Supplementary agricultural activity of citizens] (Iuridicheskaia literatura, Moscow, 1983), 108ff.

27 Tamara Timofeevna, interview, 12 September 1997.

28 Here I feel bound to make a clarification, engaging Edward Casey, who argues against the theoretical prioritisation of a supposedly abstract, empty space, over particular, grounded sites of experience. Casey's points are well taken. In this particular instance, however, the idea that plural, social places emerge out of a blanker 'space' is resonant with the experience of my respondents themselves. The *dachniki* arrive with a pre-formed set of social relations (achieved in the workplace); the landscape they are assigned is a random one, upon which they set to work, mapping out their plots and attempting to 'take hold of' (*osvoit'*) the territory. Everything outside of the confines of the comradeship becomes, for them, inexorably *peisazh*. (See Edward S. Casey, 'How to get from space to place in a fairly short stretch of time', in Steven Feld and Keith H. Basso (eds), *Senses of Place* (School of American Research Press,

Santa Fe, 1996); and Edward S. Casey, *The Fate of Place: A Philosophical History* (University of California Press, Berkeley, 1997). See also a more extended discussion of Casey in Galtz, 'Space and the everyday', 114–21)).

29 'O kollektivnom ogorodnichestve rabochikh i sluzhashchikh: Postanovlenie Soveta Ministrov RSFSR i VTsSPS ot 12 aprelia 1965 g. No. 453', *Kollektivnoe Sadovodstvo i Ogorodnichestvo, Sbornik Normativnykh Aktov* (Iuridicheskaia Literatura, Moscow, 1991), 62–3.

30 Yaroshenko, *Kollektivnyi Sad*, 54ff.

31 For further discussion, see Galtz, 'Space and the everyday', 318–21.

32 Gardening at the *uchastok* is often seen as *delo pensionerov* (something pensioners do). Common wisdom is that ageing provokes a natural affinity for the garden. But there are a number of pragmatic reasons for interest among the ageing population, beginning with the fact that plots tended to be assigned, first of all, by length of service – hence to older workers first. Moreover, pensioners are more likely to be dependent on extra produce from their plots, and more likely to have the time, obviously, to live during the week at the *dacha*.

33 Raisa Alekseevna, interview, 16 June 1997.

34 This point is very much resonant with a comment Ionin makes, in seeking to 'normalise' examination of Soviet experience: 'Soviet people proceeded from the choices at their disposal and understood freedom as a chance to choose from what was available': Ionin, 'Freedom in the USSR', 35.

35 To engage this debate, see, e.g., Michel de Certeau, Luce Girard and Pierre Mayol, *The Practice of Everyday Life, Vol. 2: Living and Cooking*, T.J. Tomasik, trans. (University of Minnesota Press, Minneapolis, 1998); Martyn J. Lee, *Consumer Culture Reborn: The Cultural Politics of Consumption* (Routledge, New York, 1993).

# Part III

THE MARGINAL AND THE SUCCESSFUL

9

MEMORY AND SURVIVAL IN STALIN'S RUSSIA

Old Believers in the Urals during the 1930s–50s

Irina Korovushkina Paert

INTRODUCTION

The remarkable revival of religious activities in post-Communist Russia gave rise to scepticism among social scientists, who characterised this religious revival as a swing of the 'ideological pendulum' from atheism to religion. These scholars represented religion in the post-Soviet era as a mechanical substitute for the Soviet ideological system, described as a kind of civil religion.[1] This argument, therefore, downplays the survival of religion in the pre-*perestroika* Soviet Union, and rules out the continuity between 'religious survival' and 'religious revival'.

However, despite this sceptical view of the post-Soviet religious renaissance, there are a growing number of studies based on recently opened Soviet archives that have countered this view. They have demonstrated that, despite the attempts of the revolutionaries to erase religion from the everyday life of Soviet citizens, it remained an important social force throughout the whole Soviet era. For example, social historians, researching the relationship between the Bolsheviks and society in the 1920s–30s, have shown how believers resisted, adapted to or circumvented Soviet policies in this period, and how religion served to mobilise popular protest against the authorities.[2]

This chapter proposes to explore the survival of religious belief during the Soviet era through oral-history interviews. While most of the studies on religion in the Soviet Union are based on official sources, derived from Communist Party or secret police archives, this study is based on the testimonies of the believers themselves. The chapter provides new evidence to assess the arguments of social historians who saw in the persistence of popular belief the presence of an unyielding opposition to the Soviet regime. Through the testimonies of believers, I am able to focus on the complexity of their relations with the Soviet regime, a relationship that combined resistance and accommodation with the regime. I aim to offer both an insight into popular representation of the state's policies, and an evaluation of the inner mechanisms of religious survival in the Soviet Union.

The chapter is based on oral-history interviews with Old Believers, a group known for its religious conservatism, traditions of local autonomy and strong sense of communal identity.[3] Old Believers were Russian Orthodox Christians who split from the Russian Church in the mid-seventeenth century in disagreement with the liturgical reforms of the Patriarch Nikon. Branding it as a schism, the church leadership and Tsarist regime severely persecuted those who refused to accept changes in ritual practices. Old Believers were divided into two main groups: the priestly ones, who had priests and did not differ in ritual and dogma from the Orthodox Church, and the priestless ones, who had substituted the ordained priesthood with elected ministers and had introduced substantial changes to rituals and the system of belief. In the Urals, the priestless Old Believers prevailed; most of our informants belonged to this religious group. Old Believers had a distinct sense of their religious and cultural identity, as expressed in rites of passage and pollution behaviour. They required newcomers to be baptised, even if they were already Christians; they used to separate themselves in food and prayer from those who were not members of their communities. Old Believers revered tradition even in most outward forms: men wore beards, and women long hair. Theirs was a patriotic religion. Old Believers were suspicious of Western secular culture, imported to Russia in the late seventeenth and, especially, eighteenth centuries during the reign of Peter I. Most priestless Old Believers lived in self-governing egalitarian communities. Lay men and women had more power in Old Believers' communities than they did in the Orthodox Church. And they tried to preserve their autonomy from both ecclesiastical control and state interference.

During the 1930s the Old Believers were attacked both physically and verbally; their places of worship were closed and turned into schools, cinemas, clubs and barns; their priests and active members of religious communities were arrested; and their objects of veneration, such as icons, relics of the saints and church bells, were destroyed. Yet, despite the efforts of the state to exclude religion from the everyday reality of the Soviet society, the Old Believers' religion survived in the Soviet collective. Described as 'a remarkable phenomenon and a paradox', Old Believer survival sheds light on the relations between the Stalinist state and the religious community, and on the ways in which ordinary men and women managed to preserve their beliefs in a changing environment often hostile to religion .[4]

The chapter has three major concerns. First, it assesses the ways in which state policies and the actions of local authorities towards believers were interwoven in historical myths and religious narratives. I employ here a concept of 'coherent narrative', which is created by placing one's personal story into the framework of a larger collective narrative, which can 'foster a sense of coherence, collaboration, competence and confidence [which is] vital in coping and mastery'.[5] Second, the chapter describes the ways in which believers tried to cope with the 'total drama' of the 1930s, and to adapt to Stalinist society, relying on strategies of survival of which some were peculiar to the Old Believers, but some common for all Soviet people. Third, the chapter analyses the survival of Old Believer religious identity through such institutions as the family, and through religious ritual and prayer.

There has also been a more personal motive for me in this research, which at an inner level is to restore a missing link in my own family history, to trace the tracks of my great-grandparents, members of Old Believer communities who were dekulakised in 1929. Four years ago my father gave me a photocopy of a document relating to the deportation in 1930 of my great-grandfather's family from a small town in the Urals to a less populated area in Western Siberia. The reason for the deportation was that my great-grandfather was a *kulak*, one of the rural rich. The document, typed on a bad typewriter with a few spelling mistakes, meticulously enumerated the number of hens and pigs my great-grandfather's family had. It was issued to confirm that the family was certainly of a non-Soviet class background, not only on a property basis but also due to the fact that some members of the family, my great uncles, had left Russia with the White Russian armies during the Civil War in 1919. Moreover, I learned from my father that my grandparents, who were brought up in Siberian exile, belonged to a conservative religious group of Old Believers. I did not have a chance to ask my grandparents about their experience of exile: my grandmother died when I was little, and I never heard anything about my grandfather (a memory gap typical of many Russian families). And the piece of official paper counting the hens and pigs is probably the only piece of historical evidence linking my generation and that of my grandparents. In my research, based on interviews with Old Believer men and women in the Urals who belonged to the generation of my grandparents, I have tried to restore both the missing link in my family history and the aspects of social history of the Soviet period.

METHOD

The chapter is based on forty oral-history interviews with members of Old Believer communities, in both rural and urban areas, conducted in 1998–9 in the Urals region (Sverdlovsk, Cheliabinsk and Perm oblasts).[6] Our interviewees were self-selected: these were men and women who agreed that their memories were being recorded. Two age groups were interviewed: men and women born between 1905 and 1920, and those born between 1920 and 1941.

I realise that my informants' memories of the past are unequivocally influenced by the present. Many old people are disappointed with the 'shock therapy' economic reforms of the 1990s; and their critical attitudes to the collapse of the state welfare system certainly influence their view of the past. Although I have tried to support my oral-history evidence with data from the archives where it was possible, placing personal accounts of religious survival in a broader social and political context of the period, I did not aim at presenting an 'objective' historical account. Unlike official documentation influenced by the Soviet anti-religious propaganda, oral-history narratives shed light on the sphere of private life and the domain of human subjectivity. The chapter aims at exploring the ways in which subjective experiences and individual narratives could open up new ways of looking at historical and sociological problems, such as the problem of the survival of religion in modern society.

MEMORY AND HISTORICAL MYTH: OLD BELIEVER REPRESENTATIONS OF THE CULTURAL REVOLUTION, 1928-32

When Stalin abandoned the New Economic Policy in 1928, religion came under systematic attack from the state, which aimed to subvert the institutions and challenge the individuals who sustained religious identity. During the forced collectivisation of agriculture in 1929-34, religion became a subject of the class struggle: alongside dekulakisation of well-off peasants, priests and ministers were also 'dekulakised'. Zinaida Moiseevna (b. 1909, Kyshtym), a housewife, remembers an Old Believer minister who came back from the forest where he was sent to cut wood for the state: 'He told me that there were many of them. Every day they buried someone. They were too old and frail for such work.' During the 1930s, local authorities arbitrarily closed the places of worship to clear the spaces for building a new socialist life. Many ancient churches and chapels were demolished, and many were converted into schools, clubs and *kolkhoz* barns. In the 1930s many Old Believer cemeteries were demolished, some being turned into football grounds. Between 1934 and 1939 the NKVD (the secret police) arrested and exterminated tens of thousands of priests, bishops, monks, nuns and active members of religious communities, the exact numbers of which have not yet been estimated. Although repression affected all religious groups, Old Believers by and large experienced a tremendous loss from which, as a non-established religion, they had little chance to recover. By 1941 only one out of forty Old Believer bishops had not been imprisoned. Only 10 per cent of Old Believer places of worship in Sverdlovsk oblast were still functioning by the end of the 1930s.

It was not only direct repression but also general economic, social and legal changes that depleted the economic human resources for sustaining Old Belief. The cessation of the New Economic Policy (NEP) suppressed private trade and family business, and dekulakisation undermined market-oriented peasants. Soviet economic policy, by abolishing private property, destroyed the basis of religious charity. Collective farms, an instrument of social control, challenged the autonomy of Old Believer communities and families: by the end of the 1930s the number of *edinolichniki* (private farmers) who refused to join the *kolkhoz* had fallen dramatically as a result of the pressure from *kolkhoz*. For example, in 1939 the collective farm authorities forced the family of Vassa Semenovna (b. 1919), from Kirov oblast, to abandon their household by cutting off their land estate.[7]

The memories of Stalinism have explosive character: the collectivisation of 1929–32 was clearly the most dramatic episode for the population of the Urals, which did not directly experience the German attack of 1941–5. Thus a single period of Soviet history became a traumatic point of reference in the collective memory. And yet Old Believer representations of the period bear the strong influence of their ethical views and historical myths.

Old Believers were consistently discriminated against by the Tsarist regime for two-and-a-half centuries, with the exception of two periods of religious toleration (1760s–1820s and 1905–1930s). In response to our enquiries, Old Believers present their recent experiences of repression in the context of the history of their religious movement: remembering Stalin's attack on religion, they often refer to the early Christian martyrdom when the Roman emperors persecuted a minority of Christians. Taisiia Ivanovna (b. 1920) calls those Old Believer priests who were arrested during the early 1930s and exiled to Siberia 'the very first martyrs', implying perhaps that the most brutal repression started in 1937–8 during the Great Terror. To restore the connection with the past, Old Believers recall in their oral and written tradition the martyrdom of the legendary leader of seventeenth-century Old Believers, priest Avvakum; they also commemorate the noble women, Fedosia Morozova, Evdokiia Urusova and Maria Danilova, who sacrificed their wealth and status for the Old Faith. 'How many people perished because of Nikon! Old Believers were stabbed and burned alive, they had their tongues cut and eyes torn out', says Vasilii Fedorovich (b. 1932). Uliana Ivanovna (b. 1931) also refers to the persecution of Old Believers as an important element of Old Believer sense of righteousness: 'Nikon tortured people who stood for the true faith!' The stories of suffering are invoked when the conversation concerns the repression in the 1930s. In one village we are told about a priest, arrested by the secret police, who was burned alive on his chair in prison. This legend (for it is unlikely that the Stalinist police would actually use medieval methods of execution) bears some allusions to the seventeenth-century accounts of Old Believer martyrdom. In prisons and camps, Old Believers suffered when they tried to defend some of their traditional ways. Agrafena Dmitrievna (b. 1951) remembers a hermit, Fr Pavel, who, arrested during the era of terror, had his beard pulled out hair by hair by other prisoners. Spiridon Fedorovich (b. 1911) remembers that his father, who was arrested in 1937, resisted when the prison guards wanted to shave his beard for hygienic reasons.

One cannot fail to notice that these often naive accounts of Old Believer purges during Stalinism do not aim at constructing a memorial to the martyrdom of Old Believers, or at promoting a mass canonisation of the clergy and believers who fell as victims of Stalin's terror. There are several reasons for this. On the one hand, Old Believer narratives largely remain localised and non-institutionalised. On the other hand, perhaps, Old Believers do not want to emphasise the fact that repression during the Soviet period represented a discontinuity of their three centuries' long antagonism with the Russian state. 'The Christian faith has always been persecuted,' says Spiridon Fedorovich, a son of a dekulakised peasant, in reply to my question as to why he thought that Old Believers suffered more than any other religious group. He rejects my suggestion that he should search for more information about his father, who was purged in 1937: 'Let's not trouble the dead.'

Although the memories of the 1930s are particularly traumatic, our informants could extract a positive message from it. For the children of purged Old Believers during the 1930s it was important to withstand discrimination and social castigation, and to gain a feeling of moral superiority over their persecutors. In discussing the violent deaths of innocent people, Old Believers indicated that the use of violence by the authorities undermined the moral basis of their power.

People who knew Vasilii Salnikov (d. 1937), a local community leader in Michura (Perm' region), say that they heard him saying that he wanted to be arrested so as to suffer for Christ's sake. Contrary to common sense and the instinct of self-preservation, Vasilii decided to stay in the village after his de*kulaki*sation, while many of his relatives left for Siberia. He said to his wife that, if he left, the authorities would close the chapel in which he served as a minister. And, indeed, until his arrest in 1937 the village of Michura remained the centre of religious life in the region. Uliana (b. 1931) remembers that Salnikov baptised the children of local Old Believers. But after Vasilii's arrest, along with another priest, Savelii Salnikov, the chapel was immediately transformed into a village club.

The memories of the struggle of the 1930s emphasised the courage of believers and their adherence to Christian values. Olga Anisimovna (b. 1937) recalls a scene that took place before she was born, presumably related to her by her mother, an active member of the Nev'iansk chapel.

> It was a long time ago. In 1930 they were demolishing our church ... They were taking icons out of the church and burning them. My mother was passing by. And at that time she was pregnant with my sister Nina. She saw them carrying a big wooden crucifix. Several people had to carry it, so heavy was it! When mum saw it [she said] 'O Lord, folks, give me this crucifix!' And they noticed that she was pregnant and allowed her to take the heavy crucifix. They did it for a laugh, because they wanted to see a pregnant woman carrying such a heavy weight. So that's what she did: she dragged the crucifix for some distance and then found a horse to transport it to our chapel at the cemetery.

The story conveys the image of Christ carrying his cross to Golgotha, the model for every Christian. The vision of a pregnant woman carrying the cross, accompanied by the laughter and insults of the crowd, had a strong emotional impact on believers and, especially, on her own daughter.

In the 1930s, when the levels of popular religiousness became subject to state monitoring and control, many believers faced an uneasy choice. For example, during the implementation of the 1937 census, which contained a question about religious affiliation, rumour spread in the countryside that believers would be persecuted. A woman told us about her mother, who felt she betrayed Christ when she hid her religious identity from a census data collector: 'She could not sleep all night. And next morning she found the data collector and told her that she was a believer.'[8] The narratives thus emphasise everyday abidance to ethical principles of Christianity, in which suffering was considered a requisite of salvation.

Old Believers' memories of terror and repression do not convey the spirit of resistance to the state, but often represent state oppression as something inevitable, as a norm rather than an exception. They would rather view the periods of religious toleration as exceptions to the rule. Isaak Mamontovich, an active member of Nev'iansk chapel, weaves the history of his community into the general narrative of Old Believer history of the eighteenth and nineteenth centuries:

> When there was Nikon's persecution, some Old Believers escaped to Taiga to look for a place to live ... then a little freedom was given (it was the next tsar after Nikon) and they began to build a plant in Nev'iansk. First, there were not too many people, but eventually, when it became more liberal, people from the river Kerzhen' came and were hired by the works ... In 1929 [the authorities] closed the chapel ... This was the time when I was oppressed very much. They gave me no freedom. They did not allow me to join the *kolkhoz*, but just oppressed me a lot ... in 1942 under Stalin they gave us [religious] freedom and from 1942 to 1963 I served in the chapel openly.

In Isaak's testimony, the periods of persecution revolve with periods of liberalisation as a natural cycle of good and bad years, of harvests and famines. It was a cycle over which the peasant had little control. Although this attitude probably has its roots in peasant mentality, it is prominent in Old Believer eschatological views, according to which humanity was on the verge of Doomsday, and the changes in political climate did not really make a radical difference to the basic issues of salvation.

What appears to be a passive attitude to state repression was an affirmation of the moral superiority of the victims over their persecutors. In their persecutions, Old Believers found proof of their righteousness. But in their affliction they appealed to divine justice to punish their persecutors, and sought consolation in the Psalms, in which the themes of messianic expectations and the yearning for God's retribution were evoked. Those who offended Christians or the objects of Christian faith were punished, either by divine retribution or, like the apostle Paul, converted from persecutors into confessors. For example, in the 1930s many stories were circulated among both Old Believers and the Orthodox about revolutionaries' iconoclasm and the miracles related to it. During the anti-religious campaigns in the 1930s, ancient icons were often attacked by local activists. To understand the rhetoric of these stories, one has to take into account the centrality of the icon in the Orthodox tradition: icons served as a means of communication with the divine, and no mystical experience was possible without the mediation of an icon (for example, apparitions in Orthodoxy usually occurred in a form of the miraculous discovery of a new icon or the renovation of an old icon). That is why it was believed that a person who stole an icon from a church, or treated it without reverence, affronted God and would be subject to God's punishment.

Anna Semenovna remembers that, in the 1930s, local activists were destroying the interior of the chapel in Nizhneirginsk, and a parishioner who was a carpenter tried to save some of the icons that were demolished by the activists:

> I remember when they started to knock churches down (some Bolsheviks volunteered for this job). They took it out [the icon of the Mother of God], smashed it as if they wanted to say that all icons must be destroyed! And then he [a carpenter] came and said, 'Give this icon to me.' 'What for?' 'I need the wood.' 'Will you destroy it?' 'Yes, I will.' He took the icon and brought it to our prayer house. And, you know, he managed to avoid army conscription. This is the Mother of God who saved him from conscription! And this young one, Victor C., who treated the icon as if it were wood (what have they done to it? I don't know ...) and soon both his legs were paralysed! Yes, his legs were paralysed, he had to stay in his bed and then he killed himself – it was the devil who tempted him. This is what happens to those who serve the devil!

Akulina Ivanovna (b. 1911) recalls a story about her stepfather: 'He was insane, really, perhaps he was a Communist. Once after having had an argument with my mother, he took a wooden icon and cut it [with an axe]. And later he became blind and perished.' The stories of the Communists being punished by divine intervention in this way can be seen in the context of traditional Orthodox culture that, through a set of taboos and behavioural prescriptions, managed to maintain some important dogmatic messages. But God did not thirst for the death of the sinner: offenders and persecutors of Christian faith always had a chance for salvation if they repented. As several people told us in Nizhnii Tagil, a woman, a representative of the city party organisation, who vigorously implemented Khrushchev's anti-religious campaigns during the 1960s, at the time of her death called a priest and made confession of her sins.

STRATEGIES OF SURVIVAL

Faced by the threat to their culture and way of life, the Old Believers resorted to a traditional peasant strategy of survival – flight and migration. Our informants' families migrated from rural to urban areas and from the Urals to Siberia for a number of reasons: to avoid persecution, dekulakisation, to escape from hunger, and to preserve the integrity of their families. Alexandra Ivanovna (b. 1918, Khokhly) was driven out of the village by the famine of 1934. First she went to live in Central Asia because one of her sisters had settled there and invited the family (the father, three brothers and two sisters). After a while all of them went to look for a better life in Siberia, where Alexandra got married and lived with her husband for a year, while her family moved to Cheliabinsk to find work at a factory. After a year she divorced her husband in order to join her family in Cheliabinsk. Among the thirty-nine men and women we interviewed, only sixteen still live in the place where they were born, and only half of this number still live in rural areas. The rapid industrialisation of the Urals in the 1930s–40s provided opportunities for dekulakised peasants to find work on building sites and to settle permanently in the cities. Isaak Mamontovich (b. 1906), when he was expelled from the *kolkhoz* in Byn'gi, went to work at a factory in a nearby town. Both Spiridon Fedorovich and Filaret Stepanovich (b. 1898), who were dekulakised but not deported, migrated from the village to towns during the collectivisation. The big cities allowed believers to escape to some extent the social control they experienced in the collective farms where they were stigmatised as believers and *kulaki*. Mobility and constant change of environment, therefore, were crucial for the survival of Old Belief.

In the atmosphere of the 1930s the reputation of being an active member of a religious congregation had often been a cause for discrimination at the workplace and at school. Deomid Ivanovich remembers that he was fired from his job in a post office on the grounds of his religious affiliation. He grew up in an Old Believer village, where he participated in church services as a singer and reader. After the collectivisation in the early 1930s he worked as a driver in the *sovkhoz* Zernogolovka (Kurgan *oblast*), but his good work was not sufficient proof of his reliability:

> The secretary of the organisation sent a request to my village. And they replied that I was an Old Believer priest [*pop dvoedanskii*]. When I came back from a trip the secretary told me to come to the office. 'Listen, Iakovlev, clear off! We have no right to keep you here. It's a known thing that you're a *kulak*. But on the top of that, you're an Old Believer priest!' I said, 'Have you ever heard of a priest at my age of 20 something? Priests are mature people, and they must study. What kind of priest am I? It's a lie! I am not hiding that I was dekulakised and that I can sing and read [in Church Slavonic]. But I am not a priest!' 'Well, comrade, for all that, we can't keep you, we must discharge you from your job'.

Despite the instances of religious discrimination, believers managed on a local level to establish good relations at their workplaces and with the representatives of the state bureaucracy. Our interviewees born between 1920 and the

1930s often emphasise that their parents, despite their religious beliefs, were highly regarded at their workplaces. For example, Olga's father trained young workers in a factory school in Nev'iansk. And, even though his pupils made fun of his beard, they had great respect for him: 'Lads, hats off! Usatik (the bearded man) is coming!'

Deomid Ivanovich managed to obtain a profession, and was successful in his career. It was his attitude to work and his good sense of humour that helped him to make his way up the social ladder. During the war, Deomid worked as a driver for a bus company in Cheliabinsk, and was selected by the secret police (the NKVD) to work in security at a military factory because he had good references from his workplace: 'A recruiter from the NKVD came to our auto park and said: "Mechanic, look, we need two persons who are the cream of your staff." He told them that Deomid was one of the best. And I always worked energetically, without accidents and in a very civilised manner: I wore a tie at work and was always jolly.'

Uliana's father, who worked in the *kolkhoz*, according to his daughter, never stole a thing from the collective farm and taught his children to do the same. Old Believers were well known for their sobriety (another factor that distinguished them from the majority of the Soviet male population). Deomid proudly told me that he never had a drop of alcohol in his life. Sobriety, however, in practice generally meant moderation rather than the total exclusion of alcohol. Uliana said that even if Old Believer men had a drink on occasion, no one ever saw a drunken Old Believer lying in a ditch. Generally the administration of the collective farms and factories tended to appreciate the industry, respect for property and restraint from alcohol cultivated in Old Believer families. Often the managers shut their eyes to the religious activities of valuable workers. For example, in the 1930s the head of a collective farm in Udmurtiia esteemed a deacon of the local Old Believer parish because the deacon was a proficient stove-maker; he helped him to get a release from the army. Even prison authorities showed some disposition towards hard-working prisoners. Ksenia's father, who was arrested in 1942 for anti-Soviet propaganda, was released from the prison in Solikamsk before his 10-year sentence had expired, as a result of his hard work and good behaviour. The prison administrators even suggested that he could stay in Solikamsk as a contract worker if he wanted to.

As far as formal relations with the bureaucratic state were concerned, individual Old Believers, like other Soviet citizens, tried to get around the impersonal bureaucratic system and use it to their advantage. Deomid Ivanovich remembers that, in the 1920s when he was deputy chairman of a poor peasant committee, he got hold of the stamped official forms:

> I was not stupid: once I stayed in the office when the chairman and the secretary were called away. Since I was there I got hold of the rubber stamp and put the round-shaped stamps [onto pieces of paper] just in case. And I used these documents – not for money, of course – to help

out people who were deported. Well, these documents were, of course, forged, but they had round stamps on them, you know ...

The last phrase suggests that Deomid saw his action not as being a criminal forgery, but rather as a little victory over the system: because the 'documents' had proper stamps, they did not look like forgeries.

Thus, if Old Believers were guided by their ethical principles at the workplace, they applied different strategies to the impersonal bureaucratic system. Survival depended very much not on resistance but on the flexibility of an individual to conform to the requirements of the system and to use it to his or her advantage.

MAINTAINING RELIGIOUS IDENTITY

Old Believers' social flexibility was vital for their survival and adaptation to society. In the following section we shall try to assess the ways in which Old Believers sought to maintain their religious identity and cultural distinctiveness, and the challenges they faced.

The problem of religious identity often arises as a practical concern when one has to think about the baptism of children, marriage and burial. The Bolsheviks saw religious rituals as an expression of superstition and backwardness, and tried to replace them with new socialist traditions. For example, Oktiabriny, a ceremony of the initiation of a newborn child into the society of Soviet people, was designed to replace the rite of baptism. Soviet propaganda repudiated baptism as harmful for the health of the baby and tried to discourage women from baptising their children. 'She exhorted pregnant women that they should not baptise their children', says Spiridon Fedorivich (b. 1911), an Old Believer minister in Nizhnii Tagil (a large industrial centre in the Urals), about a local Party official who in the 1950s carried out propaganda against baptism among mothers-to-be. A member of the same community in Nizhnii Tagil recollects that, when she was pregnant, she had to attend a course on childcare, organised by the local medical services, at which women had to promise that they would not baptise their infants – a promise rarely fulfilled.

Baptism persisted as a marker of ethnic and religious identity. A non-baptised person was excluded from both the earthly and heavenly communities of Christians. Old Believers maintained that, after death, the souls of the non-baptised ones would be locked in a dark place so that they would not see God. One could not pray for the non-baptised, and thus could not assist in their salvation. The exclusion of those who were not baptised from collective and private prayer was an important instrument for marking the boundaries of the religious community.

All our interviewees born between 1905 and the 1940s told us that they baptised their children in defiance of the exhortations of Soviet propaganda.

When the churches were closed down, both Old Believers and Orthodox baptised infants in the private houses of priests and ministers, or in their own houses. 'When our first child was born my father said that we should invite Nester Maksimovich [a minister] to baptise the baby ... He baptised my first and the second child,' says Kseniia Dmitrievna. Often the baptisms took place at night, in order to avoid conflict with the village authorities. The priestless Old Believers had an advantage over the priestly, for they allowed a lay person, not a priest, to perform the baptism. Akulina (b. 1906, Kirillovka), for example, says that she baptised her children without anyone else's assistance.[9]

It may seem a paradox, but the authorities did not seem to be concerned at the rise of clandestine baptisms. Presumably the *kolkhoz* bosses knew about the Nesters and the Akulinas who practised baptism in their domains. But, since the Party obliged local authorities to see that the level of registered rituals did not increase, they turned a blind eye to the growth of unregistered baptisms. Moreover, many of the Party officials had their own children baptised, a fact which was often recalled during the Party purges in the 1920s and 1930s. Anna Vasil'evna, for example, a collective farmer and the wife of a Party member, baptised her children with her husband's silent agreement.

Many of our informants who were not well versed in scripture and Christian dogma were not guided by the doctrinal meaning of the baptism. And yet they baptised their children and grandchildren enthusiastically. One of the reasons was that baptism drew the dividing line between the Christian and non-Christian worlds. Anna Sherstianykh (b. 1918, Nizhneirginsk) recalls the story about her mother baptising her second husband. 'Neither he nor his son was baptised. He was from a [non-Christian] village ... She baptised him, an adult man. He said that it was not very nice to be unbaptised because everyone called him a pagan [*nekhrist*].'

Baptism marked not only religious but also ethnic difference. In the Urals, where the ethnic Russians resided with Finno-Ugric and Tartar peoples, Russians who failed to baptise their children were rebuked. In 1935 the schoolchildren in one of the Urals schools mocked a girl who was not baptised, calling her a Tartar. Even if there was no peer pressure, young mothers were persuaded by their parents, especially by their own mothers, to baptise. In answer to our question about the baptism of her children, Anna replies that her mother was very strict where baptism was concerned. The relations between mothers and daughters were affected by a belief in the spiritual uncleanness of the woman who gave birth. The mother of Elena Osipovna (b. 1929, Foki) would not let her daughter, who had just given birth, do any household work until she had baptised her child and made her confession. Moreover, grandmothers often refused to care for their grandchildren, in order to increase the pressure on their daughters and daughters-in-law to baptise. 'She said she could not touch the baby before he was baptised,' Anna, the wife of a minister, said about her mother (b. 1936, Nizhnii Tagil).

Burial rituals and marriages were almost as important as baptisms. Although Old Believer cemeteries had been destroyed during the 1930s, funeral rituals were commonly performed in private houses. Traditional weddings were also performed in private before or after the civil registration of marriage.

However, although discouraged, mixed marriages were relatively common among Old Believers. And in the 1930s, marriage was one of the few instruments of upward mobility for many women, especially for the daughters of *kulaki* and disenfranchised clergy. Anna Kilina, the daughter of an Old Believer minister who was arrested in 1937, married a Communist from an Orthodox family. Fedosiia (b. 1912), a daughter of another Old Believer minister, married a Red Army officer from the non-Russian Chuvash ethnic group. Anna Ivanova (b. 1918), an illiterate rural woman whose family was dekulakised, was envied by her friends because she married a Komsomol leader, a factory activist from an Orthodox family. Nevertheless, all these women emphasised that their husbands appreciated the beauty of Old Believer worship and not only did not discourage their wives from their faith, but often expressed a wish to join the Old Believer community themselves.

As for young Old Believer men, they also often married outsiders when they left their families and traditional village community. Vasilii (b. 1935) married his first wife, an Orthodox woman, just after finishing his military service in Siberia – far from home. However, his second marriage was to an Old Believer when he returned to the place of his origin in the Perm' region.

Closing down places of worship, policing religious congregations, and purging priests and ministers, substantially reduced the opportunity for believers to exercise their faith in public. That is why the domestic sphere and the family gained a particular significance for believers. Although during the Cultural Revolution the official ideology emphasised that the family was not immune from the class struggle that sets one relative against the other, family ties became stronger in the face of external pressures.[10] Religious identity did not exist in a vacuum: the family and kin were important institutions for the preservation and transmission of Old Believer identity.

Religious identity in such families was sustained through family gatherings, common prayer and the singing of verses which reiterated themes from the Old and New Testaments and from the recent history of Old Believers. 'I remember, in the evenings mother would gather us children on the stove and we would sing spiritual verses. When dad came from work, he often joined us,' recollects Lukeria (b. 1924). Christianity was not something 'out there', it was an everyday reality in such families. Although our informants often represent their family life in idyllic terms, we should take into account the important role of religious regulations in conservative families. Prayer and blessing had to accompany each daily activity in such families. Akulina (b. 1906) explains that, in her household, one usually asked for a blessing (permission) to do something from anyone who was in the room (presumably an elder person). Praskovia (b. 1934) says that even milking the cow could not be done without a blessing from another member of the household.

Prayer must be seen as a practical way to assert one's religious beliefs. While public prayer usually requires a minister to lead the ceremony, private prayer, which can be both collective (as a family prayer, for example) or individual, does not require a special setting and a minister. Although the Soviet state restricted public worship, it failed to control private space. During the years of terror, believers gathered in private houses and prayed behind closed curtains. In the rural areas the houses at the outskirts of the village proved more suitable for common prayer. In some areas, Old Believers surrounded their houses with gardens so that the singing could not be heard from the street. Many bought houses built near the railway so that the sound of trains could cover singing and loud reading (as was the case in Leontii's family).

Given the shortage of clergy in priestly communities, some members of the congregation had to take up pastoral and liturgical duties. The authorities were puzzled by the fact that believers continued to gather for prayer even after the arrest of their leaders.[11] In the absence of the male leaders (who were arrested or deported), women took the lead in their parishes. Eight out of fourteen informants who occupied positions of leadership in their communities were women. And even if the formal head of the community was a man, the women maintained control over both economic and spiritual spheres of community life. Thus, although women had always exercised considerate informal power in church, during the Soviet period this became even more the case.

Because of their frequent migrations and their consequent isolation from spiritual centres, Old Believers developed the Orthodox tradition of private worship that allowed a believer to follow the religious calendar without feeling withdrawn from the larger Christian community. Even when liturgical books and the Bible were unavailable for sale in the Soviet Union, a believer could read short prayers and petitions remembered by heart, such as the Jesus Prayer or Ave Maria using a rosary. 'First I prayed using a rosary, and then I learned how to read canons from the wife of our priest,' says Elena Osipovna (b. 1926, Foki), who began to practise her faith after her retirement. Old Believer elders took into account that modern life did not provide good conditions for prayer, and that is why one ' ... must keep prayer in one's heart, at every place ... If you are embarrassed by people, just say "Lord Jesus Christ, forgive me a sinner in all my deeds"' (Spiridon Nasedkov).

The sphere of the everyday life and domestic activities, sanctified by prayer and ritual, was the area that was hardest for the state to police. Moreover, private prayer witnessed by no-one was an intimate realm into which the custodial state could not interfere. One could say that the more pressure the state and society put on believers, the more internalised prayer became. And it was on this level of inner spiritual life that religious identity became an integral part of selfhood which could not be affected by the external control.

MEETING THE CHALLENGES TO TRADITION

Traditional identity was maintained through cultural and social isolationism. Old Believers tended to live separately from the rest of the local community: they discouraged mixed marriages, and tried to limit communication with the outside world by a set of taboos. Some of these taboos were conditional, so that they could be applied flexibly according to the situation, while others were unconditional. In the Soviet period, some of these unconditional norms gradually became conditional and limited to the elite of Old Believer communities.

Food consumption was not free from religious differentiation in the Old Believer world. For example, in the past, many priestless Old Believers kept separate plates for outsiders.[12] Anna Vasilevna (b. 1915) remembers that her mother used to keep three separate sets of plates and cutlery: one for the members of their community, another for the Orthodox, who visited their house for interconfessional debates, and another one for the Tartars who worked as seasonal labourers at harvest time. Akulina Ivanovna (b. 1914), Isaak Mamontovich (b. 1906) and Elena Osipovna remember that, in their villages, the Old Believers did not share their meals with members of the Orthodox Church. In addition, according to Elena, smokers had separate plates.

The fear of contamination was expressed in Old Believer hygienic rules which must be seen not only as a precaution against epidemics and infections but primarily as a construction of cultural difference. Anna remembers that she always clashed with her mother-in-law, who was Orthodox, over hygienic standards:

> When I got married they [the mother-in-law and Anna's husband] treated me a little bit unfairly, because we [Old Believers] liked cleanliness a lot. Sometimes my mother-in-law would say, 'Why do you Old Believers always have wet towels?' I would answer, 'This is because we Old Believers wash our hands all the time – and you don't.'

Outsiders ridiculed the Old Believers for what they perceived was stinginess and an attitude of moral superiority. 'U-u-u, kerzhaki will never let you drink water from their bucket!' (Uliana). 'Kerzhaki' was a derogatory title for Old Believers in the Urals. Although the word derives from the name of the river Kerzhen', from where the Old Believers' ancestors came in the eighteenth century, peasants usually used it in a negative sense to criticise Old Believers for their unsociability and idiosyncrasies.

During the Soviet period many of these normative rules and taboos that constructed the symbolic boundaries between 'us' and 'them' became conditional for the majority of believers. For example, the taboo on sharing plates with outsiders had lost its significance in the Urals by the 1940s. Zinaida Fedorova, born in 1936 into an Old Believer family, grew up in the same village as Anna Vasilevna (who told us about the three-way separation of the dishes), but Zinaida never observed this ritual either in her family or among her neighbours. It was only in the 1950s, working as a teacher in a remote village of the Altai (to where some of her relatives had migrated during collectivisation) that she first observed this custom, and it seemed exotic to her. Zinaida recalls a conversation with an old woman who, selling her milk, poured it into a pot with an 'unclean' mug.

The women said, 'Keep this pot for yourself, dear, but when you go into town, please, buy me a similar one, because I made it unclean ... I poured the milk with an unclean cup, which my husband uses. You see, I am an Old Believer but he is not.' Zinaida, realising what was going on, made fun of the old lady: 'Does this mean that you eat apart for all your life?' 'Yes, my dear, we do eat apart.' 'But does this mean that you sleep apart as well?' Most Old Believers born in the 1920s and 1930s, who told us about the pollution behaviour of their relatives, did not practise this ritual in their own daily lives.

These strict rules and taboos did not become altogether irrelevant in the Soviet period, but they were applied selectively to particular members of the priestless communities, usually to the members of *sobor*, literally, the congregation (these taboos became the dividing line between the 'world' and the *sobor*). In the past, the *sobor* included both lay persons of mature age as well as younger active members, such as readers and singers. In the Soviet period, however, the *sobor* consisted of members actively engaged in church life, usually advanced in years. To be a member of the *sobor* meant to follow all the rules and regulations that became conditional for the rest of the Old Believer world.

Old Belief sought to represent the living icon of Christian tradition, or a model Christianity, as Roy Robson pointed out in his book *Old Believers in the Modern World*.[13] However, the requirements of the faith were often in conflict with the demands of everyday life for the majority of Old Believers. And this was especially true during the Soviet period. Thus, increasingly, only a minority of Old Believers carried out the guiding principles of pious behaviour, and represented iconic models for imitation by the rest of the community.

Instead, resistance to joining Communist organisations became the new instrument of transmission of traditional identity in religious families. The Communist voluntary unions practised atheism and required their members to relinquish their religious beliefs. Our informants born between 1920 and 1930 mention that their parents were generally against their membership of Communist youth organisations, such as Oktiabriata, the Pioneers and Komsomol. Lukeria (b. 1924, Al'niash) and Anna (b. 1918, Nizhneirginsk) joined in the Pioneer organisation at school but, under the influence of their parents, withdrew their application.

> Nobody warned me about it when I went to school. And there, I remember, our teachers told us what a good thing the Pioneers were. They asked, 'Who wants to join?' Well, I said, 'I do.' My friend took my bag and ran home ahead of me, and told my parents that I'd joined the Pioneers. I cannot remember exactly, but most likely I was chastised, so I never did this again.

Anna joined the Pioneers at school despite her mother's disapproval. But she left the organisation when her grandfather, who was an unquestionable authority for her, asked her calmly, 'Do you really need it?' Participation in youth organisations, however, was important for social mobility. Zinaida made a rational choice when she joined the Pioneer organisation and then the Komsomol at school. She always wanted to be a teacher, but since her mother, an Old Believer, refused to join the *kolkhoz*, Zinaida had a poor chance of enrolling in a teacher training college. She became a Pioneer and then a Komsomol member despite her mother's chagrin: 'Go ahead, join the Communist Party now!'

Membership of one family member in a Communist organisation caused difficulties for all members of the household. Anna's husband Nikolai, a Party member, was interrogated by a member of the local Party organisation on why he had icons in his house. Nikolai had to point at his mother-in-law, saying that he would offend her feeling if he removed the icons. The brother of Olga (b. 1937), a Communist, used to argue with his mother, a member of the Old Believer chapel in Nev'iansk, about religion. Eventually, she said, 'you keep your convictions to yourself, and I will keep mine to myself.'

In the post-Soviet period, many men and women who could not attend the church before due to their membership in the Party or holding a public office, again filled the Old Believer chapels. Spiridon says that many former Communist party members came to him for confession and expressed their desire to join the community. They would return their Party Card, confess, read special prayers 'rejecting their alliance with Satan', and fulfil certain religious penances, such as a number of prayers and prostrations.[14] Thus Party membership and church attendance were mutually exclusive in the Soviet period. For many Soviet men and women, membership in 'voluntary' youth and Party organisations was formal and obligatory. That is why the confession of atheism by Party members was just another formality that could easily be repudiated when an ex-Party member wanted to come back to the religious community. Old Believer rules provided opportunities for an ex-Party member to return to the community. Moreover, the renegades did not face social castigation, being perceived by the community as 'prodigal sons'. Spiridon says: 'There were many who came back. They would say, "That's it. We want to renounce Party membership and come back to the old faith!"' Coming back to the 'old faith' was a symbolic return to one's own spiritual origins, to one's parents' faith.

CONCLUSION

Old Believers preserved their faith and cultural identity despite the challenges of official atheism and the socio-economic transformation of the 1930s. Although we can speak about the limited survival of Old Belief, the fact that, through the Soviet years, Old Believers continued to gather for prayers and feasts, read and wrote theological treatises, baptised their children, and taught them how to pray demonstrates that religion survived in the Soviet Union not as a remnant of traditional culture but as a powerful source of collective and personal identity.

The Old Believer case indicates that religious identity was not fixed and immutable but was constructed through language and narrative. The stories of religious assault, situated in a larger narrative of an Old Believer heroic past, reinforced the sense of belonging to a 'storied community'. However, the survival of the Old Belief also demonstrates that identity could not be reduced to language and narrative. It was embodied in institutions and rituals, which were not necessarily discursive. Rites of passage and pollution behaviour served as the markers of religious identity and traced lines between 'us' and 'them'. Far from being just 'habits' or customs, religious rituals served as links between the religious sign and practice; they have translated symbols into concrete action and served as a practical way of asserting Old Believer cultural identity.

On the one hand, the Old Believers' survival was a result of their historical experience and culture. In the past, Old Believers had experience of social exclusion and political repression and, therefore, they possessed certain advantages in dealing with the political and social challenges of the 1930s. Restless migrants and colonisers, Old Believers developed a system of worship that allowed individuals and families to maintain their spiritual link with the imagined community of true Christians through family and individual prayer, ritual and custom.

On the other hand, the story of the Old Believers' survival suggests that, despite the scale of repression, there was an informal dimension to relations between believers and the local organs of the Party/state which could entail limited negotiation and compromise. The Old Believer case demonstrates that there were practical limits to the capacity of the Party/state to penetrate and remake all dimensions of social life, and for Soviet ideology to present a unified worldview for the Soviet nation.

Old Believer survival in Stalin's Russia demonstrates that the persistence of religion in Soviet society should be seen as an attempt to adapt to the system by establishing informal relations with local officials and maintaining a high reputation at the workplace. But the Old Believers' social accommodation with the regime did not mean compliance with the ideological premises of the Soviet state. The general principle applied by Old Believers to Soviet authorities, 'Render unto Caesar what is Caesar's, and to God what is God's', coexisted with the general Christian scepticism of the regime's promise of social paradise. The survival of religion in the Soviet Union in the face of massive anti-religious campaigns and the breakdown of traditional community has demonstrated that the Soviet project of replacing Christianity with Communist ideology as a kind of substitute civil religion has ultimately failed.

Notes

I presented earlier versions of this essay at the Pan-European Institute Seminar at the University of Essex in November 1999, and at the Annual Conference of the British Association of Slavic and East European Studies, Cambridge, in April 2000. Support for the research was provided by the Economic and Social Research Council. I would like to thank Steve Smith, Revan Schendler and Tony Swift for their comments on this essay. I would also like to thank Paul Thompson for giving me inspiration for this project.

1 James Thrower, *Marxism-Leninism as the Civil religion of Soviet Society: God's Commissar* (Edwin Mellen Press, Lampeter, 1992); Dmitrii Furman, *Stalin i my s religiovedcheskoi tochki zreniia* [Stalin and Us from a Religious Studies Point of View] (Letnii Sad, Moscow, 1989); Kimmo Kääriäinen, *Religion in Russia after the Collapse of Communism*, (Edwin Mellen Press, Lewiston, 1998).

2 Dan Peris, *Storming the Heavens: the Soviet League of the Militant Godless* (Cornell University Press, Ithaca, 1998); William Husband, *Godless Communists: Atheism and Society in Soviet Russia, 1917–1932* (Northern Illinois University Press, DeKalb, 2000); William Husband, 'Soviet atheism and Russian Orthodox strategies of resistance, 1917–1932', *Journal of Modern History* 70 (1998), 74–107; Glennys Young, *Power and the Sacred in Revolutionary Russia: Religious Activists in the Village* (Pennsylvania State University Press, University Park, 1997); Sarah Davies, *Popular Opinion in Stalin's Russia* (Cambridge University Press, Cambridge, 1997), 73–83; Lynn Viola, 'The peasant nightmare: visions of apocalypse in the Soviet countryside', *Journal of Modern History* 62 (1990), 747–70.

3 On the history of Old Believers, see Robert Crummey, *Old Believers and the World of Antichrist: the Vyg Community and the Russian State, 1694–1855* (University of Wisconsin Press, Madison, 1970); Georg Michels, *At War with the Church: Religious Dissent in Seventeenth-Century Russia* (Stanford University Press, Stanford, California, 1999); Roy Robson, *Old Believers in Modern Russia* (Northern Illinois University Press, DeKalb, 1996). See also Irina Korovushkina Paert, 'Popular religion and local identity during the Stalin revolution: Old Believers in the Urals (1928–41)', in Don Raleigh (ed.), *Provincial Landscapes: Local Dimensions of Soviet Power* (University of Pittsburgh Press, Pittsburgh, 2001), 171–94.

4 Although Old Belief did not experience such a remarkable revival as Orthodoxy in the 1980s–90s, it managed to survive through the Soviet era despite the lack of resources. Now there are about 450 Old Believer parishes registered in the former Soviet Union, and there are between 10,000 and 20,000 Old Believers living in the Urals. The number is fairly small compared to the pre-revolutionary estimates of Old Believers (for example, the 1897 census estimated the number of Old Believers in the Urals at 150,000, and in reality this number was much higher).

5 F. Walshe, 'The concept of family resilience: crisis and challenge', *Family Process* 35 (1996), 261–81.

6 The interviews, accompanied by the transcripts, are in the process of being deposited with the Library of the London School of Slavonic and East European Studies. The surnames of the interviewees were withheld; we use the first name and patronymic of an interviewee.

7 Journals of the Archaeographical expedition of the Urals State University, 1999.

8 *Ibid.*, 1992.

9 *Ibid.*, 1998.

10 Sheila Fitzpatrick, *Everyday Stalinism* (Oxford University Press, New York and Oxford, 1999).

11 Nizhnii Tagil Archive, P-70, op. 2, d. 116, l. 244. In 1940 a secretary of the town council in Nizhnii Tagil reported that the Kazanskaia parish was packed with people despite the absence of the priest.

12 This ritual seems to have more relevance for priestless Old Believers, who unlike the priestly did not have the sacrament of Eucharist, and therefore had to separate their communal body from the non-members not through the inclusions and exclusions in Eucharist but by not sharing food with outsiders.

13 Robson, *Old Believers*.

14 By 'rejection', Spiridon means the ritual of 'the rejection of Satan' that is read during the Orthodox baptismal service.

10

THE RETURN OF THE REPRESSED

Survival after the Gulag

Nanci Adler

INTRODUCTION

For Soviet Gulag survivors, the negative consequences of repression continued through to the end of the victim's lifetime and beyond, in ever widening circles. The large and small difficulties created by political repression found their way into every corner of the psychological, social and political life of the victim. While some of these 'returnees' attempted to blend into the social fabric, others would not go gently back into a society that had taken their freedom and now wanted to deprive them of their dignity by not properly acknowledging their innocence. Though the lot of returnees improved significantly as a result of the era of rehabilitation (the Khrushchev and Gorbachev reforms), the effects of their experience of Soviet repression continued to haunt their lives and the lives of everyone in their network. A great many Gulag survivors were never able to escape their sense of 'second-class' citizenship.

The title of this chapter refers to one of Freud's basic hypotheses regarding the cause and treatment of mental disorders in individuals. In the context of this discussion the term describes how a social and political system, (mal)adapted to repression, deals with disowned parts of itself. Briefly, Freud's hypothesis is that people regularly experience forbidden thoughts, feelings or impulses and, instead of finding socially acceptable ways to express or satisfy them, they repress or 'forget' them by relegating them to an amnesic section of the mind. There, these forbidden impulses persist, exerting constant pressure to have their demands satisfied. In consequence, it requires considerable mental energy to continually keep them from intruding into consciousness.

Freud's hypothesis is being appropriated here for use in the social and political arena. The 'return of the repressed' refers to the victims of the Soviet system, political prisoners who were repressed by the state, incarcerated in the Gulag where they were exposed to years of grinding deprivation, and then returned to Soviet society without any institutionalised process of re-entry.

Gulag returnees were not just individuals, they were also living memories that could not be denied. But they often were denied, because people could not find a comfortable way of dealing with them. There was pervasive ambivalence at all levels of the government and society with regard to these survivors. While there were significant changes in the post-Stalin era in the physical and legal status of prisoners and ex-prisoners, it was still a time characterised by a contradictory ethos. This was reflected in the disparity between official policy and unofficial practice.

The total number of victims of the terror who were incarcerated and/or killed in the vast network of labour camps, colonies and prisons known as the Gulag will not be addressed here, because it is beyond the scope of this chapter.[1] However, a few statistics should indicate the scope of Stalinist repression. When Stalin died in 1953, the official Gulag population was estimated at 2.5 million. About half a million of these were political prisoners.[2] These figures do not reflect the population of 'exiles', those sentenced to enforced migration. One year after Stalin's death, a report presented to Khrushchev stated that, between 1921 and 1954, 3,777,380 people were convicted of counter-revolutionary (political) crimes by the various 'organs' of the Soviet judiciary. Approximately three-quarters of them received the death penalty.[3] To this number should be added several million (perhaps between five and seven) people who filled the ranks of 'administrative exile', effectively living in prisons without walls.

Rehabilitation statistics also reflect the extent and duration of Soviet repression. For example, between 1992 and 1997, four million applications for rehabilitation (official exoneration) were filed.[4] We can infer from this backlog that, if these few million did not, or could not, obtain rehabilitation in the years immediately following their return, there were a host of official barriers during the post-release period. When asked in 2001 about the progress of the state's commission on rehabilitation, Semeon Vilenskii, member and ex-prisoner, replied, 'So far it has taken the state fifty years to rehabilitate people. Doesn't that say enough?' At the start of 2002 the Rehabilitation Commission reported that, out of well over ten million victims of political repression, so far four million have been rehabilitated since the death of Stalin.[5]

When Gulag survivors began to return to society in the 1950s, they were confronted with a host of problems: their well-founded fear of re-arrest, their struggle to attain social status equal to those who had not been incarcerated, the camp culture they could not shed, the complexities of their family reunions, and their search for justice, housing and employment. This article presents some accounts of those who, against all the odds, managed to survive Soviet labour camps. But even after that experience, their struggle was not over. It is hoped that from these narratives the predicament of the returnees in the Soviet state will emerge with a more human face.

METHODOLOGY AND SOURCES

This chapter is derived from a larger study on returnees based on oral-history, official archives (the Procuracy, the Supreme Soviet, the Ministry of Justice, the Supreme Court, the Party Control Commission and the Ministry of Finance) a selection of recently published memoirs, and the archive of Memorial. Founded in Moscow in 1987, Memorial is the most widespread watchdog organisation today dedicated to preserving the memory of victims of Stalinism and to investigating and establishing the historical record on the Soviet terror. Its archive includes unpublished memoirs and questionnaires. For this particular topic, oral narratives were a crucial supplement to the written recollections, since so little of what survivors write examines their post-camp experiences. Oral-history provided the opportunity to probe, and most subjects had to be interviewed a few times. It was generally difficult to keep their focus in the post-camp arena, since the ex-prisoners' traumatic recollections largely involved what took place inside the camps. However, the reverberations of that experience continued to echo for decades.

For this research, approximately thirty interviews were conducted and followed up, and a few hundred stories were investigated. Interview subjects were mostly chosen on the basis of availability, and are therefore not a representative cross-section of the returnee population. The advanced age of many Gulag survivors limited the selection, and some of them were still too wary to talk about their past. Moreover, most of the stories collected for this research are those of the urban intelligentsia. However, there are sufficient tales of the plight of ordinary citizens to corroborate the experience described by these autobiographers.

In general, the memories seemed to differ in focus according to the subjects' primary goals upon release. For some, restoration of Communist Party membership was a top priority, and the obstacles encountered along the way form the substance of their recollection. This group varies widely in social status. For many – elites and ordinary citizens – family reunion was the primary goal. Their memories of the difficulties of returning to their families, or forming new ones, are not markedly different from one another.

Finally, a few points should be made on the issue of men's and women's memories. This research did not centre on the camp experience, which was often quite different for men and women. Both lament their lost youth. For women, this was even more traumatic, because some were no longer able to bear children due to age, physical state or the abuse they were forced to endure during incarceration. But apart from this, few discernible differences were observed in men's and women's post-camp memories.

SEMEON SAMUILOVICH VILENSKII: PARTICIPANT-OBSERVER[6]

The first case that will be examined here is that of an individual who has made sure that the repressed return again and again. Semeon Samuilovich Vilenskii is an inspiring example of a returnee who dedicated his life to exposing the historical truth and helping others to do the same. For this reason, we will explore in depth the story of this man whose own fate is so inextricably intertwined with that of other returnees.

The historical literary society which Vilenskii founded in 1989 is appropriately called Vozvrashchenie (The Return). He, and it, have two goals: to publish memoirs that salvage repressed history so as to preserve it in the public domain, and to assist survivors of the terror. To these ends, Vilenskii has given the survivors a forum in which to tell their tales, and he has, among a host of other things, successfully lobbied the commission on rehabilitation of victims of political repression. He has pushed them to assist in the transfer of a rent-free estate in the province of Tver to Vozvrashchenie. Vilenskii's own two-room Moscow apartment is cramped because it functions as a combination of publishing house, archive, storage space, reception room and living quarters, but his efforts are aimed at finding space for others. For this purpose Vozvrashchenie created from this estate on the Upper Volga a cultural, charitable centre to which former prisoners can retreat.[7] It has the potential to become a rehabilitation centre for elderly survivors who could receive medical and therapeutic assistance. Additionally, exhibitions on the Gulag are planned as part of the centre's expanding mandate.

Semeon Samuilovich Vilenskii is an ex-prisoner who has developed the extraordinary ability to observe his personal experiences from an outside perspective, and has dedicated his life to humanitarian pursuits. His camp experience shaped his life and perspective. His returnee experience is intimately connected with shaping the lives and perspectives of other returnees. As a prisoner, ex-prisoner and a returnee, Vilenskii's story exemplifies the issues associated with the return of political prisoners to society.

Vilenskii describes two aspects of the return: the external and the internal. The external aspect includes such problems as acquiring the *propiska* (the internal passport system, giving a residence permit), finding work, securing rehabilitation and petitioning for compensation. The internal aspect addresses the problems associated with how the individual comes to terms with his or her inner psychological life. Here, fearful recollections of the past persecution merge with fearful suspicions of present surveillance. Vilenskii reports that many *ex-zeki* were (and still are) perpetually afraid of committing even such minor infractions as jaywalking, for fear of being caught and punished. The mindset of the terrorised prisoner is an enduring expectation of punishment. Vilenskii recalls that he continued to walk with his hands clasped behind his back after release, and that it took him years to break the habit. It was a struggle to get used to walking on the sidewalk, because prisoners were always marched under armed escort in the middle of the road.[8]

Early on, there were indications that Vilenskii had the kind of inquisitive mind, benevolent spirit and steadfast courage that would put him on a collision course with a terrorist dictatorship. In 1945 he entered Moscow State University as a philology student and began his development as a free-thinking intellectual in these years. Vilenskii did not mind studying Lenin, but was sceptical about the theories of Stalin. He did not like the attitude toward the intelligentsia, who, he believed, could play a special role in society that was being neglected. Furthermore, he was against nationalistic politics and opposed the deportation of peoples (entire ethnic groups who were deported during the war to the far reaches of the empire for 'suspected collaboration'). All told, these stances were later to amount to 'anti-Soviet activities'. At the age of 17 he was already questioning the system, and defending the rights of others when he spoke out for a friend who had been unjustly arrested. This was considered a form of 'anti-Soviet agitation'.

As a student he liked walking in the forest with his friends and reading poems aloud. One afternoon in 1948, in the presence of some fellow students, he recited a poem about Stalin and the intelligentsia. Its final line read, 'agents are all around, and Stalin is the first'.[9] Someone informed the authorities of this, and it was interpreted as Vilenskii's expression of a desire to destroy Stalin ('terrorist intentions'). He was arrested, and Semen's nine-month interrogation began. The following year he was sentenced to ten years under the *liter* ASA (abbreviated letters for 'anti-Soviet agitation'[10]) and the article 58–8 (article 58 was standardly applied for 'counter-revolutionary activities', point 8 referred to 'terrorist intentions').

Vilenskii spent one month in the Lubianka prison in Moscow, from 17 July until 18 August 1948. He was then taken to the Sukhanovka, notorious for its multitude of varieties of torture.[11] Those who survived the Sukhanovka were the most physically destroyed.[12] There, Vilenskii languished for a hundred days with no exercise, no interrogation, little light and the awful sound of moans and screams. He contended that one could easily go crazy there. In spite of intense pressure to sign a false confession, Vilenskii refused to do so. When he went on a hunger strike to protest the false charges, he was taken to a *kartser* (a cold, dark, special punishment cell). When he insisted on seeing a procurator, the authorities, in a Kafkaesque gesture, provided him instead with an interrogator. This is quite the opposite of what Vilenskii needed, since he had been put in the *kartser* in the first place for not signing a confession. The interrogator did not like his original story, but Vilenskii had nothing to add to it.

Vilenskii recalls that in the *kartser* he began hallucinating. The next thing he remembers is waking up in the cell to find a local doctor standing over him. She diagnosed Vilenskii as having mental problems and recommended that he be taken to the Serbsky Institute for expert examination. The role of this institution at that time was almost diametrically opposed to its later task of punishing dissidents. In the Stalinist period, the Serbsky Institute assessed the authenticity of the psychiatric diagnosis to make sure that the patient was not faking illness. There was ample incentive to fake mental illness, because such a diagnosis could save the patient-prisoner's life. Later, in the dissident era, the Institute practised the fine art of faking diagnoses and providing inappropriate, physically painful treatment in order to punish patient-prisoners. Vilenskii was in fact rescued by the Institute's validation of his psychological condition of nervous exhaustion. The doctors said that he could not be interrogated at night, and Vilenskii was sent back to the Lubianka.

According to Semeon, there was a short interval at the Lubianka during which the beating of prisoners was suspended in favour of other forms of coercion. One such form was the use of psychological torture by the arrest of family members. Another was the so-called 'conveyer' method, in which prisoners were deprived of sleep[13] in order to extract false confessions. Vilenskii was subjected to a prolonged interrogation but, because of the medical recommendations, he was allowed to sleep at night. Subsequently, he was transferred to the Butyrka prison, where he was charged under the *liter* ASA and also accused of the preparation of a terrorist act. He was sentenced by the Special Conference to ten years in a special camp in Kolyma, the harshest of Soviet labour camps.

In May 1949 Vilenskii set out on his nearly two-month train journey. Then came the ship, where they were 'transported like slaves, but that's another story', Vilenskii chuckled, as he realised how many issues he was bypassing, and how during our interview we were able to reduce such a tremendous amount of personal tragedy into this narrative of events.

At the special camp at Kolyma, *zeks* wore numbers on their backs, caps and knees. Vilenskii's number was I-1620. He recalled one camp-mate who drew his numbers larger than the standard size. When the supervisors asked why he had done this, the prisoner replied, 'I want the Americans to see me from their planes.'[14] No one saw him for the next ten days. He was confined to the *kartser*. While prisoners were allowed to write home twice a year, the 'supervisors' were not required to send the letters. Prisoners soon learned that, if they wanted the heavily censored letters they had written to be mailed, they would have to confine their writing to the subjects of working, being healthy and living well. Prisoners could ask for packages with things they needed, like blankets, so that people could guess how they were really living. They could also say they did not need blankets, which might imply that they did not expect to survive for long. There is a saying that describes Kolyma's climate as 'twelve months winter, the rest is summer'. Vilenskii remained in the special camp in Kolyma for over six years, until the fall of 1955. In the winter of 1953–4, after Beria's execution, he helped to organise the expulsion of a rebel from the camp. This 'prisoner' had started to agitate young people toward insurrection. From his experience, Vilenskii knew that such open provocation would never be possible unless the camp leadership wanted it to happen, so he rallied opposition against the provocateur. Because he had foiled their plot, Vilenskii was persecuted by the supervisors. He was sent to a camp in Kolyma where only common criminals, not political convicts, were held (political prisoners were often terrorised by common criminals). Then he was sent to a camp that incarcerated privileged criminals, the so-called *suki* (thieves who had agreed to work in the service of the camp supervisors). Vilenskii was perceived by his new camp-mates to be an agent of their arch-enemies, because he had not been killed in the camp from which he came. One of the *suki* clans set out to burn Vilenskii and the young Ukrainian nationalist prisoners with whom he had arrived in their barracks, but they ultimately failed.

Vilenskii was freed from camp in the fall of 1955. He explained that at that time Kolyma had a liberation system that was linked to work output. For example, if a prisoner exceeded the normal work quota by 110 per cent, then one working day equalled two days of the sentence; 151 per cent made one working day count for three days. Thus, extra productivity could reduce the days spent in prison and result in early release. If the prisoner had less than a year to go, he was allowed to grow hair, a mark of privileged status among the shaven inmates. *Zeki* (slang for prisoners) could also earn some money to which they were entitled upon release. However, from this sum the camp administration subtracted the costs of feeding the prisoner, clothing him and guarding him! The clothing in which the prisoner was arrested years earlier was taken out of storage (if it had survived the various transports) and returned to him. On discharge, Vilenskii received a certificate of release, and some money that his camp-mates had saved up for him.

Vilenskii was initially instructed to go to Iagodnoe, the centre of the Northern Mining Industrial Complex, where he was to obtain necessary additional documents. Those who were in the special camps did not receive a passport, but instead received a paper. Those who had certain 'points' (sub-divisions of criminal articles, like Vilenskii's 58-8) were not subjected to colonisation (compulsory settlement) in Kolyma, and thus had the right to obtain passports, albeit restricted ones. One former prisoner described these passports as an open advertisement of official disapproval. With their distinctive numbers and letters, 'as soon as the passport is opened, people know with whom they are dealing. It is like a stigma'.[15] Nevertheless, it was better than a simple piece of paper, because it gave the bearer permission to live in a certain place. In 1955, when the first soviets and *raikomi* (district committees) came to Kolyma, Vilenskii turned to the new administrators for help, since the camp administration had refused to issue him a passport. He was one of the first *zeki* to come to the secretary of the *raikom*. Fortunately, Vilenskii's father was successful in enlisting the help of the writer Il'ia Ehrenburg, whose intervention had a powerful effect upon the authorities. Vilenskii received his passport, albeit with all the standard restrictions. Ehrenburg proceeded to work on the young writer's rehabilitation.

Vilenskii's return could now begin. He describes the scene at the Ugol'naia railroad station on the Moscow–Vladivostok line: 'There were a thousand former *zeks* at the station, almost all criminals that the trains wouldn't take. I left Kolyma alive and almost got killed at the station!'[16] It was impossible to get tickets going West, so Vilenskii headed for his cousin's at Blagoveshchensk, near the Chinese border in the south-east. He had no legal right to go there because of his passport restrictions, but he got help from an unexpected source. Seated next to him on the train was a lieutenant-colonel to whom he told his story. Near the border, when documents were being checked, the officer said that Vilenskii was with him.

Vilenskii was picked up at Blagoveshchensk railway station by his physicist cousin, Iosif, who took him back to his house. That evening, when they were out taking a walk in town, Iosif pointed to a little side street and said, 'A relative of ours lives here with his family. He works for the KGB and wants to see you.' There was a meeting of sorts. Vilenskii looked across the street and saw a man, a woman and two children staring at him. There they stayed, at a safe distance – close enough to see that Vilenskii was alive and well, and far enough not to have to inform on him.

Shortly after his arrival in the east, Vilenskii called Moscow to inquire about his prospects for a legal return. He was informed that his case was being examined, and that his father and Il'ia Ehrenburg were working on it. That was incentive enough for Semeon to go back to Moscow. He returned to the communal apartment where he had been living. As a former prisoner he was received cautiously. One friendly neighbour promised Vilenskii that she would not tell the authorities about his presence in Moscow. Other neighbours judiciously refrained from asking questions.

In the meantime, Ehrenburg called Vilenskii's procurator. This young man supported the rehabilitation (official exoneration), but his superiors were against it, preferring an amnesty, because they suspected that there was a subversive quality in Vilenskii's poetry, confiscated upon arrest in 1948. In consequence, his poems were sent for review to determine if any anti-Soviet themes could be found. They were not, and the Military Collegium of the Supreme Court, which was responsible for issues of terrorism, instituted a re-examination of his case. The sentence was revoked and rehabilitation eventually followed in July of 1956. While he was awaiting the determination of his legal status, Vilenskii officially lived with his uncle in the province of Kostroma.

During this time, Semeon could not get work in his field of literature, so he took a job as a dispatcher at a trucking company. Through this job he was able (illegally) to travel from Kostroma to Moscow frequently while his rehabilitation process dragged on. Vilenskii found his co-workers in the trucking company to be much more receptive to his ex-prisoner status than were his peers in the intelligentsia. As it happened, so many of these workers had been imprisoned that they had developed the attitude that someone who had not been incarcerated was somehow inferior. In assessing this stance, we must bear in mind that many of the workers were likely to have been sentenced under criminal articles for intentional deeds. As a rule, this sentiment was not held by ex-article-58ers, since they generally had *not* been incarcerated as a result of any act they had committed.

In 1957, the year following his rehabilitation, Vilenskii obtained contract work at a publisher, *Sovetsky pisatel*, translating poems by Balkars, an ethnic group that had been deported en masse during the war and had now returned from exile. He was not allowed to express his own sentiments through publishing his own poetry, but the themes of war and deportation depicted in the Balkars' writings served to convey Vilenskii's message. In the meantime, the KGB kept a close watch on him. His apartment was once searched for the poems of an ex-*zek* from Kolyma, but nothing was found there. The rehabilitated Vilenskii wrote an indignant letter to the authorities about the invasion. Meanwhile, he kept one step ahead of them by concealing in other locations manuscripts that he had gathered. During this time he re-registered at the university, in order to finish his studies in Russian philology. As compensation for over seven years of imprisonment, Semeon was given a two-month stipend.

In 1962 Vilenskii returned to Kolyma as both a special correspondent for *Literaturnaia gazeta*, and a representative of the Writers' Union. He was not troubled by his return to the place of his imprisonment, but apparently the local authorities were, because he was not well received by them. Kolyma lagged behind Moscow in accommodating to the political changes that were taking place. In Moscow at that time many publicists valued and sought out friends who had been former prisoners because they expected that the 'thaw' would last. In Kolyma, change was much slower in coming, and harder to sustain. A branch of the Writers' Union was created there in the early 1960s. In this setting, Vilenskii made the acquaintance of Nikolai Vladimirovich Kozlov, director of a publishing company and secretary of the Magadan branch of the Writers' Union. The vicissitudes of Kozlov's struggle to publish a book on Kolyma compiled by Vilenskii, and the fate of Kozlov himself, can serve as indicators of the persistent repression in the post-Stalin era.

The book that Kozlov tried to publish was an attempt to fill a void in official Soviet history. It was an effort to present the memoirs and stories of Kolyma prisoners. Up to that time, nothing had been published in Kolyma about the camps, so the book's compilers were venturing into politically uncharted and, as it turned out, forbidden territory. Opposition did not develop immediately, because the First Secretary of the Magadan Regional Communist Party was in favour of the idea. However, when the work was compiled, and his assistant, the ideological secretary, informed Moscow of its content, things changed quickly. An order was issued from the censor requesting that the manuscript be sent to the Soviet capital, because by then it had been labelled an 'ideologically unsound volume'. In consequence Moscow decreed that the book could be published only if it was limited to the stories of those who had a *propiska* (registration) in Magadan. In other words, only the writings of those who had survived the camps (and did not mention their existence), or those who were employed in the camp press, could be published. Those writers who had perished in Kolyma were disqualified as authors. Kozlov's determined efforts to prevail against the censoring authorities resulted in his being admitted to a psychiatric hospital with the diagnosis of being 'obsessed with the struggle for justice'. The message that the authorities were sending was that it was either insane to try to challenge the system or the futility of the undertaking would drive one insane.

To make matters worse, even the attenuated and sanitised camp themes that had been initially approved for publication were gradually weeded out from the collection. The final product was described by Kozlov as being 'castrated. When it was published under the title *Radi zhizni na zemle* (For the Sake of Life on Earth), Kozlov was listed as one of its editors, even though he had demonstratively removed himself from this position. Kozlov was deeply upset by this inclusion. The date of publication was September 1963; the city of publication was Magadan. The perceptive reader could infer the book's political tale by its omission of certain authors and subjects.

Despite the testimony of the coercive influence of the state in Kozlov's determined but failed struggle, Vilenskii continued with his task – the collection of manuscripts of former *zeki*. In doing so, he was risking his own life and freedom to preserve the stories of those who had lost both. Had he been found to possess even one manuscript, he would have lost his residence permit in Moscow and perhaps much more. Nevertheless, by the beginning of the 1970s he had already gathered dozens of manuscripts, which he often placed with friends in villages outside of Moscow. This undertaking was particularly courageous: Vilenskii still suffered from recurrent nightmares about the camps. The stories that he believes must never be forgotten are also too traumatic to remember. In the interests of their mental health, he and other ex-*zeki* have become accustomed to practising a useful form of denial. He says that, when they meet, 'we don't talk about the terrible things. We all know them. We talk about the amusing things' – a particularly poignant example of gallows humour. He also wistfully admits that, whenever he sees people of the age that he had been when he was arrested, he realises that he can never replace his lost youth. But he has achieved a different form of potency. Semeon Samuilovich Vilenskii has been able to validate the suffering and salvage some of the pride of his constituency of ex-*zeki*, most of whom feel that they remain second-class citizens.[17] Through his efforts, he has made a reluctant world bear witness to their sacrifice and in so doing, give, it some redeeming value.

ZOIA DMITRIEVNA MARCHENKO: VULNERABLE SOCIAL STATUS

Fear of re-arrest was a pervasive theme in Zoia Dmitrievna Marchenko's life. Considering her history, she had good reason to be afraid. Marchenko was arrested three times, the first time in 1931, the second time in 1937 and the third time in 1949. Her brother had been a Trotskyite who was arrested in 1929 and sentenced to ten years in the far northern Solovetsky camps (Solovki) for an alleged attempt on Stalin's life. On the only visit she had with her brother after his arrest, she asked what he was in for. He responded that it was 'for purity of the Leninist line'. He was shot at Solovki in 1937.

Zoia Dmitrievna's first arrest was for the possession of 'anti-Soviet literature' – notes from the parting conversation with her brother in which he told of the torture during his interrogation.[18] She was initially held in the Butyrka prison in Moscow where she eventually worked as a stenographer. Then she was sent to

Svitlag (an acronym for the Northeastern Correctional Labour camps), where she also continued stenographic work for the remainder of her three-year sentence. Marchenko contends that she knew she would be arrested again, because (superstitious as Russians are) she had turned around and looked at the prison when she left it.[19] In view of the contrived charges that the Soviet authorities routinely used to justify their arrests, this reasoning was not so far-fetched.

In the interim period between arrests, Marchenko met and married the chief engineer of a construction enterprise, German Iosifovich Staubenberger. Staubenberger was subsequently arrested in 1936, and died during incarceration. Marchenko's second arrest, in 1937, was for refusal to sign a false deposition against her husband, and also for counter-revolutionary Trotskyite activity. She spent the first year in prison, was sentenced to eight years in Kolyma, and was held there for an additional year after her term expired. Regarding her ability to survive the notorious journey by boat from Vladivostok to the north and the subsequent years of incarceration, she reflected, 'Our organism has more strength than we think.'[20] At the age of 89 she claimed that her goal for living was to discharge a certain responsibility, 'for the sake of remembering, preserving, and passing on ... that which [she] had to endure'.[21]

Zoia Dmitrievna was released in 1946 with a 'minus' in her passport. The 'minus' stamp was a way for the authorities to restrict the movement of ex-prisoners. Marchenko was not allowed to live in the big cities. Initially, she stayed at the same job where she had worked during her last year as a prisoner, and lived in a dormitory in Magadan, outside the camp zone. In 1948 Marchenko went to live with her parents in the province of Ukraine, but not for long. She was arrested again in 1949: 'They let you out of camp too early', she was told.[22] The extrajudiciary board of the Special Conference first sent her to Sumy, where she had to endure internal imprisonment coupled with interrogations. Under such circumstances, being sentenced to 'unlimited exile' in Krasnoiarskii Krai near the Arctic Circle came as a relief. Otherwise, Marchenko contends, she would have committed suicide.

The liberty of Krasnoiarskii Krai was only relative, since travelling outside the boundaries of this region was punishable by 25 years of hard labour. There Marchenko worked as an economist on the 'dead roads', an expensively wasteful forced labour project that was abandoned after Stalin's death. In 1954, Marchenko moved to Krasnoiarsk, where she married an ethnic German, who was also a returnee with a minus in his passport. As exiles, wherever they went, they had to check in every ten days with the local authorities. One day they were told that their release documents had been received, and that their exile was over. They were still not allowed to live in major cities, however.

Returnees were constantly plagued by the threat of renewed repression. To the authorities, the fact that someone had once been incarcerated made them almost automatic suspects. This suspicion spread to the social network. Marchenko explained that, upon her arrest, a number of her friends believed that she was indeed a criminal, and avoided her after she was released. Others who understood the inequity of her predicament tried to help her after release, even at their own risk. Some old friends got together with the ex-prisoner, but carefully avoided any mention of the past. Marchenko had a deep sense of feeling like an outcast and was ashamed to tell others about her past, lest she scare people away.[23] She was so grateful to the people who 'dared give [her] work' after release that she still maintained contact with them in the 1990s.

Marchenko was rehabilitated in 1956, and many of her (non-ex-prisoner) acquaintances, whose 'eyes were suddenly opened' by the 'Secret Speech' of Khrushchev at the Twentieth Party Congress, sought her friendship. However, her circle of friends remained exclusively comprised of returnees. A group of ex-Kolyma prisoners was created; they corresponded with each other, and held regular meetings in Moscow. In short, they formed their own support network. The feeling of being second-class citizens was lessened by the Twentieth Party Congress, but it never fully went away. Moreover, the fear of renewed repression was to pervade the lives of many former prisoners. Even in 1978, when passports were being changed, Marchenko recalls how she and her friends stayed up all night, afraid, asking themselves: 'What letter or number [of the Criminal Code] will we get now?'[24]

Incarceration was a defining experience in Zoia Dmitrievna Marchenko's life. Her identification was with ex-prisoners who shared the common experience, first of being labelled political criminals, and then after years of imprisonment having the charges cleared. This was a central theme of her existence. Marchenko, like many others, felt a sense of loss for her own broken life, as well as a certain responsibility (and perhaps guilt) for those who did not survive. Hence she was motivated to undertake such tasks in the Gorbachev era as typing Anna Akhmatova's 'Requiem', an ode to prisoners of the Gulag, as well as writing her own memoirs.[25] When the Memorial monument to victims of totalitarianism – a boulder from the Solovetsky island labour camps – was unveiled in 1990 on what at one time had been called Dzerzhinsky Square, Marchenko cut the ribbon together with long-time political prisoner Oleg Volkov. Volkov was a survivor of these first correctional labour camps, while Marchenko represented the relatives of those who had perished there. Marchenko's life story is to be published in the second volume of *Dodnes' Tiagoteet* (Till My Tale is Told), a collection of memoirs of women Gulag survivors. In the late 1980s and 1990s, she became an active participant in both Vozvrashchenie (The Return) and Memorial.

TAMARA DAVIDOVNA RUZHNETSOVA: CAMP CULTURE

To appropriate a common English expression, although the repressed were taken out of the camps, for many the camps could never be taken out of the repressed. The consequences of their experience as prisoners, and the further consequences of their experience as ex-prisoners, hindered all efforts toward readjustment and re-assimilation. For their part, it was difficult for those who had not been imprisoned to engage with the prison experience, even second-hand through contact with a survivor. This was made even more difficult by the fact that those ex-prisoners who had survived, and what it was that survived *within* those prisoners, could be very unpleasant.[26]

An example of how some aspects of camp culture remained a part of the returnee and how other people responded to this can be found in the story of two sisters, one of whom was incarcerated. Tamara Davidovna Ruzhnetsova grew up with her older sister, Rita, after they were orphaned in 1931. Tamara was fourteen at the time. They had been born into a Jewish family but, because he wanted a military career their father converted to Christianity and had them baptised.[27] Ever since her father's death from a heart attack, Tamara had dreamed of becoming a heart surgeon. That was not to be. In 1938 Tamara was arrested as a British spy. The charges seemed to have originated from the fact that she had danced with a musician from a Western jazz band at the 'National' restaurant in Moscow.[28] She was shifted back and forth between camps and exile until her release in 1946. Her sister Rita was not arrested, but she was harassed by the authorities. They demanded that she denounce Tamara, which she refused to do. As a result of her refusal, Rita was stripped of the medals that she had earned for working as an interpreter in the Spanish Civil War.[29]

Upon her return, Tamara was not permitted to live inside Moscow because of her passport restrictions. However, she secretly visited Rita in her Moscow apartment. Fortunately, the building's elevator operator, whose function it was to report on residents' activities, was sympathetic towards Tamara, and would run to the apartment and tell her to hide whenever passports were about to be checked. On Tamara's first visit to Moscow, Rita arranged a whole 'festival' for her sister's entertainment. They went to the theatre, to exhibitions and to concerts. There was an activity planned somewhere for every evening.

According to Tamara, on her second visit a year later, things were different. She recalls that they sat at home on the first night and some friends stopped by. On the second night friends visited again. By the fourth day, Tamara could no longer contain her curiosity and exclaimed, 'Rita, last time I was here you got me tickets for everything, and now I'm just sitting at home – with your friends. How come?' Rita's answer surprised Tamara and reflected the personal and social problems created by the camp culture that still resided in returnees:

> Tomochka, please don't be insulted. The thing is that when you came last year you were such a *lagernitsa* (camp inmate) that I was simply ashamed to show you to my friends. You barely spoke a sentence without cursing, you were full of camp jargon. Now you have already returned a bit to your former self, and you've become an interesting person once again. And my friends want to socialise with you.[30]

To add to the misery of the returnee, the ordeal of the camp had not elevated Tamara to the status of heroine, let alone martyr, but rather profaned her in the eyes of 'proper' society. She was an outcast. Rita was not anticipating that her friends would experience discomfort or anxiety when confronted with her ex-*zek* sister. Rather, she feared their revulsion. It was not the fact that Tamara had been in the camps that would impress this complacent group, but rather that the camps were still in her. Tamara evoked images of a world that they did not want to deal with. Though it appears that her sister Rita also felt repelled, their family bond was strong enough to overcome it. Many returning *zeki* had no such family bonds, and they suffered in isolation.

When Rita was handed Tamara's rehabilitation certificate in July 1956, she received along with it a request from the authorities that she convey their apologies for past mistakes to Tamara. Tamara's response was that she would like to excuse them, but she could not because their cruelty was too great. She went on to explain that, during her incarceration, she had developed night blindness. The prisoners were forced to work from dawn until dusk, so they went to and from the worksite in the dark. A missed step to the right or left was considered an escape attempt, so Tamara lived in constant fear. She had reason to be afraid. Tamara recalls the brutality of the guards:

> We worked from darkness to darkness. There were cases in which the guards shot prisoners. We were not allowed to tell anyone, although many of us were questioned. We had to answer, 'attempted escape'. Otherwise the next day it was your turn. Our shooters also amused themselves by shouting the commands: 'lay down, stand up, lay down, stand up ... ' And since it was damp, dirty and cold, we went to work already exhausted and wet. We had to work like that until it was dark again.[31]

More than once, Tamara's life was saved by her camp-mates when they kept her from falling during the journey to and from work. But they could not save her eyesight. After camp, instead of becoming the surgeon to which she had aspired, Tamara became a typist. Eventually, she lost sight in one of her eyes. 'So what should I forgive,' she asks, 'forgive a ruined life? I have no family [her sister died in the 1990s]. I have no children. At that time they deprived me of everything of which a person could be deprived.'[32]

Today Tamara lives in Moscow and works with Memorial, transcribing oral histories. When asked on the eve of the May 1996 Russian presidential elections her opinion regarding the Communist Party candidate Ziuganov's popularity, Ruzhnetsova replied: 'I'm 78 years old. I can't cut wood, I can't do anything. They shouldn't waste a bullet on me.'[33] She had been asked her opinion of the politician. Her answer did not address the question that was posed, but rather reflected her own feelings of worthlessness and her persistent fear of the political system that he represented. Tamara Ruzhnetsova's story illustrates why the burden of the camp experience could never be lifted. It justifies the expansive title of the book in which her memoirs have been included, *Our Whole Life*.

EVGENII ALEKSANDROVICH EMINOV: FAMILY REUNION

Because the family is the most likely point of re-entry into society, the first problems of assimilation often manifested themselves in the familial setting. The returnees came back as changed people, whose experience segregated them from those they had left behind. On a practical and emotional level, families that somehow managed to remain intact during the incarceration did not quite know how to deal with the readjustment of their returning loved ones.[34]

A number of wives maintained their marriages to their imprisoned husbands, but the stresses of separation and the deforming acculturation to camp life took its toll on the marriages. According to Russian historian Roy Medvedev, few men returned to their previous wives after camp.[35] When it happened that returnees were reunited with spouses who were also returnees, their chances for compatibility were better, because at least they each had been 'there'.

Yet in spite of the official inducements to sever marital bonds, the years of separation, the uncertainty of return, the forming of other alliances, and the problems of incompatibility attendant upon return, some marriages not only endured but prevailed. Evgenii Aleksandrovich Eminov, an accomplished engineer, was drafted into the army as a specialist in 1941. His division was crushed by the Germans later that same year, and the wounded Eminov was taken into captivity. After recovery he refused to work for the Germans and was sent to Auschwitz and then Buchenwald. In 1945 he was liberated by the Americans and sent for convalescence, first to a British hospital in Hamburg and then to a Soviet hospital in Breslau. He then returned to Moscow and was reinstated in his former position of chief engineer. In 1952 Eminov was arrested and sentenced to 25 years of hard labour and five years of deprivation of rights. He believes that the reason for this was that he had let the Germans capture him alive (incarceration in Soviet labour camps, or 'filtration points', was to be the sad lot of many returning POWs). Eminov was sent to Vorkuta. He survived that, too, and was released in May 1956.[36]

When Eminov came home he was greeted by a wife who had waited for him and who had also endured her own set of problems. At the time that he was sent to Vorkuta, their son was a student, but the arrest had so damaged his son's standing at the institute that he was dismissed. Now he was in the army in the Far East. Eminov's wife was not permitted to defend a dissertation that had already been completed. In addition, she was forced to leave her twenty-year position as a specialist. In order to keep the apartment, she took a lowly engineering job. The authorities had provided her with divorce papers that she was encouraged to fill in and file, but she never completed them.[37] She did not take the proffered opportunity to distance herself from her 'criminal' husband in order to avoid hardship. But although there were a number of others who had a similar determination, such cases seem to have been the exceptions to the rule.

AINO KUUSINEN AND ROZA IAKOVLEVNA SMUSHKEVICH: ELITE RETURNEES, OFFICIAL INTERVENTION AND THE UNEVEN PURSUIT OF JUSTICE

Distinctions based on former political associations influenced for better or worse the treatment of some returnees. Some of the more prominent returnees received a 'hero's welcome', compared to the reception accorded to ordinary citizens who came back from the camps. This preferential treatment extended to a wide range of needs. There were cases in which higher officials were willing to intervene, most often on behalf of formerly privileged Party members. Aino Kuusinen, the wife of Otto Kuusinen, a Finnish Communist and member of the Praesidium of the Supreme Soviet, arrived in Moscow in October of 1955 after being liberated from the women's camp at Potma. She went to the KGB reception office on Kuznetskii Most and told an official that she had just been released from the camp and did not know how to begin a new life. When he saw her name, the official asked if she was related to the Praesidium member. Upon hearing that this returnee was indeed Kuusinen's wife, he advised her to go to her husband and live with him. She explained that her pride would not allow her to return. The KGB official had no other advice to offer.

Through old friends, Aino found a 'guardian' official to guide her through the labyrinthine process of legal return. Even so, she spent eight months going from one institution to another. The lines of petitioners extended to the ends of long corridors. At one agency, she saw an old woman faint upon hearing that many of the people who came there every day had been coming for as long as five years. Eventually, because her estranged husband still occupied his official position, and because she had help, Aino Kuusinen was offered the apartment of her choice in Moscow. In her memoirs, she addresses both her own difficulties in being reassimilated and those of others less fortunate: 'It was quite difficult for me, a [well-known] political prisoner, to return to a normal life. How much more complicated, and indeed even impossible, it must have been for simple people who did not have the support I did.'[38] Indeed, the hardships for ordinary citizens upon return, like the hardships of ordinary citizens in Soviet society, were immeasurably greater than were those of the formerly privileged. Still, even the latter group had to endure the trials and tribulations of re-entry. Let us turn to one more such example.

ROZA SMUSHKEVICH

Basia Solomonovna, the wife of an executed Soviet Army general Iakov Smushkevich, appealed personally to Voroshilov, chairman of the Praesidium of the Supreme Soviet, for help for herself and her daughter Roza. Up until her husband's arrest in June 1941, the family had lived in the building of the Council of Ministers, the *Dom na Naberezhnoi* (House on the Embankment). According to Roza (in our 1996 interview), when she and her mother Basia Solomonovna Smushkevich returned from their eleven-year sojourn in Karlag (Karaganda camp) and exile in Kazakhstan they were immediately offered their old apartment back.[39] However, according to documents that have emerged from the archives, the process was not quite so immediate or automatic. In an urgent plea to Voroshilov, Basia Solomonova wrote in May 1954: 'In my old age I don't have any place to rest my head, no corner, no roof under which I can spend my last years ... you remember my husband well ... please don't leave us in this miserable situation without help or attention.'[40] When confronted with this document, Roza insisted that it was a fabrication, because, she contended, her mother would never have written – nor would she have needed to make – such a plea to Voroshilov.[41] If Roza had known about the letter at the time, then this would be an example of selective recall. If she had not, then her insistence that the letter was a fabrication could be attributed to the human tendency sometimes to remember our roles as more heroic than they may actually have been at the time. In either case it is not logical that a letter of this nature would be falsified and preserved in the archive of the Supreme Soviet. Furthermore, Voroshilov's subsequent action supports the authenticity of the written request. He ordered that the matter be investigated immediately.

It was ascertained that Iakov Smushkevich had been executed without trial on the 'criminal orders' of Beria. The case of Smushkevich was suspended by the General Procurator, Rudenko. This suspension of criminal status was extended to his widow and daughter as well, and they were to be offered their confiscated property, the pension appropriate to the family of a deceased general, and a place to live.[42] Roza recalled that top Soviet leader Malenkov met with her mother personally, gave them some money, and offered them their former residence. Her mother refused to live there. Roza maintains that this decision was based on emotional considerations – her mother wanted to avoid painful memories. Her refusal was not due to an aversion to living in an official Soviet building. While her mother's refusal was based on sentimental considerations, Roza's refusal was more of a political protest. She thought they were better off not living in that 'accursed building where every apartment counted three, four or five arrests in its turnover of tenants'.[43] Though they chose to live elsewhere, Roza often visited, and still visits, those friends of her youth who managed to survive in the *Dom na Naberezhnoi*.

CONCLUSION

The problems surrounding the return of the repressed in the Soviet Union are aptly captured in a phrase by the great Russian poet Anna Akhmatova, whose husband and son fell victim to the Stalinist terror: 'the whole calculation was that no one would return'.[44] Though this was only partly true, because millions did in fact return, it accurately reflects the way many of the victims perceived their experience. The way they were received made a number of them feel that they may have been better off staying in camp. There were few cases in which Gulag survivors did not evoke some degree of fear, loathing, shame, pity or distress among officials and society at large. People were afraid for their positions, for their houses, and for their peace of mind.

Returnees were a force that had to be reckoned with, however. Their legitimate needs, and even demands, for employment, housing and social and legal status of a level equal to those who had not been incarcerated, served as reminders of the illegitimacy of the system – a system still largely intact. Since satisfying their demands would have been tantamount to an official admission of guilt, other means, including partial accommodation, had to be crafted.

After release, the Gulag survivors' great struggle for reassimilation began. Many eventually achieved 'rehabilitation' (official exoneration), which eased their access to employment and housing. This label, however, also confirmed their ex-prisoner status: as one KGB agent told a returnee, 'the mark was removed, but the stain remained'.[45] Those who had been 'there' very rarely could, or were permitted to, resume 'normal' lives. Hence the fates of the returnees cannot be divided into the categories which form the title of this part of the book – 'the marginal and the successful'. Russian poet and activist Evgenii Evtushenko, when asked his opinion on the social status of former Soviet political prisoners, concurred with their own description of 'second-class' citizenship. He pointed out that, with the exception of Sergei Kovalev,[46] very few of them made it to high positions.[47] No more than a handful of such individuals rose to top positions under Gorbachev and were able to build careers and recreate their social networks. Most of the survivors of the Stalinist camps maintained this lifelong sense of 'second-class' citizenship. So total was the Soviet system that, even in their eighties, nearly a decade after the collapse of the Soviet Union, former prisoners still felt vulnerable to any change in the political climate. One reason for this angst is that the issue of culpability was never adequately resolved. Russia's ambivalent struggle to come to terms with its repressive and onerous past has been going on for half a century. Many Stalinist henchmen were never put on trial, because some human rights advocates considered that revenge was not the path towards moral recovery. (Moreover, with so many implicated, there were just too many of them to try.) As for the system, Soviet Russia could not condemn its own government, because in many cases people would be judging themselves. But what about post-Soviet Russia? The 1992 trial to establish the constitutionality of banning the Communist Party might have been used to examine the Communist system itself, but it did not venture beyond the issue at hand. In fact, in the ensuing years, the Communist Party was reinvigorated, and even thrived, as worsening economic conditions turned the public attitude away from the anti-Stalinist orientation of the Gorbachev era.

Still, efforts (some of them highly dubious) at building a rule-of-law state continue. On the legal front, along with the rehabilitation of victims came the discussion in the late 1990s of the rehabilitation of Stalinist henchmen, since many had been arrested, tried and executed under the same types of trumped-up charges used against innocent victims. In the quest for freedom of information, a number of archives were opened in the mid-1990s. However, some of the archives that were declassified at that time (including collections used in this research) were subsequently closed again in the late 1990s.

There is hope, though, in the battle against forgetting. Following Europe's post-Holocaust example, the historical enlightenment society and watchdog organisation Memorial has transformed the partially bulldozed ruins of the notorious labour camp Perm 36 into a living museum of Russia's past. Visitors to this 'Museum of Totalitarianism' can enter the prisoners' dismal barracks and cells, see their uniforms, feel the flimsiness of the blankets that were allotted to them in sub-zero temperatures, and view the so-called 'exercise blocks' (steel cages) and punishment cells, and the holes in the floor that functioned as latrines.[47] But there is something even more instrumental to social Gulag remembering than a labour camp museum: the return to the public arena of the stories that victims repressed for decades. In the unstable post-Soviet era, the existence of these survivors and their accounts remains one of the few significant safeguards against the return of the repressors.

Notes

Some parts of this article are excerpts from Nanci Adler, *The Gulag Survivor: Beyond the Soviet System* (New Brunswick, NJ: Transaction Publishers, 2002).

1 For various estimates in this debate see, for example, Edwin Bacon, *The Gulag at War: Stalin's Forced Labour System in the Light of the Archives* (Macmillan, London, 1994); Robert Conquest, 'Victims of Stalinism: a comment', *Europe-Asia Studies*, 49, 7 (1997), 1317–19; R.W. Davies, *Soviet History in the Yeltsin Era* (Macmillan, London, 1997); J.A. Getty, G.T. Rittersporn and V.N. Zemskov, 'Victims of the Soviet penal system in the pre-war years: a first approach on the basis of archival evidence', *American Historical Review*, 98 (1993), 1017–49; Steven Rosefielde, 'Stalinism in post-Communist perspective: new evidence on killings, forced labour and economic growth in the 1930s', *Europe–Asia Studies*, 48, 6 (1996), 959–87; Stephen Wheatcroft, 'The scale and nature of German and Soviet repression and mass killings, 1930–45', *Europe–Asia Studies*, 48, 8 (1996), 1319–53.

2 GARF (State Archive of the Russian Federation), f. 9401, op. 2, d. 450, l. 471; see also Marta Craveri and Oleg Khlevniuk, 'Krizis ekonomiki MVD (konets 1940-1950 gody)' [The economic crisis of the MVD, Ministry of Internal Affairs, 1940–50]: *Cahiers du monde russe* XXXVI, 1–2 (1995), 182.

3 GARF, f. 9401, op. 2, d. 450, l. 30.

4 T.I. Anikanova, 'O reabilitatsii zhertv politicheskikh repressii' [On the rehabilitation of victims of political repression], *Otechestvennye Arkhivy*, 1 (1999), 110–14.

5 Semeon Samuilovich Vilenskii, interview in his Moscow home, 13 March 2001; RIA Novosti, 29 October 2001.

6 The information in this section has been gleaned from personal interviews carried out by the writer over the course of several years. Most of the interviews were held at the home of Semeon Samuilovich Vilenskii (which also served as the headquarters of Vozvrashchenie) Moscow, 2 and 5 December 1995, May and November 1996, September–October 1997, April 1998.
7 See 'Goriachii kartser diktatury' [The hot punishment cell of the dictatorship], *Vecherniaia Moskva*, 28 October 1995, 2. This newspaper enjoys a large circulation. Such a public reference to Vilenskii's project reflects the spirit of those times. Since then, interest in the Gulag question has dwindled. To date, there is insufficient funding to move forward with the rehabilitation centre, but the plan has not been abandoned.
8 Vilenskii, interview held at his Moscow home, 4 April 1995.
9 *Ibid.*, 2 December 1995.
10 The *liters* (letters) such as KRD (counter-revolutionary activities), KRTD (counter-revolutionary Trotskyite activities), SOE (socially dangerous element) and others were eventually replaced by articles.
11 'Goriachii kartser diktatury'.
12 See Lidiia Golovkova, 'Tikhaia Obitel' [A quiet abode], *Biblioteka Zhurnala Volia*, 1 (Vozvrashchenie, Moscow, 1996).
13 See Robert Conquest, *The Great Terror: A Reassessment* (Macmillan, London, 1992), 123–4.
14 Vilenskii, interview, 2 December 1995.
15 'Reabilitatsiia vracha R.' [The rehabilitation of Dr R], materials from Anton Antonov-Ovseenko sent to Stephen F. Cohen, 14 May 1980.
16 Vilenskii, interview, 2 December 1995.
17 Details of Vilenskii's story were also added in interviews held at his Moscow apartment in May and November of 1996, and on later occasions.
18 Zoia Dmitrievna Marchenko, response to questionnaire designed for this project.
19 Marchenko, interview held at her Moscow home, 6 April 1995.
20 *Ibid.*
21 *Ibid.*
22 *Ibid.*, questionnaire, p. 1.
23 *Ibid.*, interview held at her Moscow home, 12 April 1995.
24 *Liters* began to be employed for criminal articles.
25 See *Dodnes' Tiagoteet* [Till My Tale is Told], Vypusk 1, (Sovetskii Pisatel, Moscow, 1989), 309–25.
26 See, for example, Vasilii Grossman, *Forever Flowing* (New York, Harper & Row, 1972): 45.
27 Tamara Davidovna Ruzhnetsova, interview held at her Moscow home, 26 April 1996.
28 *Ibid.*, transcript of interview with Memorial members, 1990, 7–8.
29 Galina Ivanovna Levinson, *Vsia Nasha Zhizn'* [All Our Lives] (NIPTs Memorial, Moscow, 1996), 78–9.
30 Ruzhnetsova, transcript, 23–4, and Levinson, 78.
31 Levinson, 76.
32 *Ibid.*, 79.
33 Ruzhnetsova, interview, 21 April 1996.
34 For two excellent examples of works of fiction that conveyed this reality see Bulat Okudzhava, *Devushka Moei Mechty: Avtobiograficheskoe Povestvovanie* [Girl of My Dreams: an Autobiographical Novella] (Moskovsky Rabochy, Moscow, 1988); Viktor Nekrasov, *Kira Georgievna* (Cambridge University Press, Cambridge, 1967).
35 Roy Medvedev, letter to Stephen Cohen, 10 February 1984.

36 Evgenii Aleksandrovich Eminov, 'Smert' – ne samoe strashnoe, [There are things worse than death]' chast' 2, Memorial f. 2, op. 1, d. 142, l. 0008 3111 1041.
37 *Ibid.*, ll. 0008 3111 1213–15.
38 Aino Kuusinen, *Gospod' nizvergaet svoikh angelov: vospominaniia 1919–1965* [God Throws out His Angels] (Izdatel'stvo Kareliia, Petrozavodsk, 1991), 198–216.
39 Roza Iakovlevna Smushkevich, interview held at her Moscow home, 30 November 1996.
40 GARF, f. 7523, op. 107, d. 255, l. 54.
41 Smushkevich, interview, 16 May 1997.
42 GARF, f. 7523, op. 107, d. 255, l. 56.
43 Smushkevich, interview.
44 Stephen F. Cohen, *Rethinking the Soviet Experience: Politics and History since 1917* (Oxford University Press, New York, 1985), 97.
45 Nadezhda Mikhailovna Dabudek, 'Donoschik: materialy semeinogo arkhiva' [Informer: materials from the family archive] Memorial, f. 2, op. 1, d. 51, l. 1993 0511 0634.
46 Kovalev, a former dissident, rose to the position of Human Rights Commissioner under Yeltsin. After sharp criticism of Russian military intervention in Chechnya, he was forced to resign in 1995.
47 Evgeni Evtushenko, interview, New York, 7 October 1998.
48 *Informatsionnyi Biulleten', Permskogo oblastnogo otdeleniia Vserossiskogo dobrovolnogo pravozashchitnogo, istoriko-prosvetitel'skogo i blagotvoritel'nogo obshchestva Memorial* [Information Bulletin, Perm Provincial Division of the All Russian Voluntary Human Rights Historical Enlightenment and Charitable Memorial Organisation], 4, 28 February 1998.

11

SUCCESS STORIES FROM THE MARGINS

Soviet Women's Autobiographical Sketches from the Late Soviet Period

Marianne Liljeström

Explaining their methods and approaches in their book *A Revolution of Their Own: Voices of Women in Soviet History*, which consists of eight in-depth interviews with Russian women, the editors Barbara Engel and Anastasia Posadskaya-Vanderbeck state that 'we planned to avoid the narratives of "heroines" because we feared they would be too close to conventional, Soviet-style biography', and that 'precisely because of her successful career, we almost disqualified Sofia Pavlova for this book about "ordinary" Soviet women – she seemed too much like a Soviet-style heroine'.[1] Because my own interests in Soviet women's autobiographical sketches from the post-Stalin period deal especially with the construction of the 'Soviet-style heroine', the editors' statements brought me a whole range of further questions: what did they consider to constitute a 'Soviet-style heroine'; how could she be characterised; wasn't she also one of the 'ordinary' Soviet women; how did they define a 'successful' Soviet woman in contrast to an 'ordinary' woman? As well as the editors' use of the notions as if there was a common consensus or obvious understanding of them, they seemed to have a certain view on 'ordinariness': the main features were suffering and survival, including often also imprisonment or exile, or at least some 'secret dissident' views on the Soviet power system and the politics of ordinary life. For me this appeared to be a limited and universalising understanding, which constructed 'The Soviet Woman', or the 'Soviet Everywoman' as Yuri Slezkine puts it,[2] as a victimised and homogeneous category: Soviet women are described as first and foremost interested in the private, 'non-political' activities of their lives.

In the wake of *glasnost*'s search of lost memory, there is today, in a situation where the loss of the master narrative is obvious, a constantly growing literature on previously repressed remembering connected especially to the Stalin era and prison camp experiences. Increasing attention has been paid also to women's reminiscences from this period of Soviet history.[3] As memories of repression, survival and extreme suffering, the reminiscences are constructed as more 'authentic', and therefore more 'truthful', than memories of 'ordinary Soviet lives'. This has given such memories of suffering and survival a visible and dominant place in the popular and expanding research field of collective memory. Without denying the importance of this research, I want to point out another consequence of this emphasis: that Soviet collective memory is hence often constructed as the antithesis, the Other, as 'false' or ideologically strictly controlled, a memory which because of its presumed 'distortedness' can be sidestepped or even discarded. With this dissociation there is, however, a risk of a new kind of censure of the diversity of women's memories: for example, of their participation in the October Revolution and other such 'official' historical events. Surely it is a new kind of violence towards the past to delete or even downplay people's recollections of these important historical events. This desire to do away with part of the past seems to perpetuate the violence of the present on memory, that is, by acting as if a large part of the past had never taken place.[4] In contrast, my own research approach is premised on an understanding of collective memory as historically and culturally articulated and sustained realities from the past. From this viewpoint, not only repressed memories but also those of the 'official' Soviet culture, often looked upon as self-explanatory monologues, require serious, context- and text-sensitive scholarly examination.

SOME THEORETICAL PREMISES

While the 'gusdorfian'[5] generation of theorists on autobiography hardly problematised the writing self, later deconstructionist critics have argued that selves are conventions of time and place, in which symbolic systems appear in a particular testimony (*parole*). Though more recent critics have been concerned to reclaim some concept of reference for the autobiographical text, this has not brought a return to an affirmation of the factual status of autobiography.[6] Debates on autobiography have tended to polarise between an impossible demand for representational authenticity and its abandonment in a fictionalist position. Instead of inserting autobiographical texts into fictionalism, or once again in relation to the fact–fiction dichotomy, I want in this article to put the texts above all in connection with the history–memory nexus. The nature of autobiography is often derived from statements made from *within* autobiographical texts which are held to have a definitional function. This circumstance can also be seen as the ground for long-term and intensive discussions about autobiography as genre, a question which currently is becoming less topical because of the stronger tendency to consider autobiographical texts as discourse rather than genre.[7]

Foucault argues that the name of an author is not precisely a proper name among others because its presence serves functionally as a means of classification. I read the Soviet women's autobiographical texts as classificatory for the category of 'equal and successful women', and thus consider that the function of their authorial signatures is 'to characterise the existence, circulation, and operations of certain discourses within a society'.[8] In this connection, I want to underline a Foucauldian approach to biography which could be seen as including the idea that autobiographical texts serve the function of legitimating authorship and organising the Soviet women's texts around specific representations of the 'true selves' of the revolutionary women, and thus around certain representations of discourses on truth, gender and power.

The question that Foucault formulates, of 'how, under what conditions, and in what forms can something of a subject appear in the order of discourse',[9] can be seen as a sort of fundamental and overarching topic in feminist autobiographical studies and theorising: if women have been categorised as 'objects' by patriarchal cultures, women's autobiography gives an opportunity for them to express themselves as 'subjects' with their own selfhood. Feminists have pointed out that autobiographies perform powerful ideological work: they have been assimilated to political agendas, have fostered the doctrine of individualism, and have participated in the construction and codification of gendered personhood. The promise of an exploration of a 'self' has made autobiography of intense feminist interest, but simultaneously it has highlighted problems and confusions within this research.[10]

In order to analyse gendered authority and hierarchy, interpretation must attend to the cultural and discursive histories of self-representation, rather than to some overarching explanation for the gendered differences between men's and women's autobiographies.[11] Examining Soviet women's autobiographical sketches from the late Soviet period, in this chapter I try to show how women *also* used self-representation and its constitutive possibilities for agency and subjectivity. Women's short sketches were part of the boom of Soviet memoir literature in the 1960s and 1970s.[12] By relating these sketches to the practices of collective remembering, which from the late 1950s onwards were appropriated as tools for strengthening cultural management, ideological commitment and social control, I read the sketches as stories of success, both as self-representations and as narratives organising women's experiences into certain meaningful episodes, reshaping facts and producing meanings into performative discourses.

TO READ 'SUCCESS'

Engel and Posadskaya write in their introduction to the interview with Sofia Pavlova about her 'second thoughts' after the first meeting: 'she telephoned Posadskaya and said, "My God, I said so many foolish things to you – about my childhood, about my husband, about my children. Come back, and I'll tell you the truly important things, serious things about my activity in the Soviet Women's Committee and in the Soviet–French Friendship Society"'.[13] The editors comment that, in Sofia Pavlova's own opinion, her political work, that is, her work for the Party, was what really mattered about her life, even though nobody was interested in it at present. However, in their *Afterword*, the writers note that women like Sofia Pavlova chose in the interviews to emphasise 'what the system offered them and to take pride in what they achieved rather than to dwell upon the sacrifices they made'. The editors' explanation for this is that, not only Sofia Pavlova, but 'most of the women [interviewed] embraced a key element of Soviet ideology – that contribution to production and working for the public good were of utmost importance – and they apparently derived genuine satisfaction from their participation in public life'. Statements of this kind are usually referred to when Soviet women are characterised as 'strong women', a notion which in a contradictory way associates them also with the status of victims, thus implying an understanding of them as forced to be strong because of oppression and the harsh realities of Soviet life.[14] These statements indicate a materialisation of central traits of Soviet discourse on gender equality: women had in the wake of the discourse's persistent emphasis on the achievements of Soviet women as equal, empowered and active participants in main events of the October Revolution and building of the socialist society, internalised above all the 'need' to participate in the paid labour force and in public life. This 'need' was considered essential to their gendered identity, and therefore a precondition for them being defined as heroines or successful.

However, Engel and Posadskaya define success also from a slightly different perspective: they understand it as a result of utilised, unforeseen possibilities, as 'taking advantage of new opportunities', according to one of their subtitles. These were created by the new social order, especially for working-class women, on the basis of its articulated strategy of gender equality. The authors emphasise, however, that the price paid for this 'upward mobility' was to 'embrace the system uncritically'.[15] But the understandings of success either as a result of inflicted 'need' or of 'seized' opportunities are not necessarily contradictory: they point mainly to differences in how women are conceived of as acting subjects. In this article my task is to look at how women as autobiographical subjects, as authors of autobiographical sketches in the context of the 1960s, construct themselves as successful female revolutionary heroines.

Autobiographical texts are positioned within discourses that construct truth, identity and power, discourses that produce gendered subjects. This means that those women who in the 1960s were able to write their lives also had access to the successful female identities that these texts were expected to construct. My starting point in looking at women's texts is thus an understanding that the question of gender construction should be examined at the level of the texts' engagement with the available discourses of truth and identity and the ways in which Soviet women's self-representations are constitutively shaped through proximity to those discourses' definition of authority. I therefore want to emphasise that underlying my starting point for reading Soviet women's texts are the following three premises:

- First, relation to culturally dominant and historically specific discourses of truth telling, and not necessarily from women's privileged positions in real everyday life.[16]
- Second, it is necessary to differentiate between the narrated self and the narrating self, between the fictive, the historical and the writing self. I call the fictive self, the protagonist of the I-narrative, the autobiographical subject. In constructing this subject, the writing self turns the historical self into an object of investigation, which is further divided between the present moment of writing and narration, and the past on which the narration is focused.[17] The differences between and within the selves in the text and in everyday life constitute the production of autobiographical identity, the ontological being of which is manifest in the author's signature. The signature, however, has a tendency to gloss over the constitutive differences between the different selves of the autobiographical text. Simultaneously the female signature, the proper name on the title page, carries a long historical heritage of powerlessness, non-inheritance and interrupted traditions. The signature always contains a gendered hierarchy of position, voice and space. This point is especially important in my reading, because the 'success' of the female autobiographical subject must be understood as a construction, a representation of experience, which does not correspond to any true or pre-given experiences of the historical self. To extend this point even further, one could state that the autobiographical subject is first and foremost produced by autobiography; that is, by the genre and by temporal discourses on gender, truth and identity.[18]
- Third, this does not diminish the autobiographical writer as historical person and writing self; rather, it situates her as an agent in the production of the autobiographical text. At the same time her text, being constructed by certain facts and events chosen rather than others, and being a translation of them into the medium of autobiographical writing, signifies reality in a certain way: facts and events are constituted as signifiers when being referred to and constructed in the autobiographical discourses of truth and identity. This means that the writing subject constructs evidence and events into facts, to certain meanings, in accordance with some framework or perspective.

The overall condition for the sketches to be constructed as stories of success within the realm of remembrance in the Soviet context of the 1960s is their reference to the three heroic traditions in Soviet history: the revolutionary – including the Civil War of 1918–20 – the patriotic, and labour traditions.[19] These are all connected to the creation and development of the Soviet Union, its struggle for survival and triumph over numerous adversities and hardships. I have chosen three texts, the plots of which I relate to these traditions: 'Together with the party' by Alla Efimovna Arbuzova, 'With weapons in hands' by Maria Stepanovna Demidova, and 'If you work with the heart ... ' by Nadezhda

Andreevna Turetskaia. The sketches were published in the anthology *Zhenshchiny goroda Lenina* [Women from the City of Lenin] in 1963.[20]

Arbuzova recalls her experiences from beginning Party work among women in 1917. She situates her writing self in the present; that is, at the beginning of the 1960s. Demidova describes her heroic actions at the front during the Second World War, and Turetskaia writes about the all-female Communist work brigade which she was leading in the shop producing bantam tube lamps at the Svetlana factory. From a multiple – but by no means limitless – repertoire of available public, social and cultural scripts or narratives, the women writers construct themselves in their stories about action, suffering and achieving as moral agents. In Soviet women's autobiographical sketches the evaluative element – crucial in every narrative – is highly ritualised, repetitive and ideologically imperative. As Charles Taylor has argued, the capacity to act depends to a great extent on having an evaluative framework shaped by what he calls 'hypergoods'; that is, a set of fundamental principles and values.[21] In Soviet society the transcendent principle of these 'hypergoods' consisted of the norms and values embodied in the ideology of Marxism-Leninism – among them the rhetorical emphasis on gender equality. These norms and values ordered individual lives as meaningful and purposeful only in the service of and suffering for the greater political and social cause, the building of a Communist society.

FIGHTING THE ENEMIES

Narrating these specific heroic traditions as discourses of revolutionary truth and as episodes in their successful personal life stories required the women to construct their strivings for the moral good as a struggle against some sort of enemy. The face of the enemy depends on the specific plot, and therefore took many forms. In all stories the enemy, however, becomes eliminated in the process of narrating the historical and personal transformation.

Demidova's sketch focuses explicitly on the suffering she endured in order to defend her country against the Nazi enemy. She tells how she always wanted to become a doctor and how she was just about to begin her studies at the Leningrad Medical Institute in 1939, when together with her fellow students she decided, because of the threat to Leningrad, to join the front in the war as a volunteer nurse. In 1941 she was sent to the Leningrad front on a reconnaissance. In February 1942 she was seriously wounded and sent to a hospital in Vologda, but, as she writes, 'because of a mistake they informed my parents that I had died'. After this she continued her work in reconnaissance. She recalls an episode where a small reconnoitring group was sent to the other side of the front. They settled down in a village and she managed to get work in the local Gestapo office. The reconnoitring group handed over key information to the partisans. She experienced this undercover work as very hard, first and foremost because she was considered a traitor by the locals. After three months the group was betrayed by the village elder, who had been secretly following their activities: I was not afraid of death, but it pained me to tears that I had yet done very little for the victory. I am not going to recount how they questioned, tortured, and insulted us ... We all held up bravely as genuine Soviet people'.[22] Demidova's sketch highlights extreme suffering and glorious victory, and belongs to the massive production of memory markers of the 'Great Patriotic War', which as both reminiscences and physical markers – such as memorials, monuments and cemeteries – began especially after 1953.[23]

The main episode in Arbuzova's story is the first women's conference in St Petersburg on 12 November 1917. During this time the election campaign to the Constituent Assembly, which was going to decide the fate of the Provisional Government, took place. The collective enemy of the Bolsheviks is here represented by the so called *ravnopravki* (equal-righters), who also took part in the conference. As opposed to the unity and collectivity of the working women's delegation, the *ravnopravki* are individualised by detailed descriptions of their leader, *gospozha* (madame) Doroshevich. Arbuzova writes: '[she was] equipped with French stiletto heels in a fashionable hat with a veil, beautifully dressed. Already her looks woke an angry murmur among the delegates, but her demagogically false speech was interrupted by upset comments from the women workers.' By giving detailed descriptions of the bourgeois lady's dress, the 'falseness' and deceitfulness of the enemy is emphasised: Doroshevich's vanity exposes her superficial beliefs and behaviour in spite of Arbuzova's contradictory comment that she was 'beautifully dressed'. Arbuzova does not hold back on her contempt for the representative of the class enemy: 'With what a squeamish expression did she give orders to her cooks, maids and nannies, what power had she to tyrannise her servants, to degrade their human dignity.' By further constructing the dichotomy of 'us' and 'them' (or 'it'), these descriptions are contrasted with the details of the revolutionary woman's dress: 'In a black dress with white downy shawl on her shoulders, Aleksandra Mikhailovna [Kollontai] went to the tribune. This was a fascinating, thoroughly educated woman, a talented orator.'[24]

In Turetskaia's sketch the enemy takes the form of bad work discipline, being late for work, absences without reason, low quality of products, defective goods and waste, and lack of unity within the brigade. All these 'enemies' are eliminated in her narrative about the development of 'her' shop to a brigade of collective Communist work.

The sketches include as a central and necessary component of the plots the victory over these various enemies. The stories illustrate obstacles to societal, political *and* personal transformation and development, and recount an elimination of such enemies. As performances they reproduce the Soviet discourses on revolutionary truth and power, and constitute 'rites of passage' to an even firmer and higher form of political consciousness and therefore success, to a social integration of collective and individual.[25]

THE COLLECTIVE OF PROMINENT WOMEN

By referring to the speeches at the conference, Arbuzova's story reconstructs the prominence of such Bolshevik female leaders as K.I. Nikolaeva, K.N. Samoilova and A.M. Kollontai. She pays special attention to Emilia Solin – one of the speakers – and tells her life story up to her early death at the age of 29 in 1919, when she was captured by the White Army and committed suicide. By naming these individual women, the writer constructs a vanguard representing the collective of dedicated female revolutionaries and working-class women. The heroines of her story offer a strategy for both successful living and the good cause, for elimination of suffering and inequality. In their service of this strategy the women are pictured as selfless and modest revolutionaries, always prepared and willing to sacrifice the personal good for the collective. This is a common feature in women's sketches: they portray 'galleries of heroines' and emphasise through individual examples the collectivity of the revolutionary women's deeds and actions. The sketches participate in the creation of a female community of memory: 'How many energetic, outstanding working women, devoted to the Leninist party, appeared among women!', writes Arbuzova.[26]

'Indeed, there is something to tell about every member in the brigade. If not about a striking trait in the character, then about becoming a human being, about thoughts and deeds. Competition for Communist work inspires people, makes them look with new eyes at oneself, at the comrades, at life,' Turetskaia writes in her turn. By naming four particular women workers and telling about their achievements, she constructs a collective prominence based on active participation in the communist work brigade. Turetskaia begins her sketch by telling about a meeting between the 'girls' from the brigade and some student practitioners, who wanted to find out how a genuinely Communist brigade functioned. The 'girls' give precise answers to the students' questions, except for one: 'How do you differ from the backward workers?' Turetskaia explains that the reason for their lack of answer was not confusion, but fear of self-assertion: 'It is hard to talk about oneself without taking the risk that in the listeners' eyes you become immodest.'[27]

The emphasis on the collective, an inherently communal spirit as opposed to individualism, but also to individuality, is a cultural characteristic that both Russian and Western scholars have ascribed to Russian mentality, thinking, behaviour and language.[28] Referring to both Nikolai Berdiaev and Hedrick Smith, Daniel Rancour-Laferrier writes that the Russians have a public gift of submissiveness (*smirenie*) of the person to the collective, and as long-suffering people the Russians can bear the pain of misery, so long as they see that others are sharing it.[29] In opposition to this, other researchers have stressed the meaning of the collective, especially the work-collective, as a source of community, communication and mutual support in coping with daily problems of life.[30] The communality is considered a spirit or a mentality that is to be found within some formal collectives and not others, but is usually strongest in the informal circles of like-minded friends. As stories about heroic traditions, the autobiographical sketches must position the narrator as an organic but submissive part of the collective. At the same time the significance of the specific collective is brought forth precisely through narration, through the creation of the autobiographical subject in connection to a certain collective. As N.F. Sementsova puts it in her book about Soviet war memoirs, 'the memoirists talk so simply and cursorily about themselves', because 'their vital "I" is totally dedicated to the revolution, and that is why their autobiographical "I" is submitted to telling about events, which have a general revolutionary meaning. They do not give primary meaning to themselves, they do not ponder upon the individual role and achievement in victory.' According to her, the value of the memoirs can be measured only in connection with how they represent social interests, how they portray the collective and the writers themselves as representatives of the masses. 'Personal modesty is characteristic of memoirists,' she concludes.[31] However, the women writers' individual roles as both active and empowered moral agents and constructors of the plot, of their own life stories, counteract modesty and an underlining of submissiveness to the collective.

The autobiographical subjects themselves become simultaneously constituted as prominent individuals, as part of but different from other women of the collective. This means that to write the 'I' includes a negotiation with the 'we', and their individuality and 'uniqueness' entails discords with collectivity. Simultaneously, however, 'her singularity achieves its identity as an extension of the collective'.[32] Turetskaia thus tells about *her* methods of transforming the workshop into a vanguard. During the first week she just observed the women, writing her notes in a journal. Then she started to organise meetings and 'the most serious and work-loving girls supported me'.[33] However, to serve as an *example* of dedication and heroism for the readers, the I-narrator of the sketch employs a modest style of writing: she emphasises the character and achievements of the collective instead of her personal accomplishments.

Similarly, as a story about extreme personal bravery, Demidova is forced to emphasise her individuality and construct her prominence as different from the 'masses' of soldiers. Her bravery and heroism is constructed above all through two episodes. Once she was called to the commander of the division, who wanted to send her on a mission, though, as he states, he did not have any right to do it, since she was an ordinary soldier: 'But understand me right. Your personal example means very much to us. It helps us to fulfil a responsible task. We have to send a tank force behind the enemy's back. The soldiers respect you, and we rely on you.' Besides quoting these words about her prominence, she manifests the respect she had among the soldiers by recalling that, for this specific task, fifty soldiers instead of the required twenty-two offered themselves as volunteers. They fulfilled the task, but only eight persons returned from the mission, and once again she was wounded. The other incident recounts how she, 'as a surprise to myself', took command in leading a counter-attack against a heavy German attack: 'I grabbed a grenade and shouted "Forward! Follow me!"

I could not know if I shouted loudly and I do not know if the soldiers heard me in the terrible din, but everybody that was capable of moving himself and holding a weapon went with me.' For her actions in March 1944 she was actually awarded the title, 'Hero of the Soviet Union'.[34]

Arbuzova depicts her second meeting with Lenin, thereby constructing herself as an extraordinary revolutionary. She rises above ordinary women workers and revolutionaries, becoming prominent because of her personal contact with Lenin. She tells in great detail how the delegation, elected at the conference in order to bring Lenin its message of support, met with him. She describes the furniture in Lenin's reception room and the solemn atmosphere of expectation and excitement. She pays attention to Lenin's clothes ('a grey, plain costume') and his comradely, interested and warm behaviour ('the leader of the revolution talked with us as an equal to other equals'). Picturing her young listeners on the excursion as 'greedily' waiting for stories about 'Il'ich', she further contributed to the Lenin cult.[35] Thus the subject of memory in Arbuzova's story is constructed, on the one hand, through the female revolutionary collective, and on the other hand, through ritualised events. These events are reproduced because of cultural management, but as narrative tropes they give performative force to the female signature. Through this force the signature takes up and creates space in the public sphere.

CONSTRUCTING GENDER AND IDENTITY

The autobiographical subject speaks in the name of gender equality, which in the Soviet context means *both* the citation of characteristics and models of behaviour ascribed to the Revolutionary, that is, the inherently male Soviet person, *and* a simultaneous construction of femaleness. This means that, while the women as autobiographical subjects disappear into the hegemonic maleness of the discourse, at the same time by performing this hegemonic discourse they create a space for the identity of women. While Demidova's text is exemplary of this double working of the discourse on gender equality, Arbuzova's and Turetskaia's sketches differ notably from hers. In different ways the latter authors stress the importance of women's identities.

When Demidova recovered from her undercover work in the Gestapo office she was sent to the Ukrainian front as a Komsomol organiser for an infantry battalion. 'Honestly speaking,' she writes, 'at first I was rather afraid of not finding a common language with the soldiers and officers. But it so happened, that when people got to know my military biography, from the very start they approached me with respect.'[36] Thus her femaleness vanishes in connection with her military achievements. Nevertheless, she simultaneously constructs herself as female; that is, as different from men. Her worry about finding 'a common language' with the men can be read as a construction of gender in two ways. First, her femaleness means by definition a lack of the deep and inherently male experience in the military. Second, she worries about being taken seriously: in spite of all her 'typically male' military achievements, she is nevertheless a woman. However, the ambiguity between male achievements and gender does seem somewhat secondary: the difference *she* actually constructs in her narrative is less concerned with gender than her being even more daring and fearless than the best of the male soldiers.

In a more outspoken and distinct way than Demidova, both Arbuzova and Turetskaia constitute the identity category of women. Arbuzova ends her sketch with remarks about the Party work among women: 'It is necessary to say that in 1917 there was not yet a unity among the party activists about the methods of work among women.'[37] She notices that some opposed the formation of special women's groups, while others defended this strategy. Soon after the conference, however, she notices that 'the life itself' demanded the founding of special working women's commissions attached to Party organisations. By underlining the correctness in the specific historical context of attending to gender specificity in Party work, she constitutes women as a different and separate identity group. In opposition to what was common in earlier accounts, she does not make statements about the specific character of this period in Party history and about those later developments, which, as was officially stated, had shown that such work among women had made itself superfluous with the 'solution' of the 'woman question'. Thus her story informs about the certain 'reopening' of the 'woman question' and strengthening of the rhetoric of gender equality, which was made after the Twentieth Party Congress in 1956. Khrushchev's announcement that discrimination against women was a continuing problem, and his stress on women's exclusion from public life, made women's classification as an interest group with special needs since the 1920s once again visible.

Turetskaia's construction of women as an identity group is based on emphasising the importance of friendship between women of the brigade. This friendship is constituted as a source of mutual help, support and understanding. Her examples of the strength of female friendship include episodes about how other women fulfilled the production norms of those who were studying; how women collected money for one member of the brigade who by accident had lost her salary; and how a woman worker with bad work discipline was going to be sacked, but because of the other women's trust in her promises to change her attitude to work and cease her scornful tone towards the collective, she could stay.[38] Turetskaia emphasises that the resulting friendship was not an immediate and given characteristic of the brigade: the development and strengthening of friendship had required hard work.

Hence the construction of gender and identity appears to be diverse. It is therefore hazardous – in spite of the seemingly uniform character of the hegemonic ideological discourse and the mandatory ways of carrying out its edicts – to consider Soviet women's autobiographical voices as uniform and in unison. Though the writer creates order where there is chaos, narrative coherence where there is fragmented memory, and voice where there is silence, the autobiographical act is no simple reflection or mimesis, but a multiple representation.

PRODUCING TRUTH AND IDENTITY AS SUCCESS

By performing and re-enacting heroic traditions, women's autobiographical sketches fulfilled for their part the Party and state's constant need of legitimation and improved cultural management. Or, as Yuri Slezkine has put it: 'Indeed, they ["unforgettable days"] must be staged over and over again, because that is the best way to secure new conversions and because conversions are never secure.'[39] In one sketch after another the I-narrator pictures, reproduces and reconstructs the revolutionary events and women's participation in them.

The status of the I-narrator as one of immediate eyewitness implies the writer's 'closer' connection to reality. Therefore she is the possessor of the truth about women's equal and massive participation in creating the 'new society'. Thus the sketches are both performances of the mandatory, internalised codes of the hegemonic discourse, and tools of self-representation, of identity construction. This underlines the importance of comprehending the women writers as moral and social agents, as subjects actively participating in the production of meaning within the public sphere. The narratives constructed women in accordance with hegemonic male norms, reproducing features historically characteristic of the 'genderless' (male) human being and incorporating the main premises of the hegemonic ideology. In spite of these traits, the texts cannot be reduced to a fictitious, generalised, average female writer with a standardised consciousness.

Hence it is crucial to ask who is speaking in the text – a question where discourse and narrative inevitably intermingle. In this linkage the narrative has a twofold task, that of 'making meaning' and that of 'organising human experiences into meaningful episodes' through the coherent grasping of an agent who acquires a 'cognitive role'.[40] The structure of the sketches reshaped facts into performative discourses. The facts are intelligible in *one* way rather than another, thus signifying reality in a certain way. The experiences, constituting themselves as narratives, were constructed on the basis of projections, expectations and memories derived from a diverse repertoire of available social, public and cultural narratives. The basic claim here is thus that women's autobiographical identity projects should be considered as achievements and accomplishments, and as performances that have influenced transformation of the notion of what is public, first and foremost because the narratives situated difference as a public issue. Most of all, women empowered themselves by the performative effectiveness of their claim to recognition and, in doing so, they reversed the self-defeating images of women as 'victims'. By presenting themselves as strong women they became validated.[41]

CONTEXTUALISING REVOLUTIONARY WOMEN'S COLLECTIVE MEMORY

In her introduction to the collection of life stories of Russian women from 1917 to the Second World War, Sheila Fitzpatrick describes general traits in Russian women's (testimonial) autobiographical texts by focusing on certain recurrent themes, such as women's strength, victimhood, educational and professional skills, class and acceptance of a 'two camps' view of the world. Though she emphasises that 'there is great variety in the way Russian women saw their lives and times', and that 'the date of writing is often significant in Soviet memoirs', she creates a problematically coherent, century-long tradition of Russian women's autobiographical writing.[42] In doing this she does not take into account the specific historical context in which the self-representation was produced: thematically she lumps together texts written in the 1930s and the 1990s. In contrast to my reading, she understands the texts not as representations of discourses on truth, gender and power – but rather as evidences of historical facts and events. Unlike Fitzpatrick, I think that it is essential to take into account the historical context, understood as conditions which regulate the production of the texts and as the narrators' frames of reference and meaning. The early 1960s in Soviet history form a specific period of synchronic and diachronic axes of historical circumstances and meaning. The synchronic segment can be seen as the autobiographical texts' relation to specific temporal discourses on truth and identity, while the diachronic continuity can be understood as the history of Russian women's self-representation.[43]

Arbuzova's sketch begins from the time of writing: she describes a situation when representatives of 'working youth' are on an excursion in Leningrad to memorial places of revolutionary events together with 'the old guard', in order to hear stories told by participants in these events. 'All that we lived through is known to them only from books and from stories told by older generations. And good, that it is so!' She gives a description of how the young people run around and talk noisily to each other. Thus she interprets them as being 'impatient to listen to old underground workers and active participants in the revolutionary women's movement'.[44] She constructs the youth as extremely interested in the history of the Revolution. This fully corresponds to the outspoken aim, the educational function ascribed to anthologies of 'collective remembering'; that is, to hand over the experience of older revolutionaries to the younger generation, and to constitute elements in women's political education. In this perspective, the texts played a mediating, or perhaps a balancing, role between, on the one hand, increasing talk in the 1960s about the 'woman question' and 'women's special problems' and, on the other hand, women's successes and achievements under socialism. This mediating role is further enhanced if we consider the specificity of the autobiographical texts in their claims for truth and authenticity. Asserting this mediating task between problems and achievements for women's autobiographical success stories shows simultaneously that the Soviet discourse on gender equality was not a stable given, but changeable while constantly acted upon and reconstructed.

The first generations in Soviet history without any personal memories of such dramatic events as the October Revolution, Civil War and the Second World War, came to maturity in the 1960s. The boom in the publication of memoirs and autobiographical anthologies during the late 1950s, 1960s and also the 1970s can be seen as connected to the strengthening of the public collective memory of the revolutionary past. As I have noticed, the recovery of memory was a means of improving cultural management and furthering the legitimacy of the Party/state. This task was accentuated after the Twentieth Party Congress when there was a wave of rehabilitation and of declaring women (and men) imprisoned earlier in the Soviet era (usually in the 1930s) innocent of the crimes for which they had been sentenced. However, at just the time that the first wave of ex-prisoners' recollections of camps and prisons was pouring out, documentary evidence of the crimes committed by the regime was being secretly destroyed.[45]

The intensification of collective remembrance was thus conditioned by Khrushchev's revelations about Stalin. These had in part shaken confidence that the Soviet Union was set on the right path to attain the promised Communist future. The cultural concern with reconnecting with the past, which began to be especially noticeable in the 1960s, can be seen as an expression of the urge to find a new and firm sense of direction and integrity in the post-Stalin conditions. One response was a nostalgia for a mythologised past and a regard for the past as an absolute authority, irretrievably remote from the present. From the October Revolution up to the time of Khrushchev, Soviet official remembrance had its eyes set firmly on the future, being required to depict reality in its revolutionary development. This is what the women's sketches had done and continued to do. As stories about heroic revolutionaries dedicated to the 'higher cause', the sketches focused on women's struggle and achievements within the nationalist, socialist project. The sketches describe the hardships, the enemies and the suffering confronted, but they displaced these concerns onto the fight for a 'bright future'. In spite of their overt similarities in structure and rhetoric, they did this, however, in diverse ways: the sketches indicate important differences in how the autobiographical subjects constructed their narrative selves.

By including successful, revolutionary women into the mediation of the past. the sketches opened up positions of public speech and authority to women. At the same time, the texts constructed – by virtue of their female signatures – a difference and diversity into public discourses of the 'realities of the past'. As an example, the title of one of the anthologies (1975) – reiterating Lenin's famous statement – is illuminating: 'Without *them we* would not have won'.[46] Here, women are in an explicit hierarchical way marked first and foremost by gender. In my understanding, then, the sketches participated – because of their female signature, because of the difference they constructed and manifested in relation to the practices of collective remembrance – in a transformation of the public sphere.

Notes

1 Barbara Alpern Engel and Anastasia Posadskaya-Vanderbeck (eds), *A Revolution of Their Own, Voices of Women in Soviet History* (Westview Press, Boulder, 1998), 47, 222.

2 Yuri Slezkine, 'Lives as tales', in Sheila Fitzpatrick and Yuri Slezkine (eds), *In the Shadow of Revolution. Life Stories of Russian Women from 1917 to the Second World War* (Princeton University Press, Princeton, 2000), 24.
3 See Engel and Posadskaya, *A Revolution of Their Own*; Sheila Fitzpatrick, 'Lives and times', in Sheila Fitzpatrick and Yuri Slezkine (eds), *In the Shadow of Revolution*, 3–17; Simeon Vilensky (ed.), *Till My Tale Is Told. Women's Memoirs of the Gulag* (Virago Press, London, 1999).
4 Cf. Luisa Passerini, 'Introduction', in Luisa Passerini (ed.), *Memory and Totalitarianism*, International Yearbook of Oral History and Life Stories, vol. I (Oxford University Press, Oxford, 1992), 8–11.
5 George Gusdorf's influential essay, 'Conditions and limits of autobiography' (originally published in French in 1956 and translated into English in 1980), has given him the status of founding father of twentieth-century autobiography studies: see Paul John Eakin, *How Our Lives Become Stories. Making Selves* (Cornell University Press, Ithaca, 1999), 47.
6 Paul John Eakin, *Fictions in Autobiography: Studies in the Art of Self-Invention* (Princeton University Press, Princeton, 1985); Bella Brodzki and Celeste Schenk (eds), *Life/Lines: Theorizing Women's Autobiography* (Cornell University Press, Ithaca, 1988).
7 See Laura Marcus, *Auto/biographical discourses: Theory, Criticism, Practice* (Manchester University Press, Manchester, 1994).
8 Michel Foucault, 'What is an author?', in Paul Rabinow, *The Foucault Reader* (Penguin Books, London, 1984), 107–18.
9 *Ibid.*, 118
10 Sidonie Smith and Julia Watson, 'Introduction: situating subjectivity in women's autobiographical practices', in Sidonie Smith and Julia Watson (eds), *Women, Autobiography, Theory. A Reader* (University of Wisconsin Press, Madison, 1998); see also Tess Cosslett, Celia Lury and Penny Summerfield (eds), *Feminism and Autobiography: Texts, Theories, Methods* (Routledge, London, 2000).
11 See, e.g., Nancy Miller, 'Representing others: gender and the subjects of autobiography', *differences*, 6, 1 (1994); and Leigh Gilmore, *Autobiographics: A Feminist Theory of Women's Self-Representation* (Cornell University Press, Ithaca, 1994).
12 Anthologies were published in 1959, 1963, 1968, 1975 and also in 1983. See more specifically about this genre and women's sketches, Marianne Liljeström, 'Regimes of truth? Soviet women's autobiographical texts and the question of censorship', in Markku Kangaspuro (ed.), *Russia: More Different than Most* (Kikimora Publications, Helsinki, 2000), 114–18.
13 Engel and Posadskaya, *A Revolution of Their Own*, 51.
14 *Ibid.*, 219–20; see also Fitzpatrick, 'Lives and times', 9–10.
15 Engel and Posadskaya, *A Revolution of Their Own*, 47, 134.
16 See Smith and Watson, 'Introduction', 22.
17 Shari Benstock, 'Theorizing the autobiographical', in *The Private Self: Theory and Practice of Women's Autobiographical Writings* (Routledge, London, 1988), 16–19.
18 See Teresa de Lauretis, *Technologies of Gender. Essays on Theory, Film and Fiction* (Indiana University Press, Bloomington, 1987), 2–3; and Martha Watson, *Lives of Their Own. Rhetorical Dimensions in Autobiographies of Women Activists* (University of South Carolina Press, Chapel Hill, 1999), 7, 107.
19 Cf. Christel Lane, *The Rites of Rulers. Ritual in Industrial Society – The Soviet Case* (Cambridge University Press, Cambridge, 1981), 36.
20 *Zhenshchiny Goroda Lenina* [Women from the City of Lenin], (Lenizdat, Leningrad, 1963).
21 Charles Taylor, *Sources of the Self. The Making of the Modern Identity* (Cambridge University Press, Cambridge, 1989), 63.
22 *Zhenshchiny Goroda Lenina*, 208–9.

23 Specific anthologies of women's reminiscences of the war were published especially in the 1970s: see, e.g., *Docheri Rossii* [Russia's Daughters] (Sovetskaia Rossiia, Moscow, 1975); *V te Surovye Gody* [In those hard years] (Lenizdat, Leningrad, 1976) and *V Tylu i na Fronte* [At the home front and the front] (Izd. Politicheskoi literatury, Moscow, 1984). The anthologies were dedicated to the memory of the more than 800,000 women and girls who fought at the front during the war. See *Zhenshchiny Strany Sovetov. Kratkii ist. ocherk* [Women in the Land of Soviets] (Moscow: Politizdat, Moscow, 1977), 186.
24 *Zhenshchiny Goroda Lenina*, 114–15.
25 See Katerina Clark, *The Soviet Novel. History as Ritual* (University of Chicago Press, Chicago, 1981), 167.
26 *Zhenshchiny Goroda Lenina*, 121.
27 *Ibid.*, 291–2.
28 The collectivity is considered to be constructed in the Russian language through such expressions as 'my s toboi' ('you and I'), where I is always understood as part of the whole, dependent on others, and thus always in a reciprocal relationship to other persons: Hans H. Brockdorff, 'The individual and the collective: a cultural approach to the question of dualism in Soviet society', in Mette Bryld and Erik Kulavig (eds), *Soviet Civilization between Past and Present* (Odense University Press, Odense, 1998), 151–2.
29 Rancour-Laferrier's main idea is to underline the individual masochism, 'the Russian slave mentality', which is above all expressed in the submissiveness to the collective: 'The members of the collective all have to be equally miserable – otherwise it becomes too obvious that one's own personal misery is not really necessary, that is, is masochistic in essence': Daniel Rancour-Laferrier, *The Slave Soul of Russia. Moral Masochism and the Cult of Suffering* (New York University Press, New York, 1995), 207–8. In my opinion there are certain discrepancies in the author's thinking: on the one hand, he understands the slave soul of Russia as a woman, or more precisely as the Russian mother, who by definition is a sufferer, and whose 'destiny' it is above all to be able to endure and have patience (164–5). On the other hand, he defines the collective as an icon of the mother, and he also emphasises that the Party has a maternal personification (211–12). This second image corresponds badly to his understanding of Russians as individuals who characteristically welcome humiliation, suffering or defeat specifically at the hands of the collective. Besides this, he does not differ between different collectives, but defines the category as 'any group of psychological importance to the individual', be it the nuclear family, the church, the schoolroom, the Tsar's court, the Soviet collective farm, the Party or the Motherland (203). This gives his search for 'psychodynamics of individuals' an extremely abstract, generalising, ahistorical and context-free character, and therefore diminishes the credibility of his conclusions.
30 See Vladimir Shlapentokh, *Public and Private Life of the Soviet People. Changing Values in the Post-Stalin Russia* (Oxford University Press, Oxford, 1989); and Colette Shulman, 'The individual and the collective', in Dorothy Atkinson, Alexander Dallin and Gail W. Lapidus (eds), *Women in Russia* (Harvester Press, New York, 1978), 380, 383.
31 N.F. Sementsova, *Stanovlenie Sovetskoi Voennoi Memuaristiki* [Shaping the Writing of Soviet War Memoirs] (Izd. Moskovskogo universiteta, Moscow, 1981), 87, 129.
32 Cf. Jeanne Perreault, *Writing Selves. Contemporary Feminist Autography* (University of Minnesota Press, Minneapolis, 1995), 7; Doris Sommer, '"Not Just a Personal Story": Women's *testimonies* and the plural self', in Bella Brodzki and Celeste Schenk (eds), *Life/Lines. Theorizing Women's Autobiography* (Cornell University Press, Ithaca, 1988), 108.
33 *Zhenshchiny Goroda Lenina*, 293.
34 *Ibid.*, 210–13. She was thus one of the 86 women who got this title for *boevye zaslugi* (military services) during the Second World War (*Zhenshchiny Strany Sovetov*, 195).

35 *Zhenshchiny Goroda Lenina*, 118.
36 *Ibid.*, 209.
37 *Ibid.*, 120.
38 *Ibid.*, 293–4.
39 Slezkine, 'Lives as tales', 24.
40 Maria Pia Lara, *Moral Textures. Feminist Narratives in the Public Sphere* (Polity Press, Cambridge, 1998), 68.
41 Cf. *ibid.*, 71; Joan B. Landes, *Women in the Public Sphere in the Age of the French Revolution* (Cornell University Press, Ithaca, 1988), 63.
42 Fitzpatrick, 'Lives and times', 4.
43 Cf. Personal Narratives Group, 'Conditions not of her own making', in Personal Narratives Group (ed.), *Interpreting Women's Lives. Feminist Theory and Personal Narratives* (Indiana University Press, Bloomington, 1989), 19–22.
44 *Zhenshchiny Goroda Lenina*, 113.
45 Irina Sherbakova, 'The Gulag in memory', in Luisa Passerini (ed.), *Memory and Totalitarianism*, International Yearbook of Oral History and Life Stories, Vol. 1 (Oxford University Press, Oxford, 1992), 106; and Vilensky, *Till My Tale Is Told*, xii.
46 *Bez Nikh My Ne Pobedili by* [Without them we would not have won] (Politizdat, Moscow, 1975).

EPILOGUE

Researching with Interview Sources on Soviet Russia

Daniel Bertaux, Paul Thompson and Anna Rotkirch

As *On Living through Soviet Russia* has taken shape, we have become increasingly aware that we are exploring an immense theme which would take many volumes to cover. Extremely rich possibilities still remain for further research using life stories and oral history. These encompass, for example, future studies of the *nomenklatura* and of the Soviet industrial elites; of *kulak* families; and of ethnic minorities, including the Jews.[1] We have examined urban childhood here, but rural childhoods could equally be investigated, or youth or old age in city or countryside. We could look at the survival of religious practices among the Orthodox majority, as well as minorities such as the Old Believers here.

In particular, there is a need for much more information on the experience of ordinary Russian women through the Soviet period. As Barbara Engel and Anastasia Posadskaya-Vanderbeck point out in introducing their own pioneering collection of eight life stories, mainly recorded from Soviet women activists and professionals: 'We know relatively little about how ordinary Russians experienced the traumas and opportunities of the revolutionary and Stalinist eras of Soviet history, and virtually nothing about what these events meant to Russian women.'[2] And another whole series of perspectives could be opened up by exploring the immense regional disparities of Soviet Russia, ranging from the bitter Arctic to the mild south, with correspondingly different agricultures, and in some instances specific ethnic traditions. Or one might follow the production of a loaf of bread from the rural *kolkhoz* to the city breadshop, or similarly the story of the making of a car. There is an infinity of threads to follow.

While most of these topics will demand fresh interviewing, we should also wish to emphasise the importance of the growing body of autobiographical material which is now available as a resource for future researchers, both in Russia and the West. First, there is some published autobiographical material from the Soviet period, such as the women's autobiographies analysed by Marianne Liljeström in her chapter. Other examples include bizarre texts such as *Kanal imeny Stalina* (1935), a hagiographic account by twenty Russian writers on the construction of the White Sea–Baltic Canal by prison labour, in praise of labour in the cause of socialism. The first major example of a more candid use of oral accounts was by Aleksandr Solzhenitsyn. From the mid-1960s he was collecting material for *The Red Wheel* (1971 etc.), his four-volume account of the First World War and the 1917 Revolutions, notably not only seeking our manuscripts but also visiting the battle regions and interviewing Russians who had emigrated. He then turned to *The Gulag Archipelago* (1973), which was based substantially on survivors' accounts. He was forced to publish *The Gulag Archipelago* and most of *The Red Wheel* abroad. Irina Sherbakova began tape-recording Gulag survivors within Russia as early as 1978. Within Russia from the 1970s some relatively open accounts of wartime suffering were published, and also broadcast on television.[3] In most cases it is not clear whether any of the original material for this work survives. There was also important ethnographic work under the Soviet regime, and, while ethnographers did not keep any evidence of the regime's repressiveness in their public collections, many did retain their own personal fieldwork on very interesting themes, such as the survival of funeral customs after the closure of religious graveyards; but again, it is uncertain how much, if any, of this fieldwork data has now been recovered and archived.

Since *glasnost*, probably only a fraction of the immense outpouring of autobiographical evidence has been captured for the archives. Little is kept from radio or television, and typically only the printed outcome survives from interviewing by investigative journalists – we might cite as one outstanding example of this kind of half-lost evidence, just over the border, Svetlana Alexievich's graphic report on the Chernobyl disaster, built around biographical accounts. Perhaps more surprisingly, the same is true for much of the research by Westerners from the *glasnost* era onwards. Perhaps David Tuller did not keep a fieldwork diary for his fascinating autobiographical exploration of the Russian gay world, which became 'an unfolding love story between a gay American and a lesbian Russian' as much as an ethnography. But what happened to the Russian originals of fourteen of Gorbachev's reformers, interviewed at length over two years between 1987 and 1989 for historians Stephen Cohen and Katrina van den Heuvel's *Voices of Glasnost* (1989)?[4]

We know for certain that Tony Parker destroyed, as was his regular practice in all his projects, the original interviews of *Russian Voices* (1991). This is a great pity, because his version of the interviews, which were conducted through a translator, provides one of the richest available insights into the lives of everyday Russians in the late Soviet era. It has particularly strong sections on soldiers and conscripts, on health workers, on teaching – 'so we say to our pupils, "These words that are printed here are lies"' – and on faith and belief, in the churches and in the Communist Party. There is rich material on men and women, both separately and as couples, which certainly tallies with the findings reported here by Anna Rotkirch, for example in lack of knowledge about physical sex and finding the experience of it 'distasteful' and 'shocking'; the couple who are 'married in name only' and do not share a bed; the married homosexual who has 'never met a single male lover I could totally share my feelings with', and so on. There are also fascinating examples of both secrecy and fear, like the daughter of a Leningrad architect who was exiled for anti-Stalin remarks and brought up by her parents in constant fear that the KGB would take away her parents. They kept a bag for her always packed, ready to go: 'I was to go with that bag to her sister's, my aunt, and she would look after me. All the rest of my life, I have never been able to remove this fear from myself that one day something might happen like that!' What a loss that Parker's 141 interviews do not survive for others to explore.[5]

There are, however, fortunately some notable exceptions. In Russia itself the most important is the archive of the organisation Memorial itself in Moscow – and there are microfilm copies of much of its autobiographical material at the Institute of Social History in Amsterdam. Memorial's nucleus came from informal dissident networks, but it became a recognised public organisation in 1987, based in Moscow, but soon with branches in a hundred other cities. This collection was a source for Simeon Vilensky's *Till My Tale is Told: Women's Memoirs of the Gulag* (1999), as well as for Nanci Adler's chapter in this book. Although originally focused wholly on the testimonies of victims of Soviet repression, it has recently broadened with its sponsorship of schoolchildren's essays based on interviews with older family members. There are also less well organised collections at the Oral History Centre which originated from the oral-history fieldwork journeys of ethnographic students in the 1980s led by Daria Khubova; and there is the *Tsentr Dokumentatsii 'Narodnyi Arkhiv'* [People's Archive], a collection of autobiographies, life stories and other documents concerning ordinary people, with a website catalogue, founded in 1990, and now based at the Russian State Humanities University (RGGU). In St Petersburg, the Independent Centre for Social Research under the direction of Viktor Voronkov has gathered a substantial collection of life-history and thematic interviews carried out by the Centre's interviewers, as well as the written autobiographies on sex which Anna Rotkirch uses in her chapter here; and the material from several written autobiographical competitions is preserved at the Institute of Sociology. No doubt there are also other significant ethnographic sources elsewhere.[6]

In Western Europe, in addition to the Amsterdam collections, one of the most important archives is at the School of East European Studies at the University of London. The material here – all in Russian, but with a few interviews translated into English – includes the interviews used by Semenova and Thompson in their chapter in this book: forty-seven life-story interviews, which were recorded for a project led by Ray Pahl and Paul Thompson from twenty-five families who in 1991–2 were living in St Petersburg – then still Leningrad – and Moscow. These interviews were based on a new interview guide broadly structured on that published in the third edition of Thompson's *The Voice of the Past* (2000). In each family the project team normally interviewed not only one member of the generation born between 1945 and 1965, but also one of their parents or their children. They also aimed at a spread between families broadly from four main social categories: manual workers, professionals and the intelligentsia, *nomenklatura* and 'entrepreneurs'.[7] Of the entrepreneurs discussed in the chapter by Semenova and Thompson, three are drawn from this series, and a further six from family-history interviews from the Bertaux project (see below). The archives at the School of East European Studies also hold the interviews recorded by Irina Korovushkina Paert for her chapter in this book, and in addition more than 160 interviews on the experience of escape and exile by Russian refugees, recorded by Michael Glenny and his team.[8] In the British context, we must also commend two instances in which broadcast material about Russia has been made into research resources by the BBC. The first was the publication of *In the Time of Stalin* (1990), an eight-hour video set taken from the interviews gathered for the very powerful BBC trilogy 'The Hand of Stalin', produced by Tom Roberts. The second is the BBC World Service Trust's audio diary project, which was opened as an archive in Dusseldorf in 2001. This represents a different type of contemporary autobiographical source material.

Research interest on Russia elsewhere in Europe, especially in Germany and in Finland, has generated other oral-history and written autobiographical material, often collaborative, some of which is intended also to be made available for other scholars. The World Service audio diary project is an especially significant example. It is a collection of 600 audio everyday life diaries recorded by ordinary Russians and Ukrainians right across the two countries, now archived at the European Institute for Media in Dusseldorf. The largest oral-history collection in Germany is at the Fernuniversität at Hagen, and its holdings include interviews with sixteen Russians who were taken to Germany for forced labour under the Nazis; and other similar material is scattered in various local German archives. In Finland a large number of life-story and thematic interviews was gathered in 1996–8 through the research project on 'Social Change and Cultural Inertia in St Petersburg', sponsored by the Academy of Finland. These include a set of sixty-eight interviews about sexuality, and with psychologists and teachers, which can be made available to other researchers upon contacting Elina Haavio-Mannila, Markku Lonkila or Anna Rotkirch at the University of Helsinki.

In the context of this book, we should also particularly mention the interviews collected by Daniel Bertaux and his team in Russia, which are the basis not only for his chapter here, but also for those of Ekaterina Foteeva and Victoria Semenova. They consist of fifty case histories of families in Moscow taken in 1991–4, which again provide a rough social cross-section of occupations. The family case histories consist of life-story interviews with some family members, and from these are constructed accounts of the whole family network, their births, marriages and deaths, and their occupations. Bertaux terms this the method of 'Social Genealogy', in which each kin network can be analysed as a miniature mirror reflecting the grand social processes of the period. This material is in Russian and French. The intention is that it will be archived in Paris.[9]

Finally, there is a growing number of oral-history collections in the United States. One of the earliest and still the largest in scale was the State Department

Soviet Interview Project with immigrants and escapees from Russia, the interviews from which are held both in the Library of Congress and at the Russian Research Center, Harvard. The Bakhmetiev Archive at Columbia University, New York, has another large oral-history collection, including the recordings of Krushchev. The Hoover Institution at Palo Alto, California, holds more than one hundred interviews with leading Russian political figures, and also the twenty-five original interviews with women recorded for *A Revolution of Their Own*.[10] There is a more specialised collection, of unique value for the history of science, in the 600 interviews (including with astrophysicists) held at the Center for the History of Physics at College Park, Maryland. And again, we hope that collaborative projects with Russian scholars, such as those from Ann Arbor, and also the new joint Soros programme between Indiana University and the European University in St Petersburg, may soon become the basis for new accessible public archives for researchers.

Notes

1 See, for example, Viktor Voronkov and Elena Chikadze, 'Leningrad Jews: ethnicity and context', in Viktor Voronkov and Elena Zdravomyslova (eds), *Biographical Perspectives on Post-Socialist Societies* (Centre for Independent Research, St Petersburg, 1997): 187–91; Viktor Voronkov and Elena Chikadze, 'Different generations of Leningrad Jews in the context of public/ private division: paradoxes of ethnicity', in Robin Humphrey, Robert Miller and Elena Zdravomyslova (eds), *Biographical Research in Eastern Europe: Altered Lives and Broken Biographies* (Ashgate, Aldershot, 2003); and Robert J. Brym, *The Jews of Moscow, Kiev and Minsk: Identity, Antisemitism, and Emigration* (Macmillan, Basingstoke, 1994).

2 Barbara Alpern Engel and Anastasia Posadskaya-Vanderbeck (eds), *A Revolution of Their Own: Voices of Women in Soviet History* (Westview Press, Boulder, 1998): 1.
    Another useful collection, not of oral histories but translated extracts mostly from published autobiographies, is Sheila Fitzpatrick and Yuri Sledkine (eds), *In the Shadow of Revolution: Life Stories of Russian Women from 1917 to the Second World War* (Princeton University Press, Princeton, 2000).

3 Irina Sherbakova, 'The Gulag in memory' and 'Voices from the choir: reflections on the development of oral history in Russia', in Luisa Passerini (ed.), *Memory and Totalitarianism*, International Yearbook of Oral History and Life Stories, Vol. 1 (Oxford University Press, Oxford, 1992): 103–15 and 188–91. By 1991 Sherbakova had collected 250 interviews with Gulag survivors.

4 Svetlana Alexievitch, *Tchernobylskaya Molitva* (Ostojie, Moscow, 1997); David Tuller, *Cracks in the Iron Closet: Travels in Gay and Lesbian Russia* (University of Chicago Press, Chicago, 1997); Stephen F. Cohen and Katrina van den Heuvel, *Voices of Glasnost: Interviews with Gorbachev's Reformers* (Norton, New York, 1989).
    Another contrasting instance, in which the original interviews might have enabled future researchers to get behind the superficial presentation, would be Francine du Plessix Gray's interviews with women for *Soviet Women: Walking the Tightrope* (Doubleday, New York, 1989).

5 Tony Parker, *Russian Voices* (Jonathan Cape, London, 1991): 31, 61, 155, 191, 267.

6 The Memorial Archive of unpublished camp memoirs and also the Vozvrashchenie Archive are part of the microfilm collection at the Institute of Social History at Amsterdam. The catalogue of the Narodnyi Archiv is available online at http://www.pobeda.ru/na-nca/index.html. Information on the Centre for Independent

Social Research in St Petersburg may be found through its website http://www.indepsocres.spb.ru .
7 The research is more fully described in Ray Pahl and Paul Thompson, 'Meanings, myths and mystifications: the social construction of life stories in Russia', in C.M. Hann (ed.), *When History Accelerates: Essays on Rapid Social Change, Complexity and Creativity* (Athlone Press: London, 1994): 130–60.
8 Michael Glenny and Norman Stone, *The Other Russia: The Experience of Exile* (Faber and Faber, London, 1990).
9 See Daniel Bertaux, 'Révolution et mobilité sociale en Russie soviétique', *Cahiers internationaux de sociologie*, special issue, 'Les Sociétés post-totalitaires', 46 (1994): 77–97; Marina Malysheva and Daniel Bertaux, 'The social experiences of a countrywoman in Soviet Russia', in Selma Leydesdorff, Luisa Passerini and Paul Thompson, *Gender and Memory*, International Yearbook of Oral History and Life Stories, Vol. 4 (Oxford University Press, Oxford, 1994); Daniel Bertaux, 'Social genealogies, commented and compared: an instrument for studying social mobility processes in the "longue durée"', *Current Sociology*, 43 (1995): 69–89; Daniel Bertaux, 'Transmission in extreme situations: Russian families expropriated by the October Revolution', in Daniel Bertaux and Paul Thompson, *Pathways to Social Class: a Qualitative Approach to Social Mobility* (Clarendon Press: Oxford, 1997): 230–58.
10 Engel and Posadskaya-Vanderbeck, *A Revolution of Their Own*. Only eight of these interviews were used in their book.

BIBLIOGRAPHY

Adler, Nanci (2002) *The Gulag Survivor: Beyond the Soviet System*, Transaction Publishers, New Brunswick.
Aleksievich, Svetlana (1997) *Chernobyl'skaia Molitva* [The Chernobyl Prayer], Ostojie, Moscow.
Andrusz, Gregory D. (1984) *Housing and Urban Development in the USSR*, Macmillan, London.
Anikanova, T.I. (1999) 'O reabilitatsii zhertv politicheskikh repressii' [On the rehabilitation of victims of political repression], Otechestvennye Arkhivy, 1: 110–14.
Arendt, Hannah (1958) *The Human Condition*, University of Chicago Press, Chicago.
—— (1966) *The Origins of Totalitarianism*, Meridian Books, Cleveland.
—— (1968) *Totalitarianism*, Harcourt Brace, New York.
Ashwin, Sarah (ed.) (2000) *Gender, State and Society in Soviet and Post-Soviet Russia*, Routledge, London.
Atkinson, Dorothy (1983) *The End of the Russian Land Commune 1905–1930*, Stanford University Press, Stanford.
Attwood, Lynne (1990) *The New Soviet Man and Woman: Sex-Role Socialization in the USSR*, Macmillan, London.
—— (1996) 'Young people's attitudes towards sex roles and sexuality', in Hilary Pilkington (ed.) *Gender, Generation and Identity in Contemporary Russia*, Routledge, London: 132–51.
Babaeva, L.V. (1992) *Sotsial'no-stratifikatsionnye Protsessi v Sovremennom Obshchestve* [Social Processes in Modern Society], Institute of Sociology, Moscow.
Bäckman, Johan (1998) '"New Russians" and social change', in Markku Kivinen, *The Kalamari Union: Middle Class in East and West*, Ashgate, Aldershot: 15–35.
Bacon, Edwin (1994) *The Gulag at War: Stalin's Forced Labour System in the Light of the Archives*, Macmillan, London.
Ball, Alan (1988) *Russia's Last Capitalists: The Nepmen 1921–29*, University of Calfornia Press, Berkeley.
Belova, Valentina (1975) *Chislo Detei v Sem'e* [The number of children in the family], Statistica, Moscow.
Benstock, Shari (1988) 'Theorizing the Autobiographical', in *The Private Self: Theory and Practice of Women's Autobiographical Writings*, Routledge, London: 10–33.
Berelowitch, Wladimir (1993) 'De la famille patriarchale à la difficile découverte de l'individu', in Anne Coldefy-Faucard (ed.) *Quelle Russie?*, Éditions Autremont, Paris.

BIBLIOGRAPHY

Berger, Peter L. and Luckmann, Thomas (1966) *The Social Construction of Reality*, Doubleday, New York.
Berlin, Isaiah (1958) *Two Concepts of Liberty: An Inaugural Lecture*, Clarendon Press, Oxford.
Bertaux, Daniel (ed.) (1981) *Biography and Society: The Life History Approach in the Social Sciences*, Sage, London.
Bertaux, Daniel (1994) 'Révolution et mobilité sociale en Russie soviétique', *Cahiers internationaux de sociologie*, special issue, 'Les Sociétés post-totalitaires', 46: 77–97.
—— (1995) 'Social genealogies, commented and compared: an instrument for studying social mobility in the "longue durée"', *Current Sociology/La Sociologie contemporaine*, special issue, 'The Biographical Method', 43: 69–89.
—— (1997) 'Transmission in extreme situations: Russian families expropriated by the October Revolution', in Bertaux and Thompson, *Pathways to Social Class*: 230–58.
—— (1997) *Les récits de vie*, Nathan, Paris.
Bertaux, Daniel and Bertaux-Wiame, Isabelle (1997) 'Heritage and its lineage: a case history of transmission and social mobility over five generations', in Bertaux and Thompson, *Pathways to Social Class*, 32–97.
Bertaux, Daniel and Thompson Paul (eds) (1993) *Between Generations: Family Models, Myths and Memories*, International Yearbook of Oral History and Life Stories, Vol. 2, Oxford University Press, Oxford.
—— (1997) *Pathways to Social Class: A Qualitative Approach to Social Mobility*, Clarendon Press, Oxford.
Bertaux-Wiame, Isabelle, and Thompson, Paul (1997) 'The familial meaning of housing in social rootedness and mobility: Britain and France', in Bertaux and Thompson, *Pathways to Social Class*: 124–82.
Bettleheim, Charles (1976) *Class Struggles in the USSR: First Period, 1917–23*, Monthly Review Press, New York.
—— (1978) *Class Struggles in the USSR: Second Period, 1923–30*, Monthly Review Press, New York.
Bez Nikh My Ne Pobedili By (1975) [Without Them We Would Not Have Won], Politizdat, Moscow.
Boeva, Irina, Dolgopiatova, Tat'iana and Sironin, Viacheslav (1992) *Gosudarstvennye predpriiatiia v 1991–1992 gg.: ekonomicheskie problemy i povedenie* [State Enterprises in 1991–2: Economic and Management Problems], Institute of Political Economy, Moscow.
Bourdieu, Pierre (1984) *Distinction: A Social Critique of the Judgement of Taste*, Harvard University Press, Cambridge, Mass.
—— (1993) 'Social space and class genesis' [in Russian], in *Bourdieu, Sotsiologia politiki*, Socio-Logos, Moscow.
Boym, Svetlana (1994) *Common Places: Mythologies of Everyday Life in Russia*, Harvard University Press, Cambridge, Mass.
Brockdorff, Hans H. (1998) 'The individual and the collective: a cultural approach to the question of dualism in Soviet society', in Mette Bryld and Erik Kulavig (eds), *Soviet Civilization between Past and Present*, Odense University Press, Odense: 147–63.
Brodsky, Joseph (1995) 'Letter to a President,' in *On Grief and Reason*, Farrar, Straus and Giroux, New York: 212–22.
Brodzki, Bella and Schenk, Celeste (eds) (1988) *Life/Lines: Theorizing Women's Autobiography*, Cornell University Press, Ithaca.
Brossat, Alain *et al.* (eds) (1990) *À l'Est la mémoire retrouvée*, La Découverte, Paris.

BIBLIOGRAPHY

Brym, Robert J. (1994) *The Jews of Moscow, Kiev and Minsk: Identity, Antisemitism, and Emigration*, Macmillan, Basingstoke.

Brzezinski, Zbigniew (1956) *The Permanent Purge*, Harvard University Press, Cambridge, Mass.

Buckley, Mary (1989) *Women and Ideology in the Soviet Union*, Harvester Wheatsheaf, New York and London.

Bushnell, John (1980) 'The "New Soviet Man" turns pessimist', in Stephen F. Cohen, Alexander Rabinowitch and Robert Sharlet (eds), *The Soviet Union since Stalin*, Indiana University Press, Bloomington: 179–99.

Carr, Edward H. (1951–3) *The Bolshevik Revolution. 1917–1923*, Macmillan, London.

—— (1958) *Socialism in One Country*, 3 vols, Macmillan, London.

Casey, Edward S. (1996) 'How to get from space to place in a fairly short stretch of time', in Steven Feld and Keith H. Basso (eds), *Senses of Place*, School of American Research Press, Santa Fe.

—— (1997) *The Fate of Place: a Philosophical History*, University of California Press, Berkeley.

Castells, Manuel (1977) *The Urban Question*, MIT Press, Cambridge, Mass.

Chistiakova, Aleksandra (1998) *Ne mnogo li dlia odnoi?* [Enough for One?], Den' i noch', Krasnoiarsk.

Clark, Katerina (1981) *The Soviet Novel. History as Ritual*, University of Chicago Press, Chicago.

Clarke, Simon (1999) *New Forms of Employment and Household Survival Strategies in Russia*, ISITO/CCLS, Coventry and Moscow.

Clements, Barbara (1985) 'The birth of the New Soviet Woman', in Abbott Gleason, Peter Kenez and Richard Stites (eds), *Bolshevik Culture. Experiment and Order in the Russian Revolution*, Indiana University Press, Bloomington: 220–37.

Cohen, Anthony P. (1985) *The Symbolic Construction of Community*, Ellis Horwood, Chichester, 1985.

Cohen, Stephen F. (1985) *Rethinking the Soviet Experience: Politics and History since 1917*, Oxford University Press, New York.

Cohen, Stephen F. and van den Heuvel, Katrina (1989) *Voices of Glasnost: Interviews with Gorbachev's Reformers*, Norton, New York.

Colton, Timothy J. (1980) 'What ails the Soviet system?', in Erik P. Hofmann (ed.), *The Soviet Union since Stalin*, Academy of Political Science, New York: 179–99.

Conquest, Robert (1992) *The Great Terror: A Reassessment*, Macmillan, London.

—— (1997) 'Victims of Stalinism: a comment', *Europe–Asia Studies* (49) 7: 1317–19.

Cosslett, Tess, Lury, Celia and Summerfield, Penny (eds) (2000) *Feminism and Autobiography: Texts, Theories, Methods*, Routledge, London.

Craveri, Marta and Khlevniuk, Oleg (1995) 'Krizis Ekonomiki MVD (konets 1940–1950 gody)' [The economic crisis of the MVD, Ministry of Internal Affairs, 1940–1950], *Cahiers du monde russe XXXVI*, 1–2: 182.

Crummey, Robert (1970) *Old Believers and the World of Antichrist: The Vyg Community and the Russian State, 1694–1855*, University of Wisconsin Press, Madison.

Davies, R.W. (1997) *Soviet History in the Yeltsin Era*, Macmillan, London.

Davies, R.W., Harrison, Mark and Wheatcroft, Stephen (eds) (1994) *The Economic Transformation of the Soviet Union, 1913–1945*, Cambridge University Press, Cambridge.

BIBLIOGRAPHY

Davies, Sarah (1997) *Popular Opinion in Stalin's Russia*, Cambridge University Press, Cambridge.

De Certeau, Michel, Girard, Luce and Mayol, Pierre (1998) *The Practice of Everyday Life, 2: Living and Cooking* (trans. T.J. Tomasik), University of Minnesota Press, Minneapolis.

De Lauretis, Teresa (1987) *Technologies of Gender. Essays on Theory, Film and Fiction*, Indiana University Press, Bloomington.

Docheri Rossii (1975) [Russia's Daughters], Sovetskaia Rossiia, Moscow.

Dodnes' Tiagoteet (1989) [Till My Tale is Told], Vypusk 1, Sovetskii Pisatel, Moscow.

Du Plessix Gray, Francine (1989) *Soviet Women: Walking the Tightrope*, Doubleday, New York.

Dunham, Vera (1976) *In Stalin's Time: Middleclass Values in Soviet Fiction*, Cambridge University Press, Cambridge.

Eakin, Paul John (1985) *Fictions in Autobiography: Studies in the Art of Self-Invention*, Princeton University Press, Princeton.

—— (1999) *How Our Lives Become Stories. Making Selves*, Cornell University Press, Ithaca.

Elder, Glen (1974) *Children of the Great Depression: Social Change in Life Experience*, University of Chicago Press, Chicago.

Engel, Barbara Alpern and Posadskaya-Vanderbeck, Anastasia (eds) (1998) *A Revolution of Their Own: Voices of Women in Soviet History*, Westview Press, Boulder.

Engelstein, Laura (1992) *The Keys to Happiness: Sex and the Search for Modernity in Fin-de-siècle Russia*, Cornell University Press, Ithaca.

Essig, Laurie (1990) *Queer in Russia: A Story of Sex, Self and the Other*, Duke University Press, Durham.

Etkind, Alexandr (1994) *Eros Nevozmozhnogo. Istoriia Psikhoanaliza v SSSR* [Eros of the Impossible: Psychoanalysis in Russia], Progress, Moscow [trans. Noah And Maria Rubins, Westview Press, Oxford, 1997].

Farnsworth, Beatrice (1985) 'Village women experience the revolution', in Abbott Gleason, Peter Kenez and Richard Stites (eds), *Bolshevik Culture. Experiment and Order in the Russian Revolution*, Indiana University Press, Bloomington: 238–60.

Fediukin, S.A. (1965) *Sovetskaya Vlast' i burzhuaznyie spetsialisty* [Soviet Power and Bourgeois Specialists], Mysl', Moscow.

—— (1972) *Velikii Oktiabr' i intelligentsia* [The October Revolution and the Intelligentsia], Nauka, Moscow.

Fitzpatrick, Sheila (1979) *Education and Social Mobility in the Soviet Union, 1921–1934*, Cambridge University Press, Cambridge.

—— (1992) *The Cultural Front: Power and Culture in Revolutionary Russia*, Cornell University Press, Ithaca and London.

—— (1993) 'Ascribing class: the construction of social identity in Soviet Russia', *Journal of Modern History* 50 (4): 745–70.

—— (1994) 'Signals from below: Soviet letters of denunciation of the 1930s', unpublished paper.

—— (1999) *Everyday Stalinism*, Oxford University Press, New York and Oxford.

—— (2000) 'Lives and times', in Sheila Fitzpatrick and Yuri Slezkine (eds), *In the Shadow of Revolution. Life Stories of Russian Women from 1917 to the Second World War*, Princeton University Press, Princeton: 3–17.

Fitzpatrick, Sheila, Rabinowich, Alexander and Stites, Richard (eds) (1991) *Russia in the Era of NEP: Explorations in Soviet Society and Culture*, Indiana University Press, Bloomington.

Foucault, Michel (1984) 'What is an author?', in Paul Rabinow, *The Foucault Reader*, Penguin, London: 107–18.

Furman, Dmitrii (1989) *Stalin i my s religiovedcheskoi tochki zreniia* [Stalin and Us from a Religious Studies Point of View], Letnii Sad, Moscow.

Galtz, Naomi Roslyn (2000) *Space and the Everyday: An Historical Sociology of the Moscow Dacha*, Ph.D Dissertation, University of Michigan, Ann Arbor.

Gay, Peter (1994) *The Bourgeois Experience: Victoria to Freud*, The Education of the Senses, 1, Oxford University Press, Oxford.

Gerasimova, Katerina (1997) 'The verbalization of sexuality: talks about sex with partner', in Voronkov and Zdravomyslova (eds), *Biographical Perspectives*: 215–21.

Gessen, Masha (1995) 'Sex in the media and the birth of the sex media in Russia', in Ellen Berry (ed.), *Postcommunism and the Body Politic*, New York University Press, New York: 197–228.

Getty, Arch Jr and Chase, William (1993) 'Patterns of repression among the Soviet elite in the late 1930s', in Getty and Manning, *Stalinist Terror*: 225–46.

Getty, Arch Jr and Manning, Roberta T. (eds) (1993) *Stalinist Terror: New Perspectives*, Cambridge University Press, Cambridge.

Getty, Arch Jr, Rittersporn, G.T. and Zemskov, V.N. (1993) 'Victims of the Soviet penal system in the pre-war years: a first approach on the basis of archival evidence', *American Historical Review* (98) 1993: 1017–49.

Getty, Robert (1985) *Origins of the Great Purges: The Soviet Communist Party Reconsidered 1933–1938*, Cambridge University Press, Cambridge.

Gilmore, Leigh (1994) *Autobiographics: A Feminist Theory of Women's Self-Representation*, Cornell University Press, Ithaca.

Glenny, Michael and Stone, Norman (1990) *The Other Russia: The Experience of Exile*, Faber and Faber, London.

Glezerman, Grigorii (1949) *Likvidatsiia ekspluatatorskikh klassov i preodolenie klassovykh razlichii v SSSR* [The Liquidation of the exploitary classes and the overcoming of class differentiation in the USSR], Gospolitizdat, Moscow.

Goffman, Erving (1959) *The Presentation of Self in Everyday Life*, Doubleday, New York.

Goldman, Wendy Z. (1993) *Women, the State and Revolution: Soviet Family Policy and Social Life, 1917–1936*, Cambridge University Press, Cambridge.

Golod, Sergei I. (1996) *XX Vek i tendentsii v seksual'nykh otnosheniiakh v Rossii* [The 20th Century and Trends in Sexual Relations in Russia], Aleteia, St Petersburg.

Golofast, Valery (1997) 'Three levels of biographical narratives', in Voronkov and Zdravomyslova (eds) *Biographical Perspectives*: 140–3.

Golovkova, Lidiia (1996) 'Tikhaia obitel'' [Silent inhabitant], *Biblioteka Zhurnala*, Volia 1, Vozvrashchenie, Moscow.

Gorell Barnes *et al.* (1997) *Growing up in Stepfamilies*, Oxford University Press, Oxford.

Gronow, Jukka *et al.* (1997) 'Cultural inertia and social change in Russia. Distributions by gender and age group', paper, Department of Sociology, University of Helsinki.

Grossman, Vasily (1972) *Forever Flowing*, Harper & Row, New York.

Groys, Boris (1994) 'Den ryska filosofins ansikte. Från Tjaadajev till Marx' [The face of Russian philosophy. From Chaadaev to Marx], *Ord & Bild*, 4: 21–30.

Gudzen'ko, M.S. and Shul'ga, M.V. (1983) *Podsobnoe khoziaistvo grazhdan* [Supplementary Agricultural Activity of Citizens], Iuridicheskaia Literatura, Moscow.

BIBLIOGRAPHY

Haavio Mannila, Elina and Rotkirch, Anna (1998) 'Generational and gender differences in sexual life in St Petersburg and urban Finland', in *Yearbook of Population Research in Finland, XXXIV, Population Trends in the Baltic Sea Area*, Väestöliitto, Helsinki.

Haavio-Mannila, Elina, Kontula, Osmo and Rotkirch, Anna (2002) *Moments of Passion: Sexual Autobiographies from Three Generations*, Palgrave, London.

Haavio-Mannila, Elina, Roos, J.P. and Kontula, Osmo (1996) 'Repression, revolution and ambivalence. The sexual life of three generations in Finland', *Acta sociologica*, 39: 409–30.

Hareven, Tamara (1982) *Family Time and Industrial Time*, Cambridge University Press, Cambridge.

Hawkes, Gail (1996) *A Sociology of Sex and Sexuality*, Open University Press, Buckingham.

Held, Joseph (1981) 'Cultural development', in Stephen Fischer-Galati (ed.), *Eastern Europe in the 1980s*, Croom Helm, London: 257–78.

Hirdman, Yvonne (1990) *The Gender System: Theoretical Reflections on the Social Subordination of Women*, The Study of Power and Democracy in Sweden, English Series, Report 40, Uppsala.

Hochschild, Arlie R. (1997) *The Time Bind, When Work Becomes Home and Home Becomes Work*, Metropolitan Books, New York.

Hoikkala, Tommi, Purhonen, Semi and Roos, J.P. (2002) 'The baby boomers, life's turning points and generational consciousness', in June Edmunds and Bryan Turner (eds), *Generational Consciousness, Narrative and Politics*, Rowman and Littlefield, London: 145–64.

Husband, William (1998) 'Soviet atheism and Russian Orthodox strategies of resistance, 1917–1932', *Journal of Modern History* 70: 74–107.

—— (2000) *Godless Communists: Atheism and Society in Soviet Russia, 1917–1932*, Northern Illinois University Press, DeKalb.

Ionin, L.G. (1997) *Svoboda v SSSR: Stat'i i Esse* [Freedom in the USSR: Articles and Essays], Fond Universitetskaia kniga, St Petersburg.

Jones, Ellen and Grupp, Fred W. (1987) *Modernization, Value Change, and Fertility in the Soviet Union*, Cambridge University Press, Cambridge.

Kääriäinen, Kimmo (1998) *Religion in Russia after the Collapse of Communism*, Edwin Mellen Press, Lewiston.

Kenez, Peter (1985) *The Birth of the Propaganda State*, Cambridge University Press, Cambridge.

Kerblay, Basile (1977) *La société soviétique contemporaine*, Armand Colin, Paris.

—— (ed.) (1988) *L'évolution des modèles familiaux dans les pays de l'Est européen et en URSS*, Institut d'Études Slaves, Paris.

Kharkhordine, Oleg (1994) 'L'éthique corporatiste, l'éthique de samostojatelnost et l'esprit du capitalisme: réflections sur la création du marché en Russsie post-soviétique', *Revue d'études comparatives est-ouest*, 2: 27–56.

Khubova, Daria, Ivankiev, Andrei and Sharova, Tonia (1992) 'After glasnost: oral history in the Soviet Union', in Luisa Passerini (ed.), *Memory and Totalitarianism*, International Yearbook of Oral History and Life Stories, Vol. 1, Oxford University Press, Oxford: 89–102.

Kiblitskaya, Marina (2000) 'Russia's female breadwinners: the changing subjective experience', in Sarah Ashwin (ed.), *Gender, State and Society*: 55–70.

Kim, M.P. et al. (eds) (1968) *Sovetskaja intelligentsija: istorija formirovanija i rosta, 1917–1965 gg* [The Soviet Intelligentsia: A History of its Formation and Growth, 1917–1965], Mysl', Moscow.

Kokliagina, Ludmilla and Semenova, Victoria (eds) (1993) *Doklad o tret'em etape longit'iudnogo issledovaniia puti odnogo pokoleniya* [Report on third wave of longitudinal survey: paths of one russian generation], ISAN, Moscow.

Kollontai, Alexandra (1918) *Sem'ia i communisticheskoe gosudarstvo* [The family and the communist state], Communist, Moscow.

Kon, Igor (1995) *The Sexual Revolution in Russia. From the Age of the Czars to Today*, The Free Press, New York.

Kon, Igor and Riordan, James (eds) (1993) *Sex in Russian Society*, Indiana University Press, Bloomington.

Kontula, Osmo and Haavio-Mannila, Elina (1995) *Sexual Pleasures: Enhancement of Sex Life in Finland, 1971–1992*, Dartmouth, Aldershot.

Korovushkina Paert, Irina (2001) 'Popular religion and local identity during the Stalin Revolution: Old Believers in the Urals (1928–41)', in Don Raleigh (ed.), *Provincial Landscapes: Local Dimensions of Soviet Power*, University of Pittsburgh Press, Pittsburgh: 171–94.

Kozlova, N.N. and Sandomirskaia, I.I. (1996) *Ia tak tak khochu nazvat' kino. Naivnoe pis'mo'. Opyt lingvo-sotsiologicheskogo chteniia* [That's what I want to call the movie. The 'naive letter'. The experience of a linguo-sociological reading], Gnozis, Moscow.

Kukhterin, Sergei (2000) 'Fathers and patriarchs in communist and post-communist Russia', in Sarah Ashwin (ed.), *Gender, State and Society*: 71–89.

Kuusinen, Aino (1991) *Gospod' nizvergaet svoikh angelov: vospominaniia 1919–1965* [God throws out his angels], Izdatel'stvo Kareliia, Petrozavodsk.

Lachova, Ekaterina (1997), 'Vse my vhodim v "gruppu riska"', *Nezavisimaia Gazeta*, 10 April.

Lagunova, Yelizaveta (1995) 'The educated Russian woman: dominantes of destiny', *Feminist Theory and Practice: East–West*, Petersburg: Petersburg Centre for Gender Issues: 115–21.

Landes, Joan B. (1988) *Women in the Public Sphere in the Age of the French Revolution*, Cornell University Press, Ithaca.

Lane, Christel (1981) *The Rites of Rulers. Ritual in Industrial Society – The Soviet Case*, Cambridge University Press, Cambridge.

Lane, David (1990) *Soviet Society under Perestroika*, Unwin Hyman, Boston.

Lapidus, Gail W. (1978) *Women in Soviet Society. Equality, Development, and Social Change*, University of California Press, Berkeley.

Lara, Maria Pia (1998) *Moral Textures. Feminist Narratives in the Public Sphere*, Polity Press, Cambridge.

Ledenova, Alena (1998) *The Russian Economy of Favours: Blat, Networking and Informal Exchange*, Cambridge University Press, New York.

Lee, Martyn J. (1993) *Consumer Culture Reborn: The Cultural Politics of Consumption*, Routledge, New York.

Lennerhed, Lena (1994) *Frihet att njuta. Sexualdebatten i Sverige på 1960-talet* [Freedom to enjoy: the sexual debate in Sweden in the 1960s], Norstedts, Stockholm.

Levada, Yuri (ed.) (1993) *Prostoi sovetskyi chelovek* [The ordinary soviet person], Mirovoi Okean, Moscow.

BIBLIOGRAPHY

Levinson, Galina Ivanovna (1996) *Vsia nasha zhizn'* [All Our Lives], NIPTs Memorial, Moscow.

Lewin, Moshe (1968) *Russian Peasants and Soviet Power: A Study of Collectivisation*, Northwestern University Press, Evanston.

—— (1977) 'The social background of Stalinism', in Robert C. Tucker (ed.), *Stalinism: Essays in Historical Interpretation*, Norton, New York: 111–36.

—— (1985) *The Making of the Soviet System: Essays in the Soviet History of the Interwar Russia*, Pantheon Books, New York.

—— (1988) *The Gorbachev Phenomenon: A Historical Interpretation*, University of California Press, Berkeley.

Liborakina, Marina (1996) *Obretenie sily: rossiiskii opyt. Puti preodoleniia diskriminatsii v otnoshenii zhenshchin (Kulturnoe izmerenie)* [Empowerment: the Russian Experience – Ways of Overcoming Discrimination against Women (a Cultural Dimension)], Tshero, Moscow.

Liljeström, Marianne (1995) *Emanciperade till underordning. Det sovjetiska könssystemets uppkomst och diskursiva reproduktion* [Emancipated to subordination: the emergence and discursive reproduction of the Soviet gender system], Åbo Akademis förlag, Turku.

—— (2000) 'Regimes of truth? Soviet women's autobiographical texts and the question of censorship', in Markku Kangaspuro (ed.), *Russia: More Different than Most*, Kikimora, Helsinki: 113–34.

Lonkila, Markku (1998) 'The social meaning of work: the teaching profession in post-Soviet Russia', *Europe–Asia Studies*, 50, 4: 699–712.

Lutz, Emma (2002) ' "At your service, madame!" The globalization of domestic service', *Feminist Review* 70: 89–104.

McDermid, Jane and Hillyar, Anna (1998) *Women and Work in Russia 1880–1930. A Study in Continuity through Change*, Longman, London and New York.

Malia, Martin M. (1955) 'Herzen and the peasant commune', in Ernest J. Simmons (ed.), *Continuity and Change in Russian and Soviet Thought*, Harvard University Press, Cambridge, Mass.: 197–217.

Malysheva, Marina and Bertaux, Daniel (1996) 'The social experiences of a countrywoman in Soviet Russia', in Selma Leydesdorff, Luisa Passerini and Paul Thompson (eds.), *Gender and Memory*, International Yearbook of Oral History and Life Stories, Vol. 4, Oxford University Press, Oxford: 31–44.

Marcus, Laura (1994) *Auto/biographical Discourses: Theory, Criticism, Practice*, Manchester University Press, Manchester.

Marx, Karl and Engels, Frederick (1968) *Selected Works*, Progress, Moscow.

Matskovski, Michail (ed.) (1993) *Sem'ia v krizisnom obshchestve* [The Family in a Crisis Society], Institute of Sociology, Moscow.

Matthews, Mervin (1978) *Privilege in the Soviet Union: A Study of Elite Life-Styles under Communism*, Allen & Unwin, London.

Maynes, Mary Jo (1995) *Taking the Hard Road. Life Course in French and German Workers' Autobiographies in the Era of Industrialization*, University of North Carolina Press, Chapel Hill.

Mead, Margaret (1970) *Culture and Commitment: A Study of the Generation Gap*, Bodley Head, London.

Michels, Georg (1999) *At War with the Church: Religious Dissent in Seventeenth-century Russia*, Stanford University Press, Stanford.

BIBLIOGRAPHY

Miller, Nancy K. (1994) 'Representing others: gender and the subjects of autobiography', *differences*, 6, 1: 1–27.

Molotkov, A.I. (ed.) (1967) *Dictionnaire phraséologique de la langue russe*, Soviet Encyclopoedia, Moscow.

Molotov, Viacheslav M. (1937) *Stat'i i rechi: 1935–1936* [Articles and Speeches: 1935–1936], Gospolitizdat, Moscow.

Mumford, Lewis (1961) *The City in History: Its origins, Its Transformations, and Its Prospects*, Harcourt Brace, New York.

Nekrasov, Viktor (1967) *Kira Georgievna*, Cambridge University Press, Cambridge.

Okudzhava, Bulat (1988) *Devushka Moei Mechty: Avtobiograficheskoe Povestvovanie* [Girl of My Dreams: An Autobiographical Novella], Moskovsky Rabochy, Moscow.

Osokina, Elena (1999) *Za Fasadom 'Stalinskogo izobiliia'. Raspredelenie i rynok snabzhenii naseleniia v gody industrializatsii 1927–1941* [Behind the Façade of 'Stalin's Time of abundance': Distribution and the Market for the Population during the Years of Industrialization 1927–1941], Rossiiskaia akademia nauk, Institut Russkoi Istorii, Rospen, Moscow.

Osokina, Elena, Transchel, Kate S. and Bucher, Greta (2001) *Our Daily Bread: Socialist Distribution and the Art of Survival in Stalin's Russia, 1927–1941*, M.E. Sharpe, Armonk.

Oswald, Ingrid and Voronkov, Viktor (forthcoming) 'On the interview situation in post-Soviet society', Foreword to 'The "Public" in Soviet Society', *European Societies*.

Pahl, Ray and Thompson, Paul (1994) 'Meanings, myths and mystifications: the social construction of life stories in Russia', in C.M. Hann (ed.), *When History Accelerates: Essays on Rapid Social Change, Complexity and Creativity*, Athlone Press, London: 130–60.

Parker, Tony (1991) *Russian Voices*, Jonathan Cape, London.

Pascal, Pierre (1973) *La réligion du peuple russe*, L'Age d'Homme, Lausanne.

Passerini, Luisa (1992) 'Introduction' in Luisa Passerini (ed.), *Memory and Totalitarianism*, International Yearbook of Oral History and Life Stories, Vol. 1, Oxford University Press, Oxford.

Peris, Dan (1998) *Storming the Heavens: The Soviet League of the Militant Godless*, Cornell University Press, Ithaca.

Perreault, Jeanne (1995) *Writing Selves. Contemporary Feminist Autography*, University of Minnesota Press, Minneapolis.

Personal Narratives Group (1989) 'Conditions not of her own making', in *Interpreting Women's Lives. Feminist Theory and Personal Narratives*, ed. by Personal Narratives Group, Indiana University Press, Bloomington: 19–23.

Pilkington, Hilary (1994) *Russia's Youth and Its Culture: A Nation's Constructors and Constructed*, Routledge, London.

Pipes, Richard (1981) *US–Soviet Relations in the Era of Détente*, Westview Press, Boulder.

—— (1999) *Property and Freedom*, Alfred A. Knopf, New York.

Popovsky, Mark (1985) *Tretii Lishnii. On, Ona i Sovetskii Rezhim* [The Third Wheel: He, She, and the Soviet Regime], Overseas Publ. Interchange Ltd, London.

Posadskaya-Vanderbeck, Anastasia and Engel, Barbara Alpern, (1998) *A Revolution of Their Own: Voices of Women in Soviet History*, Westview Press, Boulder.

Rancour-Laferrier, Daniel (1995) *The Slave Soul of Russia. Moral Masochism and the Cult of Suffering*, New York University Press, New York.

Rasskazhi svoiu istoriu (1999) [Tell Us Your Story] Fond Nochlezhka, St Petersburg.

BIBLIOGRAPHY

Riasanovsky, Nicholas V. (1955) 'Khomiakov on sobornost', in Ernest J. Simmons (ed.), *Continuity and Change in Russian and Soviet Thought*, Harvard University Press, Cambridge, Mass.: 183–96.

Robson, Roy (1996) *Old Believers in Modern Russia*, Northern Illinois University Press, DeKalb.

Rosefielde, Steven (1996) 'Stalinism in post-Communist perspective: new evidence on killings, forced labour and economic growth in the 1930s', *Europe–Asia Studies* (48) 6: 959–87.

Rosenthal, Gabriele (2000) 'Social transformation in the context of familial experience: biographical consequences of a denied past in the Soviet Union', in Roswitha Brecker, Devorah Kalekin-Fishman and Ingrid Miethe (eds), *Biographies and the Division of Europe: Experience, Action and Change on the 'Eastern Side'*, Leske and Budrich, Opladen: 115–58.

Rotkirch, Anna (1996) 'The bourgeois housewife, the patriotic mother and the question of individualisation in contemporary Russia', in *Från skuggfält till nya yrken. Individualisering och kvinnoideal i dagens Ryssland. Licentiatavhandling*, unpublished paper, Department of Social Policy, University of Helsinki.

—— (1997) 'Women's sexual biographies from two generations. A first comparison between Finland and Russia', in Voronkov and Zdravomyslova (eds), *Biographical Perspectives*: 205–11.

—— (2000) *The Man Question: Loves and Lives in Late Twentieth Century Russia*, Department of Social Policy, University of Helskinki.

Rotkirch, Anna and Haavio-Mannila, Elina (eds) (1996) *Women's Voices in Russia Today*, Dartmouth, Aldershot.

Rybakov, A. (1988) *Children of the Arbat*, Eesti Raamat, Tallinn.

Rytkönen, Marja (1999) 'Narrating female subjectivity in the autobiographical texts of Elena Bonner, Emma Gertejn and Maiija Pliseckaja', *NORA Nordic Journal of Women's Studies*, 7, 1: 34–46.

Schlesinger, Rudolf (1949) *The Family in the USSR: Changing Attitudes in Soviet Russia – Documents and Reading*, Policy Press, London.

Scott, James (1976) *The Moral Economy of the Peasant*, Yale University Press, New Haven.

Selunskaia, Valeriia et al. (eds) (1976) *Izmenenie sotsial'noi Struktury Sovetskogo Obchshestva: Oktiabr' 1917–1920* [Changes in the Structure of Soviet Society: October 1917–1920], Mysl', Moscow.

Semenova, Victoria (2000) 'The message from the past: experience of suffering transmitted through generations', in Roswitha Brecker, Devorah Kalekin-Fishman and Ingrid Miethe (eds), *Biographies and the Division of Europe: Experience, Action and Change on the 'Eastern Side'*, Leske and Budrich, Opladen: 93–114.

Semenova, Victoria and Rozhdestvesky, Sergei (1996) 'The experience of suffering passed down through generations', paper to IXth International Oral History Conference, Göteborg, 13–16 June.

Semenova, Victoria, Foteeva, Ekaterina and Bertaux, Daniel (eds) (1996) *Sud'by liudei: Rossiia XX vek. Biografii semei kak ob'ekt sotsiologicheskogo issledovaniia* [The Fates of People: Russia in the 20th Century. Biography as an Object of Sociological Research], Institut Sociologii RAN, Moscow.

Sementsova, N.F. (1981) *Stanovlenie Sovetskoi Voennoi Memuaristiki* [Shaping the Writing of Soviet War Memoirs], Izd. Moskovskogo universiteta, Moscow.

Sennett, Richard (1977) *The Fall of Public Man*, Knopf, New York.

BIBLIOGRAPHY

Sherbakova, Irina (1992) 'The Gulag in memory', in Luisa Passerini (ed.), *Memory and Totalitarianism*, International Yearbook of Oral History and Life Stories, Vol. 1, Oxford University Press, Oxford: 103–16.

Shlapentokh, Vladimir (1989) *Public and Private Life of the Soviet People. Changing Values in Post-Stalin Russia*, Oxford University Press, Oxford.

Shulman, Colette (1978) 'The individual and the collective', in Dorothy Atkinson, Alexander Dallin and Gail W. Lapidus (eds), *Women in Russia*, Harvester Press, New York: 380–3.

Slezkine, Yuri (2000) 'Lives as tales', in Sheila Fitzpatrick and Yuri Slezkine (eds), *In the Shadow of Revolution: Life Stories of Russian Women from 1917 to the Second World War*, Princeton University Press, Princeton.

Smith, Sidonie and Watson, Julia (1998) 'Introduction: situating subjectivity in women's autobiographical practices', in Sidonie Smith and Julia Watson (eds), *Women, Autobiography, Theory. A Reader*, University of Wisconsin Press, Madison.

Soispatrova, N.E. (1981) *Grazhdanskie prava chlenov sadovodcheskogo tovarishchestva rabochikh i sluzhashchikh RSFSR: Aftoreferat dissertatsii na soiskanie uchenoi stepeni kandidata iuridicheskoi nauki* [Civil rights for non-agricultural workers involved in garden collectives], dissertation abstract 623.211.332, Vsesoiuznyi iuridicheskii zaochnyi institut, Moscow.

Solzhenitsyn, Aleksandr (1972) *The Red Wheel: Knot I, August 1914* (trans. 1972), Bodley Head, London.

—— (1974) *The Gulag Archipelago 1918–1956: An Experiment in Literary Investigation*, Collins and Harvill Press, London.

—— (1999) *The Red Wheel: Knot II, November 1916* (trans. 1999), Jonathan Cape, London.

Sommer, Doris (1988) '"Not just a personal story": women's testimonies and the plural self', in Bella Brodzki and Celeste Schenk (eds), *Life/Lines. Theorizing Women's Autobiography*, Cornell University Press, Ithaca: 107–30.

Sorokin, Pitirim A. (1967) *The Sociology of Revolution*, Howard Fertig, New York.

Stern, Mikhail (1979) *Sex in the USSR*, Times Books, New York.

Taylor, Charles (1989) *Sources of the Self. The Making of the Modern Identity*, Cambridge University Press, Cambridge.

Temkina, Anna (1996) 'Women's ways of entering politics', in Anna Rotkirch and Elina Haavio-Mannila (eds), *Women's Voices in Russia Today*, Dartmouth, Aldershot: 33–48.

—— (2000) 'Sexual scripts in women's biographies and the construction of sexual pleasure', in Marianne Liljeström, Arja Rosenholm and Irina Savkina (eds), *Models of Self: Russian Women's Autobiographical Texts*, Kikimora, Helsinki.

Temkina, Anna and Rotkirch, Anna (1997) 'Soviet gender contracts and their shifts in contemporary Russia', *Idäntutkimus: Finnish Journal of Russian and Eastern European Studies* 2: 6–24.

Thompson, Paul (1978) *The Voice of the Past*, (revised editions 1988 and 2000), Oxford University Press, Oxford.

—— (1981) 'Life histories and the analysis of social change', in Daniel Bertaux (ed.), *Biography and Society: The Life History Approach in the Social Sciences*, Sage, London: 289–306.

—— (1983) *Living the Fishing*, Routledge and Kegan Paul, London.

—— (1984) 'The family and childrearing as forces for economic change: towards fresh research approaches', *Sociology*, 18: 515–30.

—— (1997) 'Women, men, and transgenerational influences in social mobility', in Bertaux and Thompson, *Pathways to Social Class*: 32–61.

—— (1999) 'The role of grandparents when parents part or die: some reflections on the mythical decline of the extended family', *Ageing and Society*, 19: 471–503.
Thrower, James (1992) *Marxism-Leninism as the Civil Religion of Soviet Society: God's Commissar*, Edwin Mellen, Lampeter.
Titma, Michail (ed.) (1998) *Sotsial'naia Differentsiatsiia Vozrastnoi Kogorty* [Social Differentiation of an Age Cohort], ISRAN, Moscow: 64.
Trifonov, I.Ya. (1969) *Klassy i Klassovaia Bor'ba v SSSR v Nachale NEPa: 1921–1925* [Classes and Class Struggle in the USSR in the Beginning of NEP: 1921–1925], Izdatel'stvo Leningradskogo Universiteta, Leningrad.
—— (1975) *Likvidatsiia Ekspluatatorskikh Klassov s SSSR* [The Liquidation of the Exploitative Classes in the USSR], Politizdat, Moscow.
Trushchenko, O. (1993) 'Akkumuliatsiia simvolicheskogo kapitala v prostranstve stolichnogo tsentra' [The accumulation of symbolic capital in city centre space], *Rossiiskii Monitor*, 1: 13–26.
—— (1995) *Prestizh Tsentra* [The Prestige of the Centre], Socio-Logos, Moscow.
Tuller, David (1997) *Cracks in the Iron Closet: Travels in Gay and Lesbian Russia*, University of Chicago Press, Chicago.
Ulam, Adam (1955) 'Stalin and the theory of totalitarianism', in Ernest J. Simmons (ed.), *Continuity and Change in Russian and Soviet Thought*, Harvard University Press, Cambridge, Mass.: 157–71.
V te surovye gody (1976) [In Those Hard Years], Lenizdat, Leningrad.
V tylu i na fronte (1984) [At Home and at the Front], Izd. Politicheskoi literatury, Moscow.
Vatman, D.M., Lipetsker, M. and Khinchuk, V. (1982) *Kooperativy: Kvartira, Dacha, Garazh* [Cooperatives: Apartment, Dacha, Garage], Iuridicheskaia literatura, Moscow.
Vilensky, Simeon (ed.) (1999) *Till My Tale Is Told: Women's Memoirs of the Gulag*, Virago, London.
Viola, Lynn (1990) 'The peasant nightmare: visions of apocalypse in the Soviet countryside', *Journal of Modern History*, 62: 747–70.
—— (1993) 'The second coming: class enemies in the Soviet countryside, 1927–1935', in Getty and Manning (eds), *Stalinist Terror*: 65–98.
Volkov, Andrei (1990) *The 1937 Census of the Population of the USSR*, State Statistical Office, Moscow.
Voronkov, Viktor and Chikadze, Elena (1997) 'Leningrad Jews: ethnicity and context', in Viktor Voronkov and Elena Zdravomyslova (eds), *Biographical Perspectives on Post-Socialist Societies*, Centre for Independent Research, St Petersburg: 187–91.
—— (2003) 'Different generations of Leningrad Jews in the context of public/private division: paradoxes of ethnicity', in Robin Humphrey, Robert Miller and Elena Zdravomyslova (eds), *Biographical Research in Eastern Europe: Altered Lives and Broken Biographies*, Ashgate, Aldershot.
Voronkov, Viktor and Zdravomyslova, Elena (eds) (1997) *Biographical Perspectives on Post-Socialist Societies*, Centre for Independent Social Research, St Petersburg.
Walshe, F. (1996) 'The concept of family resilience: crisis and challenge', *Family Process*, 35: 261–81.
Watson, Martha (1999) *Lives of Their Own, Rhetorical Dimensions in Autobiographies of Women Activists*, University of South Carolina Press, Chapel Hill.
Watson, Peggy (1993) 'Eastern Europe's silent revolution: Gender', *Sociology*, 27, 3: 471–87.

Wegren, Stephen K. (1998) *Agriculture and the State in Soviet and Post-Soviet Russia*, University of Pittsburgh Press, Pittsburgh.
Werth, Alexander (1971) *Russia: the Post-War Years*, Macmillan, London.
Wheatcroft, Stephen (1996) 'The scale and nature of German and Soviet repression and mass killings, 1930–45', *Europe–Asia Studies* (48) 8: 1319–53.
Yadov, Vladimir (1995) *Krisis identichnosti* [The Crisis of Identity], Institute of Sociology, Moscow.
Yaroshenko, K.B. (1983) *Kollektivnyi – Pol'za Mne i Obshchestvu* [Collective Garden – Good for Me and for Society], Znanie, Moscow.
Young, Glennys (1997) *Power and the Sacred in Revolutionary Russia: Religious Activists in the Village*, Pennsylvania State University Press, University Park, Pennsylvania.
Zaslavsky, Viktor (1982) *The Neo-Stalinist State*, M.E. Sharpe, Armonk.
Zdravomyslova, Elena (1999) 'Male life histories from St Petersburg', paper presented at the 4th European Conference of Sociology, RN1: Biographical Perspectives on European Societies, Amsterdam, 18–21 August.
—— (2001) 'Hypocritical Sexuality of the Late Soviet Period: Sexual Knowledge and Sexual Ignorance', in Sue Webber and Ilkka Liikanen (eds), *Education and Civic Culture in Post-Communist Countries*, Palgrave, London: 151–67.
Zhenshchiny Goroda Lenina (1963) [Women of Lenin's Town], Lenizdat, Leningrad.
Zhenshchiny Strany Sovetov (1977) [Women in the Land of the Soviets] *Kratkii Istoricheskii Ocherk*, Polizdat, Moscow.
Zorin, Andrei (1999) 'Kak ia byl predsedatelem' ['When I was chair'], *Neprikosnovennyi Zapas* 4, 6.

INDEX

abortions 93, 99, 105, 107, 162
Akhmatova, Anna 225, 230–1
Aleksandrovich, Valentin 7, 124–5, 133
Alexeevna, Raisa 184–8, 189
Alexievich, Svetlana 253
Anatoly 33
Andrienko, Petr 8, 128, 133–4
Anisimovna, Olga 200
Anna 142
Arbuzova, Alla Efimovna 239, 240, 247; and collective remembering 247; constructing of herself as an extraordinary revolutionary through meeting with Lenin 244; contempt for leader of the *ravnopravki* 241; and gender identity 244, 245; reconstruction of prominence of Bolshevik female leaders 242
Arendt, Hannah 59, 66, 75
Ashwin, Sarah 160
autobiographical memories: interpreting 7–20
autobiography: and Foucault 236–7; as genre 236
Avvakum (priest) 199

Balkars 221
baptism: and Old Believers 205–6
baraki 14, 42; demolishment of under Khruschev 34; living in 27–9, 32, 40
Belenkaya, Anna 61
Berdiaev, Nikolai 242
Berelowitch, Wladimir 44
Berlin, Isaiah 178
Birikov, Ivan 134–5
Birikov, Vladimir 61, 123–4, 134–5
Birobidzhan 3
births: drop in numbers of 160, 162

black market 5, 157
blat 5, 10
Bourdieu: and housing as *habitus* 56–8
bourgeois specialists 81
Boym, Svetlana 178
Brezhnev, L. 14
Brodksy, Joseph 177, 179

capitalism, Russian 49–50
Centre for Independent Social Research (St Petersburg) 9
Chernov family 29–31; older generation 32; second generation 32–6
Chernov, Ivrii 35–6
Chernov, Konstantin 30, 31, 32
Chernov, Maria 29, 30, 32, 33
Chernov, Natalia 32–3, 35
Chernov, Rimma *see* Zamochin, Rimma
Chernov, Tatiana 29, 30, 31
Chernov, Tikhon 29, 30, 31
Chernov, Valia 30, 31, 32
childrearing 120–1; and extended mothering 16, 161–2
Children of Arbat (Rybakov) 58
Chistiakov, Stepan 154, 155, 156, 159–60, 164, 165, 166, 167
Chistiakova, Aleksandra 16, 146–71; abuse of by husband 155, 156; birth of children 154, 155; childhood 152; chronology of life history 150–1; construction of house 155–6, 161; and death of children 156; divorce of parents 152; early abandonment and suffering 153, 163; education 153; and famine 152–3; first love 153, 165; first marriage 154; health problems 155; help from maternal kin and relatives 161–2; and love 164–5; marriage and

INDEX

relationship with Stepan 154, 164-6; shortlisted for Russian Booker prize 146-9; turning points and generational formation 149-57; and work 153-4, 155, 157-8, 167-9
Chistiakova, Anatolii (Tolia) (son) 155, 156
Chistiakova, Vladimir (Volodia) (son) 154, 155, 156, 162
cities, migration to *see* urbanisation
Civil War 3, 7
class structure 6, 11, 15-7, 25ff, 54ff, 68ff, 43, 47
clergy 74, 195ff
Cohen, Stephen 253
Cold War 56
collective memory 236; and women's autobiographical sketches 246-8
collectivisation of agriculture 3, 27, 29, 198-9
communal apartments *see kommunalka*
communal cultural model of peasantry 40-2, 50; similarities with Stalinist cultural model 43-7
communal ethics 48-9; and market relations 49-50
Communist Party 13, 25; and Orthodox Church 41; replacement of father-patriarch figure 44
Communist Youth 34
connections *see* networks
contraception 93, 111
corruption 5, 10, 47, 48
Cossacks 4
cultural model 42-6; abandoning collectivist idea in favour of individualism 48; and collective responsibility 45; development of under Stalin 42-3; gradual distancing from 46-9; internalising of and support of 44-5, 46; replacement of father-patriarch by Communist Party 44; similarities with communal model of peasantry 43-4, 46, 47

Danilova, Maria 199
Demidova, Maria Stepanovna 239, 240-1; constructing of prominence 243-4; and gender equality 244-5; suffering endured to defend country against Nazis 240-1
divorce 99, 100, 136, 139, 151-2, 154, 166
Dmitrievna, Agrafena 199
Dmitrievna, Kseniia 206

Dobriaikova, Alina 65, 131-2
Dobraikova, Praskov'ia 61-2
DSK (*Dachno-stroitel'nyi kooperative*) 181

education 129, 140, 142; differences between working-class and middle-class families 16-17; family attitudes towards 122-5; as means for well-to-do families to restore status 80-2
Ehrenburg, Il'ia 220, 221
Elder, Glen 121
Eminov, Evgenii Aleksandrovich 228-9
Engel, Barbara and Posadskaya-Vanderbeck, Anastasia: *A Revolution of Their Own* 9, 235, 237, 238, 252
entrepreneurship 143; and family upbringing 138-42
Evgenii 31, 32
Evtushenko, Evgenii 231
ex-prisoners *see* Gulag survivors
extended mothering 16, 160-2, 163, 164

family history: concealment of and secrecy over 78-9, 130-4; transmission of by grandmothers 134-5
family models: transmission of *see* transgenerational influences
family planning 93
famine (1932-3) 10, 152-3
father-patriarch figure: replacement of by Communist Party 44
Fedorova, Zinaida 209
Fedorovich, Spiridon 199, 200, 203, 205
Fedorovich, Vasilli 199
fiction, Russian 148
Finland 98, 102, 110, 112, 115
First World War 3
Fitzpatrick, Sheila 246-7
five-year plans 3, 158
food, symbolic meaning of 88
Foucault, M. 236
France 99
freedom: Berlin on 178; Ionin on private 18, 19, 177-8, 179
Freud, Sigmund 99, 214

garden comradeship *dacha* 18, 63, 176, 179, 180-4; allocation of and number of plots 180-1; heightened freedom within limitation 188-9; property status of 183; purpose of 181; Raisa's story 184-8; size

INDEX

constraints and ingenuity by tenants in utilising space 182; as a space in the system of authority and governance 183; transformation of geographical space into social space 182
Gay, Peter 102, 106
gender: 3–4, 16, 85–6, 146ff, 235ff, and well-to-do families 85–6; and women's autobiographical sketches 244–5
gender contract 148–9, 156–7, 166, 170; and working mothers 157–60
glasnost 1, 4, 8, 95, 235, 253
Goffman, Erving 59
Golod, Sergei 112
Golofast, Valerii 99
Gorbachev, Mikhail 4, 49, 51, 231
Gorky, Maxim 72
grandmothers (grandfathers) 17, 49, 143, 160; communication between children and 8; and extended mothering 163; influence of 127, 128–9; and transmitting of family histories 134–7
Groys, Boris 97
Gulag survivors 7, 10, 19–20, 214–32; camp experiences 218–20; elite returnees 229–30; and family reunion 228–9; fear of re-arrest and threat of repression 19, 215, 217, 223, 224–5; feeling of responsibility towards those who did not survive 225; hindering of re-adjustment efforts by camp experience 225–7; problems confronting 19, 215, 217; and rehabilitation 215, 231; sense of 'second-class' citizenship 231

Hareven, Tamara 121
Hirdman, Yvonne 149
home production 121
homosexuality 108, 109, 113–14, 178
housing 14, 37, 54–67; and *baraki* see *baraki*; and Bourdieu's *habitus* 56–8; control of by State institutions and determinative character of 55–6, 57, 59; and *kommunalka* see *kommunalka*; overcrowding 4, 55; shortage of 14, 55, 128; statistics of 58–9

Iakovlev, Dmitrii 139, 140, 142
Iakovleva, Elena 62–3
iconoclasm 202
immobility, social 122

intelligentsia 6, 80–1, 107, 218
Ionin, Leonid 18, 176, 177–80, 183, 189–90
Iosif 30, 31, 32
Ivanova, Anna 207
Ivanovich, Deomid 203, 204, 204–5
Ivanovich, Vladimir 123, 130, 134
Ivanovna, Akulina 202, 209
Ivanovna, Alexandra 203
Ivanovna, Taisiia 199
Ivanovna, Uliana 199

Kanal imeny Stalina 252–3
khoziain 54
Khruschev, N. 106; criticism of Stalin in secret speech 34, 46, 225, 248; on women's discrimination 245
Khubova, Daria 254
Kiblitskaia, Marina 159, 160
Kilina, Anna 207
Kiseleva, Evgeniia G. 147–8, 154, 169–70
Klyotzin, Alexandr 94
kolkhoz 27, 29, 32
Kollontai, Alexandra 98, 125
Kolyma camp 219–20, 222, 224
kommunalka (communal apartment) 14–15, 34, 54–67; description of 59–60; different meanings for moving in 59; experience of neighbourly solidarity 64–5; experience of older generation in 59–64; fostering of 'quality in poverty' 66; indifference to living standards and everyday problems 66; interaction between former class cultures within confined space 64; lack of privacy 15; life strictly regulated 61; moving out of 58–9; overcrowding 60, 61; power relationships 61–2; and regime's strategy for seizing power in everyday life 64, 76; statistics 58–9; strategies to prevent seizure of living space by well-off families 62–3, 76
Kon, Igor: *The Sexual Revolution in Russia* 95, 96, 97, 98, 99, 105
Kovalev, Sergei 231
Kozlov, Nikolai Vladimirovich 222–3
Kozlova and Sandomirskaia 164, 167
kulaki see peasantry
Kuusinen, Aino 229

Lagunova, Liza 94
Lenin, V. 72, 244

273

Leonid 141
life-story research: differences between Western countries and Russia 11; and representiveness 11–12
love: and selective traditionalism 164–7
Lubianka prison (Moscow) 218, 219

Malakov, Stepan 141
male breadwinner ideal 170–1
Malysheva, Marina 13
Mamlin, Evgenii 60, 123
Mamontovich, Isaak 201, 203, 209
Marchenko, Zoia Dmitrievna 223–5
Marina 36–7, 50
market economy, transition to 51–2
market relations: and communal ethics 49–50
marriage(s): and Old Believers 206–7; parallel 154; as a survival strategy for well-to-do families 79; *see also* divorce, gender
Marx, Karl 13
Marxism-Leninism 43, 51, 240
masturbation 107, 112–13
Maupassant, Guy de 103
Mead, Margaret 122
Medvedev, Roy 228
Memorial 8, 10, 12, 216, 232; archive of 216, 254; exhibition on concentration camps (1988) 8; monument to victims of totalitarianism 225; and Perm 36 labour camp museum 232; sponsoring of national essay contest 9
memory, shaping of: 1, 7–20, 83–4, 130–7, 146–8, 197–202, 216–7, 221–3, 232, 235–9, 246–8
Michelangelo 104
middle-class families: attitude towards education 16–17, 124–5
Moiseevna, Zinaida 198
Molotov, Viacheslav M. 68
moral economy 51
Morozova, Fedosia 199
Moscow 14; growth in population 55; housing *see* housing
Moscow Institute of Sociology 176
motherhood 159; working *see* working mothers
mothering, extended 16, 160–2, 163, 164

Natalya V. 99, 100–1, 114

Nepmen 72–3, 88
networks 5–6, 140, 141
New Economic Policy (NEP) 3, 133, 198; abandoning of by Stalin 198; repression of well-to-do families 72–3
Nikon, Patriarch 199, 201
nomenklatura 6, 43, 47, 49, 56, 58
Novikov, Aleksei 135

obshchna (*mir*) 41
Offitserov, Viacheslav 137–8
Oktiabriny 205
Old Believers 12, 19, 195–212; attempt to use bureaucratic system to their advantage 204–5; and baptism 205–6; burial rituals and marriages 206–7; challenging of autonomy of by collectivisation 198–9; courage of during struggles 200; discrimination against by Tsarist regime 199; establishing of good relations at workplace 203–4; feelings of moral superiority over persecutors and divine retribution of 201–2; flight and migration as survival strategy 202–3; hygiene rules 209–10; importance of family and kin in preservation of identity 207; maintaining of traditional identity 208–11; maintaining traditional identity though cultural and social isolationism 208–9; memories conveying state oppression as inevitable 201; persecution and repression of 19, 196, 198, 199, 201; presenting of experiences in context of history of their religious movement 199–200; and private prayer 207–8, 212; representations of cultural revolution (1928–32) 198–202; resilience of 19, 196; resistance in joining Communist organisations 210; strategies of survival 19, 197, 202–5; traditions and beliefs 196; ways of maintaining religious identity 205–8, 211
Orthodox Church 41
Osipov, Grigorii 142
Osipovna, Elena 206, 208, 209
Osokina, Irina 170

parenting 17; emphasis on authority in 126, 127–8; mitigation of authority by grandmothers 128–9; *see also* childrearing
Parker, Tony 253

INDEX

Pavlova, Sofia 235, 237–8
peasantry 6, 16, 48; communal model of 40–2, 43–4, 44; and *obshchina* 41; repression of *kulaks* and elimination from countryside 3, 6, 55, 68, 72, 73, 85; underpaying of and facing of higher prices than urban citizens 153
perestroika 4
Perm 36 labour camp 232
Pioneers 210–11
Posadskaya-Vanderbeck, Anastasia 9, 235, 237, 238, 252
private companies 38–9
private freedoms 18, 19, 177–8, 179
private life, concept of 47–8
private sector 122
prostitution 110
pschyoanalysis, banning of 99

rabfak 15, 81
railway workers, women 158
Rancour-Laferrier, Danie 242
rasselenie 58
ravnopravki (equal-righters) 241
religion: attack against under Stalin 198; and iconoclasm 202; *see also* Old Believers
representiveness: in life-story research 11–12
residence permits 14
Riabushinskii, Dmitrii 72
Robson, Roy 210
Rotkirch, Anna 253
Ruzhnetsova, Tamara Davidovna 225–8
Rybakov, A.: *Children of Arbat* 58

sadovidcheskoie tovarishchestvo see garden comradeship
Salnikov, Vasilii 200
Schliemann, Heinrich 68
Second World War 4; communal model as key image of Russian values in 46; and discipline of workers 30–1
secret society 5, 7, 11–12
Semenova, Victoria 8, 12
Semenovna, Anna 202
Semenovna, Vassa 199
Sementsova, N.F. 243
Serbsky Institute 218
sex education 93, 99
sexual knowledge, transmission of 17–18, 93–115; children learning from peer groups 101; domestication of in 1960s 105–6; and generation of articulation 18, 109–10, 111–14, 115; and generation of learned ignorance 18, 105–7, 107–9, 115; and generation of silence 101–2, 115; introduction of the term sex in 1960s 106; lack of 95–6; lack of cultural consensus over 93–4; through fiction and pictures 103–4
Sherbakova, Irina 7, 253
Sherstianykh, Anna 206
Shiriaev, Vladimir 146
Shlapentokh, Vladimir 178
Siberia 4
Slezkine, Yuri 235, 246
small freedoms 18, 178–9, 188
Smirnov, Igor 7, 124, 126–7, 132
Smith, Hedrick 242
Smushkevich, Basia Solomonovna 229–30
Smushkevich, Iakov 229
Smushkevich, Roza 229–30
'socialism in a single country' 51
Solin, Emilia 242
Solzhenitsyn, Aleksandr 10; *The Gulag Archipelago* 11, 20, 253; *The Red Wheel* 253
Sorokin, Pitirim 69
sources and archives: 216, 252–7
Stalin, J. 34, 46, 71, 198; creation of Soviet cultural model 42–6; initiatives for new socialist state 3–4; not seen by Russians as source of suffering 4; repression and purges under 6, 42–3, 71, 72; and 'socialism in a single country' 51
Stepanovich, Filaret 203
Stern, Mikhail 96, 115
Sud'by liudei (The Fates of People) 176
survival strategies: and Old Believers 19, 197, 202–5

Tania 37–9
Tartars 206
Taylor, Charles 240
territorial mobility: as a means of survival for well-to-do families 77–8
Thompson, Paul 254–5
transgenerational family models 125–7
transgenerational influences 17, 120–43; and entrepreneurship 138–42; family attitudes towards education 122–5; and grandmothers 127, 128–30; inhibition of change 137; and moral attitudes

INDEX

83–4; transmission of family histories by grandmothers 134–7
Troitskaia, Zinaida P. 158
Tuller, David 178, 253
Turetskaia, Nadezhda Andreevna 239–40, 241, 242; emphasis on achievements of the collective rather than personal accomplishments 242, 243; and gender identity 244, 245
Twentieth Party Congress 225, 248

Ulianin, Alexander 129, 136–7, 138
Ulianin, Lydia 136, 138
unemployment 121
universities 81
upper class families *see* well-to-do families
Urals: industrialisation of 203; and Old Believers *see* Old Believers
urbanisation 3, 6, 14, 41, 55, 158
Urusova, Evdokiia 199

Valentovich, Sergei 140
van den Heuvel, Katrina 253
Vasilevna, Anna 206, 209
Vasilii 207
Vedunin, Sergei 128, 130
Victorian England 102, 103
Vilenskii, Semeon 215, 216–23, 254; arrest and sentenced 218; camp experience 218-20; collection of manuscripts from former *zeki* 217, 223; and rehabilitation 221; release from camp and issuing of passport 220; surveillance of 221–2; work following rehabilitation 221-2
Vladimir 10
Volkov, Oleg 225
Voronkov, Viktor 9, 254
Voronov family 63
Vozvrashchenie (The Return) 217, 225

Weber, Max 19, 40
well-to-do families 15–16, 68–89; concealment of family history and origins 15-16, 78–9, 82–3, 130–1; efforts to reorganise social space in *kommunalka* 63, 76; expropriation of businesses and houses 74–5; family atomisation and abandonment of family support networks 76–7; impediment of by Soviet authorities and depriving of privileged social status 71–2; and intragenerational mobility 86–7; marriage as a survival strategy 79; and NEP 72–3; official attitude towards women 85–6; and older generation 86; and personal connections 80; renouncing of old life style and learning new rules 70; repression of 72–5, 85, 86; retaining of earlier values and ethical norms 71; role of transgenerational moral attitudes and values 83–4; status restoration strategies through education 80–2, 83; survival/adaptation strategies 75–80; use of territorial mobility as means of survival 77–8
women 16, 122; and contract of the wage working mother 158–9; in industrial work during first five year plan 158; official attitude towards women from privileged classes 85–6; stereotypes 149; and work 3–4
women's autobiographical sketches 20, 235–48; and the collective of prominent women 242–4; conditions for construction of as success stories 239; constructing gender and identity 244–5; constructing of women as successful female revolutionary heroines 238; contextualising revolutionary women's collective memory 246–8; expressing themselves as 'subjects' 237; fighting the enemies 240–1; premises for reading 238–9; producing truth and identity as success 246; and reading 'success' 237–40
working mothers 146–71; contract of the wage 158–9; and extended mothering 160–2; and gender contract 157–60; *see also* Chistiakova, Aleksandra
working-class families 27–52; attitude towards education 123–4; and Chernovs 29–36; demolishment of *baraki* and uprooting/alienation in Moscow 34; discipline of workers during war 30–1; life of post-thaw generation 36–9; life of second born generation 32–6; living in *baraki* 27–9, 32, 40; migration from village to city 27, 32, 40; stability of employment 32, 40–1; working environment changes 34–5, 38–9, 40; and the Zamochins 13–14, 27–9, 51
Writers' Union 222

INDEX

Zamochin family 13–14, 27–9, 51
Zamochin, Alexandra 27
Zamochin, Egor 27–8, 29
Zamochin, Ivan 27
Zamochin, Rimma (née Chernov) 29, 30, 32, 34–5, 36, 37, 39
Zamochin, Viktor 29, 33–4, 35
Zdravomyslova, Elena 115
Zhenshchiny goroda Lenina (Women from the City of Lenin) 240
Zhurnalistov family 63
Zhurnalistova, Zhenia 135–6
Zinoviev 47, 48
Znaciecki, Florian 12
Zolotarfeva, Maria 13
Zorin, Andrei 148, 164